THE TWELFTH
POWER OF EVIL

Also by Jerrold Morgulas

THE
TWELFTH
POWER OF
EVIL

Jerrold Morgulas

SEAVIEW BOOKS

NEW YORK

MANUFACTURED IN THE UNITED STATES OF AMERICA

FIRST EDITION

Seaview Books/A Division of PEI Books, Inc.

Library of Congress Cataloging in Publication Data

Morgulas, Jerrold.
    The twelfth power of evil.

    1. World War, 1939–1945—Fiction. I. Title.
PS3563.O87158T88   813'.54   81-50325
ISBN 0-87223-704-4   AACR2

For Susan,
with love

Preface

Why were the Auschwitz death factories never bombed? No definitive answer seems possible at this late date, though much evidence does remain, diffused by time, smudged by memories grown uncertain, any possibility of verification all too frequently canceled by death.

Because of its uncertainty, and perhaps for other reasons as well, this evidence has been consistently ignored.

But much evidence *is* there. Many of the pieces can be put together, and they form a picture which, while far from complete, nevertheless has very clearly defined outlines.

The specific incidents and characters in this book are entirely fictional. The background of corporate entanglements and machinations against which the story takes place are not.

A Note on the Documents

The Documents which appear throughout this book are, unfortunately, not works of fiction. Worse still, they represent only a small part of the relevant factual material underlying this narrative.

In certain instances, names of persons, places, and corporations have been deleted for obvious reasons.

No other editorial license has been taken, difficult as that may be to believe.

There is, of course, a sort of "gentlemen's agreement" between us and our colleagues abroad that our plants will not be bombed. . . .

> Heinrich Beutefisch, production
> chief for synthetic gasoline,
> Obersturmbahnführer SS, to Paul
> Harteck, nuclear physicist

They will not dare go on with this; our American friends will come.

> Hermann Schmitz, chairman of the
> *Vorstand,* on the day before the
> I.G. Farben war crimes trials began

Of those convicted, some were released on the day of judgment because with credit for their time spent in jail, their sentences were satisfied; and the others were all pardoned by 1951.

> Josiah DuBois, chief prosecutor
> during the I.G. Farben war crimes
> trials

Prologue

November 10, 1976

New York City

It was only the third time in history that an assassination had been caught live by the television cameras, and the first time in color.

Two junior associates of the firm of Hayklut, Bard, Winston & Stropp, Esqs., had been working late in a small conference room on the forty-fifth floor of the Spire Building. On the three floors directly below, all connected by a continuous spiral staircase, the firm's other offices were mostly dark. It was a little after ten. The two young men had been putting the finishing touches on the Criterion–Eastern Sunburst Oil merger documents, checking them for the fiftieth time, collating exhibits, proofreading everything over and over and over again. If there were any mistakes, they had better be found now rather than the next morning, when the papers would be passed around the boardroom table for signing.

A dull glow emanated from the small TV set that sat on the locked bar at the end of the conference table. The picture was on but the sound had been turned down almost to inaudibility. The younger of the two men, a pale-faced former assistant SEC counsel, glanced nervously at the screen, then at his watch, then at the screen again. In a moment or two, they would have to interrupt their work and turn the sound up. The annual award ceremony of the International Academy of Petroleum Research was being televised directly from the Waldorf Astoria ballroom. The year's Medal of Merit was to be presented jointly to Marcus Trilling, retiring chairman of the board of Criterion Oil Company, now the law firm's principal client, and an equally elderly research scientist from West Germany, Dr. Ing. Golo Stellner.

It would hardly do to miss the acceptance speeches. Someone would certainly ask them if they had listened, and it would be impossible and possibly fatal to their careers to try to fake it.

Stellner's firm, one of the giant chemical companies spun off after the forcible disbanding of I.G. Farbenindustrie, had worked with Criterion's chemists to develop a new synthetic fuel process that promised both relief from the periodic gasoline shortages that had plagued the West since the Six-Day War and an unassailably superior market position for both companies.

The brilliantly lit ballroom was full to overflowing. A bunting-covered dais extended from one side of the stage to the other. A white banner carrying the initials "IAPR" stretched across the entire rear of the stage, rippling faintly in the air conditioning. At the very front of the apron, where the dance band's leader usually stood, a podium had been set up. It was at this podium that Dr. Ing. Stellner and Chairman Emeritus Trilling were positioned as the picture on the TV screen took on sound. They had just been handed a gold-faced plaque and were standing shoulder to symbolic shoulder, shaking hands across the microphone and getting ready to deliver their acceptance speeches.

The former assistant SEC counsel sighed, pushed his contracts aside, and settled back for fifteen minutes of obligatory listening. The junior associate lit a cigarette and stared blankly into space.

Marcus Trilling was no one's favorite person.

It happened just as Trilling and Stellner turned to face the audience. A small, white-haired man rose solemnly from the second row, just below the podium, slowly drew a large pistol from his coat pocket, and, just as carefully, took aim and fired.

Twice, point-blank.

The bullets struck each man in exactly the same spot. Just over the heart.

The TV announcer's voice climbed an octave and dissolved into an incoherent shout.

"This just can't be happening . . . that man, who is that man? Does anyone *know who that man is?* My God, he's just shot Marcus Trilling and the German . . . I don't believe it, it's impossible . . ."

The assassin went down at once, without a struggle. Uniformed guards fought desperately to get from their stations along the walls of the ballroom to the spot where the white-haired man had disappeared. The cameras swung away, hesitated, then settled for an unconscionably long moment on the stage.

The angular body of Marcus Trilling lay slumped over the rostrum, a ragged hole the size of an orange clearly visible where the bullet had emerged from his back. The German had collapsed over the edge of the stage and lay with one leg caught and smoldering in the footlights, hanging there like a rag doll. The blood poured down his back and over his bald scalp.

The younger associate sat stunned and blinking.

"He was supposed to *sign* this tomorrow . . ."

"Is Mr. Eisner still here?"

"He was a half-hour ago."

"Christ, we should go get him, shouldn't we?"

The younger man rose at once and ran out and down the empty corridor to the stairwell. He descended one flight as rapidly as he could without stumbling and then began to run again through equally empty but somewhat darker corridors, past the empty partners' offices and the dark conference rooms, the secretaries' deserted desks and the cavernous, empty file rooms. A distant tapping came from some far-off but still active steno pool. A few juniors were hard at work in their cubbyholes, hoping that their industry would be duly noted. They did not look up as the young associate rushed past them and down the heavily carpeted hallway.

Finally the associate smelled the coffee that Samuel Morse Eisner always kept brewing when he worked late at night. Without knocking, the associate burst into the senior patent attorney's office, an almost unheard-of discourtesy, which under any other circumstances would have meant certain reprimand and possible dismissal.

Eisner looked up slowly. For a second, the horrified associate thought that he was looking directly at the man who had just shot Chairman Trilling and the German. The assassin and Eisner were almost the same size, roughly the same age, and had the same thick silver hair. Both wore heavy glasses. Both had heavy dark eyebrows.

The associate braced himself; he had always felt cowed in Eisner's presence. The older man's stern and faintly weary manner compelled instant respect, required silence, and inevitably generated fear.

"Mr. Eisner, sir . . . I have to disturb you . . ."

"You've done that already."

"Mr. Eisner, *sir* . . ."

"You're Shelby, aren't you?" Eisner said coldly, as though marking the name down for some future unpleasantness.

"Excuse me, sir, but Mr. Trilling has just been shot. I think he's been killed, sir."

It was hard at that moment to see Eisner's eyes behind his thick lenses, but Shelby was certain that the man hadn't even blinked. Later, when he thought back on it, Shelby was reasonably certain that he had heard a short exhalation, not quite a sigh, but almost. That was all.

Samuel Morse Eisner slowly pushed aside the rat's nest of yellow pads and underlined sheets on which he'd been working and leaned forward in his high-backed leather chair.

"Where did this happen? When? Are you certain? Who told you?"

"I saw it myself, sir."

"You saw it?" Eisner rocked forward a bit more, but only slightly. "You just *saw* Trilling get shot?"

"On television, sir. If you'll come with me . . . we were watching the award ceremony up in Conference Room E." Shelby hesitated, then added hastily, "We thought that we ought to, sir, under the circumstances. The merger, I mean . . ."

Eisner got up and without another word walked rapidly out of the room, leaving the associate standing there not knowing quite what to do.

For a man of sixty-six, Eisner moved with astonishing agility and precision. He was one of those people, Shelby knew, who determinedly played handball three or four times a week, no matter what, and guarded their physical well-being—at least the outward appearances of it—with almost manic zeal. Eisner's wife was much younger than he was, Shelby knew, a pale, good-looking woman at least twenty years his junior. That probably explained many things.

Dirks, the elder of the two men who had been working on the Criterion–Eastern Sunburst merger papers, turned sharply as Eisner, with Shelby close behind, burst into Conference Room E. Eisner's face by now was as white as his hair, and he was sweating noticeably. A little wheezing noise came from his throat, but the moment he stopped moving he got it under control.

"Sir, look here, look, they're showing it again."

"Good God, instant replay," Shelby let slip. Eisner at once shot him the blackest look the young man had ever received in his life. Then Eisner turned toward the TV screen.

The whole scene was being repeated in grainy, blurred slow motion, just as it had first happened. Eisner, who was farsighted, pulled off his glasses and thrust them into his pocket.

An announcer's voice—not that of the man on the spot, but of another, calmer man—sounded clearly over the crowd noises. He was explaining as best he could what had occurred.

Eisner watched it all without moving a muscle. By then, Shelby couldn't take his eyes off the senior partner's face. No, there wasn't any real resemblance between Eisner and the assassin after all. The hair and the thick glasses had only made it seem so.

The replay film froze on the murderer at the instant just before he went down under an avalanche of spectators, then zoomed in on his face and held there for a moment.

It was a narrow, haggard face, a face that could belong only to a man who had been terribly ravaged in his life, the survivor of some unspeakable calamity. It was the kind of face that made one look away.

Then the TV shot unfroze and the camera panned again to the crumpled bodies on the stage. There was no doubt about it. They were as dead as they could be, both of them.

"That's enough," Eisner said. "We don't need to see it again." He switched off the set.

"You, Shelby," he said. "You go and find out where they're taking that man."

"Sir, how?"

"By using the brain that we're paying you to use here, that's how. Find out which is the nearest precinct house to the Waldorf. Look it up in the phone book. I'll be downstairs in my office." He paused. "And knock first this time."

Eisner descended the spiral staircase slowly, holding himself back as though certain he was being watched, though he knew perfectly well that aside from Shelby, Dirks, and a dozen or so stenos in the night pool he was almost entirely alone.

At length he reached the forty-fourth floor and went at once to his office. For a time he could still hear Shelby, arguing with someone on the telephone, trying to get information that whoever it was he was talking to wouldn't give him. The TV sound had by now been turned on full blast and filled the empty corridors like the voice of doom.

He shut the door and went to his desk, first pausing to turn on the small TV set that sat on the convector ledge, a present from Dave Bard, given years ago on the occasion of Eisner's succession to full partnership. For a moment he was doubtful that it would even work. He had never once turned it on. The set was covered with a detritus of papers and crumpled law journals. Eisner was not by nature an orderly man and never had been able to force the habit.

He took a bottle of Dewar's from a locked desk drawer, poured himself a glassful, downed it, and stood for a moment while the whiskey did its work, looking out over the jumble of lights and shapes that was midtown Manhattan at ten thirty on a weekday night in November 1976.

Then he picked up his private phone, punched out the area code —2 . . . 1 . . . 8—and rapped out the number as though he were working a code key.

He waited for a long, sweaty moment before someone picked up. His hand shook a little, the blue veins on the back throbbing visibly. The Dewar's hadn't been too good for him. It never was.

Finally he heard a voice. A woman.

"Margaret? Is that you? It's Sam Eisner here. You'd better get Wayne on the phone right away."

The woman's voice was thick, angry; she was obviously a little drunk. "He isn't here, damn it. He's never here."

Eisner drew a breath. He disliked Maggie Trilling as much as she disliked him, but he had to admit that her attitude toward her husband was as well founded as it could be.

"You know where he is?"

"Surely, *Counselor* . . ."

"Cut it out, Margaret. *Now*. Where is he? This is very important."

"You sound as though something terrible's happened. He'll be impressed, I'm sure."

"You just get hold of him, Margaret, and I don't give a damn who he's in bed with. You just do it. And you tell him to get him-

self up here to New York as fast as he can. I'll call the airport and
have Moedler get the company plane ready." He took another deep
breath. His pulse was racing now. No more whiskey, he swore. Not
now, not ever again. He'd been that route too often.

Margaret Trilling was silent for a long while. When she did
speak again there was a harsh, genuinely terrified edge to her voice.

"What's happened, Sam'l?"

"His father's been shot. He's dead. Turn on the eleven o'clock
news and you can see it for yourself. The camera work was very
good."

Her voice instantly became rock hard. Very sharp. She knew
perfectly well what Marcus Trilling's death was going to mean to
her, and it made her pulse race. Old Trilling had liked her a good
deal better than he'd liked his own son. As far as Marcus Trilling
was concerned, his son was a no-good bastard and a womanizer,
and don't bother, thank you, with all that talk about his being
presidential timber, please. He *knew.*

"You want me to call Moedler myself?" Margaret Trilling was
saying. "I think that's better, don't you? And don't worry, I know
exactly where Wayne is and who he's in. Where do you want him,
Sam'l?"

"Tell him to get himself up to my apartment. If I'm not there,
I'll leave word where he can find me."

Her voice was very low now, very small.

"What's happened, Sam'l?" she said again. "I mean *really* . . ."

"Marcus was shot right in the Waldorf ballroom, while he was
getting the award. Dr. Stellner was killed, too."

"Oh my God . . ." It had finally sunk in. Margaret Trilling had
at least some idea, and what she didn't know, she intuited.

He hung up with a momentary feeling of relief. There was nothing to do now but let it all play itself out. There were a number of
ways it could go, and he couldn't do a thing to alter any of them.
Some ways were worse than others.

In the end, though, it wouldn't really matter.

He closed his eyes. He could see Golo Stellner's face, but it was
a much younger, harder face. All of their faces had been younger
and harder in those days.

A million years ago, it seemed.

* * *

A Checker cab, the kind with lots of room in the back and two little jump seats, had whisked him first through the empty night-time canyons of Madison Avenue, then up Park past Hunter College, past the embassies with their perpetual art exhibitions, as though the never-ending slaughter, the constant oppression of governments everywhere, could be successfully hidden behind walls hung with oil paintings by native artists.

The cab slowed as it entered the Eighties. Out of respect.

He knew that the police car would be there in front of his apartment building, and he was not disappointed. The little red light on the car roof turned slowly, casting an intermittent livid glare on the windows of the maisonette doctors' offices. The doorman, Peter, was standing outside, trying to get the policemen to move away from the entrance to the building. It was just after theater time, and the usual army of cabs would begin pulling up shortly.

"Mr. Eisner?" The doorman moved in protectively between his tenant and the police officer who was waiting for him.

"It's all right, Peter. I'm expecting these gentlemen."

He nodded to the startled officer. "Peter, will you please phone up and tell Mrs. Eisner that I probably won't be home tonight?"

"We called already, Mr. Eisner. Mrs. Eisner, she's asleep. Your housekeeper tells us—"

"Just as well. You tell Lotte not to wake her. Time enough in the morning." He turned to the waiting police officer. "Shall we go? We don't want to keep your guest waiting, do we? I wouldn't want him to worry."

The policeman said nothing until they were settled in the back of the squad car.

"You know all about it, mister? I'll be damned."

"We were working late. Some of our juniors had it on television. Trilling was a client of ours, you know. His company, I mean. So it was only natural that we were watching. I saw the replay, so I suppose you could say I know all about it, yes."

"He wants you for his lawyer. That's all he'd say, sir. We're hoping you can convince him to cooperate. I know it's not the usual thing to ask, but after all, he killed two men right in front of a nationwide television audience. A million people must have seen it."

"Just like Oswald?"

"You might say."

"You might."

Fifty-first Street was jammed solid from Lexington Avenue to Third. At least fifty squad cars were crammed into the one crosstown block, bumper to bumper. A squad of mounted police were out patrolling the perimeter, looking down on the milling crowd, which had followed the police out of the Waldorf and was now trying to move in on the station house. The jam-up was so dense that the patrol car carrying Samuel Morse Eisner and his escort had to park opposite the Central Synagogue on Fifty-fifth Street. The three men proceeded on foot from that point, the way cleared by two mounted policemen.

"He asked for you for his lawyer before we even got him to the station house," the policeman said. "Do you know him?"

Eisner didn't answer. The officer shrugged. He was used to such things and knew he shouldn't even have asked. You didn't press questions when talking to lawyers. It always meant problems later on.

There were a few reporters inside. One of them shouldered a big TV camera. Others were busy popping flashbulbs at anyone who came through the door, hoping for a useful shot. The space in front of the booking desk was crowded. A trio of paramedics and a doctor were just coming out of the detention area.

The officer who had accompanied Eisner pushed his way to the desk and pointed behind him and then at the entrance to the cellblock area. The sergeant, looking distinctly harried, picked up the desk phone and spoke quickly to someone inside. A door opened. A stocky, neatly dressed man with an air of authority emerged.

"Samuel Eisner?"

"Yes."

"You may as well come right in." He shook his head. "The next thing, they'll be wearing dog tags, like the diabetics. 'In case I kill someone, please call my lawyer at the following number . . . Jesus!"

Eisner followed him through the barred doors, down a long green-painted corridor, and into the holding area. The ceiling lights were bare and harsh, protected by little wire baskets. Unlike the outer room, this part of the precinct house was deserted, calm, like a hospital corridor at night. The walls and doors were sound-proof. The only disturbance was the sound of footfalls, regular and methodical, on the asphalt tile.

"My name is Basharian," said the neatly dressed man. "Lieutenant Basharian. This is the damndest thing. Right in front of two thousand people. Is there anything you want to tell us?" His voice was tentative, hopeful but at the same time resigned. He really didn't expect anything.

Eisner ignored the question. "Has he been injured?"

"What you'd expect, nothing more. The guards got to him before anyone did any real harm. It was a reflex movement anyhow. I mean, it wasn't like with Kennedy or anything like that. I suppose if any of them had thought of it, they'd probably have applauded. Trilling wasn't too popular a person, I mean, was he? And no one here knows the German at all. I suppose the embassy will have to be contacted. Jesus, I forgot all about that."

"Don't worry," Eisner said with sarcastic kindliness. "You've got exclusive jurisdiction. The embassy can wait. And anyhow, you mean the consulate."

They went into a small room paneled with what Eisner knew was one-way glass. Lieutenant Basharian flicked a switch and the dull glass panel lit up, revealing another room beyond. A small, gray-haired man sat with his hands folded on a table before him. He was alone. There was a bandage on his head, holding a small bloody compress to his right temple; nothing more. The light in the room was dim, but the man kept blinking as though even that dim light was too much for him.

Apart from the blinking, he seemed remarkably calm.

"That's him, Mr. Eisner," said Basharian.

"I know."

"He's been read his rights."

"Of course."

"You can have as much time with him as you like. There isn't much to question about on this one, is there?"

Eisner shrugged and nodded toward the inner door.

"Anytime you like," said Basharian. "You want some coffee?"

The door was placed so that a person entering would come in behind the prisoner. Eisner pushed the door open very gently, closed it behind him just as quietly, and stood there waiting. The light in the room was even dimmer than he'd thought. He stood for a moment trying to control himself. He had to be dispassionate, as calm as was humanly possible.

It was absolutely essential that he remain calm.

He'd spent so many years being entirely in command, giving orders, controlling events, that he felt almost like an actor now, trying to feel unsure of himself and a little frightened. He didn't know quite how it should be done.

The man at the table didn't move. Perhaps he hadn't even heard the door open.

Eisner waited for another moment. Then he spoke.

"Hello, Miklos."

"You remembered," the man said, still without turning. "You *did* remember me, after all . . ."

"Why shouldn't I remember you, Miklos?"

"Haven't you read Bettelheim, my friend? He says that the only way we survive such things as you and I survived is to put them completely out of our memory. He says that the human mind removes all traces of things that it cannot cope with, until the tablet is . . . finally . . . completely erased. Freud said the same thing." He was silent for a moment. "But he was only guessing, Freud was. He could not really have known, could he?" He half turned in his seat, looking at Eisner for the first time, his eyes blinking in the gloom. His face no longer wore the expression of uncertainty Eisner had seen in the frozen TV shot, just after the two bullets Miklos Baranyi had fired had smashed home.

"Thank you for coming, Samuel."

"How could I not have come?"

"How indeed? Perhaps you could have found reasons. But you did not. For that, I thank you."

Eisner considered Miklos Baranyi's words for a moment. Then he sat down on the end of the table; there was no other chair. His hands were still shaking a little, and he knew that Basharian was watching from the other side of the one-way panel. The sound, of course, would not have been turned on—Basharian was no doubt too practiced in his profession to do something as stupid as listen in on a lawyer–client interview—but it still made him uneasy to know that someone was watching.

"They're dead, Miklos, both of them."

"I would think so. I filed the ends of the bullets myself. Also, they were dipped in strychnine, just for good measure."

"You didn't leave much room for a defense, Miklos."

"It was not my intent to take chances." He sighed and sat back. The weariness seemed to slip from his face. But not the pain. "It is written in your Testament, in *Paul* if I remember, 'Vengeance is mine; I will repay, saith the Lord.' "

"You've become God's right hand, is that it?"

"Sometimes God needs a little reminding, Samuel. That's all."

Eisner considered for a long, silent moment. He felt a faint sense of vertigo. The whiskey? No. History, more likely. He knew what Miklos Baranyi was going to say to him. He knew the words, remembered every moment of it. It was stored away in the recesses of his mind. It had been there for thirty years. Now it was going to come out again, all of it.

"What do you want me to do for you, Miklos? We'll do whatever we can, of course."

"Is the son coming?"

"I called him. He should be here within the hour."

"Does he know anything about it?"

Eisner shook his head.

"Then I want him to hear it all. That's what you can do for me. Make him listen. After that, I don't care what happens. It's all finished. Finally."

Miklos Baranyi reached into his jacket pocket and took out a crumpled, fat envelope, which he pushed across the table at Eisner. The back of the envelope was covered with dates, numbers, scratchings, cross-outs.

"While we are waiting, then, you might wish to look at *these* . . ."

"The others?"

Miklos Baranyi nodded.

The envelope was full of newspaper clippings. Samuel Morse Eisner wished desperately then for another whiskey. He avoided Baranyi's gaze; the man was watching him intently as he took the clippings out of the envelope and laid them side by side on the table.

The obituaries, the reports of accidents. The suicide of Dr. Ing.

Helmut Schragg, David Bard's fatal skiing accident, the execution by hanging in Poland of Werner Neimann, formerly Oberführer, SS, the unaccountable disappearance of Conrad Bor at sea off Riga . . .

He read slowly and carefully. The only ones missing were Lorimer, whose part in the tragedy Baranyi could not possibly have known, Stellner, and Trilling himself. All the rest were there.

"Every one of these?" Eisner breathed, incredulous. The electric wall clock whirred overhead. He could hear a faint shuffling in the next room. Basharian, of course, and possibly others. He glanced at his watch. If Maggie Trilling had been telling the truth, it would only be a matter of minutes before the door opened and Senator Wayne Trilling came in, red-faced and wild-eyed, wondering what the hell was going on, desperate over the scandal, if not the actual death of his father.

It was essential that Eisner keep calm; he would have to play it out to the end, no matter what. And there would be much that would have to be done, and done quickly.

"Could we have some coffee or a cigarette, Samuel? Do they allow such things here?"

"It can be arranged," Eisner said. "Miklos, you haven't answered me—are all of these yours? Every one of them? It just isn't possible."

"In one way or another, yes. Some actually were overcome by remorse, can you believe it? It *is* comforting to think that a constant reminder could have such an effect. Schragg, for instance, actually took his own life."

"Rather than have you expose him?"

"He *had* been exposed, if you remember. In the courtroom. And sentenced, too. Five years. Along with Ambros and Beutefisch. But they let him out along with all the others in a matter of months."

It was only because Trilling and Stellner were the last that Baranyi had acted publicly. And because they had been together. As far as Baranyi was concerned, they *were* the last. That, at least, was comforting.

It was a little after twelve when the door opened and Trilling's son, the senator, was ushered into the room by an escort of detectives and two assistant district attorneys. The younger Trilling was handsome in the same faintly dissipated way his father had been. Slightly puffy now, from too many Georgetown cocktail parties and too many nights spent with secretaries and young campaign workers. It was precisely this faintly vulnerable quality, the stamp of frailty all too visible, that made him so appealing to his constituents. They saw in that face on its way to ruin the proof that men no better than they could rise to power.

The face was that of the father, the hair like the father's thirty years before, colorless, speckled, halfway between blond and gray. Like the eyes.

"Samuel, what the hell is going on here? Is what they say true?"

"You do know, don't you?"

"About my father? Yes, of course. Moedler filled me in on the way up. Jesus, but this . . . why here?" He squinted, looked around the room, and finally saw the frail figure of Miklos Baranyi, as though Baranyi were the last thing in the room of which note ought to be taken.

"Him?"

"Yes, him," Eisner said. He turned to the policemen and the assistant district attorneys.

"We'd like to be alone, if you don't mind," he said in a cold, efficient, courtroom voice with which there could be no arguing.

"You're actually going to represent him?" asked one of the assistant DAs.

"He asked for me, didn't he?" Eisner replied stonily.

The assistant DA smiled faintly, a bit hesitantly. "But . . . after all, Counselor . . . your firm handles . . . I mean . . ."

"We represent Criterion Oil, you mean? I'm sure that Mr. Trilling's heirs and the principal stockholders will have no objection whatever to the arrangement."

"Oh?" The smile again. A little broader this time.

"They will want—*we* will want to see that Mr. Baranyi has the best possible representation. I'm sure that the senator feels exactly the same way, don't you, Senator?"

Wayne Trilling nodded, his face blank, expressionless, as though he'd hardly heard a word of what had been said or, if he had, that he hadn't understood any of it at all.

Eisner drew a breath.

"The senator's well-known concern for the impartial and full administration of justice—for human rights, if I may use the phrase —may well be tested by a situation like this. We won't deny it or try to pretend otherwise. But it's precisely tests like this that prove the real depth of the senator's commitment."

"Beautiful," sighed the other assistant. "That's really beautiful."

Eisner shrugged and nodded toward the door.

Trilling looked at him hesitantly. Eisner's glance unmistakably counseled silence. At a loss, the senator made no attempt to speak, though he had been visibly stung by the young assistant's sarcasm.

Then the other assistant said, "You know, if he says something in front of *him,* there's no privilege. You *do* know that, don't you, Counselor?"

"I knew that before you were out of grade school, much less St. John's or wherever it was you learned your manners."

"Suit yourself."

"We will," Eisner said.

When they had gone, the door closed and the one-way glass darkened so that no one could see in from the other side, Eisner poured out some coffee. It was already growing cold and tasted very flat.

"Sam, are you ready to tell me now? I mean, you *do* know where Maggie found me, and the damned inconvenience of it, and—"

"This is Miklos Baranyi," Eisner said sternly, ignoring Trilling's questions. "He's the man who shot your father and Dr. Stellner."

Eisner's matter-of-factness set Trilling back. He was neither overly bright nor overly perceptive under the best of circumstances. Now he was on the verge of total confusion. He took the cup, spilling some coffee on the table, and waited.

Baranyi stared at him.

"You don't know the name, do you?" asked Baranyi in a soft, almost gentle voice. "No, why should you?"

"He wants to explain it to you, Wayne. That's why I called you."

"Damn it, Samuel, you called *before* you got here. I know that. So what the hell do you mean 'that's why' you got me up here?"

"You should listen," said Baranyi in that same slow, measured tone. He was breathing easily now, pausing every so often to sip tranquilly at his coffee and take in a lungful of cigarette smoke. He looked like a gnome, like someone's grandfather about to tell a tale. A faint smile insinuated itself around the edges of his mouth.

Eisner sat back, resting his coffee cup on his lap. It was going to be painful, but he had to keep it all hidden. He couldn't let any of it show. Not now, anyway.

Baranyi took a final sip of coffee, lit another cigarette, and stared straight into the younger man's eyes.

"You will listen to it all, please, Senator. Do not judge before you have heard it all, yes? It would be unfair to me and to so many others if you did that. Do you promise?"

Trilling, who had no idea what the man was talking about, nodded, twisted his hands together, and listened.

"So, so, let me begin, yes? It is good that you are calm, that you will listen. You knew your father well, it would seem . . ."

"Miklos, please," said Eisner softly. "Whatever else, the man *was* his father. He'll listen to you. But don't make it any worse than it is."

Baranyi smiled faintly.

"How could I, Samuel? How could I possibly make it any worse than it was?"

What follows is not the story as Miklos Baranyi told it, limited by the necessarily narrow scope of one man's vision and experience. Rather, it is the story as it happened, with all of its sorry details filled in and its dark places lit. . . .

I

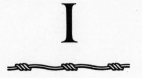

DOCUMENT

50 U.S. Code, App. § 3 WAR AND NATIONAL DEFENSE
§ 3. Acts prohibited
  It shall be unlawful—
  (a) For any person in the United States, except with the license of the President, granted to such person, or to the enemy, or ally of enemy, as provided in this Act [sections 1–6, 7–39 and 41–44 of this Appendix], to trade, or attempt to trade, either directly or indirectly with, to, or from, or for, or on account of, or on behalf of, or for the benefit of, any other person, with knowledge or reasonable cause to believe that such other person is an enemy or ally of an enemy, or is conducting or taking part in such trade, directly or indirectly, for, or on account of, or on behalf of, or for the benefit of, an enemy or ally of an enemy.

November 28, 1943
Teheran, Iran

It probably has no real beginning and will probably have no real end, but if a point and a place of beginning must be found then it may as well be a time in late November 1943 and the place the dusty, sun-blighted road leading from the airport on the outskirts of Teheran into the heart of the city, to the palace of the Shah and the legations of Great Britain, the United States of America, and the Union of Soviet Socialist Republics.

For days, squadrons of Persian cavalry had been riding three abreast between the city and the airport, practicing their formations, rehearsing their patrols, until only a deaf, dumb, and blind imbecile would not have known that something momentous was about to happen.

The Elburz mountains, soaring twelve thousand feet high to the north of the city, were wreathed in thin clouds. Dust stirred by the troops of horsemen, dust stirred by a steady cavalcade of military and diplomatic vehicles, and, most of all, dust stirred by the thousands of curious Persians who thronged by the roadside grew thicker and more dense as the way ran through the gates and into the city, between the dun-colored, shapeless dwellings of the poor and past the handsome western-style buildings and shops clustered around the northern urban perimeter.

The British had arrived by car from the airport, driven directly down the road, flags fluttering smartly, motorcycle outriders stirring up thick clouds of yellow dust, cavalry at a trot fore and aft, coming finally to a near standstill at a good distance from the British legation building. It was rumored that Churchill had turned almost purple with rage and accused his security service of making him as fine a target as a Christmas goose hung high in an Oxford Street shop window.

The Americans had made a great show of their comings and goings, and as those of the British had been genuine and the prime minister had been conveyed to the meeting with all the personal security normally afforded a condemned man, everyone had assumed that the squat black staff car and the cavalcade of armored vehicles that had accompanied the President were also genuine. In fact, the President had come into the city by the back door, through streets whose names no one knew either before or after passing through them, and in such a generally roundabout way that afterward no one could even reconstruct the route.

As for the Russians, no one knew precisely how or when Stalin had arrived; it seemed, simply, as though he had always been there, a burly presence in his specially made uniform with its shoulder boards big as trenchers and his singularly ill-fitting cap so laden with braid that it was difficult to see how he could keep his head erect. The Soviet legation building, so much larger than either the American or the British, teemed with Russian soldiery and dark, solemn men in ill-fitting, dark, solemn suits, all rushing back and forth, looking under things, opening doors, scowling, and generally making themselves so oppressive that to those few Persians who passed near enough to the legation grounds to observe their frenetic activity they became an immediate laughingstock and the joke of the city.

The British legation, less than the distance of a rugby field away from its Soviet counterpart, was surrounded by smartly dressed, turbaned Anglo-Indian troops. The Americans, when they did appear, seemed shabby by comparison—all except the naval officers, who, with accustomed neatness, managed to present an appearance entirely consistent with European standards.

The windows of the shops were full, the marketplace squares crowded with vendors. Melons, heaps of fragrant grapes, the apples of Demavend, dark strings of figs hanging from every cross-pole, fruit of every kind, filled the air with a bewildering variety of aromas. Military vehicles found it impossible to pass all but the widest streets. Squads of military police, sent ahead to clear the way, found themselves engulfed by the curious crowds. Roadblocks abounded, thrown up indiscriminately and confounding an already chaotic situation.

Inside the walled compounds of the Soviet embassy, the leaders of the three largest military forces in the world had been meeting in secret session for days. President Roosevelt, having tactfully pretended to believe Vishinsky's warnings that Teheran was alive with German agents and that a plot on his life was a real possibility, had moved with his entourage into a separate villa within the Soviet compound.

The President's Filipino messmen had finally located the necessary kitchen equipment, and the leaders of the Allies, together with their interpreters, were sitting down to the first meal prepared according to the President's standards since he had arrived in the Persian capital.

Churchill, two accompanying ministers, and a squad of interpreters had just entered the President's villa when a young man in naval uniform exited to the usual accompaniment of stiff salutes from the Russian security men and made his way down the street in front of the Soviet embassy. He could see the Secret Service men who had been placed on the roofs of the buildings opposite watching the entrances and walls with field glasses. Poor Reilly, what a job he'd been handed. A city full of Nazi sympathizers, a young Shah so anxious to please his important guests that he'd managed to ruin almost every security arrangement that had been made, the British snarling at the Russians, the Russians growling back. And an American President immobilized in a wheelchair, a sitting-duck target for anyone who could get close enough.

The young officer shrugged and crossed the street. A car was waiting for him by the opposite curb.

"Monsieur?" The swarthy driver spoke the officer's name, and the young man got into the car, sat back, and took off his white cap so as to be better able to mop his brow. The heat was suffocating. How the Russians, in their woolen uniforms, ever stood it he could not understand.

The car moved out quickly and headed north toward the blocks of new apartment buildings that had begun to rise at the foot of the gravel plains that came down from Elburz.

"It is all going well?" inquired the driver in an unctuous voice.

The naval officer hesitated. Being an interpreter in five languages often made it next to impossible to think in one. The afternoon session had been particularly taxing. So much shouting. Churchill unbelievably truculent until Roosevelt had finally come to his aid. Almost no pauses between sentences; the President had not even waited until the translators had finished before taking off with his own remarks. A quick mind, able to grasp a point even before it was completely expressed. Utterly impatient.

It had all been very tiring.

At length the car drew up before a large six-story apartment building of white stucco finish. In the distance behind it loomed the purple eminence of the Elburz, deep in evening shadow. The air seemed golden, like honey syrup.

The naval officer did not pay the driver; that had already been taken care of. He got out and went quickly into the building and straight up the stairs, not pausing to ring the bell or to announce his arrival in any way.

On the third-floor landing he paused before a door which bore on a small brass plate the name he had been given. He pushed open the door without ringing first.

The door gave onto a short hallway, which in turn opened onto a terraced living room in western style. A pudgy, elderly Persian in a white linen suit that made him look like a character out of *Rain* was having drinks with a younger, gaunt-looking man on the terrace.

The Persian was obviously the owner of the flat. The other man, the officer knew, was a naturalized Swiss, the regional deputy director of the East Persian Chemical and Pharmaceutical Corporation.

The Persian turned slightly as the naval officer entered the living room.

"Come out on the balcony, if it will please you, monsieur. What a delightful view we have. The colors are magnificent tonight."

The Swiss looked annoyed but said nothing. He took a sip of his drink and wiped away the sweat from the side of the glass.

"I'd rather not," said the naval officer. "I've seen too many pairs of field glasses already today."

"But precisely, precisely," the Persian chided. "You should *wish* to be seen. You should make it obvious that there is no reason for you *not* to be seen."

"Nevertheless," said the officer. He kept well away from the window, growing more and more edgy.

"The gentleman is correct," said the Swiss. "There is no reason to take chances. He has enough at risk already. Come, let us get on with it."

"Ah, poor me . . . and I was so enjoying the view," sighed the Persian, coming in off the balcony.

The Swiss's manner was direct and businesslike. He was about thirty, with a pale face and steely blue eyes that made the American instantly uncomfortable.

"You are what rank, *mein Herr*?"

"Does it matter?"

"Not at all. I was just curious, that is all. I am not familiar with your naval insignia. You see, we Swiss have no navy of our own, so therefore—"

The Persian again interrupted. "Drink, perhaps? Something cool?" He sighed again. "A lemonade, no alcohol? Fresher, perhaps, in this weather. Alas, myself, I cannot do without the alcohol."

The naval officer sat down, and the Swiss instantly sat opposite him. The Persian busied himself with a pitcher of lemonade, though he had had no reply to his inquiry.

"It goes well at the meeting?" the Swiss asked. It was almost the same form of words, the same intonation, as the driver's question.

"After a fashion."

"There is much dispute? The Russians do not agree with the English?"

The naval officer shook his head.

"And your President? With whom does he agree?"

"With both."

"Ah, ah . . ." said the Persian. "A wise man, very wise. In such a situation, however, there is a danger in trying to sit on the fence too long. The Bulgars used to impale their enemies on staves. The position of such a person as your President is not entirely dissimilar."

The Swiss was not amused. "Which way does he lean? Has *anything* definitive happened?"

The naval officer scowled, taking the lemonade that had been offered.

"What you want to know is this . . ." He drew a breath. "Churchill's plan isn't dead. He's pressing for it now as a diversionary maneuver only, though it's clear that *he* still considers it of primary importance."

"And your President? What does he have in mind? He sides not with the Russians and not with Churchill?"

"I didn't say that. Just listen to me. I said that he agreed with *both* sides. He's committed to 'Overlord,' of course. But this afternoon he came to Churchill's defense too. He suggested a drive across the Adriatic, to be assisted by Tito's partisans, then up the Istrian peninsula, northeast into Romania, to join with the Russians—"

"Who will be coming southward from the Odessa area, yes? This is almost the same thing that the English want. And Vienna?"

"Straight to Vienna, of course, if it's possible. And up into southwestern Poland."

The Swiss nodded. "Then the plan is still alive?"

"Yes, it is."

"Still possible." The Swiss smiled thinly. "Good, good."

"You'll see that the right people receive the information?"

"I have a board of directors meeting tomorrow. I am personally going to the airport in the morning to meet a certain Herr Grunewald, who is counsel for Chemihold of Zurich. He is a member of their board of directors and ours as well. Does that answer your question?"

"You know, I don't like this a bit," said the naval officer. "And I don't think I like you either."

"But that doesn't really matter, does it? You do what you do all the same."

"Yes, God help me, I do."

"Just as we all do. And for the same reasons."

"Here, here, gentlemen. Please," interrupted the Persian soothingly, pouring another lemonade. "Not to think unpleasant thoughts on such a hot night. All will be well when the war is ended. Be certain of that."

"If I wasn't" said the naval officer a bit uneasily, "I wouldn't be here, would I?"

"Of course not," agreed the Swiss, taking a sip of his Scotch and water.

It annoyed the naval officer considerably to note that the Swiss was not sweating at all.

DOCUMENT

Extract from the decision of the United States Circuit Court of Appeals, Second Circuit, in the case of (deleted) Oil Company v. Clark.

In September, 1939, representatives of the (deleted) group and I.G. conferred at * * *, Netherlands. At this conference the parties made a number of formal changes in their * * * relationship. A recitation was made that * * * was the equitable owner of all patent rights of the parties in the Oppanol, Paraffin Oxidation, Acetylene Arc, and Buna processes. I.G. agreed to transfer its stock in * * * to * * *. The terms of the * * * Agreement providing for division of royalties between the two parties on a percentage basis were scrapped in favor of a division of * * *'s rights on a territorial basis. I.G. released to * * * its royalty rights under the * * * Agreement. In return, * * * was to assign to I.G. all its patent rights under the four processes outside the United States and nations thought by the parties to be at war with Germany. Presumably * * * was to retain ownership and control of the processes in these nations through its stock ownership of * * * and whatever rights it had under the * * * Agreement. Other action was also taken at the * * * conference. . . .

Here we have two great industrial organizations which had shown their ability over many years to act in perfect cooperation with flexible legal devices adapted to changing industrial or political circumstances; a pressing and portentous need to make adjustments against the impending crisis foreshadowed by the war; and a formal adjustment of relations with various unusual qualities including disposition of rights by I.G. with small or indirect financial returns (quite contrary to previous habits and customs) and with concealment and furtiveness apparent. Indeed, we think this major adjudication below was quite just. [*This last remark referred to the lower court's holding against (deleted) Oil Company.*]

Unter den Linden 78, Berlin NW 7, Germany

The chairman of the *Aufsichtsrat,* the governing board of directors, put down the memoranda he had been handed only two hours before and reached for the water carafe. He looked up and down the long table, covered with green baize, on which only a half dozen pair of hands, tightly folded, now rested.

The other members of the *Aufsichtsrat,* those few who had been summoned to the special meeting, waited anxiously.

No one moved as the chairman poured himself a glass of water. To a man, the board members wore the same expression of mingled concern and confusion. What they had just been told would unquestionably have the most serious effect on their plans, perhaps on the future of their entire industrial empire.

The cable from Poland had not at first seemed that significant. But as the chairman had spoken—only a few sentences, expressing his view of what would inevitably follow—they had realized exactly how important the cable was and what a danger it posed.

"As you all know, gentlemen, over two thousand British prisoners of war have been held at our Monowitz camp since the Italian surrender. As long as they were there and as long as London *knew* they were there, our installation at Monowitz was safe. To bomb it would have meant risking the lives of two thousand Englishmen." The chairman paused. "That situation no longer exists. Our people in Office A* advise me that, over our considerable opposition, the office of the Reichsführer SS has ordered that these prisoners be removed from the Auschwitz area and transferred to camps in other parts of Poland. The reason given for this is that in the view of the office of the Reichsführer SS the continued presence of these prisoners constitutes a danger to the security of the special operations being carried out at the camp and at Birkenau in particular . . ."

* Office A of the Chief Counterintelligence Agent (Hauptabwehrbeauftrager, I.G. Farben).

"Security, is it? My God, you can smell it twenty kilometers away," muttered one of the board members.

The chairman's face darkened. He remained stiffly erect and stonily silent, as though he had not heard a word.

No one else spoke, or looked at the man who had spoken.

Finally the chairman went on.

"This all occurs at a very inconvenient time. Within the past few weeks a number of prisoners have actually managed to escape from Birkenau. We have reason to believe that a report now exists in which the SS operation there is described in great detail. This report, we are also advised, is already in the hands of the Poles and the Czechs, and efforts have already been initiated to pass it along to the Americans. Should this occur, there will undoubtedly be much pressure brought to bear to bomb the camp, the rail lines in and out, and the installations themselves. The pressure, our analysts expect, will be especially severe as Colonel Eichmann's group has lately begun to organize mass transports from Budapest. This will inevitably focus much attention on the camp itself and the fate of these people. The possible, indeed, the probable results need no further explication, gentlemen."

The six men assembled at the table exchanged glances.

One of them spoke.

"Do you have any suggestions to set forth, Herr Doctor?"

"Only that it is imperative that something be done and done at once. Our staff is working on a number of possible solutions."

"Have our business partners been advised?" asked another of the board members guardedly.

The chairman closed his eyes.

"Not as yet," he said. "There is one possible plan of action that may involve them. Until we have decided what to do, gentlemen, it would not be prudent to advise them of any of what has happened."

"And this possible plan, what is it?"

The chairman took another sip of water.

"There will be a special executive session tomorrow at ten A.M. The plan will be presented then by my staff, after I have had an opportunity to review it thoroughly, as should of course be done."

DOCUMENT

From: Edmund Veesenmeyer, Gauleiter of Hungary
To: Joachim von Ribbentrop   April, 1944

The Hungarian government proves itself serious and acts in its fight against the Jewish enemy with unbeatable speed.

March 29, 1944
Budapest, Hungary

A fierce March wind swept down from the Carpatho-Ruthenian arc to the north and blew clouds of dry, powdery snow past an Orthodox synagogue on Kazinsky Street that had just recently been converted into a stable. The Hungarian army horses quartered within, hearing the whistle of the wind loud as a freight train, whinnied in fear. For a while, the wind continued unabated. Nothing could move. The open-back Wehrmacht trucks loaded with soldiers rigid as cordwood, their rifles jutting up like fence posts, were forced to shelter wherever they could. The Hungarian Gendarmerie huddled in their greatcoats and sought out the few cafés still open. Even the little yellow prowl cars of the German police could not navigate in the blinding snowstorm.

In the building of the Jewish community on Sip Street, the president, Stern, sat with the other members of his council among their piled-up suitcases, looking for all the world like a group of travelers marooned in some deserted rural railroad station, waiting for the arrival of the German police representative. On a railroad siding behind the main station, the train that had brought the regent, Admiral Horthy, back from his meeting with Hitler at Klessheim Castle turned out to be longer than when it had left by one additional car, an elaborately equipped sleeping car that was to be the roving headquarters of the new German minister and plenipotentiary to the Hungarian government, Veesenmeyer.

Snow covered the bombed-out aircraft factories on the outskirts of the city. The brick factories, with their huge storage yards piled high with pallets of brick, vanished under the whirling white clouds. It was as though, for a few hours, the city and its furniture had been covered with sheets while its inhabitants went elsewhere.

Then, gradually, the wind shifted and began to blow toward Transylvania. A hesitant dampness crept up from the river, the temperature moved steadily higher, and the crisp, powdery snow began to turn to rivers of slush. The wind prowled through the streets, brushing away as much of the clean white cover as had not already melted.

Trucks began to move. Clouds of diesel fumes trembled in the air. Chimneys, respectfully hesitant during the storm, began to trickle smoke again.

The iron doors on the west side of the Wesselenyi Street hospital swung open. The barred windows of the wards above, where the insane were kept, glistened with a film of ice. A dozen trucks stood grumbling in the yard below, like anxious elephants, their motors running, exhaust pluming black over the slush. The sharper sound of leather whips cracking filled the air. Hoarse shouts of contemptuous command issued from the interior of the building. A low moaning, woven of many voices, rose to dispute and, at last, to subdue it entirely.

From the previously barred doorway, under a great arch of filigreed iron, a leftover from the previous century's neo-baroque excresences, debouched a triple line of men, women, and children. These all wore the blue-gray pajamas of the wards. Some wore coats or other outergarments, so that the entire assemblage gave the appearance of some sort of vagabonds' circus or paupers' carnival.

On the sleeves of their garments, where they could be easily seen, the yellow star of David appeared, sometimes, though infrequently, joined by a sewn-on cross.

Leading this moaning, groaning, wide-eyed charge and hemming it into some semblance of a line on both sides were a few men carrying truncheons and dog whips with which they struck the snowy air in constant dumb show, every crack of the thongs resounding like a gunshot from the stone walls of the building and echoing through the interior of the building like the thwacking of snare drums at a recruit.

Most of the whip-wielding guards wore the long-skirted officers' greatcoats of the Wehrmacht, some the black leather of the SS, a few the plain soldier's *feldgrau*. But from under the collar of each greatcoat could be seen the bile green of the Nyilas, the Arrow Cross, confirming the message of the identifying circlets on each arm. Toward the rear of the struggling mass came a number of police in their high, nineteenth-century feathered headgear, truncheons in hand, their breath in semaphore before them in the frosty air.

The lines spilled out into the yard, splashing in the slush. Some of the eldest slipped and fell. They were driven upright with shouts and whip cracks. The children cried and the old joined in. There was a general bedlam, leavened only by the continuous grumble of truck motors.

The tailgates of the trucks clanked down as the files of Jews, some weeping, others mouthing prayers, moved forward across the yard.

A man in his mid-forties, wearing the leather coat of an SS but the green of the Nyilas beneath, stood with booted feet planted firmly in the mud, watching the herd of patients being driven past and counting in the air with a gloved finger. He glanced now and then at a sheaf of papers fastened to a clipboard which he held in the other hand. Behind him, six of the Nyilas had formed a channel, further narrowed by inward-pointing carbines, through which the stream of inmates was now directed.

Into the backs of the waiting trucks.

A man faltered and began to howl. The officer with the clipboard—he wore the collar tabs of a captain and carried at his waist an enormous leather holster from which the butt of a Mauser protruded—plucked from his belt a dog whip of his own and began slashing the air over the unfortunate man's head. The patient, wide-eyed and still howling, tried to protect his face, regained his footing, and lurched away. Hands shot out of nowhere and propelled him bodily over the tailgate of the truck and into the dark.

"Get this shit moving, can't you?" cried the Nyilas captain. "All the same," he shouted. "Nothing but shit."

The police shouted obscenities. The women cowered and protected the children, out of instinct and a dumb compassion, for in most cases the children were not their own.

"Quickly, quickly," cried the guards.

"It's not summertime, you know. Come on or we'll have to warm you up a bit."

The yard was full of blue-gray pajamas and nightgowns now, filthy coats, blankets like prayer shawls over seamed and wild-eyed faces.

From down the street came the hiccuping siren of a police car. The captain looked around. It was one of the little yellow cars of the Nazi police that had sprouted like mushrooms all over Budapest during the previous week. Now the car bore down on the hospital yard, looking for all the world like a frosted lemon pastry on wheels. It came to a halt before the yard entrance, blocking the gate so that the trucks could not get out.

As two men in SS uniforms clambered out of the car, followed by two more in police green, the Nyilas captain shrugged, raised his dog whip, and struck out indiscriminately at the lines of passing patients.

One of the Germans, a major by his cuff title and collar tabs, and wearing the gorget of the special police, came over at quick-stride, his hand on his holster.

"You there, what the devil do you think you're doing?"

"Garbage disposal," the Nyilas captain replied, grinning. His face, now that it could be seen in the treacly light that fell from the snow-dusted clouds, was like a skull, wax white, the eyes sunk deep into the head and surrounded by circles so black and permanent that they seemed incised. A gold tooth flashed. Either a frighteningly evil face or a strangely handsome one, depending on one's point of view.

"Must you do *that?*" the SS major demanded, gesturing at the dog whip. "In public?"

"Filth. Shit," said the Nyilas captain. He shrugged and turned back to his task. Most of the patients were by now loaded onto the trucks. A few stood shivering and feverish, up to their ankles in slush.

"Who are these people?" the SS major demanded. "And by what authority are you taking them out of this place?"

A policeman, big, burly, carrying a truncheon, his quaint plumed headgear sitting high on his massive skull, came over and stood by the Nyilas captain. The loading continued. The patients, driven by an increasing flurry of blows, huddled and clambered for the shelter of the trucks.

"Shit," repeated the captain. "Jews. What more d'you need to know?" But he handed the SS major a batch of official orders, mimeographed sheets and a three-color triplicate tissue bearing a number of stamps. "Wards seven, nine, thirteen, and sixteen. Idiots, all of them. What the devil d'you *think* we're going to do with them?" He waited a second, then broke into a wide, fierce grin, displaying his gold tooth. "Why, we're going to take them for a vacation in the country, that's what we're going to do with them. You have a better idea, Major?"

The SS man hesitated; he had obviously not yet decided how to conduct himself in this strange city. The Hungarians were, after all, allies, even though the regent was then under heavy guard with two Grenadiers posted at his bedroom door, and a new government was being tailored to Berlin's order. The former Hungarian minister to Berlin, Szotjay, might be the new prime minister, but Budapest was no occupied city. Not *de jure,* at any rate. Not yet.

The hesitation flickered out under the stares of his subordinates; the SS major was young but not that stupid. He took the documents from the Nyilas officer.

The German rush to take over everything in Budapest had been so precipitous that there simply had not been enough time to find officers capable of dealing with the Hungarian language, not enough to fill even a fraction of the positions required. The major was not one of those who could cope with more than a few sentences. Therefore, he immediately lapsed back into German, thinking in German, complaining in German that he could not read the documents that had been handed him.

"*Hier, sehen sie . . . bitte . . .*" the Hungarian said with a harsh, grating accent, pointing to the official stamps. Under what appeared to be a detailed order, stamped and restamped in four colors, was a signature that the SS man recognized immediately. His instruction, brief as it had necessarily been, had at least included the names of the ranking officials in the Hungarian police service. The major knew that Laszlo Baky was the state secretary in charge of police, and thought he knew the signature, too. The document also bore a number of SS and Wehrmacht counter-stamps and scrawls. The transport manifest appeared in order, the hospital release forms had been filled out, the lists of names numbered and checked with blue pencil.

That was good. Blue pencil. Regulation.

The SS major liked order; the documents appeared to be in the kind of order he liked.

He handed the papers back to the Nyilas officer.

"Mental defectives?" he said again. "We got rid of such scum years ago."

"For summer vacation. In the woods. Yes?" said the Nyilas captain.

The SS man nodded perfunctorily, turned on his heel in a fine flurry of slush, and ordered his men back into the little yellow car. In a moment they had driven away down the street, horn tooting.

At the other end of the street, a convoy of German armored trucks rolled by solemnly, the drivers high in their cockpits like tankers, their glasses down.

"So, don't stand there gaping. Let's get these shit-bags out of here," cried the Nyilas captain, loud enough for the entire street to hear. He jumped onto the running board of the lead truck, swung the door open, and clambered inside, at the same time windmilling with his arms to signal the other trucks to follow. The rest of the guards followed suit, each climbing aboard a truck. The police remained in the yard, watching with grim seriousness as the cara-van moved out through the iron gate with a great churning of slush and coughing of motors.

In the lead truck, the Nyilas captain took a deep breath and leaned against the seat. He pushed back his cap, mopped his fore-head, and fumbled in his coat pocket for a cigarette.

The driver, a huge red-haired man, grinned widely and squinted.

"It's starting to snow again. Good," he said.

The captain nodded.

"They'll leave us alone in this mess, won't they? The Germans hate snow almost as much as we do," he said.

"After Russia, I'd think so, wouldn't you?"

The captain half turned, as though he could see behind him. He pushed open the canvas flap and looked into the dark of the truck back. Thirty or more people were huddled together for warmth there. A child was crying and complaining of the cold—his fingers hurt. A woman took him to her breast.

An old man, one of those nearest the cab, saw the captain looking back.

"God bless you," the old man said. He was one of those the captain had struck with his whip in front of the SS major.

"We're not out yet, grandfather," said the captain. Then he let the flap fall.

"We'll get out," said the red-haired giant.

"Drive like the devil, Itzhak. Don't stop until we get to Kormend. Not for anything, d'you understand?"

"Ah, Miklos, Miklos . . . do you really think you have to tell *me* such things?"

And with that the red-haired man stepped hard on the accelerator and the truck roared ahead down the street, heading south.

"Almost four hundred," the captain said. "We're going to get almost four hundred out this time, Itzhak. That's something, isn't it? That's really something."

DOCUMENT

From: The president of (deleted) Oil Company
To: Dr. Fritz Ter Meer, I.G. Farben, April 20, 1938

My view is that we cannot safely delay definite steps looking towards the organization of our Buna business in the United States, with the cooperation of the people here who would be our strongest allies, beyond next fall—and even to obtain this much delay may not be too easy.

From: The president of (deleted) Oil Company
To: Interdepartmental, April 20, 1938

Until we have this permission, however, there is absolutely nothing we can do, and we must be especially careful not to make any move whatever . . . without the consent of our friends. We know some of the difficulties they have both from business . . . interrelations with the rubber and chemical trades in the United States and from a national standpoint in Germany, but we do not know the whole situation. . . . The only thing we can do is continue to press for authority to act but in the meantime loyally preserve the restrictions they have put upon us.

April 8, 1944
Lisbon, Portugal

A cool breeze laden with the scents of a hundred African flowers stole gently down the Avenida de Liberdade from the botanical gardens above the Circo de Pombal. The palms in the garden islands that divided the north- and southbound traffic lanes of the Avenida shone a fragile silvery green in the soft afternoon sunlight. It was the first really fine April day Lisbon had seen that year, and everyone was out to enjoy it. That it was also a Sunday simply made things easier.

The Rossio below was crowded with flower vendors. Basket upon basket of fresh-cut blossoms filled the square. From the Tagus came the deep lowing of a steamer's horns. Double-decker buses lumbered up the slope from Black Horse Square by the waterside, spewing diesel fumes that mixed with the floral scents to give the city its characteristic April perfume. In rare intervals of relative quiet the shrill cry of peacocks could be heard floating down like the lament of dying angels from the gardens of the Castel San Giorgio on the western heights.

The garden islands of the Avenida were already crowded with the city's citizenry, soberly taking the afternoon sun in their accustomed shabby dignity. Here and there were persons even shabbier than the rest, men and women whose faces showed not merely the customary resignation to poverty that marked the average Lisboner even in this flush time of war, but rather the harried look of the transient who has no goal in sight and knows, too, that he cannot remain long where he is.

Germans, Poles, a few Italians, Hollanders, French, Hungarians, Greeks, people of every nationality and people so long deprived of one that they could not say without thinking long and hard where they had been born and where they had lived their earlier lives. These mingled, nervous and cautious, with gray-clad Lisboners, trying not to attract attention to themselves, trying to remain constantly alert, and so long alert that they could no longer be so.

On a bench shaded by a lush stand of palms growing somewhat taller than most sat a solemn gentleman of perhaps fifty or so, unremarkable at best, of common appearance and anonymous features. His hair was dirty speckled gray and cut a trifle shorter than was the local custom. The only thing about him that in any way set him apart was that his shoes were neither Portuguese nor Spanish nor of any other discernibly European manufacture. He wore heavy sunglasses that hid his eyes completely. Nothing unusual in this, of course, or in the sports newspaper he had been reading, which now lay open on his lap. He seemed on the verge of a doze. The cigarette in his mouth moved a trifle to one side, then to the other, the only evidence of consciousness.

On the black-and-white mosaic walk before him, a stretch some fifteen feet wide and perhaps twenty across, a number of children were playing. One little boy in a crisp white-and-blue sailor suit rolled a hoop under the watchful eye of his grandmother. Another, slightly older child, wearing a serious, intent expression, was busy bouncing a rubber ball to and fro. Bit by bit the child edged into a position directly in front of the man with the non-European shoes.

Keeping the ball going in a slow but steady rhythm, the child turned once with a quick, birdlike movement, looking back over his shoulder at the man he had come with, a small, dark, stocky person of no particular account, possibly his father or an uncle.

The father or uncle nodded imperceptibly.

The boy, making sure that no one was looking directly at him, gave the ball a slight shove, an angled bounce, so that instead of coming back to him it veered off lazily toward the bench and the palms, slowed, and rolled up finally between the non-European shoes.

The dirty-haired man at first took no notice. The child waited. Then the man with the non-European shoes smiled, leaned over, and picked up the rubber ball.

The child did not move.

The father or uncle rose and came over, an apologetic smile on his face.

"You will excuse little Jao? He is so careless. He means no harm."

The dirty-haired man nodded slightly, his eyes hidden behind the sunglasses.

"It is a pleasant day for children to play."

"Little boys enjoy playing with rubber balls," the father or uncle said. "As you see."

"As I see," repeated the dirty-haired man, smiling transiently.

He held the little black ball—about the size of an English squash ball—gingerly between thumb and index finger. He pressed slightly. The ball had a pleasing resilience.

"*Bom dia,*" said the father or uncle. He took the little boy aside, at some distance, gave him a coin, and then walked quickly across the southbound lane of the Avenida to the Tivoli Hotel.

The child scampered off to join the little boy in the sailor suit. To the discerning observer it would have appeared then that the man was not the boy's father or uncle at all but a stranger for whom the child had performed some slight service.

As it was, no one was paying any attention at all.

On any given sunny Sunday afternoon in Lisbon in 1944 at least twenty thousand little boys were out on the streets. And at least half of them were playing with balls of one kind or another.

The dirty-haired man stared at the rubber ball for a moment, turning it slowly. Then he pocketed it and went back to his dozing.

April 10, 1944
The Ljubliana Gap, Yugoslavia

The long freight train hooted southward along the line from Vienna to Ljubliana, down through the gap and into the Croatian flatlands, bearing its endless load of bricks, soap, and fodder. The last three cars were sealed, the windows boarded shut, heavy wire twisted on the door latches, tags hanging down and pocked with official blue and red stamps.

The manifests were in order. A special transport to a center being established near Skofja Loka. Three hundred and eighty-nine Jews of mixed age and sex. Police permits and transit clearances all exactly according to regulations.

The train did not stop. It rattled over high bridges spanning deep gorges, through fields in which women in black bombazine, half submerged by heavy bundles, followed hayracks past roads clotted with military trucks and concrete mixers. Into the harsh, deep blue Yugoslavian night and toward a gentler Italian morning.

At Tolmin, the border guards checked the manifests once again and waved them on. It was an odd train. At the head, the engineer, the firemen, the mechanic, all sooty in their tender, naked to the waist and swilling Slovenian beer. Thirty cars of silence. Not a living soul to be found there in the rattling freight cars.

Then three cars of Jews. Tightly packed, but breathing. Water enough in buckets. Bread enough.

In the last car, the Nyilas captain and the red-haired giant. Neither had slept for forty-eight hours. The captain's face looked more than ever like a skull. His eyes had receded even further into his head. He was reciting poetry in order to keep himself awake. In Hungarian, then German, and finally Greek, which he still remembered from the time when his mother, who had come from Salonika, had been alive.

Now and then the two men played whist or patience, games which both knew, the Hungarian doctor and the Galician mechanic, but they played listlessly and without skill.

Through the wired glass panel in the rear of the car they could see the tracks fleeing like eels into the hills and mountains behind them. The rumble of passage was lulling, almost the equivalent of a deep-sea silence.

In the second of the cars, a rabbi mumbled prayers. Someone had found candles, and even in the rank air of the car they burned and cast a wobbly glow over the upturned faces of the lunatics, the madmen and madwomen, the feebleminded children of Wesselenyi Street.

None of whom were.

All of whom had pretended.

At a siding near Glorenza there would be more trucks and the mountain men who spit on Mussolini's picture.

Then, by different routes, with different guides, Switzerland.

The train came cautiously down along the Sava River and made its way along a spur line that had been built sixty years before to take the Viennese aristocracy on holiday to the skiing villages of the lower Dolomites. The train did not stop for fuel or food or water. There was enough coal for the engines and enough bread and water to keep the passengers alive.

Just before crossing the border, they encountered a barrier thrown across the tracks by a squadron of mounted Ustashi. The word was passed at once through the cars. As the train steamed to a halt before the barrier and the Ustashi machine gun emplacements, a low moaning arose from the cars. Hebrew prayers sounded in the chill Croatian night. Children wept. The Ustashi listened, at first puzzled, then grinned with cruel understanding. The Nyilas captain in his black-and-green uniform leaned from the side of the tender and shouted imperiously. The SS seals on the low, curved-roof cattle cars were all the Ustashi needed to see, although they read neither German nor Hungarian.

At five in the morning the train pulled off the main line at a deserted siding a few kilometers east of Bolzano. It was just beginning to grow light. A steely, reluctant gray spread like a stain above the crenellated silhouette of the Rhaetian Alps.

A small switchman's shack stood like a discarded packing case near the rails, crusted with ice and fine powdery snow. In the distance, just then becoming visible, the snow-capped peaks of the Val Venosta rose, hazy and magisterial, to the north. A dark broom of snow swept down the slopes of Mount Glania, briefly engulfed the not-far-distant gothic rooftops of old Bolzano, and then whirled off towards Civedale to the west. A few empty railroad cars stood about the siding, snow heaped high on their curved green roofs, icicles hanging from their undersides. Small bonfires burned behind the shack, and a thin trickle of smoke wound up into the sky from a tin chimney. The yard was pockmarked by bomb craters, the bombs most likely having been dropped by error during a raid on Bolzano. Here and there tracks spiraled up into the air like curls of sugared pastry. Railroad ties lay on nests of rusted concertina wire.

The train came slowly to a halt, the tender just opposite the switchman's shack. The red-haired giant poked his head out cautiously. He cocked his Danuvia 43 machine gun and waited. The Nyilas captain took off his cap and pushed his thinning black hair back over his forehead. His eyes shone feverishly. His breath plumed out before him in the frosty air. It was cold, but the air was clear and fresh and a pleasure to breathe.

North Italian air.

A big, strapping man in the uniform of a Bersaglieri major came out of the shack. The red-haired giant grinned, showing his crooked yellow teeth, and leaned the Danuvia against the wall of the cabin. The Nyilas captain, in turn, holstered his Luger.

"Buon giorno, Tulio," said the giant. "Exactly on schedule."

"As always," said the major.

The Nyilas captain jumped down from the cab and puffed up a cloud of powdery snow as he hit the ground. The Italian laughed.

"Complimenti," he said, handing over a clipboard laden with official forms, sealed and stamped. "You'll find it all in order, Captain. In any event, you will not be bothered here. The route has been cleared and all the necessary instructions have been given."

"An extraordinary performance, Major Baccara," said the Nyilas captain, studying the documents.

The Italian smiled graciously. "If it is needed, there is food for your people. In the shack. Some bread, some tins of pressed meat. It should be helpful."

"It will be very much appreciated, Major," said the captain. "They've had little to eat in the last few days. Just enough to keep them alive, I'm afraid. We couldn't manage much, coming out of Budapest."

"Things do not go well there for your people," the major said.

"There's news?"

"All I know is this, that it was said on RAI last night that the Tedeschi have moved into your city in force."

"How many divisions?"

"It is not known. But there is word of the Colonel Eichmann. This is a name you have heard before?"

The captain nodded soberly.

"There will be much suffering, I fear," said the Italian. "Come, let us get the food on board, so that there will be, perhaps, a little less suffering here. You have children with you?"

Again the captain nodded.

"*Sta bene,*" the major said. "We have sweets for them. Not much, but something at least."

The red-haired giant shook his head as though trying to dislodge a fly from his ear.

"They haven't had sweets for—" He broke off, overcome.

While the major and the red-haired man hauled the sacks of food out of the shack and passed them up into the sealed cars through the sliding hatches above the couplings, the Nyilas captain spoke quietly and with great weariness.

"Almost four hundred this time," he said.

"They'll be safe soon. Will there be more?"

"Yes, but it will be very difficult."

"It has always been very difficult."

The Italian major jumped down from the roof of the car. He stood there smiling and dusting the snow from his uniform.

"So . . . *buon viaggio,* Captain," he said. "You should not remain here too long. It is safe, of course, but still, you should not remain. At Silandro there will be a checkpoint. The papers you have will see you through. The trucks will be waiting south of Gorizia. But you should change uniforms. Here, take this package. Your friend, however, must stay out of sight. I could find nothing large enough for him. You see, we are not a large people, Captain."

"You are a good people, Major."

"Some of us, Captain. By the way, you speak excellent Italian."

"And German and English, too," said the giant with a touch of pride. The captain took the package and went into the shack.

A balloon of black smoke issued from the locomotive chimney. Steam billowed between the wheels, hissing.

"Time," said the red-haired giant, looking at his watch.

In a moment the Nyilas captain had returned. He was no longer an Arrow Cross officer in green jacket and black trousers but now a captain, a *centurione* of the Fascist militia in regulation *grigio-verde*.

He saluted and mounted to the cab.

"At Silandro, remember, the papers will see you through. Try to arrive, though, at night. It will be better that way. The Tedeschi are sometimes about during the day."

The engine lurched forward. A fine spray of snow whirled up, and in a moment the switchman's shack and the major and the entire siding were lost and there was only the pungent coal smoke and the snow, spinning in the wind like a great storm on all sides of them.

Georgetown, Washington, D.C.

At 6:30 A.M., just as the first light of a fine April morning was turning the gabled rooftops a dull gold, a small gray Studebaker drew up in front of an elegant Georgetown house, not far from Massachusetts Avenue.

It was an ordinary car, without any distinguishing markings, but the emblem on the flat leather pouch its occupant was carrying as he ascended the six wide front steps proclaimed him a diplomatic courier under State Department seal.

He hesitated for a moment as he stood before the door, his

index finger hovering over the bell button. Then he touched it. Hesitantly. Very briefly, as though the very idea of pressing a doorbell at that hour of the morning was hopelessly distasteful.

The bell responded with a gentle, elegant ping.

He waited only a moment.

The door opened. He was ushered inside by a tall, craggy-faced man in his fifties, wearing a heavy ribbed sweater and canvas pants.

"Sir?"

"You've come from Lisbon?"

The courier nodded, holding out the pouch.

"It hasn't been opened, sir," he said, his eyes betraying his confusion. The pouch seemed to be almost empty. Whatever it held it was not the customary packet of letters.

The man in the sweater took the pouch silently.

"The ambassador sends his compliments, sir," said the young man.

"By all means, return them," said Trilling. Then, as if by way of afterthought, he added, "If you'd care for some breakfast, why, you can join me in the kitchen. I was just doing the eggs when you rang."

"Thank you, sir. I've eaten already."

Trilling looked vaguely cross. "Too bad. My boy's still in bed. Doesn't like early rising. So I thought you might give me some company."

"I'm sorry, sir. I'm expected back."

"Of course, that's right. You've got to go back."

"Is that all, sir?"

Disappointment settled across the older man's face. His son was upstairs, still in bed, sleeping off a late night and the whiskey and the women that had gone with it.

"Thank you for coming round," Trilling said. He turned and went off toward the kitchen, swinging the pouch.

The courier found his own way out.

DOCUMENT

Letter of (deleted), President of (deleted) Oil Company, referring to the accords reached with I.G. Farben during the meetings in Holland in 1939.

. . . We did our best to work out complete plans for a *modus vivendi* which would operate throughout the term of the war, whether or not the U.S. came in. All of the arrangements could not be completed, but it is hoped that enough has been done to permit closing the most important points by cable.

April 13, 1944

New York City

The firm name was lettered across the dark oak doors in such a restrained style that it was difficult to read: HAYKLUT, BARD, WINSTON & STROPP, ESQS. The doorknobs were polished to a dull luster suggestive of old gold and of infinite wealth and power. In the reception room, an elderly male clerk waited imperturbably behind a walnut desk, a large black appointment book open before him, his eye on an old-fashioned grandfather clock that ticked stolidly next to the brass-studded chesterfield against the opposite wall. On a side table lay a selection of magazines to be read by clients who never really were there long enough even to finish the shortest of articles: the *Wall Street Journal, Fortune, Petroleum Times,* and a half dozen other industrial and financial journals.

It was eight thirty in the evening; a tang of late snow still lingered in the city air. The winter had been unusually severe that year and long in departing. The lights along lower Broadway had mostly long since gone out. The only exceptions were the windows of the large law firms and a few insurance companies. In such places, even in wartime, the lights never went out. In such places, as in the offices of Hayklut, Bard, Winston & Stropp, Esqs., the appearance of perpetual activity was even more important than the activity itself.

The oak doors opened and a tall, middle-aged man, rawboned and craggy, and carrying a small black briefcase, presented himself to the receptionist.

"Trilling. For Mr. Stropp." His eyes were pale and ringed, his expression worried, but he carried himself erect and with an air of importance. He was, clearly, a man who knew who he was and never for a moment forgot it.

The receptionist tapped a little desk bell. A second clerk appeared, also elderly, wearing a gray cotton jacket of the kind often seen on hotel porters. He moved in absolute silence as though wearing sneakers, which he was not—as though also afraid to disturb the tranquility of the generations of former senior partners who observed his comings and goings sedately from their gilt frames on the wall. Their faces all shared a certain distasteful arrogance with the client, Trilling.

The second clerk conducted Trilling through a corridor lined with small offices under whose doors small slivers of light were to be seen. Trilling looked neither to the right nor to the left; he expected evidence of constant industry and consequently took no real note of it.

The two men ascended a circular stairway to the next higher floor, passed along another corridor, this one shadowed and dark but for the low-wattage ceiling fixtures placed at lengthy intervals. The clerk moved with the authority of a retired army officer, not even looking back to see if the client was following him.

Trilling was at last ushered into a large corner office. The room was a dark, somber place, paneled with oak and decorated with ancient maps and lithographs of the city. Bookcases crammed with leather-bound volumes of statutes and corporate mergers lined the walls. On the opposite side of a vast mahogany desk, hunched over a mass of papers which he was studying through the thick lenses of his wire-rimmed glasses, was an undistinguished-looking middle-aged man. He looked up, leaving the sentence he had been reading unfinished.

"Marcus?" The light, possibly, was too dim for him to be sure.

"Who else would they have let up here, Henry? You've been well?"

The lawyer smiled reluctantly and dismissed the clerk, who closed the door and vanished down the corridor just as soundlessly as he had come.

"Sit down, Marcus. There's coffee if you want it. Or would you prefer whiskey?"

"What do you think, Henry?"

The lawyer shrugged and went over to a sideboard to pour his client almost a full water glass of Scotch. Trilling arranged the meager contents of his briefcase on the table.

"Good trip, Marcus?" Stropp asked casually. Trilling watched as Stropp bent to secure the bottle, grimacing faintly. Stropp had a congenital spinal deformity which made leaning painful. Which, in fact, had made life in its entirety somewhat painful. Because of it, for instance, Stropp had never married.

"Trip was decent enough, Henry. I had to drive. We couldn't get clearance for the plane. Can you imagine? I couldn't get clearance to fly my own plane." He took a long look out the window and said, "You know, I don't like this damned city of yours, Henry. Be glad to leave as soon as I can. So let's get on with it."

Henry Stropp handed over the whiskey.

"You're not drinking?"

"Not now. You'll excuse me, of course. A lawyer's prerogative. It fogs the mind."

Trilling took the whiskey in one long swallow and sat down heavily, a vague, almost transfigured look on his face. Stropp eyed him cautiously and retreated behind his barricade of files. Trilling was visibly excited, his lean, hard face flushed with enthusiasm.

In the muted light of the lawyer's desk lamp, Trilling appeared worn and slightly shabby, as though the too-frequent exercise of power had somehow depleted him. His skin had the color of old newspapers, faintly yellowish, and his teeth were none too good.

Stropp avoided eye contact for a time, continuing to maneuver his papers back and forth across the desk. He had spent the last eight hours going over all the contracts, the secret arrangements and the broken deals. He had read the report that Trilling had sent on ahead and had gone carefully through the Criterion chemist's analysis. Trained as a patent lawyer, undergraduate at MIT and then Columbia Law, Henry Stropp knew quite enough about copolymers to appreciate the importance of what Trilling had set before him.

The data was not as complete as he would have liked, nor as competent. It left too many questions unanswered. But it was tantalizing. Too tantalizing not to be followed up.

Trilling had even sent along a little piece of the rubber ball. The "Lisbon rubber ball," as he called it.

Interested as Stropp was, he nevertheless resented Trilling's insisting on using him for this distasteful business. He could hardly refuse, of course; to even hint at refusal would be to risk losing Criterion Oil as a client and the annual six-figure fee that the Criterion representation meant. Nor could he deny that there were cogent reasons for singling him out to undertake the project. He, Henry Stropp, knew more about the relations of Criterion Oil of Wilmington and I.G. Farben than anyone else alive, even Trilling himself.

Stropp had been responsible for placing Trilling on the board of directors of American I.G. Chemical Corp. He had worked out the Rotterdam agreements on markets divisions with I.G. just before the war had broken out. He had obtained the assignment, again from I.G., of substantial patent rights for a number of new processes, including the new Buna rubber technique. He had done all of this. But he had made one major mistake. He hadn't quite managed to get the Germans to live up to their side of the bargains he'd made with them.

And then the war had broken out.

Now, with the tide finally turning and the frightened men on the Unter den Linden trying desperately to hedge their bets, he was going to be given a chance to "redeem" himself. That was the way Marcus Trilling had put it. There was a nasty resonance to the word: to be given the chance to redeem oneself meant that one presently lived in a state near to mortal sin. And Stropp knew that Trilling and the rest of the Criterion board regarded his failures in precisely that light, even though those failures were as much theirs as his.

When Trilling finally broke the strained silence he began, as so often he did, in the middle of a sentence, simply assuming that anyone in his presence knew exactly what he had been thinking without being told.

". . . cover, yes, they'd better. They will cover, won't they?"

"Excuse me?"

"The patents. You've checked the patents, Henry? They'll be sufficient to cover all the improvements in the process, won't they?"

"Your own legal department says they will."

"Damn it, those fellows are good for chasing bad accounts, that's all, Henry. What do *you* think? You were a better lawyer the day you got out of Columbia than our chief counsel will ever be. That's why we hire you."

"You don't *hire* me, Marcus. You retain my firm."

"I beg your pardon. We're quite touchy this evening, aren't we?"

"Plotting to commit criminal acts tends to make lawyers nervous, Marcus. Don't ever forget that."

"I'll make an effort, Henry. Now, what about the patents?"

"The patents that were assigned to you in 1938 clearly cover all improvements in the basic process. From the report you've sent me I'd say that the sample you received was definitely the result of a straight-line development of the original process."

"The hardware for which we've never seen," said Trilling sharply, his resentment at having been bilked breaking through.

Stropp nodded. "That was something we always understood."

"You did, maybe."

"We *all* did," Stropp said firmly; he wasn't going to be caught out as easily as all that. "Without the know-how, all the patents in the world were worthless. We all knew that at the time. It was the chance we took. Who can tell? Perhaps Dr. Krauch wasn't lying. Perhaps their government really was holding them back."

"*Our* people didn't say a word when we handed *them* the tetraethyl process in '38, did they?"

"Draw your own conclusions."

"I did, a long time ago. And if my conclusions weren't what they were, and still are, do you think we'd be doing *this,* now?"

Stropp shook his head and looked away. He didn't like to be reminded of the risks involved. After all, he was the one who was going to go out there and actually do it. If something went wrong, it would be his neck. If they'd been taken in before, then he'd been taken in too: he'd believed the I.G. men, Dr. Krauch, Ter Meer, and all the others, when they'd apologized for the roadblocks the Nazi government had put in their way. It was diplomatically impossible, they'd said, to turn over the Buna know-how. There was simply no way it could be done without risking arrest. Hadn't they honored their bargain by turning the patents over to the jointly owned Chemical Information Holding Corporation, or "Chemihold," as it came to be known?

Trilling, as though reading the lawyer's thoughts, was quick to remind him. "Remember, we've got a superiority position in the manufacture of butadiene. It's locked up. You people just keep the Justice Department off our backs and when you're finished you'll be on the board of Hydro-Arc. When you get back, Henry. It's been passed already. In a year it'll be yours entirely."

"Stock ownership?" Stropp was caught completely by surprise and instantly regretted his show of pleased astonishment.

"Twenty percent." Trilling smiled into the darkness. "Enough to make even King Midas happy. Frankly, Henry, I'm jealous. But then, I haven't got your adventurous spirit. Also, I don't speak German. You do."

Stropp's heart raced. He hadn't expected anything like this. Twenty percent of Hydro-Arc was enough to keep the greediest of men content for the rest of his life. The butadiene monopoly would eventually depend on the production of acetylene from hydrocarbon gases. The electric-arc process, for which Hydro-Arc held the exclusive patents, was the key to the whole thing. All they needed now was the Buna know-how.

"How am I to tell if the technical information they give me is any good? Can't you give me a good lab man to check things out?"

"Impossible, Henry. There's simply no way. We'd never get such a person past security and onto a plane, much less all the way to Zurich. Anyhow, I trust Krauch."

"I certainly don't, and I don't see why you do, not after what he did to us at Rotterdam."

Trilling's face grew dark, and when he spoke again it was in a low, barely controlled voice.

"You just do as you're asked to do, Henry, and let me worry about who to trust. Besides, if there's any real problem, there's a man already over there you can use. He used to be one of their best chemical engineers."

"Used to be? What's the matter with him?"

"He's a Jew, Henry. His name is Felix Landau. They threw him out in '38."

"Wonderful. And I'm supposed to go to *him* for help?"

"Why not? Haber was a Jew too," Trilling said. "Henry, I think you ought to have your Zurich office get hold of this fellow right away. Have him stand by. Just in case. Then use him or not, whatever suits you."

"What makes you think he'll cooperate?"

"You offer him enough, Henry, and he'll cooperate all right. They all do. Just don't start him too high. Agreed?"

"I don't like it, not one bit."

"Do it, that's all," Trilling snapped. "You wanted a chemical engineer? I'm giving you one of the best. He knows Buna, Henry. He was one of the team who designed the pilot plant at Oppau, where they perfected the chlorination process. I trust your instincts, Henry. If you have any doubt about what they give you, why then, *use him*. Have him check the data."

"You've made your point, Marcus."

Trilling sat back, looking pleased. "When do you leave, Henry?"

"Day after tomorrow. You should know. Your secretary made the reservations."

"Staying where?"

"The Baur-au-Lac."

"That's it, Henry. Go first class."

Stropp wasn't sure whether that was a compliment or a rebuke. Trilling could be enormously tightfisted at times.

"The whole thing will be first class, take my word for it," Stropp said. "We've got them over a barrel this time and they know it. They'll have to sign over the fluid-catalyst equipment this time. The whole lot of it."

"I want it all in writing from them, Henry. Something we can look to later. Grunewald can keep it safe for you. The Swiss understand these things better than we do." Trilling smiled, paused for a long moment. Then he spoke, very slowly, emphasizing each word. "We keep the bombers away from the new plant, and they guarantee that when our troops get there it's all ours. You have Grunewald check the documents that Krauch brings thoroughly. To make sure they comply with all the Swiss laws."

"As you know, we have our own man in Zurich, Marcus. I'll be working with him and Grunewald together."

"Who? Not that miserable little cocksucker, Eisner? He's an embarrassment, not a lawyer."

"Eisner is a good man, Marcus."

"Not good enough to get away with that swindle he tried to pull, was he?"

"It was no swindle. It was a simple, straightforward embezzlement. He was short and he borrowed some trust funds that didn't belong to him, that's all."

"He should be in prison."

Stropp's face went rigid. What little color there was in it all but vanished, leaving him a gray caricature of his Austrian paternal grandfather. The cold Scot's eyes that had come down to him on his mother's side narrowed until the pupils were no longer visible.

"You know exactly why we couldn't do that, Marcus. You could even say that it was your fault that we couldn't. He knew too much. Remember, he was in on your 'marriage' with I.G. right from the start. He helped draft the Rotterdam accords, and the tetraethylene purchase too. If I remember correctly, it was you who almost had a stroke when we pointed out to you what he could do if Justice ever got to him and promised him a deal. We couldn't let that happen, now could we, Marcus? It was much simpler to set up a Zurich office and put our friend Eisner in charge and out of the way."

Trilling frowned. "All right, Henry. Your point. But still, I don't like it."

"He works well enough with Grunewald. Besides, I need him."

"What for? You're a good enough lawyer for me."

"But he knows both our law *and* the Swiss. He's essential if you want everything perfect."

"You'll be there to watch him?"

"Of course. And believe me, he'll do exactly as he's told. You won't have to worry about Sam Eisner, Marcus."

"I'd better not," said Trilling. "We want internationally clean title to everything in that plant the day our troops walk in there."

"*If* we get there first."

"What, exactly, does *that* mean, Henry? *If?* We'll get there first all right. Just the way General Smuts has it planned. Up through

Vienna, across Czechoslovakia . . . why, my God, it isn't any
wider there than Rhode Island. Then we go right into the plant.
We'll get there first all right. You saw the message from Teheran,
didn't you? I.G. read it loud and clear and they're ready to deal.
The operation is still very much alive, the Russians notwithstand-
ing. We'll get there first, Henry. Count on it."

"We'd better or all of this is going to be for nothing."

"Listen, Henry . . . Churchill wants the strike up from the
Adriatic. Roosevelt wants it. *We* want it. The only ones who don't
want it are the goddamned Russians, and as long as they get what
they *do* want they won't make too much of a fuss."

"I hope you're right, that's all."

"I'm right, Henry. All you have to do is see to the assignments,
the stock transfers and the market arrangements. And make sure
that our good German gentlemen keep their word this time and
don't produce a single pound of rubber until we get there. As long
as they do that, we can keep the bombers away and everyone's
happy. You do all that, Henry, and leave the war to me."

Stropp nodded, avoiding Trilling's stare.

"One more thing, Henry . . ."

"Yes?"

"Stay away from our offices in Geneva. This trip of yours is to
remain strictly a private affair. I don't want anything traced back
to Criterion. It could be very embarrassing if anything got out."

"Nothing will get out. And nothing will go wrong."

"You see to it, Henry."

"I will, Marcus. I will."

April 16, 1944
Zurich, Switzerland

The trucks crossed the Swiss border a little after dark and by eight
the caravan had split, seven to Bern and six to Zurich. The crossing
had been simple. The Italians had been nowhere in evidence and
the Swiss border guards had been well paid to look the other way.

Miklos Baranyi had not slept for over three days, kept conscious
only by the caffeine tablets he had been taking constantly since

leaving Hungary. The red-haired Itzhak Kagan, who had the happy faculty of being able to sleep for short periods standing up, was bright and wide-awake. He still wore the remains of the Nyilas uniform he had donned eighteen days before.

The trucks had sheltered in a vast, shadowed brickyard on the far side of the Sihl River. As quietly as possible, the trucks were unloaded and the exhausted refugees moved off, one by one, to prearranged shelters, some to the country, some to apartments within the city of Zurich. The Hospital of the Sisters of Charity, acting on a sealed directive from Monsignor Roncalli, nuncio to Ankara, had agreed—very quietly, very discreetly—to take thirty of the children. Now the worst that would happen to the adults if they were caught would be internment in a Swiss camp. No longer did the Swiss send refugees back over the border. The outcome of the war was clear now, and the Swiss were not stupid.

The mud-daubed headlights of an Opel blinked twice behind the storage shed. A tailgate clanged down. Baranyi leaned against a truck, exhausted, while Kagan went over to the car.

In a moment he was back, his face creased for the first time in days by deep lines of worry.

"It's Julie, Miklos . . ."

"So?"

Baranyi could barely keep his eyes open. He had no wish to talk to Julie Malowska or to anyone else. He had been without sleep for three days, had gotten almost four hundred people out of Budapest at one time, right under the noses of the SS patrols, and all he wanted at the moment was a good Schnapps and a bed.

"She says she must speak to you," said Kagan.

"If she must, she must."

"She says it's important."

"What isn't important these days, Itzhak? Life is important, death is important. Sleep is also important."

"Please, Miklos . . ."

A line of children was being guided through the darkness to a file of waiting automobiles by one of the sisters from the hospital.

"Now let us play a game, children," the nun was saying. "There are dragons in the forest and we must not make a sound."

"What do Jewish children know of dragons?" said Kagan.

"They'll learn, they'll learn," Baranyi replied. "They learn so quickly, about everything, these children."

Baranyi looked down. Something crinkled underfoot. It was a cellophane wrapper from one of the sweets that the Italian, Baccara, had provided.

"Miklos, this is magnificent. Three hundred and eighty-nine," said Avner Liebermann, coming across the yard.

"Is it?" Baranyi replied listlessly, hardly able to focus on Liebermann's seamed, craggy face. "We left four hundred thousand or more behind."

Liebermann did not respond. Baranyi dug in his pocket for the bottle of caffeine tablets. It was empty. He threw it away.

"Itzhak, can you take care of the trucks?"

"Why not? And you?"

"My sister-in-law—didn't you say that she was waiting for me?"

With that he stalked off, still looking every inch the *centurione* of Fascist militia in the remains of his Italian uniform. As he crossed the littered courtyard, he shucked off the gray-green jacket and the mountain cap and unbuttoned his collar.

With that last gesture, a violent transformation took place: he became once again a small, almost insignificant figure, a man of no determinable age, but no longer young, of slight, wiry frame, large-headed, bent, exhausted and unsure of his footing. His arms hung at his sides. His walk became almost a lurch. He looked as though he would fall at any second.

Liebermann moved to help him, but Kagan touched his arm, holding him back.

"No," Kagan whispered. And that was that.

She was sitting there in the Opel, slumped against the seat behind the wheel and looking much as he remembered her from that day when she had rescued him and Josef at Gyrenbad—pale, exhausted, the once gold of her hair almost white. She had never regained so much as an ounce of the vitality he had once known in her. Not since her escape from Poland. She lived on air, fragile and brittle. A marginal survivor only.

Her eyes narrowed as he got into the car. "How many did you bring out this time?"

"Almost four hundred," he whispered.

She bit her lip.

He knew what she was thinking. Once, she would have said it too. "You'll never make up for *her,* Miklos, not if you bring out every Jew in Hungary." But she wouldn't say it now. It had been a long time since she'd last blamed him for her sister's death. She'd never really believed it was his fault. And certainly not now. Not anymore.

She nudged the accelerator and the car hissed out onto a gravel road between the kilns and the storage sheds. He slumped back, feeling wearier than he had felt all week.

For a moment she took both hands off the wheel in order to light a cigarette. It was the kind of near-suicidal gesture that was typical of her now. Some fought with every breath to survive for one more day. Others, like Julie Malowska, didn't seem to care anymore.

The flame illuminated her face briefly from below, giving her features a transient look of madness, like a face in a Munch painting.

"You're very tired, aren't you, Miklos?"

"I don't mind being tired. I accept exhaustion as a permanent condition of existence. But I'm not too tired to go to my son's grave. Will you take me there, Julie?"

She looked away. "Not now, Miklos. In the morning, perhaps. I'll take you in the morning. Yes . . ."

"Julie . . ."

"Paprocki wants to see you," she said flatly.

"Tomorrow for Paprocki, Julie. He's never had anything yet that couldn't wait twelve hours. The man didn't even know Poland had lost the war until he woke up one day to find a German colonel eating breakfast in his dining room. Here, give me a cigarette."

She thrust the pack at him. "We must go now. Conrad says that it's very important."

"Look, I don't really care—"

"You *know* you've got to go."

He lit his cigarette, inhaled. It was American, and very good.

"Pauer from the Czech legation will be there too. He's bringing the full copy of the report. It comes from the Czechs."

"What report?"

She ignored him, as she usually did, in her bitter, insistent way.

"The report came from Weissmandel's organization. Now are you interested?"

"Rabbi Weissmandel?"

"Whatever he is," she drawled, blowing smoke.

"And so? Tell me more, please."

"It is about the camp at Oswiecim, Miklos. Two Czechs escaped. There are thirty pages of details. Conrad has talked to Pauer about it. He says that . . ."

"Yes?"

She paused; for a moment her features softened so that she almost looked as he remembered her from before the war, his wife's lovely younger sister. Not the bitter, irrationally vengeful creature she had become.

"Conrad says that it's simply too horrible to be believed."

"Nothing is too horrible to be believed, Julie. You, of all people, should know that," he said. "Now, may I sleep for a few moments? Until we get there, at least?"

She did not answer him but hunched forward, urging the car onto the main road into the city.

Miklos Baranyi closed his eyes and in a moment had almost drifted off to sleep.

Julie turned her head slightly and stared at him with that same ambivalent look of hatred and compassion that had colored every look, every word she had addressed to Baranyi for the last two years.

The headlights picked out a No. 6 tram car lumbering across an intersection. A truck sputtered through the crossing. A few shop windows glittered with late-night lights. They were entering Zurich proper now.

In front of her, the street opened onto a view of the dark Limmat River and the Quaibrücke. She could smell the river and the familiar acrid odor produced by the converted auto motors that now burned wood instead of gas.

For a moment Julie felt herself suspended in the darkness, weightless and without any sense of time. Memories crowded through her mind.

Baranyi.

Miklos Baranyi. Her sister's husband.

She recalled vividly the day in early December 1942 when she had gone with Conrad Bor and the Polish consul, Paprocki, to the internment camp at Gyrenbad. Paprocki had made it a practice to visit the camp once every two weeks to see if any Poles had turned up. Often there was something that could be done. Residence permits could be arranged. Sometimes permission to work could even be obtained.

The day had been unusually bright and cold. The snow on the mountains to the south had glistened like cake frosting. In the shallow valley the snow was piled in high drifts against the wooden walls of the long sheds inside the wire fences. Smoke rose from a few of the chimneys and was torn apart at once by the stiff winds coming down from the Toggenburg.

Paprocki, bundled in a heavy coat and smoking a cigar, led the way to the administration hall. The camp director had arranged, as always, for the records of new admissions to be made available, and for such interviews as might be required to be conducted there.

They crossed the snow-dusted compound. A crowd of internees had gathered along the wall of one of the barracks buildings. A huge pile of what at first looked like rubbish but turned out to be a collection of shabby luggage lay nearby. A few guards, a bare-headed man whom Julie Malowska knew to be Schissl, the camp doctor, and two nurses were arguing with a wild-eyed man who stood with his back to the wall, desperately clutching a small bundle. The others, perhaps two hundred men and women, waited and watched silently.

"They refuse, always, to give up their possessions," Paprocki said sadly. "They never seem to understand their position here and why they must do as they're told."

Julie wasn't listening. She was staring at the man.

The doctor began to shout angrily. The guard lowered his rifle, not exactly pointing it but definitely threatening. The crowd of internees began to murmur.

"I'll kill you first, I swear it," the man with the bundle cried in oddly accented German. "I'll kill *him* before I let you take him."

Then she realized that the bundle the man was holding was a child. Wrapped in rags.

And also that she knew the man.

A knife suddenly flashed into view in the man's hand.

The guard lowered his rifle a bit more. One of the cantonal policemen standing nearby drew a revolver.

"Conrad, you must stop this. That man is my brother-in-law."

Bor stared at her, aghast, then turned and stepped forward with a long-legged stride that took him straight into the circle of internees and guards.

The doctor recognized him and gave way. The guards drew back. No one wanted a riot. The Swiss were harsh but not murderers.

The man with the child, his face black with grime, the pupils of his eyes dilated, backed against the wall and slowly lowered the knife. As if there had been something in Conrad Bor's voice that had instantly calmed and reassured him.

Or, possibly, because he had seen the woman standing a few meters away.

"Will you please, Dr. Schissl? The director has given us permission, explicitly. This man is a Polish national. He is known to us." Bor lied without blinking.

The crowd moved back hesitantly.

They had taken Miklos Baranyi to the empty administration hall, still clutching the child, and weeping now, violently and uncontrollably. Julie Malowska hung back, afraid that he would recognize her as she had recognized him. Afraid to ask where her sister was or how Baranyi had come to be there and in such terrible condition. Afraid to ask what had happened to the child.

In the cold administration hall, Dr. Schissl had gently pried Miklos Baranyi's fingers away from the little bundle and unwrapped the filthy scraps of blanket, knowing what he would find. Baranyi seemed to collapse, slumping back against the wall. He had finally given in to his exhaustion. Julie Malowska had leaned over, looking into the child's face—her nephew's face—for the first time.

The child's pale, glazed eyes stared off, unseeing, reproachful, sad. She touched the boy's sallow cheek. The skin was cold and hard. She ran her fingers over the shrunken chest; there was not the slightest flutter of life.

According to the doctor, Baranyi had been carrying a dead child for at least three days.

She remembered thinking, How could he not have known? In all that time, how could he not have known? He had come, like the father in Goethe's *Erlking,* desperately seeking shelter, through the storms. Across half of Europe.

But the child was dead.

And in all that time, he had not known. Though there had not been, could not have been, a single sound.

Not a single sound.

As now, in a tunnel of silence . . .

She turned again and looked at him sleeping there against the car seat. So much had happened since that day.

They had taken him in, arranged for him to live, and they had buried the poor little corpse in the Jewish cemetery south of the Limmat. Slowly, he had recovered. They had never spoken of the child, of those last few days when the boy had died. When his physical strength had returned, Baranyi had become a worker for the rescue organization of the Jews. He had gone back time and again to Budapest, to Romania, to Cardinal Tiso's Slovakia. Bringing out the doomed. By the handful, sometimes by the trainload. He had worked with the ferocious energy of a dozen men, and he had shown himself improbably brave, inconceivably competent . . . the frail former doctor from Budapest.

But it had changed nothing.

It could never change the thing that mattered most to Julie Malowska.

Teresa Baranyi, born Teresa Stefania Malowska, oldest daughter of industrialist and sportsman Adam Malowski, of Warsaw and Plotzk, was dead. And she was dead for one reason only. Because she had married Miklos Baranyi. Because she had married a Jew.

Ever since that day at Gyrenbad when all the pain Julie Malowska had experienced in her brief life had come together again in the face of a dead child, that single fact had become the focus of her existence. From it, all else proceeded. It motivated everything, justified everything, explained everything. From her weary liaison with the much older Conrad Bor to her frantic commitment to the varied causes of the Vaadah, to her strained, almost unbearable relationship with Miklos Baranyi.

All of it.

Because Teresa was dead and all that was left of her was her memory. And Miklos.

*   *   *

The lights burned late in the windows of the building occupied by the Zurich representative of the Polish government-in-exile. Vice Consul Paprocki was pacing up and down, wearing a hole in the already threadbare carpet that was the only furnishing in his office other than the peeling desk and two old office chairs. It was well past eleven. He had been waiting for the courier from the Czech intelligence bureau for more than two hours. The Jew hadn't shown up either, which was probably just as well. He was always uncomfortable when alone in the presence of a Jew. The Czechs, and Pauer in particular, always seemed to know how to deal with the men of the Vaadah. But the Czechs, as usual, were late.

Paprocki's secretary had long since finished the day's typing and was listening to Fred Bohler's swing band on the anteroom radio. Every time the announcer's voice came on, Paprocki winced. The sound of German, any kind of German, even *Schweitzerdeutsch,* grated intolerably on his nerves.

Paprocki was sweating. He knew that he would never grow used to waiting. All during his former life as administrator of one of the largest financial institutions in Warsaw, the Bank Panstwa, he had been accustomed to making others wait for him. The war had changed many things, but such firmly ingrained habits die hard.

He had smoked his last pack of cigarettes and, with a sinking sensation, realized that there would be no more for at least a week. Not that there weren't plenty of cigarettes available in Zurich, but the brand he preferred, English Sailors, arrived only every fortnight with the diplomatic pouch from London. At his age—he was fifty-six—such things took on an importance out of all proportion.

He went to the window and looked out, hardly expecting to see anything. He had, however, chosen exactly the right moment. A battered gray Renault with corrugated sides was just pulling up at the curb in front of the legation building. He recognized the car at once. It was even shabbier than the vehicles at the disposal of his own office.

He watched with a faint feeling of superiority as a man in a long leather greatcoat got out of the car on the driver's side—he had obviously driven it himself—and tramped up the front steps. The man was carrying a slim briefcase attached to his wrist by a chain.

In a moment, a bell rang in the anteroom and the portable radio was switched off. Paprocki heard footsteps and the sound of a door shutting. His secretary knocked once, without urgency.

"Come in, come in. We're expecting you."

The secretary, a plain-looking middle-aged woman who had been a flute player in the Warsaw Philharmonic before the war, pushed open the door and admitted the Czech. Paprocki whistled.

"So, it's you, is it, Pauer?"

"I thought I should bring this over myself," said Pauer. He turned to the secretary. She left at once.

Pauer was in charge of intelligence for the Czechs in Zurich, the counterpart of Paprocki's own Conrad Bor. Paprocki had hardly expected Pauer to come over himself, and the intelligence chief's presence caused him a thrill of apprehension.

Pauer, a stocky, graying man in his late forties with huge, powerful hands on the backs of which the veins stood out like heavy blue cords, unlocked the chain from his wrist and placed the satchel on Paprocki's desk. He took off his coat and settled himself into one of the two chairs in Paprocki's office. Then he took out a cigarette case and pointed it at Paprocki. "One of mine? I think they're the same kind you smoke."

Paprocki was taken aback. "How did you know?"

"Ask Bor. I'm sure he knows the brand I prefer, too."

Paprocki took the cigarette; it was, of course, a Sailors. He lit it diffidently, then unlocked the satchel and took out a thick sheaf of papers fastened by a single clip.

Across the top were written the words "Report—April 1944" and below two names: "Rudolf Vrba" and "Alfred Wetzler."

As Paprocki hesitated, Pauer looked around anxiously.

"Where is the Vaadah representative? You did contact him, didn't you? They should be the first to see this, by all rights. They're affected even more than you Poles," said Pauer.

"I sent for them. But, as you see, they're not here yet. Dr. Baranyi was on . . . an 'excursion' . . . he was expected back this evening. I'm sure he'll be here soon."

Pauer shrugged. "Then perhaps you should read the report while we wait. It comes from Rabbi Weissmandel's organization in Bratislava." There was a long silence. Then: "You'd better sit down when you read it. It's worse than you can possibly imagine."

Paprocki took the papers, sat at his desk as he'd been told, and switched on the lamp. Pauer waited, watching the older man's face intently as he read, waiting for a change of expression.

Fifteen silent minutes passed.

The radio went on again in the anteroom, the volume surreptitiously low this time. Zarah Leander, singing "Meine Leben für die Liebe."

Paprocki continued to read. The color slowly drained from his face. A number of times he stopped, wiped his forehead, and turned back to the page he'd just finished as though he could not really believe what he'd read.

Finally he put the papers down. "When did you receive this?"

"Two days ago. They escaped only at the beginning of the month." Pauer sighed. "Where is Bor? I thought he'd be here too."

Paprocki shook his head and reached for the interior phone that connected him with Colonel Bor's office on the floor below. Bor had a habit of working late and could always be counted on to be in his office until past midnight. He had the appearance of a Franciscan and the superficial habits of a Spartan. The night life of Zurich, such as there was of it, held little attraction for him. His wife, who had been a well-known dancer in the films, had been killed on the very first day of the war. What little time he spent outside of the legation building he spent with his mistress.

Which, Paprocki thought, was probably where he was now.

The phone rang for a long time. Paprocki had almost given up when Bor's familiar voice finally came on, gentle as a confessor's.

"Ah, you *are* there, Conrad. Aren't you coming up? Pauer seems to be expecting you."

"I already *know*."

"Nevertheless," Paprocki said, at a loss for words.

"As you wish" was the soft reply.

"What a trial that man is," Paprocki muttered, to no one in particular, adding, "and that woman . . ."

Pauer, who had long ago met Julie Malowska and, under other circumstances, might well have followed up on his initial interest, simply smiled.

In a moment there was a knock on the door. Paprocki knew at once that it was not Bor, who had never knocked on Paprocki's door in his life.

"Come, come, it's open."

The door swung wide and an exhausted-looking man in a shabby gray suit and open collar seemed almost to fall into the room.

"Dr. Baranyi?"

"Consul?" Miklos replied stiffly.

Pauer got up and took Baranyi by the shoulders in the compassionate way one often greets a bereaved person. It was important, that brief but firm physical contact. Baranyi understood and his red, weary eyes showed his appreciation.

"Sit down, here . . . Paprocki, you have something for him to drink? He's at the point of collapse, can't you see?"

Paprocki fumbled in his desk and came up with a bottle of kirsch.

Pauer said, "It went well this time? Good, I can tell that by your expression, tired as you are. Sit now. What I have to show you is not good, but you must see it."

Just then, Bor entered the room. "So, Dr. Baranyi, our friend Pauer here has brought you the report from those two who escaped from hell last month, yes?"

Miklos did not look around. He could see Bor in the mirror behind Paprocki's desk, a tall man, over six foot, with a large head of which the forehead and eyes seemed by far the largest portion. His hair was fine as spun glass and snow white. It had turned that color the day he had learned of his wife's death.

"You will excuse my being late, Baranyi? You understand, of course. Your sister-in-law . . ."

"Where is she now?"

"In my office. Sleeping, I'm sure. She's become positively neurasthenic recently." He smiled faintly at Miklos, as though in secret sympathy; he understood the tension that existed between Julie Malowska and her brother-in-law, and Baranyi knew, in turn, how often Bor had counseled her to compassion, but without result.

Miklos slumped down on the one free chair. The consul handed him a kirsch.

"That woman," Baranyi said softly.

"She has her uses," said Bor.

Pauer grimaced and pushed the report across Paprocki's desk.

The pages fell apart. Bor picked them up. His eyes fell on one passage toward the middle of the document.

It holds 2,000 people. . . . When everybody is inside, the heavy doors close. Then there is a short pause,
presumably to allow the temperature to rise to a certain
level, after which SS men with gas masks climb on the
roof, open a trap, and shake down a preparation in
pellet form out of tin cans . . . a cyanide mixture of
some sort which turns into gas at a certain temperature.
After three minutes everyone in the chamber is dead.
The chamber is then opened, aired, and the Sonder-
kommando carts the bodies on flat trucks to the crema-
toriums, where the burning takes place. . . .

Bor shuddered. "Read, Baranyi. I can wait. I know what's in
there already."

Paprocki's thick eyebrows went up in surprise.

Bor said, "I had a copy this afternoon. And not from Captain
Pauer, either."

Baranyi sat down. Paprocki came around the desk and stood
looking unceremoniously over the Hungarian's shoulder.

At last Baranyi finished. Not a muscle had moved on his skull-
like face all the while.

Bor spoke. "So . . . Pauer's people say exactly the same
thing as Captain Zabreski, as Lieutenant Kochel, as all the others.
The only difference is the detail." His voice became almost inaudible. "The incredible detail . . ."

Bor lowered himself into a chair. Paprocki was busy at the wall
safe, extracting the reports Bor had just mentioned, fragmentary
accounts of an unbelievable installation that had been erected just
outside the town of Oswiecim. The men who had written the
accounts, Polish officers, not Jews, who had managed somehow
to escape, had been regarded with suspicion. Their story had been
fragmentary, hallucinatory, incredible.

Bor, however, had always believed. Nothing, he had often
remarked, was too horrible for the German mind to contemplate
if only it was performed with precision and according to scientifically determined principles. "It takes a fear of the unknown, a real
imagination, a touch of hysteria, perhaps, to truly understand
horror. Such things are alien to the German mind."

"This came from Weissmandel?" Baranyi asked. He had known

about the camps, of course, about what the deportations meant, about the extermination squads. They had all known. But this? The magnitude of it and the perfection of the system was simply beyond belief.

"There's no doubt of its accuracy," Pauer said. "I had the unhappy experience of speaking to Vrba myself two days ago."

"Where is he now?"

"He's gone back, to try and help if he can. But the report is here, as you see."

Baranyi's voice was little more than a whisper. "Certainly we've had information about the camps before, the torture, the killing. But this—next to *this* the others all seem almost insignificant. This is a machine. A *factory*."

Bor nodded, imperceptibly. "At Sobibor, there is another. And at Chelmno."

"Of this magnitude? So large?"

"This one is by far the worst," Bor said.

Paprocki was the one to break the silence. "We are agreed then?"

"If by that you mean are we agreed that something must be done," said Pauer, "then the answer is, of course, yes." He took out a sheaf of papers. "We've taken the liberty of trying to work it out. Here is a map, with all the various parts of the installation drawn in. Wetzler did it for us. Quite precise, I think. It matches the aerial photos exactly. And now we know what the buildings are for, particularly the ones with the brick chimneys."

Baranyi shook his head. "Maps are all well and good. Intelligence is excellent to have, but aren't we omitting something? Consul Paprocki, how many high-altitude bombers has the Polish government-in-exile at its disposal? Captain Pauer, perhaps you Czechs have access to a squadron or two?"

There was, again, a deep silence.

Bor said, "The Americans must be told, of course. They are the ones most likely to do something. We can forget about the British. They're too concerned with what will happen to them if there is a flood of Jews into Palestine after the war."

"This is hardly a matter that involves the Jews alone," Pauer said. "Many hundreds of thousands of Czech citizens are being murdered in these places along with the Jews. And I need not remind you that second only in numbers to the Jews are the Poles who are being slaughtered. And first among them, the Polish clergy."

"You don't have to convince *me*," objected Paprocki. "The only question is what to do, and how best to do it."

Bor leaned back, fixing his pale eyes on Baranyi.

"Clearly, the Americans must be advised. Perhaps your people in America, Doctor, perhaps they can bring some pressure to bear on their government?"

Baranyi could barely keep his head up. His hands were trembling so badly that he had to hold one with the other to keep them still.

"You honestly think that we—*we,* of all people—will be listened to by the Americans? Why now? It would be the first time if they did."

"They must listen. Contact your people in New York and in Washington. You must try," said Pauer.

"What I *must* do is go back at once. Perhaps more can be saved. Ten thousand, five, even one thousand. Who knows? Horthy is not an evil man. Stupid, yes; weak, too. But it may be possible . . . I must go back to Hungary. Not to the Americans."

"They are the only ones who can do anything meaningful. We all know that. Miklos, for God's sake, what can you do? Bring out a few hundred more? What are a few hundred compared to the thousands who will stay and die?"

"Nevertheless . . ." Baranyi muttered desperately.

"Nevertheless, it must be the Americans."

"Bombing," said Pauer. "It can be done. The gas chambers are just within range. They can be hit with the Americans' high-altitude bombsights. We know that. At the very least, the railheads could be knocked out."

"If we had accurate rail maps, schedules . . ." Paprocki said. Bor exchanged meaningful glances with Pauer, but neither man said anything to the consul. Bor nodded. Pauer took note.

Paprocki said, "Even a country that has been overrun, that is occupied as we are, still has some honor left. We cannot tolerate . . ."

His voice trailed off into incoherence. He was obviously fighting a number of conflicting emotions.

"Will you go, Doctor?" said Bor. "Will you help us?"

"Help *you?*" Baranyi's laugh caught in his throat.

"We must all help each other," said Pauer softly. At this, Baranyi nodded helplessly. There was no point to it, and he could ill afford either the energy or the time for such an assuredly futile effort. But neither could he say no.

"What an insane world we live in," he said. "An asylum."

"In the morning then," Bor said. "You will go, Doctor, to the Americans. I too will go. There will be no time lost, I promise you."

"To the consul here in Zurich?"

"No. Directly to their man in Berne. We have already sent the preliminary reports there, to the military attaché, Bard. The men in Zurich are decent, Henderson and Mr. Crawley, but they can do nothing on their own. They lack authority. All reports from the Zurich consulate will go to Major Bard in any event. For clearance. So it is best to go to Berne straight off."

"Holy mother of God," said Paprocki, as though he had not been paying attention at all. He was staring at the dark window. His fingers moved flickeringly across his chest. Baranyi looked away in embarrassment.

Paprocki was crossing himself. Over and over.

"Ten thousand a day," he whispered. "Holy mother of God . . ."

Conrad Bor descended wearily to his office, leaving Baranyi, Pauer, and Paprocki to their arguments. He had had quite enough of arguments for the day, for the week, for the month. And worse than that, he knew that nothing, really, could or would be done.

He also knew that he would most likely wear himself out, possibly to the death, trying.

He was older than Paprocki—almost sixty—and burned out. There was not an ounce of strength left in him. He'd seen it all: the Russians, the first Great War, then the civil war with its unbelievable ferocity, the Bolshevik invasions, then Pilsudski and the mock republic. Finally, the last act—President Beck's mad bluff, his awful dilemma, his refusal to join with the Nazis against the Bolsheviks for fear of what the Soviets would do to Poland in reprisal.

Now, of course, the final irony loomed: because of Beck, the Soviets would undoubtedly do exactly what he had feared, even though Poland had actually stood as a buffer between them and the Nazis and had refused to cooperate.

Unless something could be done to keep the Soviets at bay. Unless the Germans could hold them back somewhere east of Warsaw until the western forces broke through the German heartland.

And saved Poland.

It was all quite obvious. If the rail lines into Oswiecim were taken out, all the rolling stock that had been diverted from the eastern front to the death camps would be free for military use. More troops, more supplies could be moved east. Every square meter of Polish territory that could be denied to the Russians would be meaningful in the end.

Whenever the end came.

And so the problems of the Jews and the Poles coincided. The solution to the one was at least a partial solution to the other. A step in the right direction.

Bor smiled at Paprocki's naiveté. If the consul really felt morally outraged, let him. If he felt that the camp was an insult to Polish honor—whatever *that* was, as of 1944—then so be it.

What served the purpose of one served the purpose of the other. Hereditary enemies would be allies. For a time.

He closed his eyes and leaned on the door. Visions of cafés and lovely women swarmed through his head. He thought he could hear the sound of Jan Keipura's grainy tenor singing a Krakowiak.

Nothing. Imagination. Warsaw—before . . .

The room was almost dark. Julie Malowska had left only one lamp on. She lay on the cracked leather sofa, her feet up on the arm, her dress up over her knees. Her eyes were closed, a beatific smile on her thin lips. Wisps of pale ash-blond hair hung over her face like the fringes of an antique shawl.

He sat down next to her and very gently took her hand. He was old enough to be her father, but that hadn't mattered at all. He was, in fact, very much like her father. He had met Adam Malowski once, at a diplomatic reception. A patent of nobility, a dozen or more sawmills and timber warehouses north of Plotzk—these had made the Malowskis wealthy and powerful.

Until the war.

"Wood burns quickly," Julie had said, and that had about summed it up. Everything had been consumed. In the flames. Her sister, Teresa, married to the Jew who now sat upstairs in Paprocki's office, had been killed in the Hungarian town of Korestan, machine-gunned by the Nyilas. The father had been blown off the face of the earth during the second day of the *Blitzkrieg* when Stukas had destroyed the sawmills at Plotzk. How Julie herself had ever gotten out of Warsaw, much less all the way to Switzerland, he would never know. She would not speak of it. Sometimes it seemed to him that the entire experience had already mercifully faded from her memory.

How many times had she been raped, how many times given herself for a scrap of bread or a cup of water? He thought that once, when he had been a young man, such things would have mattered very much to him and he could not possibly have taken her in as he had, knowing that such things had happened. But he was not a young man any longer, and if age had done little else for him, it had given him perspective, distance, and the ability to ignore things that were not really important.

He pulled up a chair and sat by the edge of the sofa, his hands between his knees in an attitude of penitence, watching her sleep. Her breathing was deep and even; a little blue vein at the hollow of her throat moved slightly. She seemed to have achieved a sense of peace that he himself would never be able to recapture.

How long he remained there by the sofa, not really watching her but, in a way, guarding her, he had no idea. A half-hour, perhaps. The legation building seemed full to the brim of time, of minutes. Like a pool of rainwater, full of drops.

He heard a breathing that was neither his own nor Julie Malowska's, then a voice.

"Is there anything you want me to do?"

Baranyi had come into the room silently. The man moved like a a cat, even when he was exhausted. A natural furtiveness. Bor had once commented on it. "All Jews move that way nowadays," Miklos had said. "We can't afford to attract attention."

Bor looked up, his long, priest's face without expression. "She's my worry. I'll take care of her."

"I'm sure you will."

Bor let it pass. He smiled faintly. "She's young enough to be my daughter," he said.

"I didn't mean to be insulting."

"I know, I know. And I didn't mean to be insulted."

"So, then . . . is there anything?"

Bor shook his head. "She's quiet now."

"Has she taken something?"

"I thought you might know. Look at her. She sleeps as though she were dead."

"I haven't given her anything, Colonel. I'm not licensed to practice here. The Swiss don't allow it, you know. I have no access to drugs."

"If I thought they came from you, I would have asked you to stop a long while ago."

"There are no drugs. She's just very tired."

"She's this way all the time now. Sometimes I think she will wake up one day and simply be too tired to breathe."

Baranyi laughed softly. "The heart beats without our willing it, my dear Colonel Bor. And we breathe in the same infuriatingly obstinate way. To my knowledge, no one has ever succeeded in committing suicide by holding their breath. The body insists on its prerogatives."

"Nevertheless," Bor said, "if you find out what it is she's taking, will you let me know? It can't be good for her."

"You care?"

"As you do, I think."

Baranyi looked away. A look of surprise had come briefly across his face, as though he had never considered matters in quite that light before and was not prepared to cope with the thought.

"I . . . pity her, Colonel, that's all. And she hates me, no matter what face she puts on for you."

"Oh? You think she blames you for her sister's death? Still? Ah, my poor Doctor, how little you understand."

Baranyi went on as though he hadn't heard. "In a way she's right to blame me, you know. If Teresa hadn't married me, she might still be alive today."

"Like her father, who did not marry you and is dead? Or her brother, who did not marry you and is also dead. Or like the millions of Poles who did not marry Dr. Miklos Baranyi but who are also dead? You do her an injustice if you think she can possibly blame you. Quite the contrary, Doctor. You are her anchor, whether you like it or not. And what a fool you are not to understand it." He shrugged, then exhaled deeply, far more than a sigh. "Go to sleep, Doctor. And leave Malowska to me."

"You *will* take care of her?"

"And I will understand her, too. If I need you, I'll call. I know right where to reach you, don't I?" Bor said. "How are you getting back? She drove you here, didn't she?"

"Pauer's waiting for me downstairs."

"Good night then. Rest. Promise me, Doctor, that you'll rest."

"Sleep, yes. That I'll promise. But rest?" He shook his head.

"Sleep then. That, at least."

DOCUMENT

From the transcript of the I.G. Farben war crimes trials. Witness Dr. Oskar Loehr.

QUESTION—When was the first time you turned over the Buna process to the American company?

ANSWER—As far as I can remember, we never did. By process, I mean detailed information as to its manufacture.

QUESTION—So, I.G. was able to suppress completely the synthetic rubber production in the U.S., was able to use an American company, (deleted), to protect I.G.'s patents in case of war between the U.S. and Germany, and . . . undermined the military potential of the United States, is that right?

ANSWER—These are conclusions which seem to disclose that I.G. impaired the military strength of the United States, yes.

Nachitoches, Louisiana

A guard in the dark gray Criterion Oil uniform, pinnacle and stars on a white shoulder patch, undid the chains, pushed open the gate in the huge hurricane fence, and waved the black Buick through. He had recognized the driver instantly and needed no identification.

"Evening, Mr. Trilling, sir."

"Evening, Jake. How's your missus?" asked Trilling, leaning out of the car window.

" 'Bout the same, sir," the guard said. "She'll be okay, I guess. Thank you for askin'."

Trilling knew the family history of almost everyone who worked for him, and he always made it a point of asking after relatives. The guard's wife was in the hospital. Criterion had sent flowers.

Little things like that went a long way.

The Buick glided almost silently along the gravel road. Ahead lay the huge complex of the Nachitoches plant. First came a row of concrete buildings stretching almost a mile east to west and connected by runways of piping and heavy conduit. Tall stacks and kettles, silo-shaped chambers that rose over a hundred feet above the Red River marshland. The sky above was bright with stars. The huge plant that lay below, all three square miles of it, was as dark and silent as the ruins of a city through which the plague had passed. Other than the guards at the gates and a skeleton force in the power station and main pumping installation, there was no one else there. The plant was deserted.

Someday, Trilling thought, the towers would be full, the sky above bright with flames, the silence of the Louisiana bayou night altered forever by the murmur of unending chemical processes. But for now there was nothing. No butadiene bubbled in the tall tanks. The plant had been built for that and for that alone; they could produce butadiene here faster and more cheaply than anywhere else on earth.

But there was no need for the butadiene. There was no use for it.

Not until they had the Buna formulas. And the know-how. And most of all, the prototype equipment.

His son, Wayne, would probably live to see it. Perhaps he would too. At fifty-two he still had a few good years left. His grandfather had lived to eighty-five, and his wife's mother was still alive, a hearty ninety-three, in Enid, Oklahoma.

Trilling got out of the car and walked slowly around his fiefdom. The air was fresh and very warm for so early in the spring. He looked skyward. Stropp's plane was up there somewhere, probably halfway to Zurich by now. It had been difficult even arranging Stropp's passage. The Justice Department was watching everyone connected with Criterion Oil like a hawk. He had no doubt that the FBI was watching too. How absurd it was, he thought, for them to be worrying about antitrust violations in the middle of a war. On the other hand, as far as he was concerned, the war hardly mattered. A momentary aberration. To be turned nicely to a profit if possible. Certainly not to be allowed to interfere.

There always had been wars and there always would be. This one was no different from all the rest.

He'd worked out the arguments and the justifications for what he was doing very carefully, but he'd never quite been able to make them all mesh. The important thing, in the end, was Criterion's postwar position. And there was no doubt that the Buna S process was essential. Particularly as it had been so improved.

The war was already won; it was only a matter of time now, a year at most. The men at State had promised him their full cooperation, and Stropp's partner, Bard, had worked hard to assure the necessary cooperation at SHAEF.

It hadn't been too difficult, really.

The only lives involved were Jewish lives. And a few Poles and Russians. They'd die anyway, most of them. For the past year, while the groundwork for the new series of agreements had been slowly worked out in Lisbon, in Geneva and Madrid, he hadn't been able to press the point. Now the British had unwittingly done it all for him. And the Germans themselves. The SS, if his intelligence was correct.

The POWs who'd been held so long at the camp right outside the gates of the Buna installation had been moved.

The question was open once again.

Something had to be done and done quickly, the *Aufsichtsrat* had decided. Before, they had held back, waiting for an advantage; now they pressed their suit impetuously. Desperately.

The moment was right. Both sides had their needs.

Therefore, Stropp, and Zurich.

The Secretary of War would cooperate. The State Department had already been silenced, to the extent that any silencing was necessary—which was very little. Promises had been made. Criterion had already begun to deliver on those promises. Trusts had been established, stock had been delivered in escrow, board of directors positions had been reserved for after the war.

It had all been done very quietly, very discreetly. And very efficiently.

It had required little effort. As far as the upper echelons of State and War were concerned, Auschwitz might as well have been on the other side of the moon.

Nothing in the world was easier, Trilling mused, than to bribe someone to do something that he was quite willing to do anyway.

DOCUMENT

From a transcript of a stockholders' meeting of (deleted) Oil Company, June 1943.

Motion—"That (deleted) Oil Company shall not resume cartel relations with I.G. Farbenindustrie after the war." [*This motion was put by a stockholder.*]

Chairman of the Board—"We do not know what business conditions will be in the postwar world. We do not know how the very intricate and complicated problems of international trade are going to be solved."

[*The motion was not carried.*]

April 18, 1944

Zurich

The four shabby rooms occupied by the workers of the Vaadah Ezra va Hazalah were located halfway down the Frankengasse, above an odd-lot print shop owned by a refugee Bulgarian. In the print shop fake passports and residence cards were printed. Here the so-called *Schutzpasses* and documents of neutral-government protection were counterfeited by the thousand and sent into Hungary and Slovakia. Above the shop, one of the four rooms had been turned into a sort of dormitory. Against the walls were crammed iron-frame double-decker cots that looked as though they'd been ripped from the rusty hold of a third-class tramp steamer. It was to this room that new arrivals in Zurich, refugees for whom no other accommodations had yet been found, were taken. At the moment, two women, one French, one Polish, and six children were asleep in a welter of long-unchanged linen and sour laundry.

A bunker had been constructed in the basement below the concrete pads on which the printing presses rested, a refuge in the increasingly unlikely event of a search by the cantonal police.

The rooms adjacent to the dormitory were filled with paper-strewn desks. Gray filing cabinets crowded every available space. The air was rank with the stale smoke of a thousand dead cigars and cigarettes. Coffee was brewed in a large steel vat that sat like a bathtub in one corner of the room that Baranyi used as an office when he was there. The floor was crowded with cardboard boxes in which Baranyi preserved a two-year accumulation of newspapers, cables, the appeals that daily poured in on his small group of workers, and the reports that filtered through the underground networks of a dozen occupied countries.

A third box remained empty. It was intended to house the records of the Vaadah's successes.

The Vaadah had been founded two years before by a group of earnest, intelligent men from Budapest: Joel Brand, Reszo Kastner, Springmann, and a half dozen other former Labor Zionists. In the early days, when Budapest had been a haven of sorts for fugitive Jews from Slovakia and Poland, they had done much good work. But now, as the noose was tightening on the Jews of Hungary, they still clung to their old ways. Reason, negotiation, "business deals." The German mind was, after all, the most orderly and rational in Europe, they insisted. In the end, one would always be able to "do business" with them, as one always had. But first they must realize that you were not afraid.

Baranyi and a few others did not agree. Most of the dissenters were young and rash. They took chances, risked their lives, behaved in ways that the solid, cosmopolitan, assimilated Jews of Budapest considered absurd, inappropriate, and nonproductive.

The group had split without really splitting; each faction tolerated the other and prayed that they would both be able to achieve their ends.

Offices had been set up wherever it was possible to set them up. A network of contacts had been established with the Jewish Agency in Palestine, with the Joint Distribution Committee in the United States, and the Aggudath, the Orthodox Rescue Committee there, with anyone who could help. The nets extended into occupied Poland and Slovakia, into Italy and Germany itself. There were even a few among the SS who, for their own reasons, rendered assistance. They were referred to as the "handwriting experts": they'd seen the letters of fire on the wall. A little earlier than some of the others.

Such staff as there was in Zurich consisted of Baranyi himself, Itzhak Kagan, a Lithuanian American named Wolkowitz who was rarely there but through whom most of their operating funds were obtained, Avner Liebermann, a number of field agents holding Swiss citizenship who regularly risked their lives in Prague, Budapest, and anywhere else that craft and bravado might save a few lives, and a few hangers-on, like Julie Malowska, whose motives no one could fathom but who were intermittently useful.

Between them, they kept the lines open to other involved organizations. They came, they went, harried men and women with feverish eyes, stinking perpetually of unchanged clothing, sweat, and railroad coal, carrying forged passports, distributing documents. Baranyi remained fixed at the hub, putting what remained of his physician's training and mind, his scientist's precision, to work trying desperately to hold it all together.

He had passed what had been left of the night on a mattress rolled out on the floor in the corner of his room, too tired even to take his shoes off. He had cried himself to sleep that night, thinking first of the words written by Vrba and Wetzler, and then of his own narrower, more sharply focused griefs. It seemed to him, sometimes, that he could no longer contain the limitless miseries of the world and that his own specific agony was all that he could possibly be asked to bear. Had he been a drinker, he would have taken a bottle that night and drained it. As it was, he smoked, until his entire soul felt indelibly stained by nicotine; a yellow soul, like the star of David he had once briefly been forced to wear on his coat sleeve.

He had to rest, to be ready for the trip to Berne. They had to go directly to the top, to the ambassador himself. There was no point in even trying to talk to the Americans in Zurich. Bor had been right enough about that. They had no power.

And they had for months been under instructions not to forward "private reports" on such matters back to Washington.

During the night a sharp wind from the Zürichsee had briefly driven a slanted rain hard against the green glass windows of the print shop below and rattled the nineteenth-century casements of his makeshift office. He slept fitfully, dreamed of Teresa, awakened, smoked fiercely and with a pyromaniac's carelessness, then slept again.

When he awoke again, drained and even more exhausted than he had been the night before, he found Liebermann watching him.

"You sleep like you were dead, Miklos. It worries me to see you sleep like that. It's not like you to sleep so deep."

Baranyi struggled up in his damp grimy clothes, pushed aside the rat-eaten Swiss army blanket, and tried to stretch. His muscles complained, his joints ached. A deathly cold filled the cavities of his body.

"I didn't think I was asleep at all. How odd."

"Oh, asleep and snoring, too."

Baranyi got to his feet. A small mirror on the wall gave him back an image truly frightening in its gray unreality, like a troll, a freshly exhumed corpse. He shuddered at the masterpiece of sallow ugliness he had achieved.

In the next room, springs groaned and a child began to cry, uncertain of where it was.

"What time is it?"

"Seven."

"Ah . . . Bor will be here at eight."

"The Pole?"

"Yes. We go to Berne. That was what it was about last night. There was a report, Avner, about the place in Oswiecim. I cannot bring myself to tell you about it. You'll read it soon enough. On account of the report, we must go to Berne."

Liebermann nodded, understanding without being told. It was the same story every time. Only worse.

"If you go to Berne—to the Americans, I assume—then you should see this also. It came while you were with the Poles."

Baranyi knuckled his eyes until the tears came. The smell of coffee wakened a dull ache in his stomach and a faint desire to live. He moved across the room unsteadily. The day outside was slate gray, still sullen with rain.

"It's not good news. I can tell from your eyes."

"Do you want to read it?" asked Liebermann, handing him a folded paper, "or shall I tell you?"

Baranyi sighed. It was like trying to hold back an avalanche. "Tell me."

"It's from Sternbuch in Basel. He's had word from Budapest that the Germans are rounding up all the Jews of the city. It started just after you left. It's for transport east. They're sending them to Poland. To Oswiecim. Oh, there's more in the cable, but that's what counts."

"What does Sternbuch expect us to do?" Baranyi poured some coffee into a tin cup and then poured some for Liebermann.

"Whatever we can."

"And what is *that* supposed to be?" Baranyi cried. He shuddered, sat back heavily. The night had been too much for him. His exhaustion, his sister-in-law, then the Vrba report. He could hear Kagan now, in the next room, talking to someone on the phone.

The cable was the worst possible news. A quarter million had already been rounded up. The Red Cross had done nothing to stop it. The infamous Eichmann sat in a suite in the Hotel Majestic drinking champagne and bargaining with Brand. Hundreds of thousands were going to their deaths. The railroad yards were full of boxcars. It seemed to mean nothing to the Nazis that their troops on the Russian front were dying for lack of transport, so long as there were cars enough to take the Jews of Budapest to the camps.

Just then, Kagan presented himself at the doorway, his leather jacket open over a black turtleneck sweater. He had the face of a Danube bargeman and the brain of a cryptographer.

"You saw this?" Baranyi held up the cable.

Kagan nodded. "Just what we expected, no?"

"But so soon, and so many . . . it's like an earthquake."

"What did Paprocki want? To rub more salt in our wounds? I wish I'd been with you. That damned fat fool . . ."

"Never mind Paprocki. Bor was there too, and he's no fool. Also Pauer from the Czech bureau. They had a detailed report on what is going on at Oswiecim. Here, you must read it for yourself."

"It's that bad?"

"The worst, Itzhak. You cannot imagine how bad it is. We go this morning to take a copy to the Americans."

"What for? They're still sitting on the last reports you gave them, the ones from the Pole, Zabreski."

"But this is so much worse . . . they *must* help this time. If what Sternbuch writes is true, then there are a half a million on their way to their deaths already. Within weeks, perhaps days. They *must* bomb the railroads, the camps themselves."

"I don't think you heard me, Miklos," Kagan said. "The Americans have done nothing. Absolutely *nothing*. The information sits there and gathers dust. Liebermann has friends in the telegraph office. The cables are watched. Nothing at all has moved, unless it's gone in the diplomatic pouch. And I can't see any reason for that, can you?"

Baranyi did not reply.

Kagan went on. "You've written to Peshko in New York how many times now? His organization can do nothing, and they're *right there,* Americans themselves. What a joke. They are Americans just as our poor friends in Germany were Germans. What difference is there really? Between pulling the trigger yourself and failing to stop someone else from pulling it when you can stop him?"

"The iniquity of the indifferent is as the tenth power of evil," said Liebermann softly.

Miklos stared at him. Kagan turned to leave. A bell jangled somewhere. A file cabinet vibrated to the sound. In the next room a child began to cry, then another.

Liebermann, who was by the window, said, "It's Bor. Your colonel. Quite elegant, too. He's found a lovely American car for you."

"Good luck," said Kagan softly from the doorway.

Baranyi nodded. "My God, how can they do this?" he muttered to himself.

Kagan said, "How?" A sad smile flickered across his drayman's face. "How indeed, dear Miklos . . ."

DOCUMENT

From the I. G. Farben war crimes trial transcript.
Witness: August von Knieriem, chief counsel for I. G. Farben.

QUES.—Now, is it not a fact that Dr. Schmitz accompanied you to London?

ANS.—Yes.

QUES.—And Dr. Krauch?

ANS.—Yes, certainly. That is stated in a prosecution exhibit.

QUES.—Now in what year did you actually negotiate this twenty million dollars' worth of aviation gasoline?

ANS.—According to my recollection, 1937. I believe that to be correct.

QUES.—Did you not know that you were acquiring the aviation gasoline for Goering's Luftwaffe and not for I. G. Farben?

ANS.—I knew that this entire acquisition was carried out at the request of the Ministry of Economics.

Wilmington, Delaware

The boardroom on the sixth floor of the Criterion Oil building looked like an Edward Hopper painting at that hour of the morning: the sun was just coming in, all soft and cream-colored over the silent concrete block buildings across the dusty road. The glow of the refinery tanks in the distance, bathed in the seven o'clock sun, rose like a mist and drifted into the room through wide, uncurtained windows. It was a good hour for a meeting. The night personnel and the guards were accustomed to seeing Criterion officers at their desks early in the morning, especially in the summer, before the heat of the day began in earnest. It was assumed that successful men were early risers. A long, sober workday was how the money was made.

Sometimes.

Sometimes there were other ways.

Marcus Trilling was concerned, deeply concerned, with one of those other ways as he entered the boardroom, a slim satchel under his arm, an envelope of coded cablegrams in his right hand. The vice president in charge of overseas operations was there already, a thin, bloodless Floridian who had been an insurance company excutive in Paris until 1937. He looked up, his eyes characterless as ever behind tinted spectacle lenses, his mouth moving in an even rhythm as he chewed on a doughnut.

Trilling grimaced. The idea of eating breakfast in the boardroom appalled him. He'd been up, had showered, eaten, two hours ago, at the crack of dawn. He expected others to do the same. Staring intently, letting his displeasure gather visibly in the seams of his face, he took his place at the table and glanced with irritation at his watch.

Just at that moment, fortunately for him, the chief chemist, Synthetic Rubber Division, made his appearance. He'd been promoted to vice president the year before and been given a large enough interest in the company and a healthy enough increase in salary to make sure that he remained loyal for at least a few years more. Trilling hadn't been satisfied with purchased loyalty, though; the man was too important. Within six months of his promotion, Criterion's bank held the mortgage on the chemist's home. Nominees of one of Trilling's private trusts quietly bought up a large number of personal gambling IOUs that the man had left scattered around North Carolina and Washington in the days before he'd come to work for Criterion.

The chemist was safe enough for a while. He could be counted on.

Two more men came in. One was the director of the Confidential Relations Department, Criterion's counterpart of I.G.'s Office A, the intelligence division of Northwest 7: a genial-looking professorial man in his late forties given to broad smiles, tweeds, and heavy shag pipe tobacco. No one would ever associate his lazy Oklahoma drawl with the kind of work he actually did. He had one of the best minds in industrial intelligence, better even than Max Ilgner's. The second man—a stocky, powerfully built New Englander with a blotchy red bulldog face—had been in charge of the Patent Acquisition and Special Licensing Division for as long as Trilling could remember. He was the only man on their legal staff Trilling really trusted. Boston-born, Harvard-educated. Tough as a railroad spike.

All of them were salaried officers. Employees. All were hungry and knew exactly where their next meal was coming from. There was no room here for idealistic directors with independent incomes, or owners whose wealth was so enormous that they could afford to temper business decisions with pseudo-moral judgments.

No secretaries were present. The meeting had not been entered in anyone's diary. Other appointments had been filled in in the early-morning spaces. No one would ever know what they had been doing that morning at seven fifteen.

Confidential Relations had brought an urn of coffee with him from the commissary, a tray, and a string of cups. Trilling nodded grudgingly. Coffee wasn't too bad. Wouldn't mind a cup himself.

But doughnuts?

Chemical pushed a fat manila file folder across the table.

"The results are conclusive, sir. We've checked everything out. Every test we can think of has been run and then some. There's no doubt about it, it's the finest cold-process synthetic rubber we've ever seen. I don't know what kind of an initiator system they're using. It's my guess they're employing some form of phosphate as a buffer. Tetrasodium salts. Ethylenediamine-tetracetic acid. But how they're doing it I couldn't begin to guess."

"Properties?" drawled Confidential Relations, lighting his pipe. "What about the properties?"

"The very best," replied Chemical. "They've managed to match all the best qualities of a high-molecular-weight product without using the normal methods. I'd say the processing characteristics are substantially better than anything we can possibly come up with for at least another five years."

"What about Du Pont or Goodrich? They haven't been exactly sitting on their hands," Trilling said.

"They haven't got anything remotely like this stuff."

"And they won't," said Confidential Relations. "Even if they did, we'd shut them down in a week. They'd never produce."

The lawyer with the bulldog face nodded enthusiastically. He knew that it would take even less time than that. Criterion had friends on the bench as well as in the legislature.

"Can the process be reproduced? Can *we* do it?"

Chemical shook his head. "I can tell you what's *in* the stuff all right, and I can even guess at some of the steps. But reproduce it? Not possible. The mechanism they use must be fantastically complex."

"Or absurdly simple."

"Whatever. It doesn't much matter. We don't have it and we don't know how to go about matching it."

"Then we have no alternative, do we?"

"I didn't know we were considering one, Marcus," said the bulldog.

"We're not, not really. I'd just like to manage without the risk if it were possible," Trilling replied. "Clearly, it isn't."

Chemical nodded agreement.

Trilling searched the bulldog's ruddy face for some sign of a reaction. "You know, of course, that we've put our New York people on this?"

The bulldog wagged his head soberly. Obviously, he wasn't pleased. He'd never been able to understand why Trilling put so much trust in his New York counsel. His own people could have done the job just as well.

And he didn't care much for Henry Stropp as a person, either.

Finally, the bulldog asked, "With what results, Marcus?"

"Everything's going very smoothly so far. That's why I asked you all here this morning. To discuss what's going to be done to help keep things smooth. We heard from Zurich just yesterday. The initial contacts have been made. It's all very gentlemanly. Precautions have to be taken, of course, and we can't move too quickly."

Confidential Relations took a deep breath, then decided not to say whatever it was that was on his mind. He was thinking, "I hope he's going to stay clear of our Geneva offices," but it was immediately clear to him that Trilling would have given exactly such instructions.

Confidential Relations lit his pipe and sucked in a mouthful of smoke. Once he had released it, he asked, "Are we going to secure the actual equipment? Is that part of the deal?"

Trilling didn't answer directly. He had a question of his own first. "Will the patent assignments cover the new cold process?"

"You know they will, Marcus," shot back the bulldog.

"I just like to hear it from you, that's all."

"I'm sure Stropp told you the same thing. He's the expert."

"He did, but he's not here now to repeat it. I like reassurance."

"Stropp's in Zurich himself?" There was surprise in the bulldog's eyes.

"Exactly," said Trilling. "Now . . . how are things holding at State?"

"So far," drawled Confidential Relations in his most amiable manner, "so good."

Overseas Operations leaned forward tensely, his knuckles white. State was really *his* territory and the most sensitive area of all. Worse yet, it was the area over which they had the least direct and least certain control.

"It's getting more and more difficult," Overseas put in. "We heard from the attaché in Berne only the other day, there's been another report. I expect it will be very hard to stop it this time."

"And I expect you'll be equal to the task," said Trilling flatly. There was a distinct edge of incipient displeasure to his tone, as though he resented even the slightest suggestion that there might be problems.

"I hope so, sir. It's not always easy to control such things. There are an awful lot of variables."

"The War Department will go along, I've seen to that—*personally*. McCloy won't give them an inch, no matter what WRB says."

"Don't worry about WRB. That's Roosevelt's sop to the Jews. Pehle's got no real authority. All he can do is whine."

"It would be a real tragedy if they destroyed the plant," Chemical said, as though talking to himself, seeing apocalyptic visions.

"It would be rank stupidity to bomb—and they know it. They trust *us* to make such judgments, and they'll go along with us, just as they always have. We've cooperated with them, they'll cooperate with us. They got their patent-pooling agreements, they've got the butadiene plant at Naches. *We* get the postwar clearance. There are a lot of reasons . . ." His voice trailed off. There was no point at all in mentioning the elaborate network of payoffs and promises that had been spun over the last few years. Stock, country homes, honors, positions, wives, sons, jobs, board of directorships. Every man in the room was involved in something similar; they all knew how it was done.

Everyone knew. Except the real owners of the company, the billionaires who never stopped to look at what their hired hands were doing. They'd have a collective fit of moral indignation if they ever found out, Trilling thought. Especially the younger ones in the family.

But all they'd ever find out would be that Criterion had somehow managed to get a complete stranglehold on the synthetic rubber industry after the war and was producing a product without comparison anywhere in the world. There would be additional billions for everyone. They wouldn't want to know more than that. They'd be too grateful to ask questions; that was the way it was and always would be.

Once the wartime patent-pooling laws had been rescinded and operations were back to normal, the others—Goodrich, Du Pont, Texaco, and anyone else who tried to get a portion of the rubber market—would find that they'd been cut off at the pass a long time before.

Particularly once Criterion got hold of the know-how for the new cold-process Buna. Which was better than anything they'd ever seen or dreamed about.

After a moment, Trilling said: "The only real problem, then, is the press."

"I'd say so," agreed Confidential Relations. "There's been a lot of pressure, though. Since the Soviets went into one of the camps . . . what was it called? Sobibor or something like that. The *Washington Post* picked that one up, and so did the *Times*."

"No one believes it, though. They're saying it's just propaganda."

"For now."

"It's going to get a lot worse. In addition to the Jewish groups, we've got two governments to contend with. The Poles and the Czechs."

"If Criterion can't handle the damned Poles and the Czechs, sir, then we'd better give up right now," offered Chemical.

"I'm glad you think so," Trilling said sarcastically. "But saying it and doing it are two entirely different things, wouldn't you say?"

"The British will throttle the Poles for us. We've spoken to our people in London about that already. No one in Whitehall wants any more Jews heading into Palestine than they can absolutely help. They won't lift a finger, you can be sure of that."

"Contingency plans," announced Confidential Relations, pushing a folder of his own past the coffee urn.

Trilling glanced down the column of names, astonished and pleased. Confidential Relations had done a fine job. The department, it seemed, had a hook into the editorial board of every newspaper of importance in the country. The advertising accounts had been deftly spun out, personal friendships exploited, a little polite blackmail employed where appropriate. It all looked as tight as it could be.

"We don't have to use much in the way of pressure, of course," said Confidential Relations. "No one really gives a hoot in hell about what happens to the Jews anyway, and they're the only ones really involved."

"You've seen the reports?" said Trilling, surprised and a little angered. The anger quickly subsided. Why should he be surprised if his expert in industrial intelligence had gotten hold of the information? Wasn't that precisely what he was being paid for?

"Pass the coffee please," said bulldog laconically.

The coffee was passed.

"Berne has the reports bottled up. The military attaché there is a partner of Stropp's and he's seen to everything. And even if the reports do get through, all that will happen is that the ambassador will get a stiff note from War Department telling him not to forward any more 'personal' reports. In short, to mind his own business and not to interfere with the censorship prerogatives of neutral governments."

"They'll try again, through London. It'll only be a matter of time before they do," said Confidential Relations.

"They'll be stopped again then. First at State and then, if they should get through by some means or other, at War."

"There's going to be no bombing, you can be certain of that," said Overseas Operations.

"As long as the Soviets don't get there first we've got nothing to worry about," put in Confidential Relations.

"And if they do, our Russian 'friends,' then we haven't got anything to worry about either," said Trilling, "because there won't be a damned thing we can do about any of it then."

April 19, 1944
Berne, Switzerland

Miklos Baranyi, age forty-three, formerly Deputy Director of General Medicine at the Bethlen Square Hospital, Budapest, later senior in charge of a hospital for Jewish military conscripts, MUSZ, at Korestan, Hungary, leaned back against the rear seat of the long black Packard and wondered why it was he was still alive.

That the sky was a perfect, translucent blue and the crisp southwest wind was already touched with the scent of spring mountain flowers only served to darken his mood. He stared ahead with unblinking eyes, never once turning to even so much as glance at Conrad Bor, who sat next to him, sunk in a mood almost as deep and sullen as his own.

Baranyi had not in fact said a word since the car had left Zurich. He had thought for a long time about his son. It was painful, but he could barely remember what the child had looked like. His memory was too crowded with the faces of dead children. It was hard to tell them apart. Something had to be done, though, about the grave. The old man at the cemetery was not taking proper care of it. He thought, too, of Julie Malowska and her perpetual reproaches. But he could not bring himself to say anything to Bor. After all, his sister-in-law was Bor's mistress, and had it not been for that simple fact he would never have been able to enlist the help of the Poles as he had. For the Poles in Zurich were as little concerned with the Jews as the Poles in Warsaw had been. Perhaps even less so. Still, Bor was a decent enough man, and the consul, Paprocki, was easily led. The Malowska woman had been instrumental in securing their cooperation. Just why was another question. Perhaps she had decided that it was the best way to ensure that Baranyi would never be able to rid himself of her. That she would always be close by, a perpetual reminder.

Of what he had lost.

And of what she too had lost.

The Packard wound its way in leisurely fashion down through

the medieval streets of old Berne, past stone buildings capped with conical towers and buttressed by curious stone wing-walls that thrust out from the façade and made it appear as though they were being held up by braces.

The American embassy building was situated in the modern section of the city halfway down the Muristrasse on the right bank of the river Aar. The car glided onto the lofty Kirchenfeld bridge, turned left through Helvetiaplatz, and proceeded slowly until at last they reached the Muristrasse.

The embassy building, its entrance flanked by the obligatory Marines in full dress uniform and rigid as the two "armed men" in *Die Zauberflöte,* came into view.

Bor remained seated for a few moments after they had reached the gates, trying to compose himself. Baranyi, morose and still sunk in thought, got out and stood on the sidewalk waiting for him.

The guards at the gate checked their papers with a brisk, disinterested courtesy and let them enter. The appointment was confirmed by a clerk seated at a wide walnut desk.

They were taken directly to the office of the chargé d'affaires. A blue disk with the great seal of the United States of America adorned the door, a welcome relief from the endless heraldic bears that were to be found all over Berne.

The chargé, Lorimer, was waiting for them behind his broad, pristine desk. He appeared clearly discomfited and kept glancing at his appointment pad and then at his telephone as though hoping that an unexpected call would relieve him of whatever problems the Pole had brought. A young secretary, clearly a Swiss from her coloring, sat to his left, a steno pad poised on her knee. To the chargé's right stood a young man with a pleasant face, thick wavy blond hair, and steel-rimmed glasses. Neither was introduced.

"Mr. Lorimer," said Bor, his English clear and almost without accent, "it was necessary for us to see you personally, and we thank you for consenting to receive us. The matter is of extreme urgency."

"Colonel . . . Bor, is it? And you, sir, must be Dr. . . . have I got it correctly? . . . Baaer-an-yee?" Lorimer spoke with a heavy Midwestern accent which even the Hungarian noticed. He wondered how long the man had been at his post. The young man to his right was already a little embarrassed.

"Is your military attaché going to join us? Major Bard?" inquired Bor.

"Why, no. He wasn't asked."

"It would have been useful. Apparently Consul Paprocki failed to mention it to you."

"Your consul did mention it, but I couldn't see the need. At any rate, Major Bard isn't in Berne at the moment, and I saw no reason to call him back."

"Perhaps *this* might be a good reason, sir," Bor said, placing his briefcase on the table, its open end toward the chargé.

"I don't quite understand," said Lorimer, pushing back instinctively from his desk. The secretary seemed puzzled, unsure whether she should take notes.

"Surely Consul Paprocki advised you of the nature of these documents. Surely the Czech legation has already furnished you with copies . . ."

"I assure you, gentlemen, I don't know what you've got there."

Baranyi sighed. Even as much as a half-hour saved could mean thousands of lives. Now they would have to start at the very beginning.

"You have heard the name Oswiecim, Mr. Lorimer? Auschwitz, as the Germans call it. It is a place in southern Poland," said Baranyi. "A little west of Breslau."

The chargé's eyes narrowed. The impression of gentle incompetence vanished from his features. His face took on a hard, uncompromising look.

"A concentration camp, isn't it? A Nazi camp. There's an industrial complex there too. Krupp has a fuse works nearby. Or a refinery or something like that."

"Major Bard, your attaché, might perhaps be better informed," snapped Baranyi. "But that's close enough. Close, but with a difference. Which you will find spelled out in these documents." He paused. "Like the others, you say? Read, Herr Lorimer. Read these." He wrenched the papers out of the briefcase and all but thrust them in the chargé's face.

The young man in the steel-rimmed glasses blanched but did not move.

"It's an industrial complex, yes, but in a way you cannot imagine, Herr Lorimer. It produces death. At the rate of twenty thousand a day when all the equipment is functioning. And when the raw materials are provided, of course. Excuse me if I sound bitter, but your country's record in this matter leaves me little cause for optimism."

"Then why bother coming to see me if that's the way you feel?"

"Only because there is no one else to turn to. Who else has aircraft capable of bombing this obscene place, of putting the gas chambers out of business, of destroying the ovens? Read, sir. We'll wait patiently. Read, and then tell us what help you can offer."

Baranyi was trembling as the chargé took up the report and began to read. Slowly, his expression began to change. Baranyi took out the second set of documents, the diagrams furnished by the Czechs. There were maps. The key cities, Kosice and Presov, were marked in red. The main rail junctions. The drawings clearly showed the layout of the camp itself, just where the gas chambers were, and the ovens. All at a fair distance from the main barracks.

As a young man, during the first war, Baranyi had flown as an artillery spotter with the Austrians. He knew perfectly well what could be done with bombs, what the new weapons could achieve.

If anyone chose to use them.

He also knew that a similar if less detailed report had been submitted to the attaché, Bard, the month before. It had not yet made its way to Washington. And no one had been able to find out why.

When it was plain that the chargé had finished, Bor said, "Now, sir, do you see the urgency?"

"This is . . . of course . . . very, very terrible," said Lorimer. To Baranyi it was impossible to tell whether the faint tremor in the man's voice was induced or genuine. He noted, too, that the young man in the steel-rimmed glasses was now reading the report, moving much more rapidly through the pages than had his superior.

"But just what do you wish *me* to do about this?" said the chargé.

"My government is most concerned," said Bor. "We have been accused of much in this matter of the Jews, and we are guilty of much. Many have assisted the murderers. *Many.* We won't deny that. But this, *this* is entirely too much to bear. That place is on Polish soil. After the war is over, people will remember Oswiecim, and when they ask where such a place was allowed to exist, the answer will be . . . *Poland.*"

Baranyi kept his eyes averted. God, the man was imitating Paprocki's hortatory manner to a *t*. And how insincere . . .

Lorimer did not reply.

After a long silence, Baranyi said, "All we wish of you, sir, is that you see to it that this report is sent at once to the appropriate officials of your government in Washington. We ask that you see that the information is made public in the American press and through your radio agencies. Silence in this matter is complicity."

"That, sir, is unfair, and you know it. This is certainly not in *my* hands," the chargé protested.

"In whose hands is it?" Bor asked icily. "There is no denying the accuracy of this information. Not anymore."

"My agency," said Baranyi, "will place copies of these documents with the Swiss press, and the Swedes will have them before the week is out. All of that has already been arranged. But—"

"Why don't you do it then?"

"Neither the Swiss nor the Swedes have bombing planes, sir. Neither the Swiss nor the Swedes are capable of putting an end to this insanity. *Your government is.*"

There was a long, pained silence in the room. The chargé's aide was visibly shaken by what he was reading. The secretary had begun to take spasmodic notes. Lorimer's face was gray.

"Such a heavy burden," he muttered. "And what if you are refused? There could be reasons. I'm sure—"

"No doubt reasons can be found. They always have been found in the past when it was a question of Jewish lives."

Lorimer had no answer.

Bor spoke again. "Sir, our government would request that we receive immediate advice of what is contemplated by way of response to our request. We are most, *most* concerned. As I'm sure you can understand. Shortly, we shall have detailed rail maps as well, and these too will be placed at your disposal. At once."

"Of course," said Lorimer quickly, nodding to his secretary. "Gentlemen, if half of this is true . . ."

"All of it is true, sir. I've spoken with these men myself. I'm not at liberty to tell you where or when, but I have seen them, questioned them. We have checked copies of the aerial photos your own planes have taken against their descriptions. We have *seen* the long lines of people in those photographs. Now we know where they were going. Those long, *long* lines of people, sir."

"A cable, please," said Baranyi. "Just a cable."

Lorimer nodded, avoiding Baranyi's stare. A few words more were exchanged. The two men got up to leave. The aide accompanied them.

"It's beyond belief," he whispered.

Miklos Baranyi took the young man's arm. "No evil, no matter how large, is beyond belief."

The aide winced, as though Baranyi's words had implied some primal ignorance and a guilt of which he would never be able to rid himself.

The chargé d'affaires sat alone behind his walnut desk for a full twenty minutes after the delegation had departed. Then, very slowly, as though moving through an underwater zone of greatly increased pressure, he rose and made his way through the anteroom, still carrying the report. This he handed to his secretary with instructions to make two copies. One was to be sent to the War Department operations office in Washington, the other was to be placed in the file of the military attaché, Bard. The original was to be locked in the embassy safe. Lorimer retained the map of the installation in his pocket. He had never seen such a map before.

He went at once to the cipher room in the cellar and composed a message, brief and to the point.

The message was to be routed through the United States embassy in Lisbon, to be picked up there by courier and conveyed by hand to its ultimate destination.

The message, duly ciphered, was addressed to former ambassador to Portugal, Marcus Trilling, now residing in Georgetown, Washington, D.C.

April 20, 1944
Berlin

In his office in Northwest 7, the Laendersbank building, over-looking the busy flow of traffic on the Unter den Linden, Dr. Ing. Helmut Schragg was busy reviewing a folder of confidential papers that had just been handed him by I.G. Farben's chief counsel, August von Knieriem. On his desk, a constant distraction, were the signal flimsies that had been coming in since early morning, detailing the almost total destruction of the synthetic fuel plant at Leuna by American bombers three days before. The magnitude of the disaster was so great that its meaning had not yet penetrated the minds of many of Schragg's colleagues. He, however, was all too keenly aware of what it meant—not only for the war economy but for the future of I.G. as well.

It was difficult, therefore, to keep his mind on his present assignment. Yet in a very real way the success of the Leuna raid served to underscore the importance of the mission to Switzerland and of the agreements drafted by Von Knieriem. His bag was packed, the transportation covertly arranged through cooperative members of the Vermittlungstelle Wehrmacht staff. A Messerschmitt *Taifun* was fueled and waiting to take Schragg and his immediate superior, Dr. Carl Krauch, chairman of I.G.'s supervisory board of directors, the *Aufsichtsrat,* and the chief of Sparte II, Dr. Fritz Ter Meer, to the little town of Waldshut near the Swiss border.

If all went well, the pact would be concluded within twenty-four hours. And I.G.'s future would be secure.

Schragg stood up and went to the window to brood. He was a tall, urbane-looking man, almost handsome, a little too dark. His body was fit, his mind honed sharp as a razor, not only from his training as a chemist at the Kaiser Wilhelm Institute but from years of service in the office of the Hauptabwehrbeauftragter, the little-known Office A of the chief of counterintelligence, I.G. Farben, where he had worked under the legendary Dr. Dieckmann. Born in Kassel to a family settled for three generations in the dry goods trade, he had gone to the University of Berlin and for a while studied under Fritz Haber. Haber had never liked him, though he'd been a good enough student. Schragg had liked Haber even less. The war had intervened, and Schragg, at twenty-three and on the verge of a brilliant career, had gone off to the front with a poison-gas company. Active service had lasted exactly three weeks. A sudden shift in the wind had blown chlorine gas back over the German positions and all but wiped out Schragg's unit. For thirteen months Helmut Schragg hovered near death, coughing his lungs out in a military hospital outside Potsdam and swearing murderously at the Jew, Haber, who had invented the gas in the first place.

The turmoil at the end of the war had coincided with Schragg's rehabilitation, and no sooner had he found himself able to navigate again than he had been swept up in the bitter warfare between the *Freikorps* and the communists. Twice he had barely escaped with his life. There had to be a better day. A chance meeting with an old classmate had led to an introduction to a protégé of Bosch's who was working for a group of dyestuff companies that had combined during the war under the umbrella title of "Interessegemeinschaft der Deutschen Teerfarbenindustrie"—the Community of Interest of the German Dyestuff Industry. He went to work at once in the newly formed Statistical Division, which was in charge of gathering industrial information worldwide.

The change of climate had been good for him. Montevideo, Vera Cruz, Buenos Aires, then New York, Chicago, Paris, London. All the places he had always wanted to visit he now visited in style, with all expenses paid. As a *Verbindungsmann,* an agent gathering economic and technical information. In short, a new kind of spy.

By 1925, the year that the new I.G. organization became a fact, Helmut Schragg was well ensconced and his talents were beginning to be appreciated. He had married the daughter of a retired naval officer from Danzig, divorced, married again—this time to a Venezuelan woman—divorced yet again, and finally taken an oath to keep himself clear of any further such entanglements.

The whores on the Kurfürstendamm would suffice. He had no emotion left to spare for a woman; from the day his second divorce became a reality, all of his emotion was channeled into his work.

Helmut Schragg became a dedicated man.

That was all a long time ago. His administrative and organizational abilities had been refined, proven, noticed. His technical knowledge had expanded apace. Finally, he had been made deputy administrator for the synthetics division of I.G., second only to Otto Ambros and Beutefisch. Schragg had lately been put in charge of the Chemie-Ausland division, the construction and operation of the Buna plant in Poland.

He had taken many precautions since his elevation. The door of his office was kept locked, and the outer corridor doors had been fitted with the best security devices I.G. Farben's electronics engineers could devise. The Waldshut matter was too sensitive to permit even the possibility of snooping by the Gestapo or the SD. Not that they couldn't be dealt with easily enough, of course. But why subject oneself to even the slightest embarrassment?

A buzzer sounded. Schragg turned and advanced on the door, confident that he would find either Ter Meer or Krauch on the other side. The only other person who had admittance to the corridor on which Schragg's office was located was Hermann Schmitz, the chairman of the *Vorstand,* whose own offices were at the other end of the floor. And Schmitz, of course, was fully aware of what was going on.

When the door opened, however, Schragg found himself staring at an unfamiliar officer whose cuff titles instantly identified him as being from the office of the Reichsminister for Armaments and War Production, Albert Speer.

"Herr Dr. Schragg?"

Schragg nodded, interposing himself between the unexpected newcomer and his desk, on which the papers he had been examining were inconveniently displayed.

"I am unable to locate Herr Dr. Krauch," said the officer. "I have an urgent communication from the highest authority, sir. Perhaps you can be of some help?"

Schragg looked down at the sheaf of papers the officer was carrying. On the edge of one single sheet of blue paper that stuck out past all the rest he recognized with a small tightening of the sphincter the personal emblem that decorated dispatches emanating from the Reichskanzler's headquarters at Obersalzburg.

Schragg's mouth went dry. The young officer stared levelly at him, with what Schragg took to be a disagreeable arrogance.

"My instructions are to deliver this message directly to Herr Dr. Krauch. If that is not possible, then to Herr Dr. Ter Meer, whom I cannot locate either. And thirdly, to you, sir. It will be your responsibility to see that it is delivered."

With that, the officer thrust the papers at the startled Schragg, turned on his heel, and stalked quickly down the corridor.

Just then the phone on Schragg's desk rang. He lunged for it without even shutting the door.

It was Krauch.

"My secretary says that some donkey from Speer's office has been running around the building looking for me. Has he been up to see you yet? For God's sake, don't let him in. I think I know what he wants."

Schragg swallowed hard. "He's just been here."

"What?"

"Just been here. Exactly that. He gave me a message. It's not from Speer at all. It's from the Reichskanzler himself."

There was a long pause on the other end; then: "You'd better open it."

"Where are you?" Schragg asked as he slit open the envelope.

"Where should I be? At Tempelhof, of course. With Ter Meer. Waiting for you."

"Von Knieriem only delivered the papers a quarter of an hour ago."

"Never mind that. What does the Reichskanzler's order say? I can pretty well guess."

Schragg read the message quickly. It was plain and to the point. Brutally so. He read it twice to make sure that he had made no mistake.

"He wants to see you both at once. To discuss Leuna."

"The fat's in the fire now, isn't it? I can tell you, my dear Schragg, exactly what's coming. Why was so large a portion of our production capability concentrated in one place? Why have we been allowed a monopoly all these years? I can just hear him now. Just as Speer warned us." Krauch paused. "Who has he asked for, did you say?"

"You, Ter Meer, and Beutefisch."

"You as well?"

"No."

Krauch swore. "Of all the times . . ."

"A pity we could not tell the Americans when to do their bombing."

"Don't attempt to be amusing. It's not your forte, Helmut. Just tell me, when are we to be there?"

"Today. The message says that a car from Speer's office will call for you at eleven. Good God, that's only an hour from now. Can you get back in time?"

"We've done the impossible on a regular basis for years, haven't we? I suppose we can manage this trick too."

"And what of Waldshut? Can it be postponed?"

Krauch did not answer at once. Schragg could hear his breathing, sharp, agitated, and annoyed.

"No. Waldshut must proceed. Who else can go? Von Knieriem?"

"Impossible. He'd be missed at once. Entirely too visible. He has too many important commitments this week."

"Then you will have to go alone, Helmut. You're the only other possible person."

"But I've never met your 'friend.' How can you send me?"

"What choice do we have?" With that, Krauch hung up.

Schragg sat for a long moment, almost in a daze. His glance fell on a batch of photos that had come in during the last hour. They showed the smoking remains of the Leuna plant. The production loss was staggering, no question about it. Goering would be livid, and that was never a pleasant spectacle. If the raids kept up, if they couldn't get Leuna back into operation, a quarter of the Luftwaffe would be grounded within two weeks.

He got up, shaking now, suddenly aware of a vulnerability he had never felt until that moment. There would be no talking rationally to Hitler. There would be rages and accusations, denunciations and recriminations. Thank God the levelheaded Speer would be there too. And Krauch and Beutefisch, to take the brunt of the Führer's anger.

He glanced over at the window, then went to it. Far below, waiting at the curb, was a long black Mercedes staff car. He didn't have to see the penant to know that it came from the Armaments and War Production Ministry.

Early, as usual. Well, they'd been given an hour. Let Speer wait. And Hitler too.

He took down the small suitcase he had packed and checked to make sure he'd put in his toothbrush and the new bottle of cologne he'd just bought.

He didn't like the idea of going alone very much. But then, as Krauch had said, did they really have any choice?

DOCUMENT

From: John Pehle, WRB
To: John McCloy, Asst. Sec. of War

If the elaborate murder installations at Birkenau were destroyed it seems clear that the Germans could not reconstruct them for some time. I am convinced that the point has now been reached where such action is justifiable if it is deemed feasible by competent military authorities. I strongly recommend that the War Department give serious consideration to the possibility of destroying the execution chambers and crematories in Birkenau through direct bombing action.

April 23, 1944
Berne

"I'm sorry, sir, but the chargé is out."

"He's been out for the last two days. When is he not 'out,' Fräulein?"

"The chargé is seldom here, sir. And when he is, he only sees people by appointment."

"Perhaps I can make an appointment then? For when? Tomorrow? Next week? Next year?"

"I'm sorry, sir."

"You have no idea, of course, and you won't care to hear this, but it's true. For every hour that this grotesque comedy goes on, for every hour that your chargé does not act, thousands will be killed. Does that mean anything to you, young woman?"

For one brief moment the receptionist looked honestly perplexed.

"Really, sir, there's nothing—"

"Then I will wait. There's nothing else I can do, is there?"

"He's not here, honestly."

"I will wait."

*   *   *

For three hours, Miklos Baranyi remained seated on the bench in the embassy waiting room. Now the porters were locking up downstairs for the night. The receptionist put on her coat and fled into the gathering Bernese dusk. Stocky Swiss women in striped aprons began to wash down the marble floors.

"You'd really better leave," said the front desk clerk. "I'll have to call the guards if you don't leave."

He got up to go.

Just then the chargé's young aide came down the main stairs, a raincoat slung over his arm, carrying a briefcase.

Baranyi turned, attracted by the sound of his footfalls. Their eyes met. The young man looked away hurriedly and went past, out the front door. Miklos could see the two Marines salute perfunctorily as he passed.

"Sir, really, you must leave," said the clerk.

Baranyi moved toward the door. There had been something in that brief glance, a flare of sympathy, perhaps of understanding. Something.

He hurried out, past the Marines and into the Muristrasse. The young man had reached the corner where the Muri opened out onto a view of the river Aar. The aide stopped once, looked back, and then turned to his left, down the Grüneckweg. Miklos followed the young man until he came to the entrance of the Schwellenmätteli, a café near the Kirchenfeld bridge. The aide went in, again pausing to look over his shoulder.

Baranyi followed him through the glass doors.

The café was crowded, smoky, the smell of fried fish heavy in the air. Miklos stopped at the entrance as an aproned waiter came to direct him to a table. The aide had just seated himself.

Baranyi gestured as though to indicate that he had recognized a friend within and wished to join him. The waiter stepped back and permitted him to pass.

He sat down at the aide's table. The young man looked up at him and appeared pleased.

"I was hoping you'd come along," the young man said.

"So it seemed," Baranyi said warily.

"Really, I do want to help."

"You know why I came back then?"

"I read the report."

"Has Herr Lorimer done anything about it yet?"

The aide shook his head.

"Why not?"

"I could guess."

"Don't. It won't do any good. But tell me, is he really that sort of a man?"

"No. At least I don't think so. He'd help if he could."

Baranyi lit a cigarette. The waiter brought over two steins of beer.

"The reports haven't gone to Washington," the aide said. "They should have, but they haven't been sent."

"Why not?"

"I told you, I don't really know. But I thought you should know that at least. If you hadn't come back, I would have gone out to look for you. Or called the Polish legation. I was going to do that tomorrow morning."

"It's nice to know that someone in this world has a small bit of conscience left."

The aide didn't respond. He lifted the stein to his lips, as though to hide his mouth. A small orchestra started to play somewhere, perhaps in a back room or in a nearby restaurant: "Brazil."

Baranyi leaned forward. "What *can* you tell me? You did want to tell me something, didn't you?"

The aide didn't answer for a moment; it was clear that he was struggling with something. Whatever it was, fear for his own position, fear of something he didn't understand, his good instincts won out, and quickly.

"Yes, there's something you should know. I don't understand it. Maybe you will."

"Yes?"

"After you left, the chargé went to the cipher room and sent a message to someone I've never heard of before. And he sent it through Lisbon, even though the address was in Washington."

Baranyi's eyes narrowed. He didn't understand at all what the young man was saying, but it was clear that the boy was troubled.

Because of the name, which he hadn't heard yet?

Because the message had been routed through Lisbon?

"Does the name Trilling mean anything to you?" asked the aide.

"Trilling?"

"Marcus Trilling. That was the name. I think he was an ambassador once, a while before the war. To Lisbon or Madrid, I'm not sure which. That's all I know, but you're welcome to it."

"And the message?"

"I only saw part of it. Such things are none of my business, you understand. But it was about the report, that your organization had it, that the Poles and the Czech government-in-exile had it. He told this man Trilling what you'd asked him to do."

"And what else?"

"That was all. It was informative, nothing more." The aide took a desultory sip of his beer. "Really, I'd better go now. I hope you can use what I've told you."

"Whether we can or not, thank you for telling me."

"That report *should* go through to the State Department," the aide said. Baranyi could see that his concern was genuine, and he thanked him for it.

After the aide had gone, Baranyi sat for a while, finishing his beer and smoking. He searched every nook and cranny of his mind but could find nothing that helped.

Trilling?

There was no connection, no resonance at all.

But why should he know the name of one particular man who lived in Washington, D.C., the United States of America? There were over one hundred and eighty million people in that country, and the only ones he'd ever heard of were those few whose names appeared in the wartime newspapers.

Marcus Trilling?

He would cable to Zoltan Peshko in New York at once. Peshko, the chairman of the Aggudath committee there, had been very helpful before, always willing to support the Vaadah. And besides, he was a *Landsmann,* a former lawyer who had lived for many years in Budapest on a street not far from that on which Baranyi had been born. When everyone else in Hungary had been hiding their heads in the sand and saying that it would all pass, that no insanity could last forever and soon everyone would forget that Béla Kun was a Jew and it would all return to normal, Zoltan

Peshko had packed up his library and his family, turned down one of the few positions on the High Court to be offered to a Jew in more than a decade, and emigrated to New York. A man of considerable wisdom and infinite common sense. There, he had quickly become a leading member of the Jewish community, a friend of judges, politicians, and bankers. With the coming of the war, he had once again given up everything, his practice, his position, and devoted himself completely to the work of the rescue committees.

Yes, by all means, cable Zoltan Peshko.

And then he would try to find out for himself what was going on.

DOCUMENT

From: WRB (London office)
To: War Department, Wash., D.C.

[*Forwarding a message from the Polish government-in-exile which read, in part, as below.*]

It is urgently requested that the WRB again explore with the Army the possibility of bombing the extermination chambers and German barracks at the largest Polish concentration camps which, they state, are sufficiently detached from the concentration camps to permit precision bombing.

April 24, 1944
Zurich

From the airport, Henry Stropp went directly to the small office maintained by his firm in one of the many imposing bank buildings that surrounded the Paradeplatz halfway up the fashionable Bahnhofstrasse.

It was early evening, a time when the New York offices of Hayklut, Bard, Winston & Stropp normally still bustled with activity. Though the lights were on and the door was unlocked, there was no sign of life in the Zurich branch. A cleaning woman was meticulously swabbing the floors outside the office door.

The anteroom was empty, the clerk's desk unattended.

Stropp banged on the table and shouted, "You've left the door open, damn it!"

There was a rattle of footsteps beyond the green glass barrier that shielded the office's few cubicles from the entrance. A startled young man in his shirtsleeves emerged carrying a stack of files. He was thin, blond, and bespectacled, and he was not Samuel Morse Eisner.

"Mein Herr? Bitte?"

"Your 'Herr' Stropp. I pay your salary. Who the devil are you?"

"Schultze I am, sir. An associate *Advokat* here."

"An associate? Indeed. And Herr Eisner is the senior partner, is that it?" Stropp knew he was being unreasonable, but the young man's wide-eyed distress was so provocative that he could not help himself. "And where, if I may ask, will I find Herr Eisner?"

"It is after seven, sir," the young man said in perfect, unaccented English. A secretary appeared beyond the barrier, her eyes owlish behind heavy glasses. Somewhere a typewriter started to clatter. Stropp grew angrier.

"He's gone home, you mean? Where is his home? You have a phone number?"

"No, sir, he does not give me the number."

"But what if he has to be reached when he's not here?"

"Sir?"

"Damn it—"

"He would often be, at this hour, sir, at the Opera café. He takes—"

"I know what he takes, thank you. All too well."

"If you would please, I could show you the way, Herr Stropp. And of course we will lock the door if that is what you wish. You must understand, it is not thought so often necessary here."

"Oh no, you stay right here and do whatever it is you're being paid to do. I know the way. This isn't the first time I've been to this law-abiding paradise of yours."

The young man gave him a bewildered and finally disapproving look. He was clearly on the knife edge of anger.

Stropp turned and marched out again, his briefcase swinging.

A cold, insistent rain was falling over Zurich by the time Miklos Baranyi returned to the print shop on the Frankengasse. A lonely, anachronistic bugle call, muffled by the downpour, drifted from the barracks across the river. It was very late and there were no taxis waiting on the Bahnhofplatz. Nor were there any trams in sight.

It was not very far to the Frankengasse, but in the time it took him to walk, he was drenched to the skin.

The lights were still on in the shop. The presses clacked steadily like railroad wheels. The long room stank of ink and naphtha.

Avner Liebermann, in an ink-stained apron, was working with one of the printers, running off counterfeit baptismal certificates. Liebermann had problems sleeping; every hour that he wasn't working, he said, meant more lives lost. How could a man sleep under such conditions? As long as he lived, he'd always wonder who had died because he'd stopped working to get some sleep.

Weary and chilled to the bone, Baranyi climbed the stairs, leaving dark, wet footprints on the treads.

Half a dozen children were asleep in one room, curled up in Swiss army blankets on the floor. The sour smell of scalded milk lingered in the air, mixing with the reek of printer's ink from the shop below.

In his warren of a room, Baranyi found his sister-in-law. She was sitting by the window, cleaning a long-barreled pistol by the light of the street lamp outside.

"Look at you, Miklos. You're soaked through."

"Why should that make any difference to you?"

She shrugged. Her eyes narrowed, and she laid the pistol down on a table, the snout pointing directly at him. He blanched. For a split second he thought that she had finally resolved to kill him. Her finger was only an inch from the trigger. It would be an accident. He took a deep breath.

"Be careful with that," he said. "Where did you get such a thing, Julie? If you're caught with it . . ."

"It belonged to . . . your father-in-law. He used it against Budyenny in '21. It's called a parabellum, Miklos. It's German, a Mauser, and it still fires quite well. I'm a good shot, didn't you know? No, I suppose Teresa never told you that. She wouldn't have. She was too gentle a creature."

Without a further word, she plugged in the electric burner and set a pot of coffee warming. He sat on the edge of the cot, shaking, his painfully thin body showing through his sopping-wet shirt like bones in an X ray. He felt both foolish and embarrassed. He would have liked to undress, but was reluctant to do so in front of her. And his reluctance angered him; he was a doctor, had *been* a doctor, hadn't he?

"Kagan? Where is he?"

"He's gone back, I think." She pushed the lank, pale bond

strands from her forehead. Her eyes shone like the little reflectors
on car bumpers at night.

"Where?"

"To Budapest. We heard this afternoon that there are rail-
equipment concentrations. Enough for ten thousand a day."

Baranyi slumped back against the wall, still shivering. Julie
poured a cup of coffee and brought it to him. He found that he
could not drink it.

"I must send a cable . . . to New York."

She shook her head. "The telegraph office is closed. The good
Swiss burghers are very regular about their business hours. They
open on time, they close on time. It would take a war—and, of
course, there is no war here."

What was the use? He sighed. Liebermann was right. By morning another thousand would be gassed. He wondered who they
would be.

"You have the look of more bad news." She came over, bringing
a blanket and a towel. He stared at her. For a moment she seemed
gentle, almost kind. Her constant shifts of mood kept him perpetually off balance. He wished she would go away, vanish, disappear.
But without her, there would be no Conrad Bor, no Paprocki.
Possibly even no Pauer.

"It's bad as it can be," he said. "The reports are still sitting there
in Berne. He hasn't sent them to Washington."

"You really didn't expect that he would, did you?"

No, he hadn't really expected anything. But he had hoped. One
could always hope.

"Look here," she said, "you've got to get some rest. You're not
twenty years old anymore. Do you want to go to your room? I'll
drive you if you do. Liebermann's car is downstairs."

He shook his head. He was too tired to move, and he knew it.
He could barely hold on to the coffee cup. Suddenly he became
aware of how frail he'd grown. His skin was white, like that of
something too long out of the light. He thought he smelled a faint
odor of decay arising from his own body. Gangrene of the soul.

"Why do you pretend to care about me?" he asked. "You'd like
to see me dead. You've said so often enough."

She put a lit cigarette between his lips and smiled. He could not tell whether from malice or kindness. Her expressions were growing increasingly ambiguous. He tasted her own mouth on the tip of the cigarette, faintly sweet from her lipstick. Her face was quite close to his now. She eased him back onto the cot and helped him off with his shirt. Then she sat next to him and dried him with the towel. He felt ashamed by his partial nakedness, but she seemed not to notice. That made it even worse.

"I'll sit with you for a while. You don't mind, do you? It wouldn't do to have you fall asleep with a lit cigarette in your mouth."

He noticed that she had the parabellum in her lap again and was toying with it as some other woman might toy with her knitting. A feeling of black exhaustion crawled over him. Socrates must have felt that way, he thought, as the hemlock worked up from his toes. Death or sleep, it made little difference.

"Close your eyes," she said. "You won't come to any harm. Not tonight at any rate."

Stropp entered the Opera café and halted by the polished mahogany bar, waiting until his eyes adjusted to the smoky gloom. The café was far more in the Central European style than most of the *bürgerlich* restaurants of Zurich, where one could get little more than a veal chop and a beer. Here, a great deal more was obviously available.

The café opened out beyond the polished bar into a series of small and dimly lit rooms. Stropp could hear the sounds of a small string orchestra playing somewhere, muffled behind many draperies. The tune was familiar, incongruous, and ultimately annoying: "That Old Black Magic."

After a while, he saw Eisner at a table far to the rear. Eisner hadn't changed much since he'd been sent into exile three years before—the same narrow, boyish face, small-boned, wide-eyed— but the expression was a little more wary and unpredictable. The features had grown a trifle sharper, more pinched. In ten years he'd be over forty and indistinguishable from any of the other gray-faced, mediocre lawyers who filled the midnight cubicles at Hayklut, Bard, Winston & Stropp's New York offices.

There was a bottle of brandy on the table in front of Eisner and a plump, not unattractive blond woman sitting across from him, feigning interest in his drawling conversation.

Stropp went directly over to Eisner, sidestepping a waiter who was carrying a steaming pot of fondue.

"Why weren't you waiting for me at the office? You knew when I was due."

Eisner jerked around, stared in disbelief at the bent, angry man looming over him.

"You've got some sort of an explanation, I suppose? You always had before," Stropp barked.

Eisner flushed, his face going a red noticeable even in the dim light.

"You don't mind, Fraülein?" Stropp said, pulling out a chair for himself. "This isn't your wife, is it, Eisner?"

Stropp knew perfectly well that it wasn't Eisner's wife. She had divorced him right after the scandal.

"No, sir. She isn't . . . she . . ."

"I'm sure the young lady won't mind leaving us alone—will you, Fraülein?"

The woman rose, angered, and said something in *Schweitzer-deutsch.* Eisner spoke rapidly to her. She calmed, shrugged, picked up her handbag, and left.

"What did you tell her?"

"I said I'd give her twice what we'd agreed on if she'd skip dinner and meet me later."

"It's going to be a lot later for you," Stropp said. He emptied an untouched glass of water into the large ashtray and poured himself three fingers of Eisner's brandy.

"You've got a lot of work to do and very little time to do it in," Stropp said. "So you leave the brandy alone. I can afford a drink. You can't."

Eisner tried to compose himself. The difficulty showed.

"If you mean the Chemihold papers, I've been working with Grunewald on them for the last two weeks. I know them by heart."

"The market divisions?"

"Just as they're supposed to be."

"And the agreements?"

"Grunewald prepared them. They're all right."

"You're sure?"

"The draft assignments are perfect according to Swiss law. They'll hold up under ours, too. Even under present conditions."

"Have you reviewed the Rotterdam accords?"

"Ten times. Plus all the confidential memoranda. I've cross-checked it all, Mr. Stropp. The only thing missing is Krauch's signature."

"We don't want any claims of duress later."

Eisner looked down. "I can't guarantee what will happen later. Who knows what retroactive statutes may get passed after the war, here or in the States? Like the contracts renegotiations act, for instance."

"No one expects you to be clairvoyant. We just need to be sure as of right now. Under the law *as it is*."

"I am sure, right now. Absolutely positive."

"What about Landau? Have you gotten hold of him?"

"Yes, sir. He wasn't hard to find. He's even got a phone listing, though where he finds the money for it, I don't know."

"How's that?"

"He's working as a pharmacist's assistant, sir."

Stropp emitted an edgy, unpleasant laugh. "One of the best chemical engineers in the entire synthetics field and he's mixing prescriptions?"

"It looks that way, sir."

"Then he's agreeable, of course. What did you offer him?"

"I thought I'd better leave that up to you. I said we'd discuss terms after you got here."

"Does he understand why he's wanted?"

"I haven't exactly explained it to him yet, no. I didn't think it would be prudent."

"You didn't think it would be prudent? That's got to be the first time in your life you ever bothered about being prudent, Eisner. Well, never mind, I suppose you did the right thing. I'll handle it when the time comes. *If* the time comes."

"I thought so, sir."

"You thought so? Jesus, Eisner . . . Give me something cold to drink, will you? The beer will do nicely. Brandy's rotten. You haven't started on the beer yourself already, have you?" He lit up a cigarette, inhaled, feeling vaguely nauseous. "Have you got a driver for me? I'll want one of our own people, not Grunewald's. Do we have anyone here?"

"Claude Ellsworth, sir. He's very good. Absolutely trustworthy. He's with Criterion's office in Basel. I'll have him up in the morning."

"Oh?"

"He'll do anything you need done, Mr. Stropp. He falls into my category, you might say. That is, he's not really in a position to argue."

Stropp smiled. He remembered Ellsworth now. There was a file on him in the office safe. Bard had gotten him off twice during the time when he'd been building a criminal law practice and doing his imitation of Max Steuer on a regular basis. Armed robbery once, attempted murder the second time around. The evidence for half a dozen more indictments lay neatly pinned up in a cubbyhole between two wills and an old corporate merger. Old man Hayklut had gotten him a job with Criterion's subsidiary in Bucharest. He'd been very good during the Iron Cross pogroms and later, breaking heads in Ploesti.

Yes, Claude Ellsworth would do very nicely. He wondered how long they'd had the man in Basel and why he'd been sent there in the first place. But he wasn't interested enough to ask. It was quite sufficient that a man like Ellsworth was available.

And expendable, if necessary.

Eisner paused, fingered his brandy glass, but, as he had been instructed, did not drink.

"Mr. Stropp, can I ask you a question?"

"What?"

"Why do you trust me?"

"Don't ask me that, Eisner. Because if you don't know the answer then maybe you're right, maybe I shouldn't rely on you." He sipped his beer, obviously displeased. "Is Grunewald ready?"

"The arrangements have been made. The border station has been cleared, the meeting site has been secured by our counterparts."

"They're very good at that sort of thing."

"That remains to be seen, Mr. Stropp," Eisner returned. "Remember, we're dealing with private interests now, not with the government. This isn't their normal way of doing business any more than it is ours. And they're just as worried as we are."

"Are we worried? I didn't know that."

Eisner took a long time considering his response.

"Sir, if we're not, we should be."

April 25, 1944
Zurich

After sending a cable to Peshko in New York City, Baranyi went directly to the Central Library on the Zahringerplatz.

He entered the building and was at once overcome by its stillness. Solid, healthy-looking guards stood by the doors, lifeless as statues. Inside, blond, stocky girls in starched dresses tended to the needs of scholars with brisk efficiency. Everyone moved quickly, silently, obeying the rules. It was, in its way, quite ominous.

How different were they from the Germans, these law-abiding Swiss? Only the rules were different. But if they had been the same? What then?

He entered the main reference room. He had no need to ask the librarian where to find what he was looking for. He'd been there many times, and although he'd never needed these particular volumes before, he knew exactly where they were located, where the entire run of them were. One for each year, as far back as the turn of the century and perhaps even further back than that.

He showed his identification, filled out the necessary slips, and handed them to an attendant.

In a few moments the young woman returned with a heavy, blue-bound book.

How absurd it would be if he could find an answer so easily. He should have come here first, before sending off the cable to the Aggudath in New York. No, it was just as well that Peshko and the others in New York were aware of what was happening. Perhaps there was something they could do at their end. Something he hadn't even thought of.

He conceded his own helplessness. Even the Poles could do nothing to move the American chargé if he didn't wish to be moved.

Other measures, perhaps more direct, would have to be considered. But before they could do anything meaningful they would first have to understand the chargé's reason for refusing to act. Only then would they know what had to be done.

He opened the blue-bound book, turned its tissue-thin pages. *Who's Who in the United States of America,* 1940 edition.

It was recent enough, certainly. The war had prevented later volumes from reaching Zurich. It would have to do.

He ran his finger hesitantly down the page.

It was there, a full, fat entry under the name "Marcus Trilling." He'd been right to look. The aide had said something about the man having been an ambassador once; such people were always listed in volumes like this.

He read slowly, growing more and more puzzled.

> Trilling, Marcus Bramwell: oil co. exec., b. 1891, Lubbock, Texas; a. Harold Whitaker and Felicia (Bramwell) t.; grad: St. James Episcopal High School, 1908, MBA Shaver College of Business Admin., 1912, B.S. in chem., Mass. Inst of Tech., 1919; m. Lydia French, 1922; children, Wayne Wallace, 1927. Assoc. w. Phillips Petroleum, Bartlesville, Okla, 1920, beginning w. staff & purch dept., successively compt., v.p., Pres. Develop & Research Corp of Am., 1928–30; assoc. w. Criterion Oil Co., of Wilmington, Del., 1931, beginning as v.p., in chg. sales, tech. dept., later pres., dir.; bd. of dir., Boys Club of America, Ten Oaks Country Club, Tech. Research Found. of U.S., trustee; member, US Govt. Research Bd., National Industrial Recovery Foundation; Amb. to Portugal, 1935–37. Home, Georgetown, Wash., D.C., office., Wilmington, Del.

Baranyi read through the entry three times. It made no sense. The aide had been right: this Trilling, whoever he was, had been briefly ambassador to the Salazar government. Apart from that, there was nothing in the entry that shed the slightest light on Lorimer's motives. It was a good thing after all that he had wired Peshko.

He left the library, more baffled than ever.

April 30, 1944
Near Waldshut, Germany

As the Rhine drops below the steel and pig-iron foundries of Schaffhausen, its flow becomes more and more rapid. The spray rises high as the river forces its way between the hard rock slabs of the Jura foothills on the one side and the sheer cliff faces that mount to the lower slopes of the Black Forest on the northern bank. The river froths and steams. The waters swell, contract, broaden, and narrow again, rolling wildly over high rock falls and into precipices which make navigation impossible. At Rheinfall, a little farther on, the river is five hundred feet wide and descends from a height of over seventy feet in a spectacle of torrent and foam that Goethe once likened to the source of all oceans. From there to the point where the Aar joins the Rhine just above Waldshut the waters move rapidly on to the west, but with a deep stillness broken only by an occasional short rapids. The forest comes down often from the German side of the border almost to the river's edge and casts a deep shadow over the swiftly running waters. From the Swiss side it is impossible to see into the forest, and the few roads that lead there, the few bridges that give access to that dark, legend-haunted wood, are devoured almost instantly by the stillness and the cold blue shadows that fall from the thick stands of pine and larch.

Henry Stropp had never been to this part of Switzerland before. He had stopped coming to Switzerland for winter vacations years before when he realized that he could no longer control his resentment at the sight of young men with straight backs moving easily over the slopes, rushing through the blue-white powder—young men doing things he could never do.

Nineteen thirty-six had been the last year he'd gone to Switzerland. Since then his vacations had taken him to warm places where deep blue water hid the grace of bodies more well formed than his own.

Now he found himself in the back seat of a large gray Daimler sitting next to a gnomish Swiss lawyer from Zurich while a border guard in a long black leather coat and high-crowned, polished leather cap checked the papers which the driver, Ellsworth, had just thrust through the window at him. Next to Ellsworth in the front seat, a briefcase on his lap, sat Samuel Morse Eisner, his face drawn, his forehead ugly and adolescent with little beads of perspiration.

The car had stopped while still on the bridge. Stropp had looked briefly out the window. Heights gave him vertigo, and the distance down to the swiftly moving black water made him dizzy. He too had been sweating heavily under his topcoat for an hour or more, ever since leaving Zurich. The law, *his* country's law, strictly prohibited any dealings with enemy nationals. He had no doubt that the law of Nazi Germany had similar prohibitions and even stricter punishments than his own. For a brief moment, he felt a wave of resentment. Trilling and the rest of the Criterion board sat safe in their Wilmington offices while he, Henry Stropp, risked God only knew what, crossing over a Swiss bridge into Nazi Germany while the war still raged on three continents.

The border guard returned the papers that the heavyset Ellsworth had given him. The documents, Stropp knew, had been carefully fabricated. He was, for the moment, one Heinrich Stropp, citizen of the canton of Thurgau. There was more than a little truth in that: Stropp's paternal grandfather had come from Bregenz, just across the Bodensee. And there were still plenty of Stropps in Ulm, Ravensburg, and Freidrichshafen as well as on the Austrian side of the line. He knew. He'd been writing to some of them as recently as November 1941.

"*Alles ist in Ordnung. Durchpassen, bitte,*" said the guard as he waved them on.

The Daimler moved soundlessly off the bridge and onto a hard-packed dirt road that led up into a pine forest. Waldshut itself lay about three kilometers to the west.

Ellsworth turned briefly and regarded Stropp with his watery blue eyes. "Was he German or Swiss, Mr. Stropp?"

"Does it matter?"

"No, sir, Mr. Stropp."

Grunewald sat back, traveling with the easy nonchalance of a man out on a pleasure jaunt. Stropp had spoken to Grunewald on the phone many times but had never met him before. The precise, almost military voice on the long-distance line had not prepared him for the man himself. Grunewald's appearance and his voice were definitely at odds. The lawyer was in his late fifties and had such a heavy shock of white hair that from a distance he gave the appearance of an animated thistle. His manner was quiet, assured and a little patronizing, as though he knew a great many things that Stropp did not know and would never know. Had it not been for his precise Swiss German and the inevitable gray of his clothing, Stropp would have taken him for an Irishman.

Grunewald was the senior of a small Zurich firm that had represented Chemihold since it had been formed in 1931. One of Grunewald's partners was related by marriage to Max Ilgner, the head of I.G.'s Northwest 7 office and its industrial intelligence operation. For the last five years, all of Criterion's business with I.G. had been handled through Chemihold, of which Criterion was a 49 percent shareholder.

Stropp had the irritating feeling that Grunewald was laughing at him. Every so often, Stropp would turn quickly, sure that he had caught Grunewald staring. But each time he had either been wrong or too late.

The car moved quickly up the hard-packed road that rose steeply between tall rows of black-boughed spruce through whose foliage only a fragmented sunlight descended. The sky was the color of slate and ribbed with long clouds that seemed incised rather than floating upon its surface. The smell of pine needles was heavy and the silence thick and enveloping. Even the sound of the car's motor seemed to have grown softer.

Grunewald reached with his right hand into his jacket pocket and managed to extract his cigarettes. He did not offer Stropp one.

The Swiss smiled amiably. "A place of trolls and witches, is it not?"

"Beg your pardon?"

"The forest, Herr Stropp. *This* forest, in particular. One always feels oneself a child here. Within such dark places the world does not enter. We come here in an automobile, to be sure, but this is not a place for such machines. It is a place for horses, for knights, for creatures with wings who fly in the night. Not automobiles, Herr Stropp. Do you feel it too?"

Stropp did not respond. Grunewald's insistence on speaking

English when he knew perfectly well that both Stropp and Eisner spoke German irritated him. He disliked being patronized and had long since decided that the use of English in a foreign country was definitely patronizing.

"And what is your opinion, Herr Eisner? How do you like our forest? Do you find that it brings back childhood memories, or—perhaps, excuse me—your childhood was of a different kind, yes?"

"Different, Mr. Grunewald. Very different, I think," said Eisner in a husky voice that made Stropp think that the man's mouth must be bone dry.

"How much farther?" Stropp asked.

"A few kilometers, no more. There was no precise location mentioned. The instructions were simply that we should proceed along the road northeast of Waldshut, through the forest, and continue until we come . . . to those we seek, who will be waiting for us."

"Or a Grenzepolizei unit," Stropp suggested.

"Hardly. There is not a border patrol unit within twenty kilometers of here. That would not be permitted. Our clients would not care to be so inconvenienced. You may rest assured that all such things have been taken care of. You forget, your partners maintain a special section whose only purpose is to ensure cooperation with the army command. The cooperation extends both ways."

The road curved sharply at a point less than a hundred meters ahead, just past a heavy stand of larch. Behind the trees a slightly darker shadow moved. A trick of the light? Two autos parked off the road. A number of men standing in the shadows.

Grunewald nodded. They had been traveling less than five minutes since leaving the river's edge.

The car pulled off the road just beyond the turn; they moved silently over the pine needles until they came around behind the larch and into a deep grove the center of which formed a natural amphitheater. On the opposite side, a dozen meters away, two black Mercedeses were parked.

"Well, then . . . to business," said Grunewald cheerfully.

Eisner let out a sigh.

Stropp leaned forward angrily. "You don't like this? It makes you nervous, is that is?"

"Mr. Stropp . . . the Trading with the Enemy Act says—"

"I know exactly what it says. What do *you* say?"

"Whatever you want me to say, Mr. Stropp."

"Precisely," said Stropp. "You stay right here. For now. You and Ellsworth. Just watch what goes on, that's all."

He waited until Ellsworth had turned off the motor before getting out. The briefcase hung from his arm by a chain. It was only half full: the market-allocation agreements, in blank. He intended to make the trip back to the car with the case fully loaded.

Stropp stood by the side of the car, eyeing the three men who waited by the Mercedeses. It took a second for him to become accustomed to the gloom. Grunewald was already halfway across the clearing when Stropp called sharply after him—to stop.

"What's that, Herr Stropp? Is something the matter?"

"Where the hell's Krauch? I don't see Carl Krauch there. What's going on?"

Stropp had known Krauch for years, and he knew Ter Meer, Ambros, and Von Schnitzler almost as well. He would have recognized any one of them at a hundred yards in a rainstorm.

The men standing by the Mercedeses were strangers. He had never seen any of them before in his life.

With a few quick steps, he caught up with Grunewald and pulled him back. He could hear Eisner move heavily against the car door. There was a sharp metallic sound. It had not even occurred to him to ask, but it was just possible that Eisner was armed. Ellsworth certainly was. And he was a damned fool for not having taken a weapon himself. The precariousness of his position suddenly struck him like a ton of pig iron. A heavy sweat broke out all over his face and neck.

One of the Germans stepped forward, a tall slender man with a high-domed forehead, his sparse black hair brushed back flat against his skull like a cap. His hands were thrust deep into the pockets of a gray tweed coat. He looked the picture of an Englishman out for a walk on the moors.

"Here, here . . . you are Henry Stropp?"

"Sir?" said Grunewald, interposing himself between Stropp and the German. "Who are you, if you please?"

"I can speak for myself," Stropp said, pushing forward. The German's hands had come out of his pockets; he was not holding a weapon.

"Yes, I'm Stropp. Who the devil are you?"

The German smiled nervously. "You are dismayed to see me here," he said in English. "Of course, of course, I can understand that—you expected—"

"Krauch," Stropp shot back. "You're damned right." Stropp drew back, hefting the briefcase as though ready to use it as a flail. The two other Germans watched closely but did not move.

"Permit me, Herr Stropp. I am Dr. Ing. Helmut Schragg. Deputy director of Sparte II, production division."

"Where's Krauch? Why isn't he here? Or Ter Meer?"

Grunewald stepped aside. "You must give us an explanation for this, please. We were expecting Dr. Krauch and—"

"I understand perfectly," said the tall German. "I was not expecting to be here alone either. Would you mind identifying yourself?"

Grunewald held out his passport. Schragg read it quickly.

"And you? You also have papers for me?"

"You still haven't answered me. Where's Krauch?" Stropp turned to Grunewald. "Max, I think we'd better go back. That is, if we still can."

Schragg didn't move a muscle. "If you wish," he said.

"What I wish is to see Carl Krauch."

"Unfortunately that is quite impossible. At the moment he and Ter Meer are at the *Führerhauptquartier* trying to explain to our leader how they are going to repair the damage your bombers did at Leuna the other day."

"So *that's* it," breathed Stropp. "And they sent you instead?"

"Not exactly instead. I was to come with them, as production chief. Now, as you see, I am alone."

Grunewald said, "I think you should listen to him, Henry."

"How do I know he's who he says he is? For all I know he's a Gestapo agent."

"I appreciate your concern, Herr Stropp," said Schragg. "The possibility of such a thing concerns us just as much as it does you. Consider that I am as suspicious as you are. I do not know Herr Grunewald except from photographs. I do not know you at all. You do not know me. Yet we have business to transact. Shall we talk? If, after we talk, you still do not trust me, then by all means . . . go back."

Stropp considered his alternatives. He had no choice, really, but to sound the man out. He knew of the Leuna bombings; they'd made the front page of the Zurich *Tageblatt* the day he'd arrived. It was certainly possible that Hitler had called Krauch and Ter Meer on the carpet in the aftermath of the raid. Almost half of the synthetic aviation fuel capacity of the Reich had been destroyed at one time. That was certainly enough to warrant a command performance.

"Alone then. Just you and I," Stropp said.

"As you wish. My companions will stand aside."

"Max, wait for me there. Keep an eye out."

When they had moved a distance away through the woods, Schragg asked, "Do you have the papers with you?"

"What papers am I supposed to have?"

Schragg laughed. "The market agreements. For after the war, of course. You are testing me, naturally. I don't mind. Believe me, you are not the only one to be nervous. Consider—I was told only a day ago that I would have to take Dr. Krauch's place in this matter. Alone. I am just as concerned as you are about the problems involved in this meeting. Many would not understand exactly why we are doing what we are doing. They would misinterpret our motives. The Gestapo, for instance. Kaltenbrenner, I am sure, would not understand. Nor would the SD. If you will permit me, I think they would take as dim a view of these proceedings as your own people would."

"That hasn't stopped you, though."

"No more than it has stopped you. Come, shall we discuss what we came to discuss?"

"Why not?"

Schragg pointed to the two Mercedeses. "Good, then. We have brought with us the patent assignments in blank. Everything that was requested. The entire polymerization process is covered."

Stropp did not let him finish. "You gave us the patent assignments the last time, too. They're worthless without the technical information."

Schragg hesitated. "We have brought as much of the technical information as we could. It was not easy, Herr Stropp. The danger was great."

"*Some* of it? Not *all* . . . ?"

"Enough, I think, for you to satisfy yourself that we are sincere. It is in our best interest to be sincere under the circumstances. Wouldn't you agree?"

Stropp could hardly argue with that. This time Criterion was handing over nothing of its own. The quid pro quo was simply an agreement to keep the bombers off the new Buna plant. The instant anyone thought that I.G. wasn't playing straight, that there was going to be a repetition of the Rotterdam fiasco, the bombers could be let loose and the plant destroyed within a week.

"The equipment? Have you brought diagrams? Plans? How are we to be sure?"

"You've seen the product. Obviously we cannot bring the equipment," Schragg said. "Be reasonable, Herr Stropp. We have brought as much of the technical data as we could safely carry with us. And we have executed assignments of all rights in the equipment located in the Monowitz plant. We are under no illusions as to the outcome of the war. Your people will have control of the process for some years to come. The assignments, of course, must run to Chemihold, to the Swiss corporation . . ."

"And you people have a two percent edge on my client in ownership there. It's rather like moving your wallet from your left pocket to your right, isn't it?"

Schragg frowned. There was a long silence. Then he said, "Dr. Krauch anticipated your . . . reservations. And so, we have also included in the package a transfer, by deed of trust, of three shares of voting stock in Chemihold. From ourselves to your client. To be held by Herr Grunewald and turned over to your people when the war is concluded. All strictly according to Swiss law."

Stropp smiled faintly. That was far better than he'd hoped for.

"I've got to talk to Max for a moment."

"Of course," said Schragg. He took a heavy cigarette case from his coat pocket and offered it. "French. A bit strong, but better than ours. Perhaps I.G. will get into the tobacco business someday and then Germany will have a decent cigarette. But for the time being . . ."

Stropp permitted himself a pleased expression. It was more than Grunewald had thought to do, to offer him a cigarette.

Stropp moved silently over the pine needles to the other side of the clearing, where Grunewald waited by the car. Eisner was still in the back seat. Doing just what he'd been told to do.

"Yes?" the lawyer said as Stropp approached. "Everything is well?"

"Everything is not well," Stropp replied. "You don't know that man, do you? Of course you don't. And the others? Are any of them familiar to you?"

"There are over a hundred executives in the upper echelon of I.G. Farben. The *Vorstand* alone has perhaps two dozen members. I only know by sight the ones who are also on the board of Chemihold."

"Which leaves us just where?"

Grunewald sighed. "What shall we do, Herr Stropp? Shall we go back? Shall we simply forget the entire business? It will suit me, if that is your wish."

"You know perfectly well it isn't."

"What then?"

Stropp could see the three men in their heavy overcoats by the Mercedeses. Besides the one called Schragg there was a short stocky man of about fifty who looked like a banker and a small, somewhat younger man with the wary look of a Levantine trader. Certainly not the kind of assortment one would have expected to represent an *echtdeutsch* organization like I.G. The three of them looked distinctly like a third-rate-movie version of Gestapo agents.

He noticed with sudden horror that one of the men had a camera in his hand.

They'd been photographed. *He'd* been photographed, talking to Schragg.

Grunewald's question hung in the air like a wisp of fog. Stropp swallowed hard and pulled at his collar.

"They say they're giving us the technical material. If Krauch had told me that, I'd have believed him, I think. But how do I know what this man is handing me? I'm not qualified to tell."

"You have no technical expert with you?" Grunewald said in astonishment.

"There isn't a first-class technical man in this field in the whole United States who isn't under close FBI surveillance. There's a crisis in the synthetic rubber industry. No, of course I couldn't bring anyone with me."

Grunewald threw up his hands. "Under such circumstances . . ."

"Damn it, I need a man who can look at the stuff they're handing me and tell me whether it's genuine or not. And, more important, someone who can tell me whether *he's* genuine, this man Schragg."

Stropp's brain was racing now. He could see it all slipping away from him. The deal, the stock in Hydro-Arc, the board of directors, all of it.

And that damned camera in the German's hand. That was part of it now too. They hadn't missed a trick.

He took a deep breath. "All right. I've got no choice. We have to use Landau."

Grunewald's face went slack, as though someone had let the air out of it; his glasses seemed to slide down the bridge of a nose suddenly too slender to support their weight.

"Felix Landau? But he—"

"He's in Zurich. Eisner knows where. He's spoken to him already, just in case."

With that he turned his back on the Swiss and walked across the clearing again. Schragg took a few steps toward him. This time they met within the shadow of the Mercedeses.

"All right," Stropp said. "We'll proceed. But there will have to be another meeting."

Schragg looked pained but not negative. "If it is necessary, of course. It is only natural that you don't trust me. On the other hand, what have you got to lose? You're giving us nothing this time."

"Nothing at all, Herr Schragg. Only the status of an open city for the Buna works, that's all."

"We agree to produce nothing. Not one kilo. Not until the war is over."

"And if we find that you've hoodwinked us again, then all we have to do is tell our air force people, 'Sorry, the gentlemen at I.G. haven't lived up to their side of the bargain, so please go ahead and bomb now'? Sure, that's just what we'll do. And no one will ask a single question about it. No thank you. We make sure. *First.*"

Schragg's face grew dark. Little liver spots appeared at his temples. He forced a polite smile.

"But of course. You are cautious. It is good business to be cautious."

"In, say, three days? Grunewald will set it up. On our side of the river this time, though. Agreed?"

"Do I have a choice?"

"None."

"Agreed then." Schragg made a move as though to hold out his hand, then withdrew it before it was refused. It was clear that the man had no illusions about Stropp's attitude.

The auto with Swiss plates moved quickly out of the grove and slid soundlessly back onto the road leading to the Rhine and the Waldshut bridge.

Grunewald's face was almost invisible behind a screen of smoke. The interior of the car stank from it.

"Felix Landau," Grunewald brooded. "You say he's here in Zurich? How do you know that?"

"Oh, he's here all right," said Eisner from the front seat. "I met with him two weeks ago. He's expecting us to contact him."

"Does he understand why?" Grunewald asked, incredulous.

"Not yet, but it won't make any difference to him," said Stropp. "Eisner tells me he's not very well off at the moment. And it seems that he has his little girl to support."

"They did not pension him off as they did with Weinberg and with Mendelssohn-Bartholdy? I've heard—"

"Weinberg was a member of the *Vorstand,* remember? Upper-class. That was different. For such people, yes, a pension. For Landau, who was only an engineer, not a pfennig."

"So you think this will be sufficient? That he will cooperate because he is poor? Herr Stropp, remember, Landau is a Jew."

"I don't care what he is. He'll cooperate. We know our man, believe me. Besides, I have Eisner's assurance."

Eisner looked pained but said nothing. It was hardly the time to interrupt.

"You have a very harsh view of human nature," said Grunewald. "Do you know that?"

"I'm surprised to hear you, of all people, say so. But perhaps you're right," Stropp replied. "But I hardly think 'harsh' is the right word. 'Accurate' is what I'd say. Yes, 'accurate' is the right word really, don't you think?"

May 3, 1944
Zurich

West out of the city, in the direction of Fällenden, a narrow road ran, first through the crowded side streets surrounding the Polytechnicum, the hospital, and the observatory, then running out into more open country and climbing slowly up the slopes of the Zürichberg. The trip to the old Jewish cemetery took over two hours if one walked from the Limmat, a half-hour or less by car. On days when the cold was not too sharp and there was no rain, Miklos Baranyi took the No. 9 tram to Romerhofplatz and walked the rest of the way from there. He had done so this day, though it was cold for spring and threatening rain.

He wished, as always, to be alone, and as he could neither drive himself nor stand to have either Kagan or Liebermann with him, he braced himself against the nipping wind, lowered his head, and trudged alone through the weed-filled streets in the direction of the old cemetery.

As long as it took, it would take. He would get there soon enough. Josef would wait.

It had been more than a month since he had last been there, though he had promised himself that he would visit the grave every week that he remained in Zurich. What he would do when he finally left the city, he had no idea. He preferred not to think about it.

Ahead, down a rutted lane that rose between poor but neat little stone houses, he saw the field and the iron fence of the cemetery outlined against the gray sky. A cowbell clattered somewhere nearby. He heard children laughing at play.

How Josef would have loved it in Switzerland. The cows—Josef had always loved cows. And goats. Anything that was warm and soft and could be loved.

What a waste it had all been.

Miklos's eyes were dry and hot. He'd shed the last of his tears long before. For Teresa. For the boy too. His own small griefs seemed insignificant now, but at the same time the only true, important griefs. It was odd. He tried to rationalize his feelings, to understand them, but could not. Not with his doctor's mind, nor with what was left of the Jewish theology he had learned as a child.

Unless one accepted the ancient prophecy that the way to the Messiah had to be washed in blood, that it was necessary that evil grow so great that it nearly eclipsed the vision man had of God; unless one accepted that rationale, none of it made sense.

He hadn't brought himself that far yet.

The gate was open. Thank God the old *Shamus* wasn't there—a tallow-faced man from Bessarabia—how he'd wound up in Zurich no one knew—who lived in the stone gatehouse and chanted prayers for a few francs.

How many Jews were there left in the world, Miklos wondered, who couldn't say their own prayers?

Along the tree-shadowed path between the gravestones, spring flowers had begun to push up among the weeds that the *Shamus* had neither energy nor reason to trim. Some of the stones were covered by grass. Others, a very few, were marked by little pebbles left by mourners. A few recent graves had begun to sink.

The rain began, broken by the trees, only a faint mist settling to the graves. He turned up the collar of his coat, stopped by the familiar site, small, fenced in by a little black iron railing he'd carried out one day and set in place himself. Next to the grave was a larger empty space, big enough for two. Someday he would go back to Hungary, to Korestan, and bring out not the living but the dead—Teresa—if he could ever find her. The space was for her, next to her son.

And later, the other space . . .

He stood looking down at the little stone marker with its simple inscription in the Hebrew letters the child hadn't had the time to learn.

JOSEF BARANYI. 1938–1942.

The rain slowly pooled around his feet, turning the ground to mud, soaking his shoes. He felt nothing at all. For the first time, tears came to his dry eyes, only a few at first, a faint irritation, then suddenly a flood.

The sobs were soundless, a dry heaving in his chest, little more than labored breathing, but loud enough so that he did not hear her approach behind him.

It was the strong fragrance of flowers in the rain that made him turn, not the sight of her or the sound.

She was standing there with a bunch of blue mountain flowers in her hand. She was shivering, and her shoes, like his, were soaked black from the rain. How long she had been standing there behind him, afraid to intrude on his mourning, he had no idea. She acknowledged his surprise with a slight nod. Then, without a word, she stepped past him and laid the flowers on the grave.

For a moment she stood, head bowed, her hands in the pockets of her shapeless raincoat. Her wet hair hung in disordered strands like a fringe over her forehead.

"You followed me here?" he asked.

She looked up. Her expression was ambiguous, half defensive, half angry. "No need to follow you. It's always the same, the same time, the same day of the week."

"I haven't been here for almost a month."

"That's why I thought it was time you came out. I was right, it seems."

"Yes, you were right." He searched her pale, once beautiful face for a reason, found nothing. "But why did you come?" he asked.

"For her, for myself. Maybe even for your sake. How should I know? I don't try to understand what I do anymore. That's for when you're a student. I'm not a student anymore. I just do what I do, that's all." Her smile was quick, nervous, almost afraid.

"Well, for whatever reason, thank you for coming. The flowers are beautiful, Julie. Josef would have loved the flowers."

She shrugged, suddenly and transiently vulnerable. "He liked flowers, Miklos?"

"Yes, very much . . . You know, it's funny. It's one of the few things I remember clearly about him. Flowers and animals he loved. But I suppose all small children do, don't they?"

"I don't know. No one else in our family had little children. They didn't have time. He was my only nephew."

"You would have liked him, Julie. He would have liked you, too."

"You think so? I wonder why . . ." She stared at him, a vague, distant look in her eyes. "I like children. Really I do."

"Do you know, it's so strange, they suffer more than anyone else, the children do. But they don't hate. They seem incapable of hate. I wish, sometimes, that I was a child again, so that I wouldn't have to hate."

"You'll stop someday. We all stop sometime. It's too exhausting. You just have to stop."

"I think the hates of this war will last forever."

"Nothing lasts," she repeated dully, like an echo, her voice trailing off.

He looked at the grave again. "You're wrong. Some things do last, they go on forever, growing and growing. The need for justice, the need for judgment. You come to a place like this and you understand that. Look around, Julie. Cemeteries are a place for judgment. It cries out from the stones . . ."

"Miklos," she began.

He was aware of a hand on his arm. It was the first time his sister-in-law had ever touched him so gently.

"You must be strong," she said with a surprising and, it seemed to him, deceptive calm. "God willing, there will be an end to it all someday."

"So," he said, "you didn't come just to torment me?"

She hesitated, caught off guard.

Then she sighed. Her expression changed, became resigned. "Liebermann is looking for you. That's why I came."

With flowers? he thought. But he said, "More bad news?"

"I don't know. There is a cable from New York. I haven't read it, and even if I had I probably wouldn't have understood it. After all, what does a stupid Pole like me know of such things? And a woman besides . . ."

God . . . Miklos shuddered. It was her sister's voice for a second. Her injured pride, her contempt. She would be a doctor too. Not merely a nurse. Someday.

But that someday had died in the hospital courtyard at Korestan.

Because of Korestan and the Nyilas. And because she had married a Jew.

Miklos and Julie Malowska exchanged glances. There was nothing more to say.

They hurried on. Liebermann was waiting.

II

May 4, 1944

Zurich

A bank of heavy clouds over the Zürichsee obscured the higher peaks of the Alps to the south. Now and then a spear of sunlight broke through, touched the surface of the waters, glanced off and leaped in a sharp, dazzling zigzag into the steel gray sky. Stropp had left the shades of his hotel-room window up; he always slept with the windows uncovered so he would be awakened by the first light of day. A cold bath was already running in the deep iron tub. But the porter had not yet brought up his coffee and roll.

The phone rang. It was Eisner.

"He's expecting you, sir."

"Who?" Stropp was still a little groggy. Age was creeping up on him. He wasn't as quick as he used to be.

"Felix Landau. You said you wanted me to set it up as soon as possible, didn't you? He leaves at seven thirty, right on the dot, every morning. You want to get to him before he gets to the pharmacy, don't you? The address is 97–94 Spiegelgasse."

"You're getting better, Eisner."

"Thank you, sir."

Stropp hung up, took his bath, and toweled himself red. In the hall he encountered the porter, advancing on his room with a rolling breakfast tray. Stropp angrily waved him away. He didn't need the damned breakfast now. He'd do without.

He stepped out into the chill spring morning, walked as briskly as his deformity would allow, north up the Talstrasse and past the big gray buildings on the Paradeplatz. The address Eisner had given him was not far off, just across the nearest bridge, in the old part of Zurich. Landau's flat lay in the welter of old houses with oriels and wrought-iron signs that crowded between the Limmat and the Seilergraben on the right bank of the river. Narrow streets, clean as always but shabby, full of shadows even during the day-time, and curious fecal odors. Roofs reaching across from one side of the street to the other, shutting out what little light there was. He seemed to hear the whir of the silk mill machinery in the chill damp air. It was a good thing, Stropp thought. It marked the tempo of life. There were those who could move to it and those who couldn't. That was the way it was.

He looked up the narrow street. Number 97–94. The nearest doorway showed a set of black iron numerals: 87–83.

Just then he saw a door open a little way ahead. A small, gaunt man in his mid-forties wearing a long topcoat that reached almost to his ankles and a worn black felt hat stepped into the street. The man caught sight of Stropp, eyed him hard, hesitated. There was something about the movement, the sudden start and the drawing back, that struck Stropp as out of keeping with the usually aggressive movements of the average Zuricher.

Stropp stared back at the man. His face was narrow and singularly triangular in shape, the forehead high, the lips full but compressed, barely visible, the nose prominent, thin, with flaring nostrils. Ears a trifle protuberant under the heavy ledge of the hat brim. The expression instantly wary.

The iron numbers over the man's head read "97–94."

"Herr Landau?" Stropp called.

The man did not move.

"You are Felix Landau?"

The man's face relaxed slightly. He took a tentative step forward and responded, also in English. "You are Herr Eisner's . . . employer?"

Stropp reached into his pocket and took out a fold of papers: his inoculation certificate, his passport, his driver's license. He handed them to Landau.

On the top, sticking out of the upper compartment of the wallet, was a plastic corporate-identity card that Trilling had given him with the pinnacle and stars of Criterion Oil in yellow and red.

"May I speak to you, Herr Landau?"

"Of course," the man replied, returning the wallet. "We will walk, yes? I have certain business I must attend to this morning."

"You are employed as a pharmacist's assistant, Herr Landau. What business can you possibly have that cannot wait for five minutes?"

"Whether I am employed and at what is my affair, not yours."

"It's my affair at the moment," Stropp said. "I have something very important to say to you."

Landau nevertheless began to walk, rapidly, as though on the verge of flight. Stropp had difficulty keeping up with him. Damn the arrogant Jew, he thought, no wonder everyone hated them. He knew he would end up detesting Landau, no matter what the man did for them.

"I want to offer you work," Stropp said.

"So your Herr Eisner has said. But why? What kind of work can I possibly do for you?"

They turned a corner and entered Pelikanstrasse. Carefully modulating his voice and speaking very slowly, Stropp began to explain.

"Felix Landau. Age forty-seven. Formerly assistant to Dr. Otto Ambros, Development and Production for Buna N and S, I.G. Farbenindustrie. A protégé of the late, great Fritz Haber. Graduate of . . . Shall I go on, Herr Landau?"

"Yes, by all means. You arouse my curiosity."

"You were one of the best, Herr Landau. You were very, very good. They made a bad mistake letting you go."

"They made no mistake. I am a Jew. I'm sure your dossier on me does not omit that particular fact."

"Nevertheless, a bad mistake."

Landau uttered a grating laugh. "A penniless Jew. They *gave* to Weinberg, they *gave* to Merton, they *gave* to Simson. To me? Nothing. You had to be a member of the *Vorstand,* not simply an engineer. Engineers and chemists they chewed up and spat out. No matter how good."

"A mistake, Herr Landau."

"Perhaps. In their place, who knows, I might have done the same thing." Landau had slowed down a little now. "Bosch once warned Hitler that if he persisted in forcing Jewish scientists to leave Germany he would set chemistry and physics back a hundred years. Do you know what Hitler said? He said, 'Then we'll work a hundred years without physics or chemistry.'" Landau laughed again. "That's the kind of mistake they made. It was no mistake, believe me."

"We are not so foolish," said Stropp.

"And exactly who are you? Your card with its elegant symbol means nothing to me. The name, of course, I know. I could not have worked sixteen years at I.G. without knowing that name. But just what is it you want from me?"

They turned another corner. A wash of dingy sunlight fell into the street, making it seem even colder than before. Somewhere up the Limmat a barge horn hooted. A horse cab clopped by, the driver bent forward on the seat, his whip trailing.

"Ah, *there* . . ." said Landau suddenly, pointing to a shop on the other side of the street. In the window were a number of large dolls and a dozen or more brightly colored toys. "Excuse me, but this is most important."

"I don't follow you," said Stropp, irritated and puzzled.

"The 'business' I spoke of before. It is *there* that I have my business. It is the birthday of my daughter, Ilse, you see. This morning she is ten years old. Quite a significant event, even in these times, would you not say? And for a present, what does her father give her? A set of Braunfelder's *Encyclopedia of Science for Children*. A fine set of books, let me assure you. Just what a father like me would want his daughter to wish for. I scrimped and saved for a year to buy them for her. She accepts, of course, but I am not so stupid that I do not see that there are tears in her eyes. She tries to appear grateful, poor child, but the truth comes out soon enough. What she really wanted was a doll, a big, enormous, pink doll with bows in its hair and a dirndl around its fat little waist. How easy it is to injure our children, Herr Stropp, by forcing our own desires on them. It will be a great hardship for me, and perhaps we will have little to eat for the next few months, but she will also have the doll. She has little enough else."

They entered the store. The shopkeeper, a granitic woman with pale blond hair done in a massive bun, turned and stared at Landau as though she had seen him before. He smiled back weakly; he had often been before the shop window, with the little girl. Every evening for weeks.

While Stropp waited by the doorway, Landau made his selection. A huge blond doll, almost half as tall as Landau himself, the hair done in braids, dressed in a flowered blue dirndl. Huge blue eyes. Chubby pink arms.

The shopkeeper stared at Landau, who at that moment appeared not only shabby but faintly unhealthy. The way he handled the doll made the shopkeeper scowl. Stropp could see the disapproval in her eyes. It was simple enough to guess what she was thinking.

Landau was obviously one of *those* people. He did filthy things with dolls. A Jew. A degenerate.

Landau dug in his pocket.

"Forty francs," said the shopkeeper.

There was a moment's pause. Landau flushed. "One moment, please. Just a moment."

"Forty francs," said the shopkeeper again.

Stropp moved quickly to the counter, took out his wallet, and began counting out the bills. Landau shook his head, flustered, almost angry.

"I cannot permit that—"

"For the child," said Stropp. "Not for you."

"Please . . ." Tears began to gather in the corners of Felix Landau's eyes.

"Wrap it up, please," Stropp said in English. "Nicely. It's a gift."

The shopkeeper nodded briskly, taken aback. She picked up the bank notes and did as she was told.

When they were back outside on the street again, Landau barely able to manage the enormous box, Stropp said, "Now, let's talk about *my* business, if that's all right with you."

It was clear that Landau had not eaten in some time. A plate of hot croissants and a pot of marmalade began to disappear before the waiter had even brought the coffee and cocoa. Stropp could barely restrain an expression of disgust at the way Landau jammed food into his mouth.

Finally, still chewing, Landau said, "So . . . you still have not told me what it is exactly that you want me to do."

"Two things. First, you identify this man Schragg, if that's who he actually is. You tell me whether he's who he says he is, or not."

"This is easily done. I have known Helmut Schragg for over ten years. All I need to do is see him. The rest you will have to judge for yourself."

"Not exactly. He will also have certain documents with him. Technical information that must be evaluated."

"And this you cannot do yourself?"

"I'm a lawyer. I know nothing about synthetic rubber. You do,"

Stropp lied. It was partially true, partially not. But there was no reason Landau had to know that. It was far safer if the man believed that he had no expertise at all.

Landau spread more marmalade on his croissant. "Of course. I was Ambros's chief engineer. I could do this for you. I could tell you whether the information is genuine or not."

"It's supposed to be an improvement over the old Buna S method. Could you tell if *that* was genuine too? It won't be exactly the same as it was when you . . . when they asked you to leave."

"When they threw me out, Herr Stropp."

"As it was then?"

Landau took another mouthful and chewed thoughtfully, his small eyes narrowing until he looked for all the world like a marmoset.

"It would be simple enough for me. The new catalytic dehydrogenation process was developed in my department. We were working on it already when I . . . left. Or perhaps it is now a development in the area of fluid catalysts. Yes, that too."

Stropp nodded. "Will you do it?"

"One question, Herr Stropp. And that is—why do you come to me? Why not one of your own people? Surely Criterion has skilled research chemists who—"

"I asked the same question, Herr Landau. The answer is quite simple. There are perhaps two or three men in Criterion's employ who have the requisite knowledge. If we could have gotten one of them out of the country and over here, believe me, we would not have come to you. But as things are, they are each of them involved in high security work and I could no sooner put one of them on a plane to Zurich without a satisfactory explanation—which of course I could not give—than I could float an elephant across the Atlantic. So. Will you do it? Yes or no?"

"For what price? Please realize, I don't ask you *why* you wish this done or how it is that you are dealing with these people. I think I understand that well enough. But what I do wish to know is what you will do for me if I . . . accommodate you?"

"Ten thousand dollars, American."

Landau stared at him. His eyes widened; then he laughed. "No, no, that will not do at all."

"That's a fortune."

"The sum is tempting, particularly for a man who has absolutely nothing at the moment. But—excuse me—I am not stupid either. This is clearly very important for you. Otherwise you would not have come to me. Why would you take the risks?"

"I don't for a moment assume that you're stupid," Stropp said, "and I'm prepared to meet any reasonable request. What, exactly, do you want?"

"Let us say, first, the ten thousand dollars you offer."

"And what else?"

"One other thing only."

"And that is?"

"When the war is over, I want my position with I.G. back. Just as before. No, perhaps a little better. A small promotion, perhaps. A safe position in my old department."

"When the war is over?" Stropp was astonished.

"The Nazis are finished. Everyone knows that. But the people at I.G. will survive. They always do. What you are doing now, what I guess you are doing, is the best proof of that. I am not, as you say, a stupid man. I understand these things. So . . . so . . . what I want is a document, signed by Dr. Krauch, also by Schmitz and at least two of the other *Vorstand* members. This document must say that when the war is over Felix Landau will have his position back. That he will have a small financial interest as well. Yes, some stock in one of the reconstituted companies perhaps. I would like this drawn up and signed and put in a vault here in Zurich. Then I'll do what you ask. With pleasure."

May 5, 1944
Zurich

Baranyi sat alone at a table in the corner of the Hauptbanhof restaurant. Over the clatter of dishes and the rattle of silverware he could hear the clipped Swiss voice on the station loudspeaker calling out the departure times for trains to Lucerne and Schaffhausen. The restaurant smelled of cabbage and cheese, the entire station of coal, oil, and damp. It had rained heavily the night before and the pavement outside was glossy, the tracks under the main arrival shed covered by pooled water. The sun had finally managed to break through the heavy clouds that had gathered over the lake. A wash of cold, pale sunlight the color of cough syrup trickled down the Banhofstrasse and into the vaulted confines of the station.

It was early, a little past seven. Baranyi was groggy, his head full of cobwebs and phantoms. His frail body seemed held together by little more than willpower and coffee. He munched absently on a hard roll; it had no taste. Food seldom had any taste for him these days. Often, he forgot to eat entirely. He was beginning to understand how easy it would be to turn to alcohol. Already he had had to take pills to help him sleep for three out of the past five nights—even though he had been working at a pace that would have killed a far stronger man and by all rights should have collapsed each night into the deepest of all possible sleeps.

A voice on the waiting-room speaker announced a departing train. In three languages. Baranyi took a sip of coffee and glanced at the crabbed front page of the *Tageblatt*. There was not a word about what he knew was happening in Budapest, not a word about the deportations. Sports and the usual cantonal news. A table comparing the prices of foodstuffs and selected consumer goods for the last five years. Farm prices. The *Landesgemeinde* would be held at Glarus the following week. The schedule for the summer symphony concerts at Interlaken would shortly be available. A few words about the war, mostly concerning butter coupons and the Russian front. That was all.

No wonder he still saw mounds of corpses every night. If *he* didn't see them, who in Zurich would?

The swinging doors to the restaurant opened. Miklos had not even heard the train announcer call out an arrival, but there in the doorway was Zoltan Peshko, fresh from Geneva by way of Lisbon, a bundled, dwarfish figure with the face of a disgruntled mole. He wore a fur-trimmed coat far too heavy even for this dismally chill spring day. And his eyes were, as always, mere ciphers behind his thick, tinted lenses.

Miklos had not the strength even to rise and wave him over to the table. There were few people in the place; Peshko would see him soon enough.

Peshko was carrying a battered cardboard suitcase done up with straps, and a folder of the kind solicitors use for their papers. Peshko's eyes were deeply circled; he had been traveling for two days and probably had not slept at all. A frayed cigar, unlit, was clamped between his teeth. He had been, in his former life, a lower court judge in Budapest and still retained the briskness of movement and angular gesture that bespoke absolute authority. Though a small man, a head shorter than Baranyi—who was by no means large himself—he could easily command men far bigger and stronger. Had it not been for this quality of self-confidence, he never would have gotten out of Hungary in the first place.

"No welcoming committee? A fine thing," Peshko said, pulling out a chair for himself. "You look rotten, Miklos. Have you seen a doctor?"

"You don't look so well yourself, Zoltan."

"I can't afford to," Peshko said. "No one has any compassion these days for a healthy-looking Jew."

"Is that what we must rely on now, compassion?"

Peshko grimaced. He took the unlit cigar from his mouth and laid it on a plate. "No enthusiastic welcome and you don't even offer me a proper breakfast either."

"You never eat breakfast. Not since I've known you."

"That's beside the point."

"Also, you don't make jokes like this. It's not your custom." Baranyi paused. Only a Peshko on the brink of despair would be behaving in this bizarre way.

"Is the coffee not too poisonous?"

"I've survived it. Nothing the Swiss make has much taste anyhow. Except the chocolate." There was an empty cup at the unused second place-setting. Miklos took it and poured in half his coffee.

"From you I'll catch nothing I don't already have," Peshko said. He took a large swallow; his face grew instantly red. "What's the matter with you? That's obscenely good coffee. Do you know, Miklos, I haven't had anything to eat since Lisbon?"

"If you starve to death you'll be of no use to anyone."

"How much use am I as it is? How much use are any of us?" An expression of infinite pain suddenly darkened his face. He pushed the solicitor's folder across the table and at the same time at last opened his coat. He was beginning to perspire. "The Czech reports still sit in the American embassy?"

"We've spoken to Mr. Henderson at the consulate here, but he knows nothing. His orders are that everything must go through Berne. His hands are tied, he says." Baranyi took a parcel wrapped in butcher's paper from the adjacent seat and handed it to Peshko. "A copy for you. Perhaps in New York . . ."

Peshko shook his head. "Not even in Washington have we been able to break through the wall of silence. This is far worse, this statistical nightmare the Czechs have produced, than anything we've had so far. But it still makes no difference. They do nothing. Our friends in the War Refugee Board, young John Pehle and DuBois, they are outraged. But so far it all ends at the State Department. They look at the reports and say to us, 'Are you *sure* this is the truth? How can you be sure that this is the truth? Who will believe such things? Remember all the atrocity stories during the first war, nuns with their breasts cut off in Antwerp, and so on? Propaganda. No one will believe it, even if it *is* true.' "

"This time they will believe. No one could invent such horrors."

Peshko shook his head sadly. "You really think that they tell us the *real* reason that they refuse to help? Here, my friend. Read *this,* and then perhaps you will understand at least a little of what is actually happening."

"What's in there?" Baranyi's fingers hovered warily over the portfolio.

"The information you asked for, my friend. You will read it and you will understand what we are up against in this thing."

Peshko retrieved his cigar and placed it between stained, irregular teeth. "Then we will walk together in the clear, fresh Swiss air and talk about the consciences of men, yes? You and I . . ."

The sun had broken through the clouds at last. A flood of amber light streamed in through the single window of Colonel Bor's office. The room was cluttered. Encyclopedias in three languages crowded the shelves of a rickety bookcase. Cabinets ranged along the walls overflowed with papers. There was no desk, only a wide trestle table on which Bor had arranged a cracked globe, a number of paperweights, heaps of papers, a microscope, and a light. On the walls were pictures of Polish film stars. A large phonograph with a curved, domelike top stood amid heaps of records. All Chopin, mostly played by Brailowsky and Cortot. Baranyi knew that Bor had a mania for Chopin.

The colonel was listening with his chin on his hands.

"So, you see," Miklos went on, "there can be no doubt about it now. Peshko's information shows that the blockage of information from the embassy in Berne can be traced directly to this man Trilling and his associates and their friends in the American State Department. Even before the Vrba report, there was evidence that almost every initiative of the War Refugee Board relating to the Oswiecim camp had been throttled by the same group. Every man on our list has a direct connection to the Criterion Oil Company. Every one of them is either a major stockholder, a director, or an officer. In some cases they are former officers who have given up their posts for wartime government positions. In some cases they also still retain their corporate positions. And if not they themselves, then their sons or sons-in-law or some other close relative."

"And this interference occurs only where the Oswiecim installation is concerned?" asked Bor.

"There is no question about it. As far as the other camps are concerned, there is indifference, but in the case of Oswiecim it is direct, deliberate obstruction. One might even think, though it is so horrible, that all the rest, the indifference to everything else, is simply so as to bury the deliberate obstructions concerning Oswiecim. As though they had decided to wreck an entire railroad train in order to kill one man."

"The eleventh power," Liebermann said, so softly that only Baranyi heard him.

"What?" Miklos asked.

"No," Liebermann went on, as though to himself. "This is not mere indifference or even anger. It is far worse. These people destroy without even thinking about it, out of blind greed. They don't hate. They don't even *notice*. . . . The people they destroy are nothing at all to them. Surely that must be the twelfth and final power of evil."

"But why, why?" Bor demanded. "What possible reason can they have?"

Peshko shook his head sadly. "It is all too clear. Miklos, show him the second report."

Baranyi handed Bor a few sheets of paper clipped together by a metal fastener. The top sheet looked like an army organizational chart.

"This man, Trilling, is the president of one of the largest oil companies in the United States. This company is not only very important in the petroleum field but has subsidiary interests in every major chemical and pharmaceutical field as well. The chart you are looking at, Colonel, shows just how and with whom Criterion's cartel agreements have been made. The next chart shows all the direct connections that these people at Criterion Oil have with one concern in particular. These arrangements have been carefully concealed by the use of a number of intermediary, jointly-held stock corporations both in the United States and in Europe. There is, for example, a company in New York City which handles particular statistical information for them, another company in Zurich through which patent assignments are pooled and distributed. There is yet another company in the state of Illinois, America, which handles research and the distribution of technical information. And so on and so on. Each block on the chart shows the respective stock participations of Criterion and . . . the other organization. Note also that all of the various boards of directors overlap. There are names common to almost every one of them. And where the names do not appear to be common, please to consult the list on the next page and you will see that we are dealing with sons-in-law or brothers or cousins. Some of these people have become residents of the United States and in some cases have also become citizens. In short, these people are all so intertwined that it would take, if you will pardon me, an expert in Gordian knots to ever untangle them."

"Criterion Oil Company of Wilmington, Delaware," said Bor.

"And Interesse Gemeinschaft Farbenindustrie. Exactly. I.G. Farben. They are, these two, what could properly be called 'married.' "

"Which, of course, may answer some questions." Bor paused, seemed to be reaching back deep into his memory. "They were the ones who were responsible . . ."

"For what?" Peshko said. Obviously Bor knew something that neither Peshko nor Baranyi did.

The Pole sat back in the chair behind his trestle table and closed his eyes.

"In 1936, these people at Criterion Oil transferred to the Nazis, through their friends at Farben, the formulas and technical information for tetraethyl lead."

"What?" exclaimed Peshko, genuinely puzzled.

"Tetraethyl lead, sir. A vital additive for high-octane aviation fuel. Without which the Luftwaffe would have been to all intents and purposes grounded."

"In 1936? And so . . .?"

"That, of course, is not all. The Nazis took the formulas and the know-how and began to build plants to produce their own. These plants, however, were not to be finished until the end of 1939. There were meetings between the Farben people and Criterion's representatives. In London, of all places. And as a result, Criterion sold to the Nazi Air Ministry—again through Farben—twenty million dollars' worth of tetraethyl lead. Some five hundred tons of it. All of this had the approval of your American ambassador to England, Mr. Joseph Kennedy, without whose assistance the sale could not have been consummated. The Stukas that smashed Warsaw in September of 1939, my friends, flew only thanks to these people, to these Americans of the oil company." Bor at last opened his eyes. "Yes, these people interest me very much. These people of Criterion Oil. I would put nothing past them if it served their own interests. But their interests—just what can they be in this case? We must be objective, gentlemen. Absolutely objective." He took from under a pile of papers on his desk a large diagram of the Oswiecim installation—the sketch that had accompanied the Vrba-Wetzler report.

"True," he continued, "according to the Czechs, at the camp that is now called Monowitz, within the Oswiecim complex, there is an I.G. plant. It is still under construction. It is intended to provide fuel and synthetic rubber." Bor's long, elegant finger wandered along the lines. His voice softened. "But, gentlemen, what you seem to be suggesting makes no sense. The fuel plant is at a great distance from the main camp. While the Buna installation is much closer in, of course, it is by no means complete. And then," he said, again burrowing under the papers on his table, this time opening up a folded newspaper, "there is *this*."

He passed the paper across the table to Baranyi. Peshko leaned over to see it. The headlines were unusually strident for a Swiss journal. The article described the massive bomber strike at the Leuna synthetic fuel works. The Swiss journalists seemed as much taken by the technical accomplishment of the raid as by its tactical significance.

"If what you are suggesting is true, how can we explain *this?* After all, Farben installations have by no means been immune to bombing. If you are suggesting that the influence of this American petroleum company is so strong that it could actually protect its 'marriage partner' in Germany, then you must be mistaken. If that were so, there would be no purpose in proceeding with the war. Farbenindustrie accounts for perhaps half of all German war production. To spare them would be to spare the entire German war economy." He shook his head. "And in any event, it has *not* been spared. No, gentlemen, we will have to find some other explanation."

Peshko and Baranyi exchanged glances. Of course, Bor was quite right. The theory didn't make much sense when one looked at it that way.

Miklos considered for a moment; he had his teeth into the thing and was not about to let go.

"There are I.G. representatives here in Zurich? Also in Basel and Berne?"

"Of course. They come quite often. There are also Swiss corporations through which they act. These things can be checked quickly."

"The charts show a jointly-owned stock company located here in Zurich, Chemihold, as it is called on the chart. I assume that the company has offices, a board of directors? Perhaps their counsel would be the best place to start. Do we have his name?"

Peshko nodded. "We have compiled a list. The names always appear on the papers filed in New York. Here . . . Chemihold, Zurich, Aktiengesellschaft, A.G. Yes?" There was a pause. Just enough for Peshko to take a deep breath. "One Max Grunewald. Offices on Paradeplatz. Number seven."

Bor reached for the phone. "Are we all agreed that he should be watched?"

"By your people or ours?" Miklos asked. He was not certain that he trusted Bor entirely. Or any Pole. Particularly with the

Russians now smashing deep into Poland and the government-in-exile afraid for its political life.

"By ours," Bor said calmly. "And Pauer's too."

Baranyi nodded.

He thought, "Yes, and also by Kagan. Just to make sure."

May 5, 1944
Near Freiburg, Germany

Nine o'clock in the evening. Schragg had dined alone in the office of the manager of I.G.'s fuse works near Freiburg. A plate of sausage, hot potato salad, and cabbage with caraway seed; there was little to console a man in that. A bottle of Steinhäger, half consumed, sat on the table next to the phone. Through the windows—entirely too grimy to suit him—Schragg could see the huge, two-story metal sheds of the fuse works stretching endlessly across the fields. Surrounded by wire, partially hidden by nets, their outlines were broken and reshaped until, from the air, the entire installation appeared as no more than an irregular mass of forest and low hills. The blacked-out windows shone palely, a little light leaking through despite the slathering of paint. The constant hum of machinery and the slam of metal stampers formed a low ground bass, like the murmur of a forest.

Schragg wiped his boots and took another sip of his Steinhäger. He was glad to have gotten rid of the two men who had accompanied him to Waldshut. They were superfluous and, on a mission of that kind, potentially dangerous. Krauch had insisted on their going along. Well, if he continued to insist, let him extricate himself from the conference at the *Führerhauptquartier* and come himself. Otherwise, everything would have to be as he, Helmut Schragg, wished it. And that meant both without interference and without surveillance.

The plant manager had put his office at Schragg's disposal, which meant simply one small room and access to the "covered" phone system connected directly to Northwest 7.

Schragg took from his pocket once again the notes he had made during his recent phone conversation with the Swiss lawyer. A second meeting had been arranged. In two days. Near Zurich this time. That would just give him enough time to attend to the other incredible business that had been thrust on him. At first, when Grunewald had told him what would be required, he could not believe his ears.

Only after the connection had been broken and he had had time to think had it begun to make sense.

He picked up the phone. Had the operator managed to put him through to Berlin yet? If only the Herr Doctor would be patient; there were bombing raids in progress. Things were very difficult. A few moments more would be required.

Schragg replaced the phone on the cradle and took another drink. It was warm now and not particularly pleasant. The sausage was giving him gas. He was not as young as he had been nor in as good physical condition. He would have to watch what he ate from now on.

He would have to watch many things.

The SS security man back at the camp, Neimann. His colleagues. And most of all, Felix Landau.

He opened the window of the director's office. What a depressing place it was, with its neat filing cabinets, its bulletin board with the latest tissue orders pinned up in rows, its photos of Hitler and Speer, the latter autographed to "My dear Hanke." Production figures in neatly typed rows, goals on pink sheets. A large map on which the recent Allied air strikes had all been marked.

The phone buzzed suddenly. The line was remarkably clear now. Another tribute to I.G.'s engineering staff. A covered, safe line, run from the plant directly to Berlin. No need for ciphers, for scramblers. It was all underground, laid in concrete conduit. Only a mole could have listened in.

"Stellner? Can you speak a little louder? I can barely hear you."

"I shouldn't be speaking to you at all," said the voice at the other end. "I'm mad to be here in the first place. Can't you hear? There's a raid on."

"I can hear it," said Schragg uninterestedly. All he could make out was a dull rumbling in the background. It could just as easily have been the toilet overflowing.

"Half the British air force must be up there."

"And half of ours, I hope."

"Half of what's left of it," said Stellner.

"Listen, can you hear me? Is Krauch back yet? Or Ter Meer?"

"They're still at Obersalzburg. You have no idea how bad things are. Have you seen the reports from the Leuna plant?"

"They'd only just come in when I left. But I have some idea."

"He's had Krauch and Beutefisch on the carpet up there for two days now. Speer's trying to soften things a little, but they still can't get away, if that's what you want to know. Not for a few days."

"Then you'll have to prepare the papers yourself. With Von Knieriem, of course. And send someone up there to have them signed."

"What are you talking about? I thought all of that was taken care of weeks ago. Von Knieriem is up in Schweinfurt now."

"Does the name Landau bring back any memories, Golo? Felix Landau?"

There was a long silence on the other end of the line, punctuated by the thud of bombs exploding nearby. Schragg felt a faint thrill of *Schadenfreude*. He knew how skittish Golo Stellner was. What a shame he could not be there himself to watch the raid, to watch the searchlights against the sky, the brilliant pyrotechnical display. And Stellner's fear.

"What has Felix Landau got to do with any of this?"

"A great deal, it seems. Because of this idiocy at the Leuna plant, we seem to be in a very awkward position. The man on the other side doesn't know me, and what he doesn't know, he doesn't trust."

"But *Landau* . . . my God, what has *he* to do with it?"

"He's living in Zurich apparently, and he seems to have been appointed as their expert. Not only as far as identifying me is concerned but also to check the technical material. Actually, he's not a bad choice at all."

"This could be very dangerous, Helmut. He'll realize at once what's missing, that the data are incomplete."

"They know that. Their man has already been advised that we can go only so far and no further with the technical material. He accepts that. What is really important to them is the equipment itself."

"Which, for the moment, is safe in the Monowitz plant."

"How safe is anything in Poland now?"

"As safe as we can make it. Come to the point."

"Our friend Landau has made certain demands. He wants . . . certain things as a quid pro quo for his cooperation."

"From *us?* I would have thought he'd be asking for payment from *them.*"

Schragg laughed, instantly aware of the insincerity of the sound. Then he told Stellner just what it was that Felix Landau wanted.

"Incredible," came Stellner's reply. "He can't be serious. I mean, after all that has happened . . ."

"Perhaps he sees things more clearly than we do."

"It's out of the question."

"It's *not* impossible, Golo. And it can be done. Believe me, I understand exactly what he has in mind, and I'm sure that Krauch will, too. After all, if we can send Weinberg a pension, if we can take care of the others in the way we've done, and if they can accept it from us, then certainly we can do what Landau asks. Remember, he's a fine engineer, whatever else he may be."

"You sound like Bosch."

"Bosch was right. You and I both know it."

There was no reply. Only the continued thudding of bombs.

Schragg spoke again. "You can have it taken care of? At once, please. Send up to Obersalzburg and get Krauch's signature, also that of Schmitz. Landau will recognize them both, of course. All the formalities must be observed. Make copies. And see that they're buried in an appropriate place."

"What precautions have you taken at your end?"

"Photographs, for one thing. Their man will be most cautious, believe me. He will not want a picture of himself talking to me to turn up in the wrong place."

"Neither would we," Stellner said. "Some people might not understand."

"Don't worry. I have the film on me at all times. And as for our friend, we have the best guarantee of his discretion that we could ask for. Better, even, than pictures."

"And that is?" Stellner demanded, exasperation and fatigue mixing in equal proportions in his voice.

"Greed, my dear Golo. Greed, pure and simple. And *that,* you will agree, is something that we all understand quite well."

May 6, 1944
Zurich

He knew he was dreaming but could not wake. He knew that in that dream he had just seen and would see again the face of his dead wife, Teresa. He would see her with a clarity no conscious effort of memory could duplicate, and so he was content to repeat the agony of that dream again and again.

The hospital at Korestan, where they had sent the Jewish Labor Battalion conscripts who had come down with typhoid during the epidemic of '41.

Where they had sent him, as a doctor, and his wife, as a nurse. And their child, Josef.

The low, dark shape of the hospital barracks, pressed heavily into the earth like ancient ruins in the Carpathian blackness. Sheds, two stories and one, black and barely visible. Rutted hills. The long lines of beds within, mounds of filthy blankets, and the stench of pus and disinfectant. He could hear the moaning of the fever-mad. Green walls and the flushed faces of the dying.

He saw for a second the dark outlines of the paths leading to the sheds where the doctors and the nurses slept. Then, with a sharp dread undiminished by repetition, he saw the trucks suddenly lumbering onto the roadway bordering the hospital. Canvas-backed army trucks, the tops down and the shapes of machine-gunners caped against the rain that had begun to slash down through the forest in wind-driven sheets. Then the searchlights on the trucks winking on, lancets of light flying through the filthy hospital windows, throwing shadows against the flyspecked walls.

In his dream he ran to the window, straining to see, just as the grenades began to explode.

"My God, they're burning down the hospital!"

And the flame throwers hissing and pluming. In the light of the flames he saw figures running from the doctors' sheds. Not toward the woods and safety but toward the hospital. Three men, one woman in a white coat, her blond hair almost white in the glare of the searchlights.

The machine guns began to fire, the tracers groping lazily over the cinder paths. His wife's face, upturned, toward him. Then his fists, crashing through the windowpanes.

One instant, frozen in time, as the machine-gun bullets ripped across her body and she fell, his Teresa, so gracefully, almost floating. So he remembered it.

He began to scream and at the same time to blot out the remembered scream that was once again laced through his nightmare, through the screams of the conscripts racing through the smoke-filled rooms of the hospital, trailing their smoldering blankets. The odd roar of men being burned alive.

He continued to scream. The machine guns continued to pound. There was another, sharper, less methodical pounding.

He woke.

Slowly, he raised his head, almost too weak to move. His body was drenched in sweat. The threadbare blankets were twisted about his legs just as the blankets had been twisted that night around the bodies of the dead.

He realized that he had fallen from his cot. He was on the floor, his wrist bent under him. For a long moment he lay there, trying to bring back that one instant when he had clearly seen, for the last time in his life, the face of his wife.

The knocking continued. He gathered strength.

"A moment. In a moment."

It was dawn. He was in his shabby, cramped room. The cracked sink stood in the corner, the toilet concealed only by a low wooden screen. One window looked out on a narrow shaftway, and a corner of the steel-gray Zurich sky showed high to the upper left.

Throwing a blanket over his shoulders, he went to the door and opened it. Itzhak Kagan stood outside, his cap pulled down to his eyebrows, wearing a long coat that made him look like an army officer.

"What have you done to yourself. You're sick?"

Miklos shook his head, still unable to speak.

Kagan understood. "Teresa?"

Miklos nodded.

"Ah, Teresa, Teresa. Poor Teresa. I wish I had known her, Miklos." He came into the room, shut the door. With a gentleness no one would have expected in a man his size, he half carried Baranyi over to the sink, turned on the tap, and helped him clean the dirt from his face. Then he went to the stove, lit the gas ring, and put on a pot of coffee.

"Miklos, shall I call someone for you? You look like hell."

"Why is today different than any other day?"

"Very amusing, Miklos. You look like the wrath of God himself and you make sacrilegious jokes. Have some coffee, Miklos. And shut up until it's ready. You don't expect sympathy from me, do you? We've all got our Teresas. Mine was named Rosa."

"Itzhak, for God's sake." Miklos winced. He knew all about Kagan's wife, Rosa. She'd been a student at the university in Berlin, an intellectual and a communist. They'd fallen in love, impossibly, but with a kind of elemental force that still brought tears to Kagan's eyes when he remembered it. He had never quite understood why such an impossibly beautiful, incredibly intelligent creature had married a big lummox like him. A truck driver. A brewery worker. It hadn't lasted long, though. She'd been arrested one night during a Stormtrooper sweep-through only a month after they'd been married. She'd vanished off the face of the earth that night. It was only months later that he found out that she'd been thrown into Plotzensee and beheaded after only two weeks there, along with a half dozen other students.

Sometimes Kagan spoke of her as though she were still alive, as though the whole thing had only been a rotten practical joke someone had played. He really couldn't believe it. Someday she'd come back to him. She had to.

Miklos hadn't heard Kagan mention her name in months. It was a sign of just how agitated he was that he had.

Slowly, Itzhak Kagan composed himself and came back from wherever it was he'd been for those few seconds.

"That wasn't fair, I know. I'm sorry," Kagan said softly.

"I thought you'd gone back to Budapest. They said . . ."

"I was going to go, but something came up. You should know about it, Miklos. That's why I came."

"More from Sternbuch? Or is it Riegner in Geneva this time? How many more on their way to Poland?"

"This is from Bor. Not about the transports. There's nothing about the transports at the moment. Do you want to hear what Bor has to say? It may be important."

"Of course, go ahead."

"It's simply this," Kagan said, pouring the coffee. "His people have been watching the *Advokat,* Grunewald. He has a visitor, it seems. An American lawyer named Stropp."

"Is he important? Who is he?"

"Our friend Peshko is very thorough. His files inform us that this man Stropp is from the firm of attorneys in New York City who represent the oil company."

Baranyi said nothing but reached for a cigarette. The pack was crumpled and empty. Kagan handed him one of his own, Turkish and dark.

"How long has this man Stropp been here?"

"A few days, it seems. Your sister-in-law spoke to a friend at the police bureau and checked the passport entries," Kagan said. "And that's not all."

"More?"

"A little more, and I'm afraid it all goes to support Peshko's theory. The American, Stropp, made contact yesterday with a man living here in Zurich. It was someone we know. His name is Landau. Pauer checked him. He was a chemical engineer with I.G. Farben until '38. They threw him out then, with all their other Jews. No pension, no special arrangements. He's been scraping by as a pharmacist's assistant since 1940. We tried to enlist him a few times but gave it up. In spite of all that has happened he still thinks of himself as a German, can you imagine?"

Baranyi did not reply directly. He sipped the hot coffee. Warmth, and guilt at feeling warm, flowed through him at about the same time.

"The meeting, do we know where it's to be?"

"Ah, you're coming alive again, aren't you? Good, good, Miklos, get angry, get interested. To answer your question, we don't know exactly, but Bor has a man on the main switchboard at the Baur-au-Lac. He'll call when anything happens with the American. You can follow him if you like. Perhaps something will turn up."

Baranyi rose and put his hand on Kagan's shoulder.

Kagan looked away. "I know . . . it's the only way to make it go away, even for a little while. To do *something*."

Miklos nodded.

Even for a little while.

May 7, 1944
Zurich

The gray Renault had picked him up near the Quaibrücke just after nine. Baranyi had expected Liebermann to be the driver. Instead, he had found Julie Malowska behind the wheel. She wore a heavy, shapeless coat of dull olive-drab and a knit cap that pulled her hair well back from her face and gave her an oddly androgynous look. On the seat next to her were a leather binoculars case and the parabellum in a huge wooden holster.

"Where's Avner?"

"Avner is busy printing baptismal certificates," she replied. "Someone had to drive you. You can't manage a car properly by yourself. You never could."

"It seems I can't escape you either," he said.

"No, you can't," she replied. "Conrad likes me to be around you as much as possible." She laughed in a vague, hesitant way. "He thinks you're a good influence on me."

"What he thinks is that you're on drugs of some sort and that I'll talk you out of it. You're not on drugs, are you?"

"No, I'm not," she snapped back, indignant. "Though God knows there's no reason why I shouldn't use them. It wasn't pleasant, you know." She shuddered faintly. He nodded and looked away; she tried to be hard always and pretend that what had happened to her on her journey from Warsaw to Switzerland didn't matter—others had had much worse times—but Miklos knew. Bor had told him once that when she had finally arrived in Zurich she had looked like a woman of sixty and had been almost out of her mind with shame and fear. It had taken three doctors almost as many months to bring her back to some semblance of sanity. Many nights, Bor had said, he had sat up by her bedside, holding her hand, even singing to her, old Polish children's songs, while she writhed and screamed, reliving the memories that she refused to share with him when conscious.

She thought that the dead were lucky; nothing could change her mind about that.

It was odd, Miklos thought—so many people he knew were like that, had undergone experiences that should have left them complete cripples but functioned now with the strength of ten, as though the limits of mind and body were no longer even remotely relevant to their condition.

He nodded finally and said in a low voice, "I know, I know. As your Colonel Bor cannot possibly know." He touched her hand fleetingly as though to reassure her that some small amount of human contact was still possible between them. "We're the same in many ways, you and I, Julie. And for that reason we don't need to speak of any of it. Now tell me, what did you come to tell me, what are we to do?"

She composed herself, her eyes seeming to focus on something far distant down the road. The Polish legation had called to say that the American, Stropp, would shortly leave the Baur-au-Lac in the company of three other men and proceed to wherever it was the meeting was to be held. Bor's man at the hotel had listened in on the conversation that had set up the meeting.

"Bor knows this for certain?"

She nodded.

"So," Baranyi said, attempting humor, "you're good for something, you Poles. If not for fighting, then perhaps for sticking your noses into other people's business."

"I'll be sure to mention that to Conrad."

"Excuse me, I'm not in the best of moods today."

"Are you ill?"

"No more so than usual."

"A doctor is always the last one to know he's sick."

The Renault turned a sharp corner and came in view of the entrance to the Baur-au-Lac. Julie Malowska guided the car to a curbside spot and turned off the motor.

"They should be coming out soon."

"How do you know?"

"Conrad's man specifically mentioned the front entrance."

They sat and waited in silence for ten minutes. Miklos was content to wait, his eyes half shut, listening to the sound of his sister-in-law's breathing, the noise of traffic on the street, the clatter of tram cars going by. He realized that at that moment what he dreaded most was silence.

Malowska's low whisper interrupted his musing. "There, you see? Conrad knew what he was talking about."

Two men were just coming out of the hotel's front entrance. Miklos did not recognize either of them. One walked with an odd, lurching gait. The other man was much younger, dressed in a suit that did not fit too well.

Baranyi nodded. Julie Malowska turned the motor over and put the car in gear. It moved into the street with a shudder. The two men got into a large black Buick that had just been driven up to the hotel entrance. There were two other men already in the car.

"Shall we?" Miklos said.

"A lovely day for a drive," Julie said. "They'll be heading north, I think. Shall we pretend we're off for a day in Otwock?"

Miklos said nothing but settled down in the seat. The Buick moved out over the Quaibrücke and onto the Ramistrasse, heading toward the north road. To Schaffhausen.

They had been driving in silence for almost an hour, the Buick just in sight, far ahead up the road. Baranyi had to admit she was a good driver. She kept just far enough back to avoid being seen yet never lost sight of her quarry for a moment. It was, in a chilling way, quite characteristic of her.

The Buick had taken the northwest road, up through Winterthur. The heavy Swiss mountains closed in, oppressive in their purity, the walls of firs rising inexorably on either side, the air obscenely cool and bracing. The road wound through deep valleys, heavy forests of fir and larch. They drove for a long while in silence. Baranyi took out the binoculars and tried to keep the Buick in view. At the rate they were going, they would be at the border in another half-hour.

Julie Malowska touched the brake and the Renault slowed. With the perspective distorted by the binocular lenses, Miklos had not noticed that the Buick had slowed down and was now angling up a steep dirt road toward a farmhouse on a low rise near a small stream and a covered wooden bridge.

"We'd better stop here," Malowska said.

"They may go on."

"No. The road stops at the house, can't you see?"

She pulled the Renault off the road and hid it in a strand of Norway spruce. "You see? Good thing you have heavy shoes on. The ground is wet."

He got out and slung the binoculars around his shoulders. He had no idea where they were. Only that the border could not be more than a dozen kilometers away.

And that, therefore, anything could happen.

They lay in the tall, cool grass, next to each other. He could feel the slight warmth of her body through her coat. From somewhere she had produced a second pair of glasses, a small set of Zeiss binoculars of the kind used to watch birds. She had them trained on the path that led to the farmhouse. Through his larger pair, heavy, reticled military-style glasses, Miklos could see the farmhouse, the path, and the poultry shed to the side. Behind the barn a small black car was parked, partly concealed by the hayracks and wagons. By the door of the house stood a man in a black leather coat, carrying a shotgun. A little farther down the path was another car, with Zurich plates. Two men were standing by the hood: one was the lawyer, Grunewald, the other a middle-aged man in a long topcoat. The Buick had stopped a little farther down the dirt road.

The two groups greeted each other and proceeded toward the house.

"Four of them? Bor said nothing about there being four."

"Two are lawyers," Julie Malowska said matter-of-factly. "One is Swiss, the one with the limp is the American. The other, the young man, is from the law firm of the American. The fourth man I do not know."

He lifted the binoculars and watched intently. He noticed that the license plates on the car parked by the hayracks were painted over. It was a Mercedes, sleek and polished.

The door of the farmhouse opened and the man in the long over-coat waved the party inside with his shotgun and then followed them in.

"We must try to get closer. You wait here. There's no point in both of us taking risks."

"You prefer to take risks?"

"Wait here," he said angrily. It was a long time since he had given orders that anyone had obeyed. He wasn't used to the tone of command anymore, and Julie Malowska knew it. But she nodded and pressed herself down into the high grass. A few insects leaped up with whirring wings.

The farmhouse consisted of one large room with a brick fire-place at one end and a tier of bunk beds screened by a curtain at the other. In the center was a large wooden table. At the table, a briefcase open in front of him, Helmut Schragg sat, hands folded, an expression of infinite patience and forbearance on his face. He had on a disturbingly informal hunting coat of salt-and-pepper tweed, high boots, and a woolen muffler. On the table, next to the briefcase, was a small flask of brandy.

As Felix Landau came into the room behind the two lawyers, Schragg's face came apart. Though he had been trying very hard to compose himself, all his efforts failed when the moment came.

"Dr. Schragg," said Landau in an oddly respectful voice.

Schragg looked right through him. "Ah, Herr Stropp, you've brought your assistants with you. Everything is well? A marvelous day for a drive, is it not?"

"You could have picked a spot a little closer to Zurich. We accommodated *you* the last time," Stropp said.

Schragg was startled. Stropp was evidently in a bad mood. His carefully planned manner had better be changed at once. His expression grew instantly harder, his speech more clipped.

He pointed to Eisner, the question hanging in the air without having been spoken.

"My lawyer," Stropp said.

"I thought *he* was your lawyer," Schragg replied, pointing to Grunewald. "I thought you too were a lawyer."

"He's *our* lawyer. I wanted to have *mine* along too."

"Point well taken. But I think it is an unnecessary complication. The fewer people involved in this transaction the better."

"Mr. Eisner is completely trustworthy. He is in no position to cause any difficulties," Stropp said sharply. "I want a double review. Swiss law and ours as well. And I don't want to be my own counsel. Now . . . you know Felix Landau, I assume?"

"We have met before, yes."

Stropp waited. His pale eyes remained fixed on Landau's face. "Before we go any further, Landau, is he Schragg or not? Is he who he says he is?"

Landau nodded. "The man is who he says he is. Dr. Helmut Schragg. He is deputy production chief for the synthetic rubber. Also for poison gases. His direct superior, unless things have changed markedly, is Otto Ambros. Ambros, in turn, reports directly to Fritz Ter Meer, who is head of the *Vorstand*'s technical committee. He is also chief of Production Division Number Two, which is called Sparte Number Two by our system of identification. The line is direct. I know this man's authority. Is that sufficient for you?"

"You know him personally then?" Stropp asked. What he really wanted to know was why Landau had used the pronoun "our."

"I said I did. You have my word on it. Dr. Schragg and I have met many times before. I was one of Ambros's chief engineers. One of his best. I was one of the leading workers in the development of the synthetic processes. I was—"

"We understand all that," Stropp said quickly, noting the effect that Landau's words were having both on Schragg and on Landau himself. "Good, so that's settled. Congratulations, Dr. Schragg. We can go on to the next step now. You've brought the technical materials?"

"Excuse me," said Landau. "The agreement? You've brought the agreement?"

"Herr Landau," Schragg began. "I am simply amazed by your question—"

"You are amazed that I would want what I'm entitled to? From you?"

"That you would *question* whether we have kept our part of the bargain, that's all. Herr Stropp has made a request of us. We agreed. Otherwise you would not be here."

"The papers then. The matter of your honor is something for another time."

"This is strictly a business transaction, Landau. Your feelings about me personally—"

"Have nothing to do with the case. Obviously. Or *I* would not be here."

Schragg took out of the briefcase a document of a half dozen pages, backed in the manner of a legal paper. This he handed to Landau.

"You will want your lawyer to examine this, of course?"

"I'm quite capable," said Landau. "And if I have any questions, the examination will in any event be done back in Zurich. As will my examination of the technical material."

Schragg's face darkened. "That was not part of the agreement."

"There was no agreement about where the documents were to be examined," Stropp interrupted. "I understand Herr Landau's reluctance. That man over there . . ." He pointed to the man with the shotgun. "It wouldn't be unreasonable for Herr Landau to imagine that if he examines your technical material here and passes it, he might be shot right on the spot."

"Thank you," said Landau, his voice low and a little hoarse. "You do understand these people, don't you." He stared down at the document in his hand, moved his finger slowly over the face of it, turned the pages. "Yes, yes, it would seem correct. I know Ambros's signature well enough. And this is Schmitz's, certainly. All right. Give me the papers I'm to examine."

"Why this should be necessary," Schragg muttered, reaching into his briefcase, "I cannot understand."

Landau handed the document over to Grunewald. "What do you think? All legal? All in proper form?"

"The correct forms, as required by the present government—" Grunewald began.

Landau interrupted him: ". . . are no legal forms at all? Is that what you want to say? Of course. We understand that. But tell me, does it *seem* in proper form to you? Binding according to Swiss law? Does it restore to me what is rightfully mine?"

"Really, that is no question to ask me," Grunewald replied.

Eisner took the papers and studied them for a moment. Then, with an authority that to Stropp was totally unexpected, he said,

"It's all in order. I'll vouch for it. Provided the government doesn't pass some new law."

Landau laughed. "A new law? What *government*? What *laws*? Do you take me for a fool? Only if they lose this war will the agreement be honored. We both know that. If they win, neither you nor I will be here to worry about whether the signatures are legal or not. But Herr Dr. Schragg does not expect Germany to win the war. And Herr Dr. Schragg is never wrong, is he? There will be a peace. An armistice, perhaps. Or a debacle. But there will be no victory for those people."

Schragg drew himself up, his face dark and angry. He was straining visibly to control himself.

"You have wrung this agreement from us, Landau. Now let us see you live to enjoy it."

"Is that a threat?"

Stropp took him by the arm, digging his fingers in hard. "You agreed, Landau."

Landau could barely contain himself. "Have you any idea what this man has done to me? All of them, Schmitz, Ter Meer, Ambros, these sanctimonious scientists and businessmen? They are the worst of all. They pretend not to see what is going on around them, they do not deign to notice. What swine they are."

Schragg stepped around from behind the table.

"I do not understand you, Landau. I must confess, I do not understand you at all. We, at least, are beyond misunderstanding. We say what we mean. We've told you as clearly as we can what we think of you. Yet you insist on thrusting yourself on us. What do you hope to gain by this? If you are in a position to enforce this agreement then you will also be in a position where you don't need anything from us at all. You'll have it all by then. You and your kind."

"You would like me to believe that, wouldn't you? But I am a realist, Dr. Schragg. You will have your peace, you always do. You people will survive without a scratch. It will be business as usual. When the war is over there will be different rules, but you people will continue to play by your own rules, as you always have, and nothing will have really changed. Don't I know what you did? As long as it was possible, you retained us. We built you up. We gave you your best ideas, and when the Nazis said get rid of the Jews you did so. Because it was the expedient thing to do. After the war there will be a new expediency."

"Enough!" shouted Schragg. Before anyone could stop him, he struck Landau across the face, sending him reeling backward over the table.

"Jesus!" cried Eisner, backing away. The man with the shotgun swung around and pointed it at Landau, who sat on the floor, rubbing his face and laughing.

Stropp pushed down on the barrel of the shotgun until it was pointed at the man's own toes. Not a word was spoken. Stropp turned and went back to the table, took the briefcase, and handed it to Landau.

"I don't like you, Felix. And I don't like you either, Dr. Schragg. You don't behave like gentlemen, if you want my opinion. Either of you. You, Schragg, you're as arrogant as a *Junker,* and in my book that's no damned good. But if I have to do business with you, then we'll do business. Exactly that. But there'll be no more of this crap, do you understand?"

"My dear Herr Stropp, are you telling me—"

"I'm telling you to mind your goddamned manners. We've got something you want. Maybe you've got something we want too, but that remains to be seen. If you don't cooperate with us, then you've got nothing, now or later. Let's not forget that." He turned to Landau. "How long d'you think it will take you to go through the data and tell me whether it's genuine or not?"

Landau smiled. "A few days. It depends."

"That's preposterous," cried Schragg. "He can tell you in an hour."

"I'll examine the papers, but only in Zurich. Not here. If I don't go back to Zurich, excuse me, there is no deal. You can have your agreement back, Dr. Schragg. And you, Herr Stropp, you will have to take your chances. But without my advice."

"You heard him," said Stropp. "We'll let you know in a day or two. Where?"

Schragg hesitated. It was clear that he had not expected yet another delay. "At your hotel, tomorrow afternoon or the next day. At one o'clock. Let me know through Herr Grunewald. You can be my host at lunch and tell me then whether this . . . *per-son* . . . is satisfied or not."

"Happy to," said Stropp. At that moment he disliked the German even more than he disliked the Jew. "But we'll make lunch at two. I never eat before then."

"And if it is all satisfactory, then we have an agreement?"

"We'll do the best we can. That's all I can promise you. I think it will be enough. But if we can't manage it, then we lose as much as you do."

"There will be no bombing?"

"As long as you don't produce."

"That is agreed. Not a kilo of Buna will come out of the Monowitz plant as long as the war continues."

"We can make no commitments concerning the synthetic fuel plants, you understand that, don't you?"

Schragg nodded. "The fortunes of war must control. As they have already at Leuna."

"The agreement holds only as long as the plant is within reach of our troops. If the Russians get there first, there can be no promises. That's understood, isn't it?"

"It will be up to your people to get there first."

"Or up to yours to hold off the Russians long enough."

"You will check over the market agreements also? For after the war?"

"Grunewald will check those for us. I assume that Ter Meer remains a man of his word. You're to get Germany and Eastern Europe. We'll have exclusive rights to Buna distribution and manufacture elsewhere. The synthetic oil markets division remains as it was set at Rotterdam."

"Exactly. You'll find everything in order."

"That's a strong point with you people, isn't it? Order?"

Schragg said nothing. He was staring at Landau.

Stropp added, "The signed agreements are in the Chemihold vault. We've brought unsigned copies for you to examine."

Grunewald took another cluster of papers out of his briefcase. Schragg barely looked at them.

"Our undertaking to stay out of the synthetic fuel business in Europe . . . after Himmler has managed to arrange an armistice," said Stropp.

He turned to go. Landau stood by the door, still rubbing his jaw. There was an angry red blotch from his chin almost up to his eye.

"You will let Herr Grunewald know when I am to come?" Schragg asked.

"Understood."

"I await your call."

"I hope this works out better than the last deal we made with you people. For both our sakes," said Stropp.

Schragg, for a number of reasons, all of which seemed very good to him at the moment, did not reply.

Baranyi came back through the thickets, his jacket clotted with brambles, the binoculars strap twisted around his arm. As he reached the rise where he had left Julie Malowska his heart stopped and his stomach felt as though it had been filled with ice water.

She was not where he had left her.

He stood there for a moment, not knowing what to do. What a fool he had been to leave her, even for a little while. But what could have happened to her? All the men from Zurich had been at the farm until a few moments before. There had been only one Mercedes, one other car. Had there been lookouts in the woods?

At that moment his sister-in-law stepped out from behind a thick row of bushes. She had taken her coat off. From her neck, in addition to the small Zeiss glasses, hung a camera with a large telephoto lens.

"Did you find out anything?" she asked.

"Thank God," he said.

"What?"

"You're safe."

"Why shouldn't I be?"

"You said nothing about having a camera."

"Would it have made any difference to you? You'd still have wanted to go down there."

He hung his head. How well she understood him.

"So, you haven't answered. Did you find out anything?"

"Only that the license plates on the second car were German. I got that close. I have the number, for whatever good it will do us."

"It can be traced," she said. "Pauer can manage it."

"And you?"

"Oh, it's a good day for picture taking. Good sun. In just the right position. We'll have some faces to look at, at least."

"You were able to do that?"

She smiled. "Right through the window. You'd be surprised what a lens like this can bring in. Of course they helped me a bit. Perfect poses, right in the window frame. The whole lot of them."

Night settled prematurely over the wooded heights to the north of the city. The sun sank red and bleeding into the Zürichsee, and was interred quickly by a counterfeit night of heavy black storm clouds blown up from the southern Alps. The streets of the old section of the city between the Limmat and the Seilergraben were submerged so rapidly in shadow that householders in those narrow byways barely had time to light their lamps and turn on the electric doorlights before the heavy spring night swept in on them.

Felix Landau did not return at once to his rooms on the Spiegelgasse, though the rented Buick had made the return trip to Zurich well before six. Stropp had gone back reluctantly by himself to the Baur-au-Lac. He disliked leaving Landau alone, but counted on the fact that he had not yet paid the man the promised ten thousand as sufficient to secure Landau's discretion. At first he had suggested that Eisner go with Landau and remain with him for the night. But Landau would not hear of it. How could he concentrate under such conditions? How would it be possible for him to give Schragg's technical work sheets the attention they required with someone looking over his shoulder? Of what were they afraid? That he would betray them? To whom and for what purpose and for what gain? The Schmitz–Ter Meer commitment would be meaningful only so long as the rest of the arrangement between the Americans and I.G. was carried out. Restoration to his former position, with a promotion to chief of department guaranteed by year's end. A liberal pension when it came time. Rights to the pension vested in his daughter, Ilse, in the event of his death. All meaningless if Farbenindustrie did not survive the war with its interests intact.

At length Stropp had agreed. Eisner had been anxious to get away. He would check in in the morning. That would be time enough. Grunewald had, in any event, insisted that he needed at least a day to go over the assignments and escrow agreements that Schragg had delivered.

Felix Landau stood for a long while on the same quay bridge over which they had passed that morning on the way to Winterthur. The lake water below ran black and swift, with a bone-chilling cold that reached up brutally and firmly from the surface. He leaned far out over the rail. Traffic passed behind him, the headlights of the automobiles sending strange and frightening shapes leaping out of the water, then slipping back silently into the dark. The smell of burning wood was sharp and heavy. A barge moved slowly against the current, out into the lake. A steamer hooted somewhere in the direction of Rüsnacht down the shore to the south.

He stared into the blackness. A stiff wind ruffled the surface of the lake. Why not throw the briefcase in? What a lunatic he had been. It seemed impossible to him at that moment that he could actually have done what he had done. Yet, once the opportunity had presented itself, what else could he have done? He hadn't gone out looking for the chance—it had presented itself and he had simply accepted. Just as they would have done if they'd been in his place. He was no better than they were. Well, had he ever contended that he was? To be persecuted for one's religion did not automatically make a man a saint.

What did they want of him? Was he to be the world's conscience? He had to look out for two people only. Himself and Ilse. It didn't matter that they'd thrown him out, that they'd turned on him because he was a Jew. Fully a third of the I.G. supervisory board had been Jews. The Weinbergs, Merton, Peltzer, Mendelssohn-Bartholdy, Schlieper, and Simson. When the Nazis had first come to power hadn't they railed at Farbenindustrie and called it "I.G. Moloch" and "Isidore G. Farber" in their newspapers and magazines? Hadn't Carl Weinberg himself—foolishly as it turned out, but perfectly in keeping with his character—found the Nazis' ideas so much to his liking at first that he said so, publicly, over and over again? Ter Meer had always been decent to him. And Schmitz, too. Landau wasn't going to blame them for what they'd had to do. Everyone else had done the same thing, the university men, the judges, businessmen of all kinds, doctors, the heads of medical schools. Everyone. I.G. had been no different, and no worse. The important people had been pensioned off. They were still getting their money in South America and the Orient, wherever they were. War or no war. I.G. had gotten a lot of "their Jews" out of harm's way by posting them to foreign offices and discharging them there. There were many—most, in fact—who hadn't even done that.

The Schraggs—people like that—were in the minority. The rest were only ordinary business people who did what they did only in order to survive.

When the Nazis were gone everything would get back to normal. That, too, was only a matter of natural law.

All of this Landau repeated to himself over and over again. But try as he might, he still could not wholly convince himself that he had done the right thing. For him, certainly, it had seemed right. If everything worked out, it *would* be right. And sooner or later, after the war, there would be a decent life for him again. Doing what he knew how to do. It all depended on how the war ended and on what would be left to whom. After all, no one really believed the American Roosevelt's pious trumpetings about unconditional surrender." No one in his right mind could expect Germany to accept that. No, a deal would be made. Concessions would be given. The fighting would stop before everything was destroyed.

It would have to.

He moved away from the railing, tightening his grip on the briefcase. He walked slowly back to the east bank. The lights were blazing now in the windows of the Baur-au-Lac Hotel and he could hear a salon string orchestra playing somewhere: "Roses of the South." A wall poster announced a lieder-abend by Erna Sack. *Fidelio* was at the Stadttheater, and a "Moulin Rouge" ballet at the Corso Palais. It was all very reassuring. Almost the way it had been before.

He walked slowly back along the Fraumünsterstrasse, past the now darkened municipal building. Another steamer hooted mournfully at its moorings, south, beyond the bridge. Landau turned up the collar of his coat, as though to hide his face.

Why should he hide? He had done nothing. Nothing, surely, any worse than any of them had done. He was trying to live, that was all, to get back what was his. Who could fault him for that?

The lights of the Odeon on the Sonnenquai across the river caught his eye. He crossed on the Münster bridge and went in.

The café was crowded. No one would notice him. Why should they? He ordered a large cognac and sat at a small side table, well away from the door. Someone had left a newspaper on the opposite chair. He picked it up. The headlines were uninteresting. Rumors, unfounded speculations. No one knew just what was going to happen. American troops had landed at someplace called Hollandia in the South Pacific. In New Guinea. The Russians had entered Romania. A Hedy Lamarr film—*Ein Nacht in Saigon*—was opening at the Acadilli. There was little more.

The waiter, seeing Landau's glass empty, returned. Landau ordered a second cognac, then a third. He sat watching the customers solemnly downing their drinks. Just like the joyless Swiss, he thought. Solid, uninteresting. What did they have to worry about, after all? Nothing. And without worries there could be no real relief either. Thus, no pleasure.

Time fled by. The street outside grew darker by imperceptible degrees. There were no stars. A stiff south wind raised furrows on the river outside. Small boats banged against their moorings. From another room came the sound of a radio, Lys Gauty singing throatily in French: "Un Petit Bouquet de Violettes." He could not understand the words.

A woman's laughter suddenly reminded him of his daughter. She would be waiting for him, of course. Poor child. He should have phoned. But she would be occupied with the huge, wonderful doll he had given her for her birthday. She would not have noticed the passage of time. A resourceful child, she would have fixed herself something to eat and gone on playing, patiently waiting for him to come home. If she'd needed anything, there was always Frau Birkli on the floor below. She had an inordinate fondness for the child.

He paid his bill and left a good tip.

There was still money in his pocket. Stropp's money. He started back to his rooms, walking slowly, then more rapidly as the chill wind cut through his threadbare coat and the cold came up from the pavement through his paper-thin soles.

He stopped at a candy shop and purchased a small box of Lindt chocolates. It had been months, perhaps a year, since Ilse had had any decent sweets.

He hurried on, urgency in his walk now. He was anxious to see the child and sorry that he had stayed away so long.

As he turned into the Spiegelgasse, he stopped short. At the far end of the street the blue lights of a police car winked ominously in the gloom. There were a number of people standing, as they inevitably did, next to the car. One of them was pointing to the house into which the police had obviously gone. All the lights in the building were on.

It was his building.

His knees grew weak. The right leg started to shake. Steadying himself, he moved as quickly as he could down the street without actually running.

At least there was no ambulance.

What had seemed from a distance like a crowd turned out to be only a few neighbors and passers-by. One policeman was still sitting in the little car.

"Excuse me, what has happened here?"

The policeman looked up; he had been reading the sports paper. "Do you live here?"

"Yes, on the third floor."

"Well then, you'd better go up."

Landau stared at him, terrified. "What do you mean, the third floor? Does it involve a child?"

"You'd better go up, *mein Herr.*"

Landau needed no further prompting. He ran into the building and up the narrow, damp-stained stone stairs. On the third landing, a door was open, *his* door, and a bright rectangle of light cut by the shadow of another policeman fell onto the stones.

The policeman turned, attracted by the noise; his expression was noncommittal.

"I am Felix Landau, sir. These are my rooms."

The policeman, a stout, fatherly-looking sort in his mid-fifties, shrugged and turned at once to say something to someone just inside the doorway.

"You see, *Kinde,* there was nothing to worry about. Here he is, just as I promised you." He turned sharply back to Landau, who stood flabbergasted in the doorway. "Really, *mein Herr* . . . I can smell the brandy on you. You should have a little consideration for the child, no? Shame on you."

The child, Ilse, came running past the policeman and threw herself into her father's arms. She was strong and wiry, lean from a slow, never-satisfied hunger. Stringy ash-blond hair framed a wide forehead and narrow eyes set in a perpetual squint, as though she were never sure that what she thought she saw was actually there.

The girl was incoherent with tears. Over the policeman's shoulder Landau could see Frau Birkli rise from her knitting in the next room, placid as always, and bear down on him with a distinctly disapproving look on her face.

"How *could* you, Herr Landau? The child was *so* worried . . ."

"Who called the police?"

"Why, the little girl, of course," volunteered the policeman. "Poor thing. She hasn't had enough trouble in her life already, is that it? Your neighbor has told me everything. Ah, you Jews . . ."

Landau stood aghast as the policeman produced a sheaf of official forms from his pocket. "These will have to be filled out, of course," he said.

"These papers?"

"Reports, *mein Herr*. We cannot jump up to answer a missing persons call and then simply pretend it never happened. We have our records to complete, just like everyone else."

Landau stared at the little yellow pad of forms, with its tissue copies and carbon sheets.

"This must be done?"

"Absolutely, *mein Herr*." The policeman's fatherly expression took on a sterner aspect. "Is there some reason, perhaps, that you do not wish to fill out the forms?"

"Papa," the little girl said, "it's not my fault. I didn't do anything." The tears continued to pour down her narrow cheeks. The policeman searched in his pocket and at length produced a toffee wrapped in green cellophane.

"Here, *Kinde,* you take this while your father does what is required."

Frau Birkli, ever helpful, and at the moment disapproving in the extreme, handed Landau a pencil.

The box of Lindt chocolates lay on a chair, forgotten.

* * *

The red safelight cast a theatrical glow over Baranyi's face, accenting his sunken eyes and high forehead. It was the first time that Julie Malowska had ever seen him wear glasses.

Slowly, with a steady rocking motion, he dipped the film back and fourth through the developer. A little ceiling fan moved the stagnant air in the basement darkroom, causing the few prints still hanging on the line to dry to tremble faintly and cast moving shadows across the opposite wall. A pot of coffee and an untouched plate of cold sausage sat by the old Zeiss enlarger. The smell of hypo was deep and, he thought, medicinal—reminding him of other places and other times.

"Do you do this often? I didn't think you knew how," said Julie Malowska.

"I sometimes had to develop my own X rays. This is no different. Look, the images are starting to come."

Slowly, through the clouded emulsion, shapes were beginning to appear, large, round black faces captured by the telephoto lens.

"How long does it take?"

"For the images to come up? A few minutes, that's all."

"We'll know then?"

"Not unless you can read black for white and white for black."

"You read X rays that way, don't you?"

"Faces are different, Julie. Bones are clear and precise. It doesn't matter with bones. The outlines are there, one way or the other. But a face is unrecognizable in the negative. It is the nuance, the shading, not the shape, that makes the face recognizable."

"Like the soul?"

"What?"

"Oh, nothing, really," she said. "You've got to print them then, I suppose. How long will that take?"

"An hour more, even with the dryer. Our good friend Avner rigged up a negative drying box out of an old fan and some light bulbs. Why don't you go home to sleep? The morning will be time enough."

"Home in this case means to Conrad. I'd rather stay here."

"Then have a bit of the sausage at least."

"I'll fix you something too, Doctor."

"When I've finished and washed. The chemicals are poisonous, I think."

She nodded. "I'd suppose so—they must be if they can bring out the black image of a man so easily."

He looked across the little room at her, puzzled. He had never known what to make of her, and now was no exception. She was barely recognizable in the unearthly glow of the red safelight.

Then he realized what it was.

The red light made it look as though she were rising from a conflagration, surrounded by flames. He recalled clearly someone else, framed by just such a red light.

Teresa.

He looked away and stared fixedly at the film.

The emulsion had cleared entirely. All that was left now were the negative images. Clear and sharp.

Like bones.

When they reached the street, Julie Malowska turned and, after studying him for a moment, smiled and said:

"Take me to dinner, Miklos. I'm hungry."

"I haven't any money."

She shrugged. "So? Conrad has enough for both of us. Certainly enough for the best the Ali Baba has to offer." She showed him the folded bills in her purse.

"A plate of *Wurst* and a beer would do," he said longingly. He had not realized until just then how hungry he was.

The rain drifted down, a fine cool mist, brushing their faces gently. He turned up the collar of her coat for her.

"Why did you do that?" she asked.

"So the rain won't go down your neck," he said. "I've enough problems without having to tend a pneumonia patient."

They walked the short distance to the Ali Baba, a restaurant near the Bürkliplatz where White Russians, Poles, and Romanians gathered. The man at the door had on a garish blue turban with a yellow feather in it. He seemed uninterested and a little embarrassed.

"It's too expensive here," Miklos said. "We could go someplace else."

She laughed. "Conrad won't mind. And the Polish government won't mind either. Besides, if you're taking me to dinner, I have a right to choose where I want to go, don't I?"

The doorman in the turban opened the glass doors. They went in. "Pani" he said, acknowledging her as she passed. Miklos shot her a questioning look.

"They're all from Warsaw." She laughed. "Even the 'Indian.' They call him Gandhi. That's why I come. For the Poles."

The restaurant was smoky and dark. A rotating mirrored ball suspended from the ceiling caught the beam of a single spotlight and sent the reflections fleeing all over the room. The interior of the place looked like a ballroom or a dance hall. It stank of heavy Turkish tobacco, Bulgarian, and Gauloises. It was all most un-Swiss.

He sat down and looked at the menu.

"It's too expensive," he said. "Even for Conrad. Tournedos for fifteen francs. Let's go somewhere else."

She laughed again.

"Order, Miklos, order. The shashlik is excellent. They'll even make a good *gulyas* for you if you like. One of the chefs is from Veszprem."

A waiter in a shabby blue jacket came over. He was about forty and looked twenty years older.

"Good evening, Pani," he said.

Julie Malowska nodded. "As usual, Andrej. Bring a vishniac for the gentleman, please."

"No," Miklos said, "I'd rather—"

"You're cold and wet," Julie said firmly. "It will do you good. Why shouldn't you have a vishniac?"

The waiter shrugged. He brought the vishniac, a bottle of calvados, and two glasses.

"Does Bor drink vishniac?" Miklos asked.

"No, only kirschwasser. The best there is. And French wines. God, you should see the man do away with his French wines."

Miklos drank the vishniac sullenly. It burned his throat. For a moment, until the shock of it wore off, he felt dizzy.

She noticed it.

"Some food, Miklos. You'll feel better after you've eaten."

The waiter came again and took their orders. The winking light from the mirrored ball gave Miklos a headache, and he tried to keep his eyes averted. The place was crowded. A jumble of languages could be heard, mostly Slavic, with some Romanian and French. But no German at all. Of any kind.

The innocuous dance music that had been playing since they came in stopped. A new record was put on the phonograph. Hanka Ordonowna. She began to sing—"Milosc Ci Wszystko Wybaczy"— in her throaty little-girl voice.

Julie smiled and closed her eyes for a few seconds.

"God, that makes me feel homesick," she said. "She was my favorite when I was a little girl. I worshipped her."

"What a lucky accident for you, then."

"What accident? They do that whenever I come in here. Andrej thinks he gets a bigger tip by making me sad."

Miklos ate wolfishly, digging into his food with violence. Then he stopped, suddenly aware that she was watching him and that she hadn't touched a thing on her own plate.

"You weren't hungry, Julie. You were lying," he said.

"Yes," she replied." But *you* were hungry."

He looked at his plate, embarrassed. Half the food was gone already.

"Why?" he asked. "Why?"

She poured herself a second calvados and drained it in one swallow.

"Because you're mine. You're my responsibility."

"That's presumptuous, isn't it?"

"But it's true. And that's why you're angry when I say it." She reached for the calvados again.

"No."

"In vino veritas," she said, pouring another glassful.

"That's not 'vino,' Julie. It's ten times as strong."

"So? Then my truth will be ten times as strong too."

He closed his eyes and leaned back. A deep, pained breath whistled between his lips.

"Suppose you tell it to me then, this ten-times-stronger truth of yours."

"Which particular truth do you want to hear?"

"The one that explains why I'm your responsibility."

" 'Expiation' would be a better word."

"Why?"

"Because of her. Because of Teresa. Do you know, I was actually jealous of her, Miklos. I couldn't understand why you preferred her. I was far better looking. Everyone always said so."

"Yes," he replied absently.

"Yes. *Was* . . . but no more."

"You need rest, Julie, you drive yourself too hard."

"Not as hard as you, Miklos, not nearly so hard. But I *was* more beautiful than Teresa. And smarter, too. I would have thought that *that,* at least, would have appealed to you. They say that you Jews like smart women." She lit a cigarette. "And so, I was jealous, Miklos. In such an odd way. I think for a while I truly hated her."

"There's no need for guilt," he began.

"There's always need for guilt. Guilt is always there. You have it, for the child. Don't say no. I have it, for *her.* And because the guilt is there, so is the responsibility."

"You're not making sense."

"No? Perhaps not. But I'm making truth. *Zrodvy,"* she said, lifting her glass again. Her blond hair hung down lankly in strands over her forehead. Her face was damp and flushed.

She had been speaking a little too loudly, and a couple at a table not far away were staring.

"Do you know them?" Miklos whispered.

She glanced in their direction, shook her head. Her eyes suddenly filled with tears.

"No, I don't know them, and I don't give a damn for them, either. Or for anyone else. Take me home, Miklos. I want to go home."

"You haven't eaten."

"But you have. That was the point."

He got up. There was to be no arguing with her, he could see that.

She threw a few bank notes on the table without counting them.

It was still raining outside, a little heavier now. The night air was sharp, more like fall than spring. There even seemed to be a faint odor of decay coming in with the rain, sour and autumnal.

The drifting rain obscured everything. Miklos seemed to hear

Hanka Ordonowna's voice. The record had still been playing when they left.

The stairwell and landing were dark, the house silent except for the insistent meowing of a cat somewhere behind a closed door.

"Poor thing, she's in heat. They should let her out."

"There's no point," he said. "Why bring more kittens into such a world? It isn't even fit for people anymore."

She turned on the light in her room and shut the door behind them. He was surprised by the disorder. Somehow he had imagined that her room would be neat, precise, everything with a hard, sharp edge to it.

"Well, take off your coat."

"I should go back. You're home safely now."

"Safely? My God, you were worried about my getting home *safely?*" She began to laugh. "My God, for two years there's been nothing *but* safety. Sometimes I think I'd almost prefer the way it was before. With the Germans."

"You don't mean that, Julie. Don't say it."

"No. I don't mean it. Take off your coat. You're wet through again. I've never seen a man get wet through so quickly."

He shook his head, a little bewildered.

"I've got to go back."

"For what?"

"For what?" he repeated dully.

She threw her coat on the disordered sofa. A water spot promptly spread on the upholstery.

"Don't you know when you're being propositioned, damn you? You're supposed to be so smart. Where's all your Jewish intelligence?"

He stood there unable to think of a word to say to her. Her face was even more deeply flushed now, and a little ugly, he thought.

She took hold of his shoulders, hard, and moved him across the room to a little corridor and into the tiny bedroom. The room reeked of perfume and powder. A little light entered through the slats of the blinds on a small window opposite the bed.

"This is absolutely wrong," he said.

"It is absolutely right. If you're to be my responsibility, then you should be mine altogether, shouldn't you?"

"I'm not your responsibility."

"But you are," she said. "Do you want a drink? I've got some of Conrad's best kirschwasser in the night stand."

To his surprise, he found his hands moving gently over her back. He could feel the bones, the shoulder blades in particular, sharp and cleanly articulated under the skin. She seemed frail to the point of weightlessness, as though the only thing solid about her at all was her face and her eyes.

The clothing fell away slowly. He felt the damp cool of the air on his own skin, then the startling warmth of her body, the nipples like tiny points of heat against his chest.

She strained against him, as though somehow she were trying to bore her entire body into his. A feeling of inevitability stole over him. If it was good for her, what difference did it make to him? He owed her . . .

He was lying to himself, of course, and he knew it. He was not indifferent. At that moment he wanted her very much.

It was the first time in three years, and he had forgotten how good it was. But not for a moment was he able to forget what had happened and what he had yet to do.

Even at the moment of climax he was fully conscious of it all. There was no forgetfulness, no oblivion in the act.

It surprised him, in the end, that the semen came at all; he had thought of himself for so long as dried out, empty, a walking ghost.

"What are you thinking?" she said, rolling away from him on the bed. A rivulet of sweat ran down between her small breasts; her face was faintly red, her eyelids puffed.

"I?"

"Who else is there?"

"I was thinking," he said slowly, "what if we should have a child?"

She laughed and reached for the kirschwasser and the tumblers.

"That's the kind of thing you would think of," she said, laughing with real mirth for the first time. "Only you, Miklos. Only you."

DOCUMENT

From: Col. H. A. Gerhardt, executive assistant to John J. McCloy, Asst. Secretary of War U.S.A. [*Attached to a forwarding transmittal containing a plea for the bombing of the railheads through which the transports from Budapest and elsewhere were carrying victims to Auschwitz.*]

I know you told me to "kill" this but since those instructions, we have received the attached letter from Mr. Pehle (WRB). I would suggest that the attached reply be sent.

[*The attached reply was substantially the same as those which had been addressed to earlier pleas of the same nature:* No.]

Washington, D.C.

The memo from the War Refugee Board had lain on the desk of the Assistant Secretary of War for three days. Attached to the top of the first sheet by a small bulldog clip was a blue tissue endorsement from the office of the Assistant Secretary of State that read simply: "Deal with this."

The memo was a half dozen pages long. The top sheet was signed by John Pehle. Stapled to it were copies of cables from the Polish and Czech legations in London and Zurich, and letters by two prominent American rabbis.

A few lines caught the assistant secretary's eye.

". . . the whole relief action, commissars, pity, all of this is useless unless decisive steps are taken. The camps must be put out of business, the rail lines destroyed, the rail hubs at Kashau-Presov obliterated. . . . It is urged by all sources of information in Slovakia and Hungary that the bombing take place at once, as the only possible means of slowing down or stopping future deportations and the killing of those who have already been deported. . . ."

He checked the incoming pouch for the morning; there was

nothing from Berne, no message sent through the chargé's office there, nor any private communication from either Criterion or its attorneys.

Everything, then, was still in a state of stasis.

He knew exactly what was expected of him.

The assistant secretary considered for a moment whether or not to dictate his response. He was not at all sure of what his stenographer's reaction would be and, curiously, found himself very apprehensive. Of course, she could be replaced easily enough. But she had been with him for so long . . .

After a moment, he picked up a pen, loaded it in the silver-capped inkwell on his desk, and scratched out a reply in longhand; at least he would not have to look his typist in the eye.

"In the opinion of the department," he wrote, "the suggested air operation is impracticable. It could be executed only by the diversion of considerable air support essential to the success of our forces now engaged in decisive operations and would in any case be of such doubtful efficacy that it would not amount to a practical project."

It would have to do for the moment. In fact, he concluded on reflection, it was quite sufficient regardless of the moment.

Had he received information that the arrangements had been concluded, he would have done exactly the same thing.

May 8, 1944
Zurich

It had not occurred to Felix Landau that one of the Americans would be waiting for him he returned from the bank. The whole transaction had taken less than a half-hour and it was still early in the morning. The older man, Stropp, did not like to take breakfast early; he'd said so himself the day before. The early morning had therefore seemed safe enough.

But the young lawyer had been there instead, standing by the entrance to his building, smoking a cigarette and looking unhappy.

Thank God he'd bought a newspaper on the way back. It would provide an excuse for having been out.

"Where've you been, Landau? You shouldn't have gone out. No one said you could go out. It's not safe," Eisner said in decent enough German.

Landau smiled wryly. "And who, sir, is going to harm me? Not you, certainly. Not Herr Schragg. Who else then?"

Eisner shrugged. They entered the building and climbed the stairs. From above came the sound of a piano, played not very well. A Mozart sonatina. Landau's daughter, Ilse, at her exercises.

"No," said Landau. "What you meant is that it wasn't safe for *you* to have me leave the building, isn't that it?"

"I suppose so. Where did you go? Stropp will want to know."

Landau held up the morning edition of the *Neu Zurcher Zeitung*.

"Oh, for Christ's sake," said Eisner.

Laudau smiled in a faintly superior way. "Have you eaten? I can't offer much, but since your employer was good enough to advance me some funds the other day, at least we now have some decent coffee in the house."

Landau pushed the door to his lodgings open, releasing a flood of clumsily executed arpeggios into the stairwell. Eisner took off his coat and pulled out a week-old copy of the *New York Times*.

"How long are you going to be?"

"All day, at least," Landau lied. He'd finished at about two that morning. There hadn't been that much for him to do. After all, he'd been one of the four engineers who'd worked out the basic innovations on the original process, and it had taken him only a few minutes to recognize what was really only an extension of his own handiwork. It was just as he would have developed the ideas had he remained. A little neater perhaps, but no different. But he had to make it seem more complicated than it really was. Stropp would not be pleased with too fast an answer; he felt he had the measure of the man already, at least in that respect.

Also, it wouldn't hurt to keep Eisner tied down in the apartment all day. He already had the distinct impression that the young man would just as soon spend the day reading the paper and drinking coffee as doing anything else.

Landau sat down at the table he had arranged by the window. Schragg's papers were all there, laid out in orderly piles. It was obvious that he'd been working.

The perfect theatrical set.

Ilse continued to thump away at the old upright in the next room.

"Doesn't she have school?" Eisener asked at last.

"Not until the afternoon. Do you want coffee, yes or no?"

"I live on coffee, Mr. Landau. Never turn it down."

"A true Viennese response. Do you have relatives there?"

"From Mecklenburg. An uncle. My father's parents came from somewhere near Königsberg."

"Oh, I see," said Landau. He called in to the child and told her to turn on the burner under the coffee, then settled down at his table, immensely pleased with himself.

It had taken only a half-hour to secure a safe-deposit box. With Stropp's money. To fill out the necessary papers. The box was in sealed trust for his daughter, her property now under Swiss law. All it had taken was a signature, a notary's certificate, and two officials' attestations. No one could touch the box without his signature and hers together. The box was small, and he'd paid the rental for it in advance for the next ten years.

It was just large enough to hold the agreement that Hermann Schmitz, Fritz Ter Meer, and Carl Krauch had signed. Too bad Helmut Schragg hadn't signed it too. That would have been even better.

Just then Ilse came in with the coffee pot and two cups.

"Sugar?" Landau inquired, raising his head from the polymerization flow charts. "I'm afraid we haven't got any cream. Can you imagine, in this country, not to have cream?"

The presses on the ground floor were going full tilt, emitting a sound like that of an asthmatic metal-stamping works. False Swedish passports, immigration permits for Palestine through Romania, and baptismal certificates were all being produced in record quantity. In the upstairs room, behind the now empty dormitory, a half dozen experts were putting the finishing touches on the documents.

All destined for Budapest.

Julie Malowska had just climbed the stairs and now sat poised like a famished bird on the edge of Baranyi's cot. Peshko paced back and forth before the window, looking out now and then at nothing in particular. Baranyi sat at his desk, the photographs spread out before him. He was no longer looking at them.

Itzhak Kagan had come in a few minutes before with the news

that a meeting of railroad officials had just taken place in Vienna. Sufficient rolling stock for four transports a day from Budapest had been authorized.

"In round figures," Kagan had announced, "that means twelve thousand to Oswiecim every day. Twelve thousand, and we just sit here."

Baranyi's head ached from lack of sleep. The photographs, so far, had yielded nothing. No one recognized any of the men in the pictures other than the American, Stropp, whom they already knew, and the Swiss lawyer, Grunewald.

With Pauer's help, Bor had managed to add a few bits and pieces to the mosaic. The license plates on the second car at the farmhouse were definitely German. The Czechs had learned that a border guard at a post above Rheinfall had let through an auto carrying two German nationals without observing normal crossing regulations. The bribe had been substantial. And the description of one of the men matched a face in one of the photographs perfectly.

"There are a few other things," Julie Malowska added. "Not very cheerful."

"What is cheerful these days? One is cheered merely by the absence of total calamity," said Peshko.

"Out with it then," Miklos said wearily.

"A transport from Kistarcsa to Oswiecim. About three thousand. I suppose you know all about that."

"We know," said Peshko, "but thank you all the same."

Julie Malowska said, "There's been another roundup in the Carpatho-Ukraine region."

"How many?" Baranyi looked up. This was news.

"About eight thousand this time. Conrad doesn't have exact figures yet."

"It's the same as we had from Weissmandel. Pauer's people let us know last week," Peshko said. "It came through the Czech minister in Geneva, Kopecky. God, what are we to do? What?"

"And then there are these," Malowska added quietly, pushing across the table a sheet of handwritten notes and a yellow tissue flimsy with official markings on it. Baranyi glanced quickly at it. It appeared to be a police report of some kind.

"Yes?"

"Conrad thought you might be interested. Does the name mean anything to you?"

Baranyi picked up the report and read it. A Zurich metropolitan police report? Someone—a child, it seemed—had called in to say that her father was missing.

What had that to do with anything they were involved in?

"Felix Landau," said Julie Malowska.

"Landau?" repeated Peshko, his voice suddenly taking on an apprehensive edge. "Felix Landau? This is a familiar name, yes?"

"The chemist? The one who was with I.G. before the war?" Miklos intoned. He was on the verge of collapse now. He looked down at the still damp prints on his desk. Obviously, one of the unidentified men at the meeting had been Felix Landau. It all tied together.

"At what time was he reported missing?"

"Late yesterday afternoon. He turned up again much later that evening. It's all here," Miklos said. He turned to Julie. "What else is there? There's more, isn't there? I can tell from your expression."

"Conrad believes that the license plates on the German car are registered to I.G.'s Freiburg factory."

Baranyi pushed the photos at Peshko. "Can we make a positive identification?"

"I've never met the man. I know only the name."

"That's hardly a problem," said Julie Malowska. "It will take me less than an hour to get Landau's passport photos. There's a woman at police headquarters who takes care of such things for us. She'll surely let me have a look."

"For us," Miklos thought gloomily. For her and Conrad. For the Poles. Damn them all.

"You can do this?" said Peshko.

"Of course. I'll be back in less than a hour. It's not far. Felix Landau? Do you have an address?"

Baranyi read it off the police report.

While they were waiting for her to return, Peshko sifted through the papers that Julie had brought. Miklos went over to the window, taking Peshko's place. He stared out into the gathering dusk.

"The reports we send through the American embassy do not go

through. Neither do those we hand over to the military attaché, Bard. Nor do those we give directly to the chargé, Lorimer," mused Peshko.

Baranyi nodded. "The aide to the chargé tells me, out of what I can only assume is an attack of conscience, which means to me also that he must understand more than he has told me, that immediately after our visit, the chargé sent a cable to the man, Trilling . . ."

"Who is an officer of the American oil company . . ."

"And which company sends a representative to Zurich almost immediately afterwards, the man Stropp . . ."

"Who then has two meetings with the Germans, who are at pains for some reason to keep their meetings very secret. Which is very odd . . ."

"Because after all, the petroleum company has had many dealings with the I.G. people for the last twenty years. Everyone knows this. It is no secret. It is no crime for an American to talk to a German here in Switzerland. It is done every day of the week, at all levels. So why do they meet in the woods? Why all this skulking about?"

"Assuming, of course, that the Germans *were* from I.G."

"The license plates would seem to prove that."

"All right then," said Peshko. "The representative of the oil company meets with the I.G. people. Possibly as a result of the cable sent by the chargé, possibly not. It could be purely accidental."

"And then there is the question of the identity of the two men who accompany Stropp and the Swiss. One of whom may just possibly be this man Landau. And if *that* is true, then what possible connection . . ."

"What possible connection indeed," Peshko said quietly. "Perhaps there is none at all. And while we sit here, quite safe, trying to put together the pieces of what may not be any kind of a puzzle at all, twelve thousand more are being sent to their deaths. Even now, as we talk. Twelve thousand a day. My God, Miklos. Who can comprehend such a thing?"

The presses continued to clatter. Liebermann came up the stairs carrying a large box and vanished into the next room. More baptismal certificates. So far, the Hungarian government and Cardinal Seredi had at least been able to prevent the deportation of converted Jews.

Baranyi came away from the window. "She's back."

"So soon?"

"She walks like a mountaineer, that woman."

In a moment, Julie Malowska was at the door, carrying a brown folder.

"A lovely lady, our Frau Loewe. She's actually loaned them to me. I must return them first thing in the morning."

She put the passport folder down on the desk and leaned over it. Miklos flipped the folder open. A small photo of Felix Landau was pasted on the left-hand side, above his signature.

He glanced quickly at the clearest of the photographs. The sun had been at just the right angle. The shot was perfectly exposed and in focus.

Peshko adjusted his glasses. Miklos didn't have to.

It was clear. The faces were identical.

May 9, 1944
Zurich

The banker brushed the lint from his trousers, straightened his tie with a smooth, unselfconscious movement, and rose without hesitation. He nodded once, the corners of his mouth arranged in a practiced institutional curve, a half-smile intended to inspire confidence.

Max Grunewald did not smile. Nor did he feel particularly satisfied with himself. He noticed that his fingers had whitened markedly on the handle of the briefcase he carried. When he let go with his left hand the pressure of his fingers left small indentations on the padded handles.

He followed the banker out of his office and down a short corridor lined with paintings of former bank officials and members of the board of directors. The papers had all been completed and signed. The banker carried a slim folder of Venetian leather, tooled with the initials of the bank in subdued gold lettering. Elegant and tasteful. Very restrained.

The banker had not spoken. Unlike Grunewald, whose very art was in his words, the banker considered his art to reside solely in figures and discreet silence. He moved along a few feet ahead of the lawyer, like an Armenian leading his wife.

A uniformed guard opened a door. A buzzer buzzed and a steel panel slid back, revealing a stairway. A light blinked, and from somewhere deep within the building came a faint electrical humming.

Grunewald followed the banker down the stairs.

The vaults were deep beneath the streets of Zurich, and as the two men descended there was a noticeable change in temperature. The air grew damp. Carefully as they had been sealed, the stone walls were nevertheless old and could not keep out the damp entirely.

Grunewald wondered idly whether the damp got into the vaults too, into the safe-deposit boxes. Perhaps papers left there mildewed and in time became unreadable. The prospect did not dismay him.

Finally they arrived at a landing. The stairs continued down, penetrating even deeper into the rock under the lake. A clerk sat at a desk behind a heavy steel door pierced by a small window of heavy wire-reinforced bulletproof glass. The clerk rose, removed a ring of keys from a hook, and opened the door. He nodded to the bank officer and permitted them to pass into the small antechamber beyond.

Ahead was an enormous door made of steel bars, not unlike the door of the elephant house at the Berlin zoo. The clerk produced another ring of keys, and in a moment the door swung open.

Without a word, Grunewald handed the clerk the folded escrow papers. Under the terms of the agreement, the box into which he was about to deposit the agreements that the I.G. representatives had delivered could not be opened until after the war or the passage of twenty years, whichever was to occur first. No one other than an authorized representative of Chemihold could present the key. The escrow letter also stipulated that in the unlikely event that Switzerland was drawn into the war and Germany somehow emerged victorious, the box should be destroyed. The timing of such a move was left to the discretion of the director of the bank.

The banker moved briskly into the vault and fitted a large iron key into one of the many locks on the wall of boxes. The wall reminded Grunewald of the wall of coffins he had seen at the cemetery in Fiume on vacation years before.

The banker turned and, without inquiring whether Grunewald wished the privacy of a room, simply set a large steel box on a table reserved for that purpose, opened the lid, and stepped back.

He knew exactly what the lawyer wished to do.

The documents had been placed in separate envelopes, three altogether. Grunewald put the envelopes in the box. The banker shut the box and replaced it in its niche in the wall.

Grunewald was the first to leave the room. He did not even look back, such was his confidence in the institution.

The banker slipped the key into a little blue envelope made of stiff paper and gave it to Grunewald. The other was already in the lawyer's pocket.

They climbed the stairs, slowly, solemnly. As there was room for only one man at a time on the stairs, Grunewald led. The banker followed decorously behind. It occurred to Grunewald that Orpheus's moment of apprehension must have been just the same; he inclined his head slightly and caught out of the corner of his eye a pink blur a few meters back on the stairs. The banker, soundless as a phantom, was still there.

Not a word had been spoken the entire time.

At length they emerged onto the marbled ground floor of the bank. The door closed behind them and they walked suddenly into a corridor, not solitary and deserted as had been those below the street level, but full of busy clients and tellers. A gold clock high above the cages read a few minutes before noon. The entire process had taken less than sixty minutes.

"It is always a pleasure, Herr Grunewald," said the banker.

"A pleasure indeed," said the lawyer.

May 13, 1944
Zurich

It seemed to Felix Landau as though he had been walking the streets for hours, though in fact it had been less than forty-five minutes since he had tucked his daughter in for the night, left her in Frau Birkli's charge, and gone out into the chill Zurich night.

Though it was well into spring, the night still had the bitterness of winter about it. Landau had lived in this dank, river-ridden city for almost five years but still could not get used to its climate. The lake with its dark, freezing undercurrents dominated everything. The Limmat and the Sihl seemed like the black rivers of a prehistoric mythology, hiding guilt and the soul's decay.

The chill was everywhere. Nothing ever seemed dry. He hated water, rivers, seasides, but it seemed his fate never to escape them.

He turned a corner and passed down a dark, medieval street. The oriels of the houses on either side loomed out of the night like heads mounted on the walls of ancient hunting lodges, each with its own eyes, its own individual silhouette. Chimneys sprouted like the trees of a forest. Smoke rose, shimmering against the night. He breathed in the cold air, vastly relieved to be out of the apartment, if only for a little while. It had become, in twenty-four hours' time, the worst kind of prison for him.

He huddled into his coat. His fingers felt the memory of frostbite.

What a despicable person he was that he should wish to please men like Schragg and Henry Stropp. They had driven him out. They had destroyed how many like him? For no other reason than that they were Jews. Was *he* really a Jew? He had never thought of himself as a Jew until the first of the Nuremberg laws had been passed. Even then there had been exempt classes, and even outside of the officially exempt classes there were still other exempt groups. By agreement, by consensus. People who were needed, who were somehow above it all, were spared. Weren't the decrees really aimed at the *Untermenschen?* And he was certainly no *Untermensch.* Not Felix Landau.

He would show them. The writing was already on the walls of

Berlin, on the walls of the factories of Essen, of the chemical plants, of the *Kasernen.* The war couldn't last long now and everyone knew it. A man had to look out for his future. And his children's future. He was still alive, and that placed on him certain obligations.

A cold sweat trickled down his neck. His body was hot. He had to relieve himself. But there was no place to go.

The Swiss arrested you for pissing against a wall.

He walked more quickly, moving deeper into the old section of the city. A sour wind broomed the streets, bringing with it a stink of cow dung from the mountains. The smell of turned earth was everywhere, and the smell of potatoes which the Swiss had planted in every available patch of soil, even in the park in front of the opera house.

He turned a corner. As he did so, he noticed two figures not far behind him. The streets up until then had been almost deserted. The Swiss were early to bed. The only lights to be seen were in the occasional windows of cafés and wine cellars and those of the lake steamer riding silently in its berth at the quay above the Bürkliplatz.

He paused, catching the reflection of the two figures in a grated shop window. They were now only ten or twenty meters behind him.

Stropp? Eisner? Impossible.

Schragg?

But why? The Nazis would have no compunction about murdering anyone, even on the streets of Zurich if it suited them. But Schragg was no Nazi. He and his associates feared them almost as much as they cooperated with them. Which made it far worse. Besides, the agreement with the signatures of Ter Meer and Schmitz was already in the vault, where it could not be touched. Surely Schragg must have understood that he, Landau, would take at least that elementary precaution.

He began to walk more quickly. The figures behind him moved with equal speed, always keeping their distance, never closing.

He turned into the Rennweg. He could smell the coal and oil of the railroad station not far off, and the potatoes again, even stronger here. Suddenly he found himself running. The few other people still on the street turned to stare.

He stopped short at the intersection of the Rennweg and Oten-bachgasse. A large man in a leather jacket was standing there as though he had been waiting for him. He had red hair, huge shoulders, and fists like hammers. Landau drew back. The man advanced on him, seemed for a second to move forward, then faded into the shadows.

Landau hesitated. The wind slicing up from the quays was damp and bitter cold. He shivered and hurried on.

The street was deserted. The muffled voice of a radio announcer speaking in harsh Swiss French snapped down from an upper window. A record of a dance band played somewhere: "Besame Mucho." He went quickly into the stairhall of his building. There he paused, leaning against the wall and breathing only with difficulty. His forehead, despite the chill, was running with sweat. The urge to urinate was almost overpowering. He climbed quickly, afraid that he would wet himself.

There was a light under the door. Eisner was still there, of course, waiting.

He went in.

Eisner was there, but so were two other men. They sat on the sofa with the child between them. One of the men was playing patience with Ilse. Some of the cards had fallen on the floor. Eisner sat by the window, his hands in his lap, tied with a length of kitchen rope, a blank look on his face.

Landau gasped and turned to run. As he started back into the stairwell, he saw the red-haired man coming up the stairs toward him.

"Felix Landau?" asked one of the men on the sofa. He was short, stocky, wearing a long overcoat that reached almost to his ankles. A broad-brimmed felt hat like those worn by actors in American gangster movies lay on the lamp table next to him.

"Who are you? What do you want of me? Herr Eisner, who . . . ?"

"If you are not Felix Landau, then we want nothing from you. If you are, then we simply wish to talk to you, that is all."

"To talk?"

"Only to talk," said the man in the long overcoat softly.

"Shall I close the door, Miklos?" said the red-haired man, who had come up the stairs and stood at the threshold.

"You *are* Felix Landau, aren't you?" said Baranyi slowly.

The child put down her cards. "I win, Papa," she said.

"Sit," intoned Kagan.

Landau held out his arms, and the child went to him.

"It would be better if she was in bed, don't you think?" asked Peshko quietly.

"You won't hurt her?"

"What do you take us for? Of course we won't hurt her."

"The child, please—she should not hear this."

"Ilse, yes . . . be a good girl. Go to bed, yes?"

"May I have a cookie, Papa?"

"A cookie. Oh God, yes, find a cookie. Take two cookies. Yes, take two cookies. But do as they say. Bedtime now, please." Landau was having difficulty keeping calm.

The girl gave him another kiss and ran off into the kitchen, closing the door behind her.

"I don't know who you are. I've never seen you before."

"But we've seen you." Baranyi thrust a packet of photographs at Landau. "Do you recognize yourself?"

Landau looked down and groaned. It was all there, the farmhouse, the car with the German plates, Schragg, Stropp. And Felix Landau. Clear as could be.

"So . . . *that* is established, Herr Landau?" Baranyi settled back on the threadbare sofa. "You may start, please, by telling us exactly what was going on in that place."

Eisner strained forward. "Wait one minute, you can't ask him that, you have no right. Mr. Landau, don't—"

Baranyi whirled. "So far you have been treated very gently. That could all change in an instant. I suggest you keep your mouth shut until we get to you."

Eisner slumped back. He saw the butt of a Luger sticking out of Kagan's belt.

"But who are you?" cried Landau.

"Germans," Eisner said. "Can't you hear?"

Miklos laughed harshly. "No, no, Felix Landau. *You* are German. Not us. Not at all. We are called the Vaadah Ezra va Hazalah, the Council for Assistance and Rescue. My name is Miklos Baranyi. I am a medical doctor and Hungarian. This man is Zoltan Peshko and he is from the United States of America. Our friend Kagan there prefers not to remember where he is from. We are all Jews, Landau. Not Nazis. So, does that answer at least some of your questions? Yes? Now, if you please, answer ours. You will tell us exactly who these people in the photos are and why you and this American from the oil company were there. And also what this all has to do with the camp at Oswiecim."

It took Landau almost a half an hour to explain what had gone on in the Waldshut farmhouse. The words spilled out, coming faster and faster, until Landau was hardly intelligible. Eisner sat deathly pale through it all, not making a sound. By the time Landau had finished, Baranyi's hands were shaking. He could not even look at Peshko, who was close to tears. It was left to Kagan to take from Baranyi's briefcase the copy of the Vrba–Wetzler report.

"Read this. Both of you. Then you will perhaps understand the enormity of your crime."

Miklos sat with his head in his hands, overwhelmed. Peshko lit a cigarette, took a few puffs, stubbed it out, then lit another. This performance was repeated four times. They could hear the child singing to herself in the next room as Landau and the American read.

Ten minutes passed, then twenty. The singing stopped.

"I'm going to bed now, Papa," the little girl called from the other side of the closed door. "Will you kiss me good night?"

Landau did not answer. His face was white.

The child's footsteps could be heard, fading down the hall. Then an absolute, deathly silence settled over the room.

At length, Landau looked up.

"How could I have known this? Who could believe such a thing, even of *them*? You should not have waited. You should have come to me with this sooner."

"We only knew of your involvement a day ago."

There was a long silence. Then Landau put down the report.

"What is it you want me to do? I am so ashamed."

"If you could give us copies of the patent assignments and the market agreements . . ."

"I still have all the technical data. I was to return it tomorrow."

Peshko shook his head. "The technical data alone will not be enough. It would prove nothing. Only that it had come into our hands somehow. It could have happened in a hundred different ways."

"I could give testimony," said Landau. "I could make a statement."

"They would say that we had made it all up. No one would believe you. Or us. Not without more. We must have more. We must have the assignments, the cartel agreements. Then they would *have* to listen. We could go directly to the War Refugee Board in Washington, to John Pehle. He would go directly to Roosevelt. You would not read a word of it in the papers, but the bombs would start to fall."

"I told you, it's impossible. I don't have them."

"Where are they then?"

"One set went with Schragg, the other set is with the lawyer, Grunewald, Chemihold's lawyer."

"You, Eisner, you can obtain copies for us?"

Eisner didn't respond. His eyes were clear and sharply focused. He leaned forward.

"Listen, I'm willing to help you. Believe me, he isn't the only one. I had no idea . . ."

"You had no idea? You expect us to believe that? You read the documents, *you drew up the agreements yourself.*"

"For Christ's sake, of course I did, I know that. But what I mean is, I didn't know about *that place,* what they do there. I thought it was just another factory. And besides, they promised not to produce a kilo of the stuff. How was I to know about the camp?"

"Even so, what you did was treason. You broke the laws of your country by dealing with those people."

"I swear, I didn't know. How long have *you* known? Tell me that? Where am I supposed to read about it? Who's going to tell me? There hasn't been a word about it in the papers here. The radio says nothing. *How am I supposed to know?*"

Miklos sighed. "He's right, of course."

Peshko refused to let go. "It is precisely because of him and his employers that *no one* knows. They're the ones who've blocked every attempt to get the information out. And now we know why."

"I told you, for God's sake, I'll help."

"Oh yes, you'll help, Herr Eisner. And for the most elementary reason. Because if you don't you are a dead man. Oh, we could turn you over to your own government, and perhaps they would deal with you. The photos would be sufficient to ensure that. But to a man like you, what would prison mean? Nothing, I'm sure. But a bullet in the back of the neck? That's another story."

"You wouldn't!"

"No, *we* wouldn't. But others would. If need be, we will simply call our friends in Polish Intelligence. Or the Czechs. Together they may even advise the English, and if they don't, we will. We will also provide them with the photos, with a dossier, with copies of the technical information. Herr Eisner, you would have perhaps twelve hours to live after we did that. No more."

"You don't have to threaten me, damn it. I told you, I'll help."

"Yes, you certainly will," said Baranyi.

"This is not wise," Peshko added. "I don't like it."

"Is it any less wise than trusting to *that* man's sudden change of heart?"

"That is unfair," cried Landau.

"It is not unfair," Baranyi said wearily. "You knew that the Americans were trading protection for that hideous place for the patents and the equipment rights, didn't you?"

"Not at first. I swear it. But after Waldshut? Yes. How can I deny it? But I did not know what kind of a place it was. I thought it was only . . . another camp. A bad place, but like any other concentration camp."

"Would it have made a difference to you if you had known?"

Again, Landau was silent.

Baranyi said, "So . . . we will put aside questions of guilt and responsibility for the time being and do whatever we can do. Herr Eisner, you will obtain copies of the assignments for us, yes?"

"I don't know what Grunewald's done with the papers."

"Find out," Kagan snapped. "That shouldn't be too difficult for a man of your unusual abilities. At Sachsenhausen they said it was impossible for a man to carry the big stones in the quarry all day, that he would die in twelve hours or less. I carried those stones for two weeks. Because I insisted on living. Now, if you do not know where the papers are, then I suggest you find out. Insist on living, Herr Eisner. As I did. It is no small thing, in times like these, to keep on living."

DOCUMENT

Leaflet distributed to the Hungarian Christian Community,
May 1944.

In this eleventh hour of its tragic destiny, Hungarian Judaism addresses this appeal to the Hungarian Christian community with which it has shared for a millennium, within the common fatherland, the best and worst moments. We have silently endured deprivation, the loss of our citizenship and of our dignity as human beings. We have been expelled from our homes. Now that our very existence is at stake, we launch this last appeal.

We must inform the Hungarian Christian community that, for weeks, hundreds of thousands of Hungarian Jews have been deported abroad in cruel and tragic circumstances, without precedent in the history of mankind.

Through the Jewish Council, the German and Hungarian authorities had guaranteed the security of Jewish goods and persons—on condition that the ordinances of the New Order be respected. The Hungarian Jews have respected the laws. But the promise made them has been violated; the death trains have been dispatched from every part of the country. To this day, nearly 500,000 people have been deported. Although the ordinances referred only to regrouping the Jews, the areas set aside for these regroupings have quickly been transformed into veritable concentration camps; from there, the Jews have been sent to brickyards, flour mills, factories, etc., where living conditions are even worse. Then the Jews have been huddled into trains, 70 or 80 people to a car, under the blows of rifles, clubs, and whips. These cars, sealed, with only one outlet for ventilation, filled with humans deprived of everything, furnished only with two pails—one of water, the other for human necessities—have ridden for days and days into foreign lands. . . .

The Hungarian nation has the right to reject its Judaism. But for that, will it sentence women, children, severe war

casualties, without weapons and without defense, to a pitiless
death? Would that not be in violation of all the nation's tradi-
tion of honor?

In the name of our children, our aged, our wives, in the
name of all of us, doomed to near extermination, we address
a last appeal to the Hungarian Christian community. We keep
our faith in its sense of justice, which cannot allow this massacre of innocents to be carried to completion.

If this last plea is denied, we ask the Hungarian nation to
spare us the tortures of deportation and to exterminate us at
home, on our native soil.

———————

May 20, 1944

Berne

When Henry Stropp entered the office of the chargé, Lorimer, he
found the weary diplomat standing alone before a large wall map
on which the gradual widening of the Normandy beachhead was
depicted by an ordered profusion of colored pins and paper flags.
As yet, Stropp noted, there was no indication of a strike north
toward Vienna from the head of the Adriatic.

Lorimer inclined his head slightly toward the door and took his
cigarette out of his mouth absently, letting the ash fall.

"Mr. Stropp?"

"Mr. Lorimer?"

The chargé extended his hand in perfunctory greeting.

"To get right to the point," Lorimer said warily, not pleased at
all at the position in which he had been put, "I must tell you that
I consider this all most irregular."

"I'm sure you do. But sometimes there are no other ways of
doing things that must be done. The irregular sometimes becomes
obligatory."

Lorimer blinked at him, not sure he'd gotten Stropp's real meaning. He noticed with some distaste the man's angular, gimpy walk

and his slightly hunched posture. His mouth wrinkled in dismay. Then he went to his desk and retrieved the envelope he was to deliver.

"Yes, yes, I suppose so," he said. "Nevertheless, to use the diplomatic pouch as a private mailbox, particularly in these times, well, it's . . ." His voice trailed off.

"It's quite all right, I assure you, sir. Former ambassadors *do* have certain privileges."

"Nevertheless, I really should ask you to let me read that letter."

"Out of the question. I'm sorry. You'll have to take Ambassador Trilling's authority on that."

Lorimer shrugged and returned to his desk. He gestured toward a small door on the left side of his office. "You can read it here, if you like. That's a comfortable chair over there. Or, if you prefer, the office next to mine is vacant at the moment."

"I'll take the office, thank you."

Stropp shut the door firmly, so that there could be no possible misunderstanding about his insistence on privacy. The room was small, had a table, a desk, two chairs. The window looked out on the Mutistrasse.

Stropp drew the curtains, switched on the lamp, and opened the envelope. It bore the seals and stamps of the diplomatic courier service to the U.S. consulate in Lisbon.

Inside was another envelope.

He took out a double fold of paper, instantly recognizing Trilling's looping script. No secretary had been involved; the contents, therefore, had to be treated with the utmost confidentiality.

Dear Henry,

We've just had some very disturbing information and I pass it on to you with full assurance that you'll know exactly what to do. This comes from your own office in New York. I think you'll have to be very careful from now on. As you know, we keep a close watch on the record room at the Federal Courthouse in New York City, where the files on the Justice Department suit against our joint subsidiary "Chemihold New York" are kept. An awful lot of dangerous material got into those files, mostly in the depositions, and the worst of it is that they're open to the public. Any damned busybody can stick his nose in there if he wants to. The clerk gets a good bonus from us every year just to let us know who's been looking at those files. It's the least we can do. A few weeks ago, someone spent a couple of days poring over them. We got a copy of the requisition slip and just now ran down the man's name. I don't think it was idle curiosity or coincidence either. You'd better look for a man named Zoltan Peshko, from New York City, and a refugee organization, called the Aggudath or the Vaadah Ezra something or other. A copy of this Peshko's passport is enclosed. He's in Zurich now. You'd better find him and keep an eye on him. He's probably involved with the same people who've been trying to push those reports through Berne. So far we've managed to keep them bottled up and to keep the Air Force from even looking at the "place." But I don't have to tell you what may happen if these people get too much information. They could ruin our plans entirely and cost us billions. You have our full authorization to do whatever you think is necessary. We'll back you to the limit. Just try to be discreet, but whatever you do, be effective. I know I can count on you. The chargé, Lorimer, will do whatever you need done, however disagreeable he may be about it. And don't forget Dave Bard. He'll give you all the help he can. Just don't ask too much of him. His position is very sensitive, I don't have to tell you. By the way, we've got Wayne posted up to the Aleutians, how do you like that? He's furious. Hates the cold. Good for him, I say. Let's hear from you as soon as possible. With good news.

Yours, Marcus

It was a measure of the seriousness with which Trilling regarded the situation and the degree to which he felt the successful resolution of his problems rested entirely with Stropp that he had signed himself "Marcus."

It was, in Stropp's memory, the first time even a memorandum, much less a full letter, had been signed in such a fashion.

It pleased him and at the same time made him feel distinctly uneasy.

He took out the little passport photo. It showed an ugly, round-faced, balding man in his mid-fifties. Definitely a European face. Stropp wondered how he'd ever gotten into the United States in the first place with a face like that.

He'd check with the embassy clerk and then with the consulate in Zurich in the morning. No point in even mentioning the man to Lorimer. The consulate in Zurich would have a record of his whereabouts. So would the police. And his passport.

After that, it shouldn't take Claude Ellsworth too long to run him to the ground.

And to do whatever might be necessary.

DOCUMENT

From: U.S. State Department, Wash., D.C.
To: U.S. Minister to Switzerland, Harrison.

You are to stop sending reports to private persons in the United States except under extraordinary circumstances. Private messages circumvent the censorship of neutral countries and these neutral countries might respond by closing their lines to confidential official matter.

[This transmission referred to cable 482, to the Undersecretary of State, in which Minister Harrison had transmitted the first reports of the death factories at Auschwitz.]

Mid-June 1944

Arlington, Virginia

The locker room of the Ten Oaks Country Club smelled of old men and aftershave lotion. Major Bard was relieved to have finished dressing and be out of the steamy, sickeningly fragrant place. Its mingled odors made him faintly ill. He much preferred the straightforward odor of sweat.

The day was blazing hot, and humid to boot. The grass everywhere else was turning yellow from lack of water. But the links at Ten Oaks were deep emerald green—official priorities. The club was the private preserve of senators, Pentagon staffers, and State Department officers, and if not a blade of grass got watered anywhere else in Virginia, it would get watered here.

Bard wiped angrily at the back of his neck. He could hardly complain, though: the prematurely fierce spring heat would keep all but the most fanatic golfers off the course. The older men would sit inside and sip their gin and tonics at the Nineteenth Hole clubroom and play gin rummy while the fans cooled the sweat off their backs. And there were no younger men around. They were all off at war. In the Pacific, or in England, getting ready for the invasion.

David Bard had business on the golf course, and that business was best done in the kind of privacy that the heat would afford.

He shouldered his golf bag and went out. A cluster of expectant caddies lounged drowsily by the clubhouse exit. He noticed with distaste that they were all older men, most of them suffering from a visible deformity or disability of some kind. The generals and senators played golf and the rejects carried their clubs. It was the way of the world.

He gestured to a short, balding man with watery eyes on the end by the water fountain. The man was Trilling's regular caddy and could be trusted not to be too nosy.

"Sir?" said Watery-eyes, catching the gesture.

"Nine holes. You think you can make it?"

"It ain't *that* hot," the caddy said and took Bard's bag.

Pray God he wasn't going to be like that when *he* got older, thought David Bard. He was still relatively young, in full command of his faculties. The juices still flowed despite the long, enervating months behind a desk in Berne. The few hours he'd spent with his wife after landing at Washington Airport—he'd gone straight home, expecting but not exactly receiving a hero's welcome—had been totally unsatisfactory. Absence had neither made the heart grow fonder nor improved her technique. She was still as hopeless and inept as always. But what could he expect from a woman who knew that he'd married her only to gain a position in her father's law firm? That had been a long time ago but she hadn't forgotten. It took the edge off things, no question about it.

He wasn't looking forward to the next few days, having to listen to her constant inconsequential chatter. She was a trial under the best of circumstances, and now he had other, far more important things on his mind than listening to gossip about her cousins and friends.

So after he'd unpacked, he'd gone to a place he knew in Georgetown, an elegant little house. For an hour, no more. When he'd finished, he'd felt like a man again.

He needed reassurance then, and now, too. The stakes were too high and the part he'd been assigned to play was too little under his own control. He didn't like having to rely so heavily on other men. Particularly men like the Undersecretary of State he was to meet shortly. One wrong move could jeopardize everything.

He teed off. Watery-eyes watched disinterestedly. He'd seen worse, and lots better, too.

The course was almost deserted, the sun a blazing hole in a sky only vaguely blue, a sky that looked as though it had been dusted over with graphite. Over a rise in the course he could see a single white cart moving slowly like a dung beetle over the links. The flagstone terrace of the clubhouse behind him was empty and forlorn, the venetian blinds screening the Nineteenth Hole clubroom down and closed. The sun buzzed angrily overhead, and the sweat poured down his neck.

The ball had gone straight and true, and a long way down the fairway.

He followed it with his eye, then walked slowly after it. Watery-eyes grunted, hoisted the bag, and labored after him. Glancing at his watch, Bard confirmed the time. Eight forty-five. The meeting was to take place on the green by the third hole, at about nine. The undersecretary had sent word that he would be there.

And if he wasn't, what then?

He'd have to arrange a meeting with Trilling directly, though Stropp had warned him repeatedly not to risk it. Yet he had to do something. The Poles were becoming more insistent than anyone had imagined possible. He had to be sure that the cork would stay tightly in the bottle.

Only State could give him that assurance.

He saw the undersecretary and his caddy far down the fairway, a slender, middle-aged man in a white, short-sleeved seersucker shirt, white duck trousers, and a floppy blue cap. Bard tried to visualize the face beneath the cap visor as he had once known it, the sharp, penetrating, wily eyes. The eyes of a banker, which was what the undersecretary was. A very successful banker. He hadn't seen the undersecretary for over a year. Men changed a great deal under stress, particularly during wartime. He wondered if he'd recognize the man.

Bard drove the ball again, relying on a skill acquired at much expense in both time and concentration. The shot went high and landed very close to where the undersecretary stood.

Bard came up to the pair, a little out of breath, his forehead dripping. The heat was taking more out of him than he'd imagined it would. He wasn't used to it; Switzerland got a man used to cool, refreshing temperatures, not the steam-bath atmosphere of Virginia in a premature summer. Maybe he was getting a little like the fat old men in the locker room, with their iced drinks and lavender-scented shaving lotions. The next thing, he'd be flat on a table, having the fat pounded off him by a black masseur. Jesus, what a future that was to contemplate.

He checked himself; what was the point in thinking that way? If there wasn't any point, there certainly was a reason. Everything had started to go a little sour recently and he didn't like thinking about what he was doing, not at all. Maybe the others didn't understand the implications, but he did. Maybe their greed was so intense that they actually didn't see what it all meant.

He saw.

He'd read the reports. And he'd been having nightmares ever since.

"Hello there," Bard called. "Mind if I play through?"

He came up closer and pushed his cap back. The undersecretary's eyes narrowed just a little. Then a relaxed smile spread over his face.

"Well, it's David Bard, isn't it? What a surprise. Aren't you supposed to be in Berne?"

Not very good acting, but the undersecretary had never been much of an actor, in private or in public. Everyone knew it. Transparent as a good condom, that's what they said of him. Well, why should he act? For the caddies' benefit? Or just because that was the way the undersecretary was, always trying to act—and doing it badly, too?

The undersecretary clucked approvingly, went over to his tee, selected an iron, and addressed his ball. The shot went far down the fairway in a high, looping arc. A perfect drive. Bard had to admire the man's skill. He certainly didn't give the appearance of an athlete.

The undersecretary's caddy moved out after the ball. Bard followed at a distance, thinking about what his life would be like after the war if he didn't do what he'd been told to do. No partnership, no security, no stock interests in the half dozen companies he'd been promised a piece of. All down the drain if Criterion didn't pull off the Buna transaction. It wasn't a very pleasant prospect.

All he had to do was keep on doing what he'd been doing in Berne and, now, exploit a few old school connections. Not that there was anything new in all of it; he'd done it half a dozen times before.

When his caddy had gone limping down the fairway together with Bard's man, the undersecretary took out a handkerchief. The smile on his face vanished at once, as though he'd wiped it off along with the sweat.

"Isn't it Rita Hayworth who's always saying 'we've got to stop meeting like this'?"

"Yes, sir, it's Rita Hayworth all right," said Bard. "If you can think of a better way, though . . ."

The undersecretary didn't reply. His face was very composed, his expression extremely businesslike.

"I hit the damned thing as hard as I could, but Pauly's good. He'll find it in a minute or two. That gives us . . . maybe three to five. Let's start walking."

"I don't need more than a minute, sir."

"Good. I hate this damned heat. Makes a man smell like a goat in five minutes. I don't like that, do you?"

"No, sir," Bard replied.

"Didn't think you would. Not a man of your . . . sensitivities. Marcus speaks very highly of you, did you know that, Bard?"

"Glad to hear it, sir."

"Thought you'd be. We'll see what we can do for you next month. A promotion isn't impossible."

Bard hardly heard him. What was the point of a promotion in a place like Berne? Whether he was a major or a chicken-colonel, it would be the same desk, the same musty building, and that same horse's ass of a sanctimonious ambassador.

"Let's get down to cases, what do you say, David?"

"That's what I came for, sir."

"Well then?"

Bard hesitated. He wasn't exactly sure how much the undersecretary really knew. A lot of what was being done was being done because of friendships and natural tendencies. There were plenty of men who did what they were asked simply because an old school friend or a former business associate or someone else's business associate had asked them to, or because they sensed with that fine sense of smell that the old boys always have that being helpful would be to their advantage later on.

In a way, they weren't doing anything different from Trilling. Or the I.G. people.

And then, there was the ever-present dull hatred. If they could be accommodating and at the same time put it to the kikes who were still trying to take over everything, well, why not? And nobody was going to tell them that it wasn't still going on. Look at that bastard Baruch, and Morgenthau and all the others. Who did they think they were kidding?

The undersecretary had to know. Or if he didn't—exactly—then he had to sense it.

Bard said, "The deal's almost closed."

"Good, good. I was beginning to wonder. I don't trust your 'friends' over there as much as you do, you know."

"Who does? But they know where their best interests lie."

"Just as we do," said the undersecretary. "Why should they be any different? Well then, what can *I* do for you?"

"It's the reports. We've bottled them up pretty well, but there've been leaks. They *know*. The pressure is getting harder to resist."

"Oh, I think we can resist it for a while longer, don't you think?"

"*These* reports—"

"We've had reports before, David. Means nothing."

"These do. Eyewitness, Mr. Undersecretary. Thirty or more pages. I've read them, and believe me, they're really horrifying. If they get into the wrong hands, if they get out to the public . . ."

"Easier done than said. I'll get hold of Gilbaine at the *Post,* Hereford at UP. It'll be taken care of, I promise you. I think I can count on the press secretary to cooperate. And if worse comes to worst, there are certain sanctions available."

"It's very important," said Bard.

"Oh, you don't have to explain it to me. They can make a lot of noise, your Jews."

"It isn't just the Jews. It'll be the Poles this time too. You'll hear from the London government. And the Czechs. They're all very jumpy about the thing."

They were getting near the spot where the undersecretary's drive had come to rest. The caddy had already located the ball and was standing there smiling, about fifty yards away.

"Do you want me to speak to Spaatz again?" the undersecretary asked.

"If you think it's wise, sir."

"Can't hurt, can't hurt. Maybe we won't have to go that high though. There'll be no problem in any event. Bank on it."

"I will. So will you."

The undersecretary smiled; he wondered if Bard really meant that. Not that it was particularly important; the undersecretary was already a very rich man.

"Tell Marcus he doesn't have to worry. And he doesn't have to pay me off, either."

"We never thought we did," said Bard. "Not for a minute."

"Anything else, Major? We're almost there."

"Just this. No matter how tough it gets, the War Department has to keep saying no."

"You people really think you have it locked up, don't you?"

Bard nodded. "As long as the Adriatic landing goes forward and we get into southern Poland before the Russians do, then yes. We've got it sewn up. There's no doubt about it. It will all be waiting for us. Everything that we need."

"You make it sound so easy. Like picking up the marbles after the other boy's gone home."

Bard forced a smile. Maybe it wasn't going to be that easy. But for the moment, Trilling thought it was. And the members of Hayklut, Bard, Winston & Stropp, wherever they were, all thought so too.

A DC-3 passed overhead, high in the blast-furnace sky, the sunlight dancing off its silver wing-tips. Bard looked up anxiously, apprehensive. All at once, he wanted desperately to be on a plane like that, heading away, fast and clean, getting away from where he was and what he was.

It was astonishing, but Major David Bard was feeling just a little bit guilty.

For the first time.

As the undersecretary walked away swinging his chalk bag, Bard called after him impulsively, surprising himself.

"Just one more thing, sir . . ."

"Yes?"

"Do you think you could arrange something . . . for me?"

"For you personally?" The undersecretary looked startled.

"I'd like to get out of Berne, sir. If there are any openings, say, in England . . . I want to be there, where it's happening. Or France . . ."

The undersecretary's face went slack. He didn't answer. Lines of concentration slowly creased his ruddy face; he was trying to understand.

Then he shrugged and turned his back, walking over to where his caddy was standing, to choose a club for his next shot.

DOCUMENT

From Weekly Report No. 11, August 3–9, 1941, I. G. Farbenindustrie Aktiengesellschaft, Auschwitz Werke.

Various conferences with the commandant and his assistants about the assignment of inmates have taken place. As you know, the assignment of two more guard companies has been refused. Through the intervention of the Reichsführer SS, it has now been ordered that all concentration camps are to detach 75 guards for duty at Auschwitz. Of this number, 40 have already arrived during the week covered by this report. In this way, it is possible for the concentration camp to assign another 1,000 inmates in addition to the 816 already employed at present. Of course this could not be done from one day to the next. * * * The assignment of inmates is causing difficulties due to the lack of guards—1. They can always only be assigned in groups of at least 20 or more. The consequence of this is that, in some places, they are working together so closely that they are hindering each other. That is just a fundamental difference between the working methods of a concentration camp and of a free enterprise. The concentration camp has no need to consider economic principles but in a free enterprise this must be done; particularly when it is a case of firms working at standard rates. This is not always sufficiently taken into consideration and recognized by the officials of the concentration camp. 2. The inmates can only march out in daylight and must return to the camp in daylight. If it is foggy in the morning, the inmates are also not permitted to leave the camp. Therefore it is not possible to employ the inmates on shift work; they can only be considered for the day shift.

The conditions will naturally improve once the construction site has been fenced in. The preparations for this have been made so that the fencing can be done by the end of the month. It is now planned to use concrete posts, which are being made in the concentration camp, and barbed wire and wire netting, which we are obtaining from the wire drawing mill in Gleiwitz. We have furthermore drawn the attention of the officials of the concentration camp to the fact that, in the last few weeks, the inmates are being severely flogged on the construction site by the Kapos in increasing measure, and this always applies to the weakest inmates who really cannot work harder. The exceedingly unpleasant scenes that occur on the construction site because of this are beginning to have a demoralizing effect on the free workers (Poles), as well as on the Germans. We have therefore asked that they should refrain from carrying out this flogging on the construction site and transfer it to the inside of the concentration camp.

Zurich

Stropp was sitting at the desk in his room at the Baur-au-Lac re-reading Trilling's letter when the phone began to jangle. He snatched it up, annoyed at having been disturbed.

"Yes? What is it?"

"You said to report in, sir, when I picked him up." It was Ellsworth's voice.

"Yes?"

"Well, he was at a print shop on the Frankengasse all morning and he's been at the library all afternoon, sir. He's in there right now."

"When he comes out . . ."

"I'll follow him, yes, sir."

"Don't lose him."

There was a short laugh. "He's not easy to lose, Mr. Stropp. You should see him, the way he's dressed."

"You stick with him."

"Yes, sir."

"And if you get the chance, go ahead. Do what you've been told to do."

"Tonight?"

"There's no reason to wait. We can't take any chances with a person like that."

"What about the police, sir?" There was an edge of concern to Ellsworth's voice.

"I'll handle the police if that should be necessary. Don't worry. Things are no different here than anywhere else. The police didn't raise a fuss in Bucharest, did they?"

"I'm not worried, sir."

"Good. Now go and do it."

"Yes, sir."

Kagan switched off the motor. A little way up Münsterstrasse the lights of the Grüne Fahne threw a pale golden glow onto the paving stones. A pall of smoke hung about the entrance, and the sounds of crockery clinking and glasses rattling against each other could be heard as far as the next corner. It was a perpetually crowded, convivial place, and it was there that the bachelor Grunewald often took his evening meal.

Kagan glanced obliquely at the American. He disliked looking directly at that pasty, whey-white face. The pale eyes disgusted him. The expression, servile and fearful, made him want to retch.

"I'll be outside. Right in front, watching you through the window."

"I suppose there'll be someone in back, too?"

"Why should we bother? If you betray us, all it will take is a phone call."

Eisner shuddered and got out of the car. As he opened the double glass doors of the restaurant, a wave of warmth swept over him. The smoke was heavy in the large, open room. It was a typical Zurich restaurant, the ceiling crossed by heavy beams from which heraldic symbols and racks of steins were hung. It was very little different from its German counterparts just across the. border. There was a strong smell of beer and damp sawdust.

Grunewald was sitting in a little booth near the back, looking smaller and more gnomelike than usual. The proprietor waved at Eisner pleasantly. He was a familiar face there and often during the past few weeks had dined either alone or in the Swiss lawyer's company.

Grunewald's expression changed almost at once from startled pleasure to a wary surprise. Eisner sat down quickly.

"Herr Stropp needs something further?" the lawyer asked. "Why didn't he call me at the office? Surely it was not necessary to interrupt my dinner. What could be so urgent?"

"Are you finished now?" Eisner said, ignoring the complaint.

Grunewald shrugged. He preferred to take his meals alone but could not see a polite way of putting Eisner off. The waiter came over.

"As it happens, I am only through the soup. So if you would care to join me . . . ? of course, do so."

Eisner ordered a cutlet with asparagus, and a beer. The waiter moved away.

"Now," said Grunewald, "what is this about? You are fooling no one, Mr. Eisner, least of all me. Let me tell you straight away, while I will do anything for my clients during office hours, whatever the exertion, my private time is my own. I resent intrusion."

Eisner leaned forward and without even attempting to apologize began to speak.

Half an hour later, Kagan saw the two men come out of the restaurant. Eisner stopped and pointed toward the Renault. For a moment, Kagan tensed, waiting for something to happen.

The little American bastard had betrayed them after all.

Then Eisner did a strange thing: he walked directly over to the Renault, with Grunewald by his side, opened the door, and crowded into the front seat.

"This is Kagan, the man I told you about, Herr Grunewald."

The lawyer looked at him, wide-eyed. "Herr Eisner has told me terrible things. Yet, if even some of what he says is true . . ."

"It's all true. Every bit of it. You probably knew most of it already."

Grunewald's face grew dark. It was noticeable even in the shadowy interior of the car.

"I did not know. I assure you. Had I known, I could not have possibly permitted—"

"Of course," said Kagan flatly. Where was all of this leading? Obviously Eisner had not done what he'd been asked to do.

"If I could be certain," the lawyer began. "Can you show me

anything? I am a lawyer, you understand. Even in this, I must be sure of my facts."

"I can show you everything. There are no secrets."

"When?"

"Right now. We will go to our offices. There you will see it all."

The lawyer nodded and closed his eyes.

Grunewald sat on the edge of Baranyi's cot, bent deep over the papers Miklos had given him. The clock ticked loudly on the desk. Baranyi tugged at Kagan's shirtsleeve.

"Where is Zoltan? Shouldn't he be here?"

"He was all afternoon at the State Library, looking up American law cases involving the oil company. He went back to his room with a headache. No wonder."

"He's unwell? Perhaps I should see him?"

"A headache, Miklos, that's all. You'll see him in the morning."

By the time Grunewald had finished reading, his seamed face had taken on the appearance of a ruined monument. Where there had once been confidence, pride, now there was confusion and shame. He pushed the papers aside, the Vrba–Wetzler report, the fragmentary reports drawn up by the escaped Polish and Czech officers, the Criterion dossier brought by Peshko from New York, the notes prepared by Landau. All of it.

Baranyi lit a cigarette. "Well?"

Again there was silence. Grunewald's small, clear eyes were clouded over. He was trembling. When he spoke it was in a small, broken voice.

"There are some things that even a lawyer must not be asked to do. He should not be made an unknowing accomplice to a crime. When this happens, his responsibility to his client is at an end." He struggled to regain his composure. Baranyi handed him his cigarette case, and with uncertain fingers Grunewald tried to extract a cigarette. Baranyi had to help him light it.

"I am not a murderer," Grunewald whispered. "And I will not allow anyone to make a murderer out of me."

"No one has said that you did this with knowledge. But now you have that knowledge."

Grunewald nodded. "Herr Baranyi, I cannot do the impossible. Anything that is within my power . . . anything you might ask of me I will gladly do. But what Herr Eisner has asked is not within my power to do. It is simply impossible."

Baranyi's mouth went dry.

Grunewald went on. "The documents are in a vault at the Crédit Suisse. The letter of consignment provides that the box cannot be opened until the war is ended. Those are the terms of the deposit. It is entirely out of my hands now."

"You could sign for their release, surely?"

"I could not. You must understand, there is simply no way. The banking laws in this country are very strict and their observance is a point of honor with our institutions. No matter for what reason, these laws cannot be broken and the confidence of the customers violated. I acted for a client, not for myself. I am not the party in interest. Even if I had been, once having made the deposit according to the letter of consignment, I could not change its terms."

"There is always a reason. When it comes to killing Jews, there is always a reason why murder cannot be stopped," Kagan said.

"Without the documents, there is no chance that we can convince anyone. No one will lift a finger to help."

"Wait."

It was Landau. No one had paid any attention to him up till now. He had been sitting in the corner of the room, in the shadow of Baranyi's file cabinet. He jumped up, electrified. His body trembled and his eyes shone feverishly.

"There *is* a way," he cried. "There is another way entirely."

Then he began to speak. The words tumbled out in a torrent, so precipitously that he became almost incomprehensible.

And as he spoke the others listened, more and more intently.

When he had finished, Baranyi stood up, silent and unsure.

"I must talk to Peshko about this. And Bor as well."

"It will work," said Landau. "I know these people. Believe me, it will work."

"Why should they believe it?"

"Precisely because it is the kind of thing they themselves would do without a moment's hesitation."

Grunewald agreed. "So it would seem," he said.

Kagan watched, waiting for an order.

"I'll go to Peshko at once. Headache or no headache, I want his opinion. You, Herr Landau, you will stay here."

"My daughter?"

"Is being looked after by Frau Birkli, yes? We will check up on her or bring her here, whichever you wish. The Malowska woman can look after her. But you must stay with us," Miklos said. "I'm sure you can see why."

Landau nodded.

"If I were in your position, I would not trust me entirely either," he said. "But I promise, you will trust me soon enough. You'll see."

The pension in which Zolton Peshko had taken a room was not far from the Frankengasse. Baranyi walked quickly, taking deep gulps of chill night air and fighting hard against the vertigo that had overwhelmed him as he listened to Landau explain the way out of their dilemma.

An insane plan that just possibly might work.

Baranyi was both stunned and angry. Landau was right: his scheme was sound and took good account of the peculiar psychology of the Germans as well as of the oil people. On a personal level, the risks were enormous, but no greater, really, than those he had been running routinely for the last two years.

What most disturbed him, in the last analysis, was the clarity with which Landau had seen both the situation and the character of the people they were dealing with.

God, Baranyi thought, it takes one to know one. But one of *what,* exactly? He could not get over his confusion. Landau had him absolutely baffled. And what was worse, he knew that the world was full of Felix Landaus.

He pushed open the door of 26 Brennergasse. The concierge was asleep in her cubicle by the door, a dumpy old woman slumped like a heap of rags in an old armchair, the newspaper open on her lap. A canary was chirping somewhere, and he could hear the fish tank bubbling in the next room.

The stairwell was dark and full of indistinct, musty odors. How like Peshko to have chosen such a dismal place instead of a decent hotel, which surely he could have afforded.

He paused at the third-floor landing. There were two doors. Which was number six, Peshko's room?

He froze. In the dim light of the landing, he could make out the enamel *6* hanging on the door panel; the door was ajar, a slice of light showing at the jamb.

He knocked softly before pushing the door open.

No response.

Then he caught a whiff of a strange but familiar odor and his stomach began to churn with sudden nausea. He shoved the door open, acutely aware that it was a very foolish thing to do.

The room was a shambles. The bed was overturned, the sheets in a tangle on the floor. The contents of Peshko's suitcase had been dumped out. A bottle of purple medicine had been ground underfoot. There was broken glass everywhere.

A few of the little steno notebooks that Peshko always used were scattered on the floor near the bed. The pages were covered with a tight, neat scrawl, a mixture of Yiddish and Hungarian. The ink looked fresh and the books were of Swiss manufacture. They had obviously been filled in since Peshko's arrival in Zurich, perhaps even that very afternoon.

Baranyi's gaze followed the finger of twisted sheet that seemed to point directly toward another door on the opposite side of the room—the door to a water closet or toilet of some kind. It was from there that the odor came.

Baranyi kicked open the door and almost fainted.

Zoltan Peshko hung upside down, suspended from an iron bar across the top of the water closet. His throat had been cut so fiercely that his head hung at an odd angle, almost severed. The blood had drained out of his body and over his face, obscuring his features and filling the toilet bowl beneath.

Trussed and slaughtered exactly as pigs are trussed and slaughtered for Easter. Baranyi had seen that done to human beings only once—in Bucharest in 1939, when the Iron Cross fascists had gone on a rampage and murdered hundreds of Jews.

He fell back, retching.

. . . like a pig, the blood draining into a bowl below. For sausage meat.

He knelt in the center of the room, his body heaving convulsively until he had nothing more to vomit. From the water closet came a steady dripping sound.

He would not turn, would not look again. Nothing would make him look again. Somehow, he got to his feet and managed to reach the landing. All of the other doors were closed, on the third floor as well as the second. A radio played softly somewhere, hardly denting the dense silence. Tino Rossi's androgynous voice crooning a tango.

He would have to call . . . whom? Bor? Kagan? Pauer? Perhaps they could explain why someone had wanted to kill Peshko, so badly that they would do it in such a terrible way.

Call the police? The Swiss cantonal police? An inquiry, precise, dispassionate, cold. Please tell us nothing about the war, Herr Baranyi. We do not wish to know about such things. Do not tell us what men do to each other. Only what *one* person has done to this *one* particular other person.

He could not stand such a thing, he knew that. And none of them could afford the scrutiny that such an investigation would bring.

The concierge was still asleep, snoring under her tent of newspaper. He rushed past, silently.

Once outside he looked up and down the street for a *Telephon*. Nothing.

For a few seconds he did not even know which way to go. It had not really registered. No—it hadn't even really *happened*. That was it. It had all been an hallucination. He was simply overtired. He looked back and at the same time smelled the acrid odor of his own vomit.

His trousers were streaked and his hands slimy with it.

The street seemed deserted. Which way to go? He set off, stumbling.

Where the devil was a phone? There had to be one.

Somewhere.

He hurried down the street, finding it difficult to keep his balance, now and then thrusting his hands out to steady himself against the walls of buildings as though he were drunk. He was as close to being in a state of shock as he could ever recall. His heart was racing madly and his skin was cold and clammy.

He slumped against the wall and jammed a cigarette into his mouth, cupping a hand over the end to shield it from the wind. He struck a match, then a second, with no success. His hand was trembling too badly.

But in the flare of the match he noticed a large man standing halfway down the street. The odd thing was the cut of the man's hat. It was not the kind of hat that the Swiss wore, though the coat was of the same cut. The man was pretending to look in a shop window. But there were no lights. How could he see anything?

Miklos crossed the street to a point where he could place the man's reflection in the angled window of a dry goods shop.

The man was still there, following him, his tread measured to Miklos's own.

Baranyi found his pulse slowing, his control—oddly—returning as his fear mounted. A tram car went by on the next street, shedding blue sparks that were instantly whipped from the wires and scattered over the cobblestones by the wind. A horse-drawn beer wagon lumbered by, the driver hunched down on the seat, his long whip trailing on the horse's rump.

Thank God there were others around. He was not alone. No one would dare . . .

What was the matter with him? For a second, a memory of the streets of Budapest, of the Nyilas uniforms he had worn, of the trucks, the trains, the escapes, all flashed before him. Was he the same man now as then? Why was he so terrified? He had faced far worse than this before.

Peshko's dangling body. That was why. *Peshko.*

He turned into a narrow alleyway, passed down it for half its length, and then pulled back into a doorway. The mouth of the alley was lit by the street lights. Anyone presenting himself there would make a perfect target.

Then he realized one awful fact: he was unarmed. He had not carried a weapon since the day in Budapest when he had impersonated the Nyilas officer. In Zurich there had been no need.

Until now . . .

The man was still there. He moved at once into the alley, without the slightest regard for his visibility. That was bad. Either the man was impossibly clumsy or he had decided to put an end to the game.

A beam of light lanced down the alley, unexpected, driving Baranyi back into a doorway. The man had a flashlight.

In his other hand, the man held an object of indistinct outline. Baranyi did not need a better look to tell him that it was an automatic, not the knife he had expected.

The alley was dark. The windows, all barred, appeared to be the side windows of shuttered warehouses and shops. Miklos reached behind him, fumbling for the knob of the door against which he had pressed himself.

The knob would not turn.

The beam of the flashlight prowled slowly down the alleyway. He realized now that he was caught. By his own stupidity. From the corner of his eye he could see past the edge of the wall to the end of the alley. It was blocked by debris.

The tip of the beam hesitated, stopped, remained fixed on the stones just a meter away from the doorway in which Baranyi had sheltered. The length of the beam shortened without the tip's moving. The man was advancing, keeping the light lowered on that one spot. Baranyi could see him clearly now, a big, shambling man, the head unexpectedly small, the features pinched.

Baranyi's fingers moved cautiously in his pockets. They were full of small coins, dozens of little copper centime pieces.

He waited until the man came almost even with his hiding place. Then, as the man stopped, Miklos doubled over and rocked forward, almost to his knees, at the same time pitching the coins directly at the man's face. He heard a furious, baffled cry; the flashlight beam swung wildly. In that second of confusion, he ran as fast as he could for the alley exit, head down, crashing against boxes and cans stacked on the sides, zigzagging so as to make a more difficult target.

He heard a muffled pop in front of him, a sort of hissing, squirting sound. Something flashed past and splattered against the wall. He rolled forward, down, reaching out to anchor himself to the corner of the wall and use it as a pivot.

Then there was a deeper, different, pounding sound—still muffled, but much stronger than the first had been. Then another and another, at regular intervals.

The beam slid away from the wall and remained angled across the alley. Rigid.

Miklos turned and looked back. An unbelievably foolish thing to do, but he could not help himself.

There was a second figure silhouetted against the entrance to the alleyway. It was a woman, unmistakably Julie Malowska, her hair whipped to one side by the wind, standing with her feet planted well apart, the parabellum fitted with a silencer held forward in both hands.

Slowly, she pumped the entire magazine into the huge figure now sprawled against the alley wall amid the garbage cans. The body jerked convulsively each time one of the 9-mm slugs bit into it. The ridiculously small head lolled to one side, flopping back and forth.

At last Julie Malowska stopped firing, the magazine of the parabellum empty. For a moment she remained stock-still, as though expecting that the man had survived somehow, was capable still of a renewed assault.

"All right, Miklos. You can come out now."

Shaking, he moved back to the center of the alley. The whole thing had happened so rapidly, so silently, that in all likelihood no one in the street had taken any notice. The man hadn't uttered so much as a single cry. Malowska's first bullet had shattered his face, splashing blood and bits of hair all over the wall behind him.

She came over to him.

"Of all the brothers-in-law a woman could have . . ." she said. "What a trial you are."

"You followed me here?"

She ignored the question, knelt, and began calmly rummaging through the dead man's pockets.

"Nothing. Not a thing. Look." She held up a breast-pocket wallet. "Not a scrap of paper here."

"You *followed* me," he repeated, dull, incredulous. It was almost an accusation.

Slowly she turned and looked up at him with fierce, narrowed eyes.

"You're mine, Miklos. Do you understand that? You belong to me and to no one else. I'm not about to let you get yourself killed," she said. "Now do you know who or *what* this thing is?"

"I think he's the one who killed Peshko."

"What? Peshko's dead?" There was real shock in her voice.

"His throat was cut. They hung him up to bleed to death like an Easter pig."

"Jesu Maria . . ." she breathed. "Who would do such a thing? And why? The Germans?"

"This one isn't German. Look at that face."

"What's left of it."

"Where did you learn to shoot like that?"

"I told you, your father-in-law was a fine hunter. You never took the time to get to know him, did you? He taught his daughters to shoot well. Teresa was even better than I am, particularly with a rifle."

As she said these words, his fingers touched something in the dead man's coat pocket: a heavy Swiss army clasp knife. Even in the dim light of the alley he could see that it had been only partially wiped clean.

"He's the one all right. He must have seen me go up there, waited for me to come out . . ."

"And I for you as well. You need a full-time guardian angel, don't you, Miklos?"

"And what do we do now? With . . . *him*? And with Zoltan? We can't have the police." His mind whirled back to the conversation with Landau less than an hour before. If the police were allowed to interfere now, there would be no possibility of doing anything at all. "We will all end up in prison or an internment camp, at best."

"I'll call Conrad. He has people who can clean this up."

"And Zoltan?"

"He can deal with that too." Suddenly she straightened up. Her probing fingers had found something that Baranyi had missed.

"This . . . what's this? It was on his lapel."

"A party badge? The SS wear such things," said Baranyi with something like relief; it would be far simpler if the man had been a German agent.

Julie Malowska shook her head and handed the button over.

Miklos squinted, brought the flashlight beam full on it under a cupped hand.

He pronounced the words slowly, letting their import sink in like acid.

"Elks . . . Club . . . Lakeville . . . Illinois."

Greifensee, Switzerland

It was less than ten kilometers from Zurich to the lake. The trip had taken less than a half-hour.

Eisner's teeth were chattering, from fear and from the unexpectedly cold night air. He felt Kagan's hand on his arm, slowly, irresistibly forcing him to bend close over the ruined body that lay in the trunk at the lake's edge.

He shivered; the mud oozed under his shoes.

The beam of Bor's flashlight swung down slowly and lingered on the shambles of a face for only the briefest time. The nose had been smashed by the first slug and there was little left of the mouth, either.

But it was enough.

"That's Ellsworth," said Eisner, gagging. "It's Claude Ellsworth all right."

Bor switched off the light. For a moment no one could see. Then the dark outlines of the two cars parked at the lake's edge and the seven people gathered there came up out of the slightly less intense dark of the Swiss mountain night.

"He has given us all a great deal of trouble, your Mr. Ellsworth," said Bor. One of the Poles slammed the lid of the trunk closed and began to wrap it with boat chain. Another trunk lay nearby, already at the water's edge, by the stern of a small powerboat that had been pulled partially up onto the shore of the Greifensee.

In the second trunk was Zoltan Peshko's body, also wrapped in chains.

Baranyi glanced quickly at the trunk, then away.

Julie Malowska noticed his movement.

"He'll understand," she said. "Your friend. He will know that it is necessary to do this."

Baranyi nodded slightly, feeling—with some surprise, but more a quiet sense of reconciliation—his sister-in-law's hand on his arm. Firm but gentle.

He, in his turn, tentatively touched her hand. He was afraid to feel anything, to give in. But how could he not, now?

She did not pull away, but allowed his hand to cover hers.

He wished at that moment that he could see her face clearly, but it was too dark and Bor had pocketed the light.

Bor went over to Eisner.

"This man, Ellsworth, who do you think sent him?"

"It had to be Stropp. It wasn't me."

"But he was the chauffeur for your law office." Bor's voice was hard, a knife edge on it.

"I swear, I lent him to Stropp a week ago. He said he needed a driver, someone to do odd jobs for him while he was here."

"Odd jobs? Yes, I'd say so."

Kagan's flat voice cut through the darkness. "If we thought otherwise, you'd be with him in the trunk."

The trunks were loaded onto the boat and Bor's two men, huddled in their leather coats, climbed in. The motor turned over. How they had managed to get both bodies out of Zurich without attracting attention was a mystery to Baranyi. But never again would he underestimate the cunning and artfulness of the Poles.

The boat moved out from shore, soft as a whisper, its delicate wake catching the light of those few stars that now and then emerged from behind the clouds.

Bor turned to Baranyi.

"So . . . and now must we not pray?" He paused for a moment. "Does your Herr Landau know about this?"

Baranyi shook his head.

"He should not be told then," said Bor. "Do you agree?"

"Not for now, at any rate. There is no point in frightening him."

Bor laughed. "He is not frightened by what he proposes to do and you think he would be frightened by *that?*"

"Who can tell? He is a desperate man, I think. He almost lost his soul and he knows it. No matter what the risks, he will be willing."

"Perhaps," Bor mused. "Perhaps you are right. We'll see."

Out toward the center of the lake there was a soft splash, then another. The powerboat turned and headed back toward shore.

"We will help Landau all we can," said Bor.

"I'm counting on that," said Miklos.

"Pauer will also help."

"Yes."

Kagan said, "A moment, please—a prayer for Peshko's soul . . ." Julie Malowska held tightly to Miklos's arm. Kagan began to recite the *kaddish*.

When he had finished he went over to Bor.

"When it's time, not now, but later, when it's time, we will deal with this man Stropp. Will you help us in that too?"

"To kill a man is one thing, to slaughter him like an animal is another," Bor replied. "Even if your friend had been a German I would help you even the score with a man who would do something like that."

"Good then. When the time is right."

"When the time is right, Itzhak, but not now. For the moment the time is not right. After he has done what we ask him to do, then he must simply be put out of the way for a time. Not killed. We cannot afford to frighten the Germans. He must only be neutralized so that he cannot interfere. And this must be done in a way that will not arouse suspicion of any kind."

Bor looked at him in dubious silence. Kagan scowled.

"I will tell you exactly how it will be done," Baranyi said. "And with your help, Colonel Bor, we will succeed."

There was also the matter of the notebooks.

For a time, sitting in the rear of Bor's Packard on the way back from the Greifensee, Miklos found himself unable to focus on anything except the lake and the trunks. He saw the trunks slowly twisting down to the bottom of the lake, through successively colder levels of black water: a gentle, almost beautiful descent. He shivered, tried to clear his mind. He knew he could not afford the luxury of such feelings. Not for long, at any rate.

Finally he took out the notebooks, in order to give his mind something else to focus on. He had almost forgotten about them.

He snapped on the overhead light and flipped open the first pages. It was impossible to make out Peshko's cramped Yiddish script. But there were a few numbers and European letters scrawled across the top of the page. Two digits followed by a letter, *F*, followed by a smaller number, followed by three larger digits. He squinted at them hard, as though by so doing he could force the meaning out of them.

Eisner, sitting next to him, looked over.

"I know what that means," he said quietly.

Miklos stared.

"The Yiddish? You can read that scrawl?"

"No. Only the numbers on top. They're a citation."

"A *what?*"

"It's the way American law decisions are identified. By the volume, the *Reporter* series, and the page."

"These are notes of a court decision? What sense does that make?"

"He was at the State Library this afternoon, wasn't he? He must have been taking notes on a reported case."

"If you're right . . ."

"I'm right, you can be sure of that."

"Then in the morning we can see. When the library opens."

"You don't have to wait until morning. We have the books in my office. I think I know what the case is, too."

Kagan, who was driving, turned his head slightly. "You don't have to say anything, Miklos. I heard."

The small Zurich office of Hayklut, Bard, Winston & Stropp was deserted. The clerk had long since gone home. Unlike the New York and Washington offices, no night staff was maintained here. The Paradeplatz was similarly deserted. In order to avoid attracting attention, Kagan had dropped Eisner and Baranyi off at the entrance to the building and then parked farther up the Bahnhofstrasse where he could keep an eye on who went in and out.

The library was maintained on rows of steel shelves in the corridor between the reception room and Eisner's dingy office.

Eisner went directly to a row of books bound in tan cloth with gold and red stamping on their spines.

"This one," he said. "We can take it into my office."

"No. Better in the reception area. There's no outside window and the light can't be seen."

Eisner nodded and then went back to the secretary's desk.

"You don't have to read it," Eisner said, lighting a cigarette with shaking hands. "I can tell you exactly what's in there."

"You know what he was looking for?"

"I couldn't ever forget those numbers. I can give you the decision by heart if you want, word for word."

Baranyi shook his head. Was it really possible that Peshko had been butchered because of something that was printed in a law book and available for *anyone* to read?

"Give me a cigarette. And a drink, if you have one. Then talk, Herr Eisner. Tell me the whole thing."

"It all ties in to what happened to me. If you want that too . . ."

"Everything."

Eisner passed Miklos a cigarette and a bottle of brandy. He took a long swallow, and for a moment it made him feel warm and comfortable. Then he thought of the trunks and the lake and the freezing black water.

"Talk," he said.

Eisner licked his lips, wiped the neck of the bottle fastidiously, and took a swallow.

"In a way it's thanks to what happened in that case that I'm here in Zurich. It wasn't because of the money I stole that they sent me. You know all about that, I'm sure, but that wasn't the real reason. It was because of the case. They couldn't trust me and they couldn't get rid of me any other way, either. So they sent me here. Little Siberia in the Alps. The case is why they didn't throw me to the wolves after the business with the money."

"Get on with it, damn you."

Eisner took another swallow and put the bottle down. His eyes were bleary and raw with fatigue.

"I'm older than I look. I'll be thirty-four next September, if I live that long, and I've been with the firm since 1933. But what I know goes back even further than that. They put me to work on the agreements right away, right out of law school, can you imagine? I was at the top of my class. Very proud and very pleased with myself. I was going to have a really great career. Oh Jesus, and I walked right into *this* . . ."

"Herr Eisner," Miklos said coldly, "tell me about the case, whatever it is. Not about yourself. I want to know why Peshko was killed, not why you are unhappy. Now, the *case*. What has the *case* to do with all of this?"

"Be patient, will you? I'll give you the whole story. Not just what's in the judge's decision, though God knows that's enough by itself." He took a deep breath and began again. "It all started in 1929, when our client, these fine gentlemen at Criterion Oil, got themselves together with those equally fine gentlemen at I.G. and they got themselves what they were pleased to refer to as 'married.' "

Miklos could see the brandy working. Eisner was talking more and more rapidly. But it seemed as though it was not only the alcohol. A strange catharsis was taking place.

"A marriage, Mr. Baranyi. That's what they called it and that's what it was. They signed an agreement not to compete in each other's fields. I helped draft it. The fine gentlemen in Wilmington got clear sailing in the petroleum market and the fine gentlemen in Berlin got a promise that Criterion Oil would keep their hands off the chemical industry in Europe. Oh, they each took a minority interest in each other's prime areas and they pooled their technology. I worked on some revisions to those agreements only a month after I got to Hayklut. Can you imagine? I suppose none of that shocks you, Mr. Baranyi, being a European. But for a nice American boy like me who's been taught that cartels are the worst thing next to heresy, it was quite a shock. The *Herren* in Berlin saved the skin of the gentlemen in Wilmington, let me tell you. That was the year there was a big scare about the oil running out and everyone suddenly got interested in synthetics. Then I.G. handed Criterion its hydrogenation process and that about locked up the synthetics field for them. Which is just the way Criterion handled it. They organized a licensing subsidiary and made the terms so tough that no one wanted to bother getting into the field. Natural petroleum was safe and a lot cheaper, even if it was supposed to run out soon. No, sir, there wasn't going to be any competition from synthetics, not for a long while.

"And in return, Berlin got all kinds of agreements from Criterion, including the know-how to produce tetraethyl lead for aviation fuel. And with their market agreements they all but stopped development over here in the methanol and synthetic rubber fields. That's when the tug-of-war over the Buna rights started. We were supposed to get Buna as part of the quid pro quo but the *Herren* in Berlin held back and made all kinds of excuses. Then in 1930 we formed another dummy for them—'Carco,' they called it, Combined American Research Company. Carco got all the patents for new processes developed either by Criterion or I.G., it didn't matter which, with a split-up of profits and rights. Berlin was still being very smart. They gave Criterion's people the electric-arc process, which got them really panting over the Buna rights. But that was it. That was all they got. The Criterion people went crazy, believe me. They didn't know what to do then. Well, what *do* you do if your partner is still reluctant to give you what you really want? Why, you give him presents, don't you? Butter him up. So next thing, Criterion handed I.G. their new process for making rubber out of butyl. It was still experimental and not too well worked out, but maybe it would turn out well. Nobody knew. And after that, how could I.G. refuse to turn over the Buna rights in return? But—of course—there was still no Buna.

"You'd think they'd have learned, but oh no . . . and here's where it gets much, much worse. It's '38, right after the *Anschluss*. I.G. gets a call from the air ministry . . . Oh, I saw all of it, the memoranda with General Milch's signature, the letters, the whole lot. Even some cables from Goering himself. They were strapped. They didn't have the tetraethyl factories finished yet and it looked like war was going to start at any minute. How do you fight a war when you can't gas up your planes? So they got hold of Trilling and they ask, couldn't they please just *buy* five hundred tons of the stuff? Only about twenty million dollars' worth. And you *know* what they're going to use it for. So, of course, what happens? Who turns down a twenty-million-dollar deal even if it means sitting on your scruples? You shove your scruples under the rug until you've banked the check. Time enough for scruples later. And besides, there's the Buna to think of. They still haven't got the technical details and they still can't actually manufacture the stuff. They haven't even got the patent assignments yet, even though they've managed to keep every major chemical company in the country out of the synthetic rubber market while they're waiting for I.G. to hand over the new Buna process. Even Trilling had qualms about that one, and he checked with the embassy in London before we went on to Rotterdam. The embassy people almost stopped it until our ambassador, Mr. Kennedy, got wind of what was going on and told Criterion to go right ahead, he didn't see what was wrong with it at all. After all, it was only the lousy Poles who were going to get bombed.

"That's when they sent Henry Stropp and a few of us expendable junior attorneys over to Rotterdam. I worked on those papers too. The *modus vivendi* agreement they signed was drafted by *me* the first time around. They knew the war was coming and they wanted to make sure that none of the I.G. patents were grabbed by the alien property custodian the way they'd gotten grabbed in 1917. So we drew up an agreement for them; it was to control everyone's rights during the war. We set it up so that I.G. would assign all its patents in the United States to our people, or to American citizens under Criterion's control, 'for the duration of the war,' and then afterward it would be business as usual.

"We signed, all right, but even I.G. hadn't been prepared for Hitler's impatience. Poland was invaded while we sat on our camp chairs in the hotel garden, and we had to backdate the signatures two days in order to make it all legal.

"And, of course, the fine *Herren* in Berlin continued to stall on the Buna process. They assigned the patents, all right, but they also sent a very polite telegram saying how sorry they were but they still couldn't turn over the know-how.

"I started to think, what was the point of being honest if they weren't? I mean, if they could get away with things like that, who could complain if I took what I needed? And I certainly needed plenty at that point. You do if you haven't got anything at all." Eisner laughed, a faint, embarrassed sound deep in his throat. "It was really like Jean Valjean, in a way. I mean, I didn't take much, and I took it only because I really needed it. Money wasn't exactly in good supply in those days. They caught me at it, and while they were trying to decide whether to throw me out or have me jailed, the Justice Department hit them with an antitrust suit. It was about then that they decided that what I'd done wasn't so terrible after all and that it would be a good idea to open up a branch office in Zurich. With a staff of one or two. Me and a secretary. Under the circumstances, I could hardly refuse, could I?" He stopped and fumbled in his pocket, looking for another cigarette.

Miklos took out a pack of Gauloises and handed it to him. He was stunned. From what Peshko and Bor had told him before, he had begun to get some idea of the extent of the Criterion–I.G. dealings, but he had never imagined that they had been so incredibly close.

"It's all here," said Eisner in a voice weak with shame and fatigue. "All their dancing around the issue didn't do them any good. The government was even smarter than they'd been and they found it all out. Or most of it, anyway. What came out was enough. Read it yourself. Judge Lowenthal laid it all out very nicely. Better than I could ever do. It's even indexed. We call them 'head notes.' Tells you where to find everything. Ironic, isn't it? All things considered, I mean. Judge Lowenthal being Jewish, I mean. It's quite a story, isn't it?" He took a long, deep draw on the Gauloise. "But they're right, you know. It'll all be forgotten in a year or two. It's probably almost forgotten already. After the war they'll build their big plants and go on making their big deals and no one will remember what they did. Or if they do, they just won't care. That's the worst part of it all. No one will care at all."

Miklos said nothing. He was not concerned with what would happen in two or three or five or twenty years. He had the morning to worry about.

And the next step.

Knowing what Eisner had just told him was going to make things just a little bit easier.

Or, if not easier, at least it would be possible for him to see a little more clearly what he had to do.

DOCUMENT

From: Major General Frederick L. Anderson, Deputy Commander serving under General Carl Spaatz, Commander in Chief of the United States Strategic Air Force (USSTAF)
To: United States War Department, OPD (Operations Division) [In response to a transmittal from OPD forwarding a message from WRB, London, pleading for bombing of the camps; copy to Spaatz.]

I do not consider that the unfortunate Poles herded in these concentration camps would have their status improved by the destruction of the extermination chambers. There is also the possibility of some of the bombs landing on the prisoners as well, and in that event, the Germans would be provided with a fine alibi for any wholesale massacre they might perpetrate. I therefore recommend that no encouragement be given to this project.

The mountains above Laufenberg, Switzerland

Pauer adjusted the rucksack on his shoulders and shifted the shotgun under his right arm. The forest was cool and fragrant, and for a moment it was even possible to forget that there was a war on and that he was dangerously close to the German border.

He had arrived at the inn near Laufenberg just after the noon meal, had refreshed himself with a nap and a plate of soup. Then he waited. Shortly after three, a chambermaid had knocked at his door and delivered the message he had been expecting.

The contact had been arranged. In the forester's cabin, six kilometers up the path from the inn toward Brugg.

He walked slowly, cautiously. There was no alternative but to take the risk himself. The contacts with the Wehrmacht had all been made through the Slovak organization. He, Pauer, was known. Others were not.

He knew he was dealing with desperate men and was ready for anything. Once again a devil's bargain was in the offing. The German army was being slaughtered by the Soviets, largely for lack of supplies and mobile reinforcements. A red tide was about to overwhelm Poland, then East Prussia. OKW saw the writing on the wall. Hold off the Russians for a while, time enough for a peace to be arranged. There were rumors that someone high up, perhaps Admiral Carnaris, perhaps even Himmler, was already secretly negotiating with the Americans. They had to buy time. And time could be bought only with rolling stock.

Knock out the rail lines into Oswiecim and the other camps and the rolling stock that had been tied up transporting Jews to the gas chambers could be freed and used where it was needed—to carry troops and supplies to the east.

To hold the Soviets back just a little longer.

Pauer understood. It was to the advantage of the Czechs, too. Far better the Americans and the British in Prague than the Russians. If the eastern front didn't hold, then it would be all over within a year. Hitler's prophecy would come true over the ashes of Hitler's Reich.

The Soviets would rule all of eastern and central Europe.

The path angled up into a heavy pine wood. Cowbells clattered in the distance, the sound carried clean and clear in the still mountain air. Birds flitted in the treetops. The sun, pale and surprisingly wintry, moved at an infinite distance. The air was fragrant with wildflowers.

Ahead he saw the forester's shack. He'd met the German there before a number of times. Once, after they'd transacted their business the two of them had done a little hunting together, drunk some brandy, and exchanged stories. They had even promised to meet each other with their wives and children. After the war.

The door to the shack was open.

The German was inside, whittling a walking stick, a machine pistol within inches of his right hand. He looked up and smiled.

"*Gott Gruss,*" he said. "Punctual as usual."

"A good day for a climb, yes?"

"There have been worse."

The German knew what Pauer wanted. The word had gotten back quickly, and had he not been prepared to provide it, he would not have come.

Pauer sat on a bench by the window, where he could keep an eye on the trail.

"A long walk," Pauer said. "Too bad I couldn't have ridden."

"By railroad?" said the German.

"Railroads run, these days, everywhere but where you want them to go."

The German smiled ruefully. "It can be arranged," he said.

"Do you have anything for me?"

"In a few days. I assume that we both want accuracy. It takes time to achieve accuracy."

"Understood. A few days then?"

"You'll have everything you need. Maps and schedules. The railheads and junctions will all be clearly marked."

"Flak installations?"

The German smiled. "There will be no flak. You see, there is no ammunition for the guns. That's one of our problems. The trains bring bodies to burn, but no shells."

"Aircraft? Will the fighter strength be given?"

"Again"—the German shook his head—"there is none to speak of. What is left has been shifted either to the front to meet Konev's Stormaviks or to Berlin."

Pauer almost felt sorry for the man.

"The courier? When and where?"

"There is one condition my superiors have imposed."

"Yes?"

"We cannot deal directly with you, nor with the Poles."

"Who then?"

"The Jews. The Vaadah. They are sufficiently apolitical. You see, if it turns out that we must eventually make our peace with the Soviets, despite everything we may do, then it is better that we deal with the Jews than with you. Wislicency says the Vaadah people can be trusted. Even that swine Eichmann seems to think so. And so, we are also willing to work that way."

Pauer considered for a moment.

"It can be arranged. There will be no problem."

"At the usual place then? Hansi's? Say, in three days?"

"I will send you a Hungarian doctor and his bodyguard."

The German smiled. "Our man will be immediately identifiable. He is only partially intact, and as a result has no particular love for the Ivans."

"Agreed then," said Pauer.

"Now, shall we go for a walk in the woods? I understand that the cinquefoil is out."

"An expert?" Pauer said, surprised.

"Flowers are a hobby of mine," said the German.

"A hobby . . ." repeated Pauer.

Zurich

Stropp was soaking in the deep steel tub in the hotel bathroom when the phone began to ring. He swore under his breath and climbed out, pulled a towel off the rack, and struggled into the bedroom. Of all the damned times for Ellsworth to call; he'd told the man not to bother him until after breakfast.

But it wasn't Ellsworth. Felix Landau was on the line.

Something, he said, was wrong. Terribly, terribly wrong.

Stropp dressed as rapidly as he could. His mouth was dry and he had difficulty buttoning his shirt. What the hell did Landau mean, something was "terribly wrong"? He'd been checking the papers for days now and hadn't said a word. Everything had been calm, orderly. No problems. Stropp had gone walking in the botanical gardens, had taken the railway up to the Uetliberg and looked at the city from the heights. He'd sent a cable to Trilling through the embassy in Berne. His plane tickets back to New York had been confirmed already.

What the hell did Landau mean—*now*—that something was "terribly wrong"? The son of a bitch . . .

Landau was waiting for him in the foyer of the hotel, sunk deep in an armchair by a stand of ferns. Without a word, the two men went outside and turned along the terrace overlooking the quay and the steamer berths. It was a bright morning and the surface of the Zürichsee shone like a polished silver dish.

"It wasn't enough money for you?" said Stropp. "Is that it? You want more money?" He sensed a trap, yet he saw genuine dismay scrawled all over the Jew's face.

"We all make mistakes, Herr Stropp. You must understand, I have been away from this for so long. It's more than five years since I was in a laboratory. Perhaps you should not have relied on me."

Stropp's mind was racing now. The Jew had what he wanted. What was he trying to pull? What could he possibly gain by trying to back out now? Nothing. It didn't make sense. He didn't like it at all, not one bit.

Maybe there really *was* something wrong. Maybe Landau had found a real gap, a mistake or a critical omission in the data. After what they'd pulled at Rotterdam, he wouldn't put anything past the men of Northwest 7.

"Sit, Herr Stropp, I will explain it to you. It has to do with an element of the basic process. Something I alone was working on at the time they . . . removed me."

Stropp began to sweat. He leaned out over the terrace railing and averted his face.

"We are talking, Herr Stropp, about the process by which the copolymerization of the butadiene with the styrene is to be achieved. The emulsion process—there is a serious doubt in my mind concerning the oil extension procedure. The equipment—"

"You realize," Stropp interrupted coldly, trying desperately to control his rising temper, "that I don't know *what the hell* you're talking about. I'm a patent lawyer. I know something about chemistry, certainly. But nothing about synthesis. If I did, I wouldn't need you to begin with."

"But surely you understand at least the basic process that is involved. The addition of the antioxidant to the blending tank must be carefully controlled. The oil must—"

"What is it you're trying to say?"

Landau took a deep breath. He reached into his pocket and, to Stropp's astonishment, took out an envelope.

"You will find here the payment that you gave me, Herr Stropp. In full. Also the agreement that Schmitz and Ter Meer signed. I cannot accept any of this."

Stropp's hand froze. He pushed the envelope away.

"I doubt the equipment, Herr Stropp. The couplings from the antioxidant tank to—"

"The equipment? Why aren't the formulas enough for you? Are the formulas all right?"

"Like so many other things in science, Herr Stropp, having an idea that is theoretically sound is one thing and making it actually work is quite another." He thrust the envelope at Stropp again.

Stropp backed away as though the whole thing might burst into flames like Creüsa's wedding dress.

"What are you telling me?" he asked thickly. "Say it plainly, damn you." He could see the whole thing suddenly slipping away from him. The shares in Hydro-Arc, the seat on the board of directors, the lucrative law practice after the war, the fees from Criterion. All of it.

"I have to see the equipment," Landau said. "That is what I am saying. The papers are not enough. Not if you wish to make sure that you are not being fooled again. I *must* see the equipment. Only then can we be sure."

"You're crazy. Jesus, you Jews are all crazy. How can you see the equipment, for God's sake?"

"You must arrange for me to go there, to the plant."

Stropp was sweating a flood now. He rubbed his hands together convulsively. "Just like that? Pick up the phone and arrange a guided tour for you? Let you go in there, to the plant, and take a look? My God, you *are* insane."

"It's the only way," Landau said softly. "The blending-tank valve system is clearly suspect."

"The hell with the blending-tank valve system, Landau. Either you're lying or you really have gone crazy."

"As you like," said Landau calmly, putting the envelope between Stropp's hands. "You understand, of course, that this means as much to me in my own poor way as it does to you in yours. It is *my* future too. But if you do not believe me, very well, nothing more needs to be said, does it? Remember, you sought *me* out. It was not the other way around."

He turned sharply and began to walk away.

"Wait," Stropp called after him.

"Yes?"

"You're telling the truth?"

"As I see it, yes. There is a distinct possibility, a probability in fact, that the entire antioxidant feed system will not work. Without that, there is *nothing*. The process is worthless."

"Then I don't really have any choice, do I?"

"Neither of us does. Listen . . ." Landau's expression darkened, his hands trembled visibly. "If you think I like the idea of going into that *place* in order to do your dirty work for you, you are very much mistaken. But there is no other way and it simply must be done. Unless you wish to trust Herr Dr. Schragg and his fine friends."

"And if you're right, if the process still doesn't work, do you think they'll let you out again to tell me the news?"

Landau smiled. It was an ugly, unsettling smile that showed crooked yellow teeth with a flash of gold to the right. He nodded.

"Oh yes," he said.

"And why is that? They'd have to be crazy to do that."

"They will. Rest assured, they will."

"You're so sure?"

"Because if the process does not work, then, Herr Stropp . . ."

"Yes?"

"I shall make it work for them."

DOCUMENT

United States War Department to the British Government (1944).

It is not contemplated that units of the armed forces will be employed for the purpose of rescuing victims of enemy oppression unless such rescues are the direct result of military operations conducted with the objective of defeating the armed forces of the enemy.

July 1944
Zurich

The Packard circled the botanical gardens once and headed north along the Pelikanstrasse toward open country.

The three of them sat in the wide front seat, Bor driving, Baranyi in the middle, and Pauer by the door.

"I don't believe it," Miklos said. "It makes absolutely no sense."

"Yet it's true," said Bor. "Their man will be here by tomorrow night."

"But why should they do it?"

"Because they wish to survive. Believe me, they have no particular love for you or for us. But they have seen the word of fire on the wall very clearly, Doctor," said Pauer. "And the word is clear. The word is 'Soviet.' "

Baranyi laughed gratingly. "So the German army is willing to help *us* arrange for the bombing of the rail lines into Oswiecim, to give us the necessary maps and schedules."

"All of it," said Pauer. "In the hope that once the lines are out, all the trains that have been commandeered over their protest to carry Jews to the death camps will be free once again to carry munitions and supplies to the armies facing the Russians." Pauer put a hand firmly on Miklos's arm. "And they trust no one but you, the Vaadah. Can you understand? How the world has turned upside down."

Bor guided the car onto a narrow mountain road. The slopes rose green and peaceful on either side, dotted with wildflowers. Cattle grazed in buttery clumps on the steep meadows. The air was fresh and cool, even in summer.

"With the maps in hand, we can manage extremely convincing forgeries of SHAEF targeting proposals," Bor said calmly. "I begin to think that they may actually believe you, the gentlemen at I.G."

Miklos nodded. "Those, together with the other details. The documents from Washington will be in tomorrow's pouch. Thank God the man at the Zurich consulate is more cooperative than that swine in Berne."

"Only because he doesn't understand what's going on," said Pauer glumly.

Baranyi had no answer to that; besides, it was probably true.

"The American has already obtained the necessary stationery to forge the letters. Grunewald has been most cooperative. Not only has he had a shock to his moral system but I think he smells a real scandal. The two together make a powerful incentive to do what is right."

"I am even beginning to think that it just might work," sighed Baranyi.

Pauer took a deep breath. "Insanity. The entire business is insanity."

"Colonel Eichmann offers to trade Jews for trucks. The Germans murder ten thousand a day in a factory designed scientifically for that sole purpose, industrial concerns whose nations are at each other's throats carry on their business as though nothing at all was happening and plan calmly for future division of markets, and you call what *we* do insane?"

Pauer shook his head and said nothing. What, after all, was there to say?

DOCUMENT

Extract from Weekly Report No. 30, December 15–21, 1941 —I.G. Farben/Auschwitz.

On this occasion the mistreatment of the inmates on the working sites of the firm Schultz, which is still continuing, was discussed repeatedly. Herr Wernicke expressed his very serious objections to these occurrences and his fear that the German employees would not put up with it very much longer. We will talk about this to the commandant once again. . . .

The work, particularly of the Poles and inmates, continues to leave much room for improvement. The amount of sickness constitutes a great nuisance. * * * The lack of discipline at work of the Polish workers is also shocking. Many of the workers work a maximum of 3–4 days per week. Every type of pressure, even sending them to the concentration camp, remains without result. In this respect, it is only to be regretted that the construction management itself has no disciplinary powers. Our experience so far has shown that only brute force has any effect on these people. But this is absolutely taboo here, as incidentally it is in the Government General too. As is known, the commandmant always argues that as far as the treatment of inmates is concerned, it is impossible to get any work done without corporal punishment.

Apart from the many other difficulties which prevail on the construction site, caused by present conditions, this situation must also be mentioned. There is no doubt that it will again and again have a deterrent effect on the schedules and will increase costs considerably. Although, until now, we have been able to keep the standard prices comparatively low, on the basis of our experience, we feel that it will be very difficult to maintain this for any length of time, particularly since the firms employed up to the present have now also had their experience over a period of several months.

Rheinfall, Switzerland

They met this time in the courtyard of Laufen Castle, above the cataracts of the Rhine falls. They sat in the restaurant which had been created in the castle proper, looking out over the illuminated spume which Goethe had once called the "source of the oceans."

Stropp stared across the table at Helmut Schragg. A plate of consommé lay cooling in front of him. Schragg was toying with his wineglass. By his elbow was a small envelope.

The photographs.

Very clear: perfect shots taken with the best Leica equipment. The faces were precisely in focus. Unmistakable.

For the first time, Stropp was extremely uncomfortable in Schragg's presence. It was the photographs, of course. He had put them entirely out of his mind during the past few days. Now, here they were.

He wondered how Schragg was going to take the news.

"So," said the German, nudging the envelope, "for the moment the photos remain with me. An interesting souvenir. No more. But I am becoming impatient. Nervous, if you will. There was another raid last night. On the refineries near Brüx this time. Very near, Herr Stropp. Only about two hundred miles away."

"Close," agreed Stropp.

"Very close, Herr Stropp."

"We must move very cautiously. I'm sure you can understand that, Dr. Schragg. The risks are considerable."

"For both of us, I imagine. I would not care to think what would happen to us if the Gestapo should become involved. Every day that we delay it becomes more of a possibility."

Stropp could hardly argue with that. The worst that could happen to him would be a trip to prison. Schragg clearly had other, more serious things to worry about. Still waiting for the right moment, Stropp temporized.

"You've nothing to complain of," he said. "We're honoring our part of the bargain even though we haven't made it yet. As you see, no bombers have gone anywhere near the plant."

"For the moment, that is true." Schragg's face relaxed.

Stropp leaned forward. The spray from the falls rose up beyond the tinted windows of the restaurant. The searchlights touched the edge of the spume and struck a rainbow against the night sky. The roar of the waters was so loud that they could barely hear each other. Schragg, irritated, leaned forward himself.

"There is a problem I must discuss with you," Stropp said.

"A problem?"

"Landau isn't satisfied. He's convinced that the equipment for the antioxidant feed system won't function."

For a second Schragg did not register what Stropp had said; then, all at once, his face darkened so that Stropp thought he was going to have an apoplectic seizure.

"That filthy little Jew? He's lying, of course. You don't actually believe him, do you?"

"Why should he lie? For what purpose?"

"What does he want now? More money? Another 'agreement' from us?"

Stropp took a breath and told him.

What Landau wanted was to go to the Monowitz plant and inspect the equipment. Only then would he commit himself.

Schragg was losing control. The veins stood out on his high forehead as though molded there in ropes of clay. His cheeks flushed purple.

"No, no, no, this will not do. This is insane," he said in a suffocated voice. "Insane for us, insane for you as well. We have been very lucky so far. Everything has been done discreetly. But to bring this—this *Landau* to Monowitz, with that insufferable man, Neimann, skulking about? With all the risks? No, it's out of the question."

"Nevertheless, my hands are tied. I would like to believe you, Dr. Schragg, believe me. It would make things much easier for me. But why should I, after Rotterdam?"

"You prefer to believe a lying little Jew?"

Stropp nodded. "That's the way it is, I'm afraid."

"I see, I see. That is the way it is." Schragg lapsed into a long silence during which his fingers worked the edges of his napkin to shreds. Suddenly he smiled; it was an ugly spectacle. "We must trust each other, Herr Stropp."

Stropp shook his head. "Can you do it?"

"I *must,* Herr Stropp. You leave me no alternative. I will arrange it. Provided Northwest Seven consents."

"As you say, we must trust each other, Dr. Schragg."

"How can we not? You have what *we* want, we have what *you* want. I have the photographs, you have the agreements we signed. Each of us holds the power of life and death over the other. An equitable arrangement, wouldn't you say? Most equitable. It gives us both the incentives we need. You have no interest in going to prison and I have no desire to be beheaded. *Prosit,* Herr Stropp," Schragg said, lifting his wineglass.

Stropp had almost forgotten that the waiter had also poured a glass for him. He fumbled for it, almost knocking the glass over.

"*Prosit,*" he said.

Zurich

The bar near the Bürkliplatz was small, inexpensive, and displaced in time, the kind of place at which refugees inevitably gathered. At the rear a small man with delicate, almost feminine features and prematurely white hair played the piano and sang in a soft, lulling voice:

> "*Reich mir zum Abschied noch einmal die Hände*
> good night . . . good night . . . good night . . .
> *Schön war das Marchen und ist es zum Ende,*
> good night . . . good night . . . good night . . .*"*

Kagan's face was a mask. Not a flicker of emotion showed. His eyes hardly moved as he searched the room. Baranyi had never been able to see well in the dark. Itzhak Kagan could see like a cat.

The room was heavy with cigar smoke. A faint odor of disinfectant mingled with the steamy damp of Zürcher beer.

"Over there," Kagan whispered. "That must be him."

Miklos could not see where. The piano player went on, sighing "good night, good night, good night," making the word "night" into two syllables, long, drawn out; a lament.

"Good ny-eet, good ny-yeet, good ny-yeeeet."

Kagan was right. The man he had indicated was sitting in a booth by the back wall, just behind the piano player. He alone, of all the people in the place, seemed alert, watching. Waiting for someone.

They went over.

Miklos spoke the arranged signal.

"Do you care for Strauss?"

"I prefer Paul Lincke," the man said. He looked very military close up, and very tired.

Kagan and Miklos sat down. The man in the booth had chosen his location wisely. They were close enough to the piano player so that the music would effectively cover everything they said. No one else could possibly hear them. Hidden microphones would be useless.

The man was stocky, gray-faced, powerfully built, in his mid-forties. He wore his civilian clothes uneasily. His eyes darted about the room as though to make sure no one had followed them in.

No one, at least, whom he recognized.

Then, finally, he allowed the lines of his face to relax a bit. There was a bottle of whiskey on the table and three glasses. He pushed the bottle over.

Kagan poured.

"*Santé,*" said the German.

Miklos drank silently, only nodding in response. Kagan did not drink.

When they had put the empty glasses down, Miklos leaned slightly forward and asked:

"Your credentials?"

"There were to be no names."

"Understood. But you can also understand that we must be cautious."

"Our concern for caution," said the German, "is mutual." He moved his left hand out onto the table. In the dark, neither Miklos nor Kagan had noticed before that the hand was artificial. Wood, with a black leather glove covering most of it.

"Stalingrad," said the German. "Eleventh Corps, Sixth Army. We were the last of Paulus's boys to give up. I didn't, as you can see." He attempted a smile, failing markedly. "As a result, I have a keen appreciation of the problems involved. And also a wooden left foot, if you'd care to see that as well."

Miklos exchanged glances with Kagan. "Enough," he said.

"And you? What have you to offer besides a decadent taste for Strauss?"

It had not occurred to Miklos that more would be needed. He hesitated. Kagan leaned suddenly across the table, pushing his arm forward, just as the German had done.

"An arm for an arm," he said and shoved his sleeve back. There was a blue number tattooed just inside the elbow.

"Sachsenhausen?" said the German quietly.

"Very good. *Very* good."

"One must know such things," the German said.

"Are we agreed then that for the moment at least we must trust each other?"

"Under the circumstances . . ."

"You've been paid," said Miklos, half a statement, half a question.

The German's face grew dark. "I would not do such a thing for money, you bastard."

"Why then?"

He sighed. "The war is over. We all know that. The only question is whether we surrender to the Americans and the English and somehow survive, or let our bones be ground to fertilizer by the Russians. We prefer the possibility of survival, however faint, that the West offers. It seems in our own best interests to do anything we can to hold the Russians back long enough to allow the Americans to overwhelm us from the opposite side. A grotesque logic, but a logic nevertheless, yes?"

"And the railroad lines? How do they—"

"Please, is there really any need to go over this yet again?" The German grew agitated. "I bring you what you want. It serves both our purposes. Why must you Jews forever be asking questions?"

Kagan smiled faintly. Miklos shook his head. There was no need. The German was right. There was no need for questions.

If the rail lines into Oswiecim were destroyed, the rolling stock that had been preempted by the SS for their nonstop transports would be freed up for military use. On the eastern front. That was part of the understanding. A bizarre echo of the deal that Eichmann had offered Joel Brand in Budapest only the month before: trucks for Jewish lives. Trucks to be used only against the Russians. The Americans and the English had professed to be shocked and had refused. The Vaadah could not afford even the pretense of such a dubious morality.

If, in fact, there was any question of morality involved at all.

"Where are the papers?" Kagan asked.

The pianist was singing a tango now.

> *"Ich hab an dich gedacht, als die tango notturno*
> *Zwischen Nacht und Morgen, von Ferne geklagt. . . ."*

The German took hold of his left hand. The index finger came off. It was hollow. Miklos could see a little roll of film curled up inside.

"It has its uses," the German said grimly. "The ladies, also, seem to find it very romantic."

Kagan took the little roll of film and put it in his pocket without looking at it.

"It's all there?" Miklos asked. "And accurate?"

"All the junctions are marked. The lines are precisely located. The switching yards are shown. We have indicated the points at which the system is most vulnerable, in particular those which will take the longest to rebuild if they are destroyed."

"The gas chambers and the crematoria?"

"Also located exactly. By coordinates. You could lay artillery fire on them and score a hit with the first shell."

"What guarantee have we?"

"None," the German said. "Other than this: I'm going back there myself now, to join General Model. If the information I have given you is not accurate, if you do not knock out the rail lines into the camp and restore to us the rolling stock that lunatic Eichmann has commandeered, then I expect Marshal Konev will be having us all for breakfast within the month. I do not want to die, gentlemen. Not now. Not for what's left, and not for such an obscene reason."

It was insane, Miklos thought. Yet it was just as Pauer had promised. The German army was conducting its own private war with the SS, trying desperately to salvage enough equipment from the extermination operations with which to fight a war.

To hold back the Russians for at least a little while. Long enough to allow the western powers to conquer Germany.

They got up to go.

The pianist had shifted to a waltz from *Frau Luna.* Some of the patrons were humming along.

Kagan chuckled grimly. "Lincke . . . you see? Everyone likes Lincke."

The German was not amused. He poured himself another whiskey and looked away.

Morning. The black medical bag sat on the table, open. Kagan could see that it was still full and gave off, as such bags always did, the inevitable mingled odors of medicine and pain. He had not seen the bag for over two years. Not since Baranyi had first come to the Vaadah offices in Zurich.

Miklos sat back, blowing smoke, his eyes partly shut.

"Landau's employer—I should say his former employer, the pharmacist—was most helpful. No questions asked. You see, he too is a *Landsmann.*"

Baranyi pushed the little brown glass bottle he had been toying with across the table toward Kagan. It had a glass stopper of the old-fashioned kind, tightly fitting and large enough to get a good grip on.

"You're sure you can manage it?" Miklos asked.

"The head chef at the Baur-au-Lac is from Lodz. Bor says he's absolutely reliable. The only thing we have to worry about is whether they've got a white jacket my size." Kagan tried to laugh, but the sound came out like a muted groan. He stared at the little bottle.

"What's in it, Miklos?"

"Exactly what's needed. We want to put this man Stropp out of the way so that he can't interfere, yes? But we must do it in a way that will look perfectly natural and arouse no suspicions, yes? Therefore, we cannot kill him; that would certainly frighten the wolves away. So we must simply incapacitate him."

"But what is in the bottle?"

"Foxglove, Itzhak. Tincture of digitalis leaf. A very ordinary compound. Every doctor uses it. It contains four glucosides, of which three act vigorously on the heart. A total of from twelve to twenty ccs, given in successive doses over the next few days, will do the job. It is absorbed very slowly. By the time we have reached the twenty-cc level, he will begin to feel nauseous. He will perhaps start vomiting. His pulse will become very slow and very irregular. He will suffer from fainting spells. He will probably collapse."

"A heart attack? I thought that digitalis . . ."

Miklos smiled. "Yes, in small doses it serves to counter some of the effects of a heart attack. But in the amounts we will administer it will do just the opposite. If enough is given, it will even kill. So we must be careful. If it is done right, with precision, by the time they get him to the hospital both he and anyone who examines him will believe that he's had a serious heart attack. If they use an electrocardiograph on him—assuming that they have a machine—the readings will most certainly confirm the visible symptoms. There will be no question in anyone's mind and no reason to look further. Particularly with a man of Stropp's age and profession. Lawyers are very prone to heart attacks. It will seem the most natural thing in the world."

"How long will he be in the hospital?"

"The half-life of the compound is a few weeks. The symptoms will persist. If I was an attending physician I wouldn't let him out in anything under twenty days."

Kagan nodded grimly. "By which time . . ."

"By which time we will have gotten in and, I hope, out of Poland, with our work done."

"And how long will it take for the drug to be effective?"

"He will feel nothing at all until we approach the critical cumulative quantity. Then, from the last dose, it should take eight to twelve hours, possibly less, depending on how good his kidneys are. It will hit him quite suddenly. He will panic, I'm sure."

"I'll call Bor at once. When should we start?"

"As soon as possible. As I say, it will take two or three days of cumulative doses to reach the critical level, which will give us just enough time to complete our arrangements."

Kagan took out a few crumpled papers: order slips for the

breakfasts Stropp had regularly had sent up to his room at the Baur-au-Lac. "The man from Lodz was very obliging," he said. "What sort of things does he eat for breakfast? The tincture has a faintly bitter taste. We must select the right medium." His eye ran up and down the scrawled orders. "Yes, here, in the orange marmalade. He has orange marmalade every day. He'll never notice it in there."

"In the marmalade then."

"And also in anything he drinks. Have you spoken to the man at the hotel bar? Is Stropp a heavy drinker?"

"Every afternoon at about five he has at least two or three whiskeys."

Miklos nodded. It was going to be very easy.

At least this part of it.

Colonel Bor leaned over the table and adjusted his glasses and then the overhead light, which he brought to bear full on the out-spread map. Directly over the area marked in small black letters: *Oswiecim.*

Baranyi watched, fascinated, as Bor drew on the celluloid overlay with a large compass and red grease pencil a series of inter-secting areas which perfectly matched those shown beneath the overlay on the map itself.

"Here you see the bases," Bor said, indicating with the pointed end of the dividers the origins of the arcs. "The Eighth Air Force here, the Ninth here at Sunninghill Park. The aircraft are all heavy bombers of the Fortress and Liberator types. All have a range in excess of thirty-four hundred miles. For the bombers to reach Oswiecim is no problem. The camp is also within range of the Fifteenth Air Force units in Italy and the Twelfth as well. We know from our people in London that even now plans are being drawn for strikes at the refineries at Blechhammer, which is only—here —some seventy kilometers away. No, it is not the range of the bombers that is a problem. The problem is the range of the fighter escort. They cannot make the round trip and must refuel at Soviet bases. But the Soviets have refused to allow this. They say *they* must have control of all bombing targets in their area of operations. Perhaps there are other reasons why they too wish to keep the bombers away from Oswiecim. In any event, this may no longer be a problem. There are rumors that the Americans have found a way to stretch the range of their escort fighters so as to be able to provide cover to and from the targets. But even that is of little importance now. The Germans have no defensive fighter strength in this area at all. Only flak guns, and fighters are no protection against flak. Hence the issue of the range of the escort fighters is also no longer of importance." He pushed a typewritten list across the table. "Here, gentlemen, are the targeting proposals."

Baranyi scanned the list: Blechhammer, as Bor had said, but also Odertal, Morovska-Ostrava, Bohumin, and Trzebinia.

He gingerly lifted the targeting schedule. It was official-looking enough; it had been borrowed from the files of the London office of USSTAF, the United States Strategic Air Force, Unified Command, by a Polish intelligence operative, copied perfectly, and then returned.

Baranyi hesitated. "But to give them *this* . . ."

"Would be to tell them nothing they don't already know. Ever since the bombing of Leuna it has been obvious that these plants must eventually be struck. The list does not say *when* the raids will be. It only says that there *will* be raids, which is already well known and inevitable in any event. Hence no harm will be done, but it will add considerably to the persuasiveness of your argument. As will the maps."

The maps showed the targets listed, the rail lines, the plants at Auschwitz, the industrial complex within the main camp itself, consisting of the Krupp and Siemens works and the I.G. installation directly to the west. And they were all authentic. Bor's forgers had done wonders with the microfilms provided by the Wehrmacht courier. They were perfect. It would take weeks of chemical analysis to detect the tampering.

"A strike could also be accomplished," Bor went on, "with medium bombers. The distance, as you see, is only a little over twelve hundred miles, round trip. There are refueling stations available in the Adriatic, at Vis in particular. Last week the oil fields at Ploesti were attacked, not even using medium bombers, but with fighter planes, the P-38s, or *zweispitzen Teufels,* as the Germans, with good reason, call them. There are a dozen different ways it could be done, and the men at I.G. will need no detailed explanations. They are all too keenly aware of the fact that it *can* be done. The only thing they count on is that it will *not* be done. And you will disabuse them of that notion with these." He pointed to the maps and the target schedules. "And the material your American associate will obtain for you."

Baranyi nodded. Eisner was still working in Grunewald's office under Kagan's watchful eye, preparing bogus letters from Stropp to the Criterion home office in Wilmington and interoffice memoranda between Trilling and his liaison to the operations division of the War Department in Washington. In the letters Stropp complained bitterly of another double-cross. The memoranda confirmed an intention to withdraw protection. The Vaadah in New York had sent a copy of a memorandum by Pehle of the WRB to the Assistant Secretary of War, McCloy, detailing an attack by English fighter bombers on a Gestapo prison in France; the prisoners had been kept on the upper floors of the building and the raid had been so skillfully carried out that only one prisoner had been killed. The rest had escaped. The building, thanks to the availability of detailed plans, had literally been taken apart from the ground floor up by low-level bombing and machine-gunning. Pehle suggested that the same be done for the gas chambers and the crematoria. A copy of the report had arrived in the courier's pouch at the American consulate in Zurich, thanks to Henderson in particular.

It was the kind of precise detail that would be most persuasive to the Germans. As was the forged reply by McCloy rejecting the idea and opting for high-altitude saturation bombing.

Baranyi looked across at Landau; the chemist had sat there in stony silence, taking it all in. As it became possible to distinguish faces again, as Bor raised the shade on the room's single window and admitted a pale wash of afternoon sunlight hazed by a fine summer rain, Baranyi saw that the expression on Landau's face had not changed one bit.

It was almost as if the man were already dead.

"And so," Bor was saying, "it will be clear enough to them that it can be done. All that remains is to convince them that it *will* be done. Then they will have no alternative but to move the critical equipment. After which, gentlemen, there will be absolutely no reason for the Criterion people to interfere further. After which, gentlemen, we can also be sure that that hellish place *will certainly be destroyed.*"

Miklos watched critically as Landau left the room, alone. Bor understood the narrow, squinting glance at once and smiled.

"Nothing to fear, Doctor. I have two men on him, wherever he goes. Semkowski and Prus. Very good men. You met Semkowski at the lake the other night. And, by the way, Landau's phone has an intercept on it. We record everything."

Baranyi lit a cigarette. "I was wondering just how far you expected me to trust such a person."

"Not far, but a little, Doctor. A little. Not so much as to be foolish. We must hedge our bets, like all reasonable gamblers."

"I can't understand the man. To me, such a mind is incomprehensible."

"Oh, he's easy enough to understand. You simply need practice with the type. I've had plenty of it, and believe me, he's nothing unique. He's much easier to understand than some of the others, I'd say."

"The others?"

"Sit down for a minute, Doctor. There's something else I wanted to tell you. But not with Landau in the room."

Bor pushed a bottle of vishniac across the table. Miklos declined. Bor shrugged patiently. "As you wish. Really, it's very good. Particularly for chilly weather." Bor sat back, lacing his hands across his lap. "You realize you will probably never come back from this trip."

"It must be attempted," Baranyi said.

"I know, I know."

"Do you? Perhaps you think you do. Perhaps that's enough."

"You think that you Jews have a monopoly on suffering? Were you in Warsaw when the Stukas came, Doctor? Have you read the reports from the camps thoroughly? Do you know how many Christian Poles have been murdered in those places. Do you know how many have died so far in this war? My wife, for example."

Miklos was very quiet in reply: "My wife too was killed. I did not mean it that way, Colonel."

"No, I thought not. You're tired, as we are all tired."

"Dead."

"Not quite yet, I don't think. And I will do my best to put off that time, no matter how reckless you wish to be. You are a good man, Doctor."

"For a Jew?"

Bor did not respond. Miklos had touched a nerve: the Pole straightened, pulled himself up erect.

"Listen to me, Baranyi. I am going to tell you something now that may be very important to you. In Oswiecim . . ."

Baranyi leaned forward, his weariness so great that he thought he would collapse entirely.

Bor went on. "This may come as a surprise to you, Doctor. But we have a man inside the camp."

"A prisoner?"

"Hardly, Doctor. Surely you know that many in the Abwehr and even a few in the SS itself have assisted us and others like us in our endeavors. Some do it for the most laudatory of motives—patriotism, a sense of outraged morality. There are not many of them, and they are the least trustworthy in the end. Self-interest, as in the case of the man who brought the plans, this too is a motive. Most do it simply for the money or because they know how the war must ultimately end and they wish to survive. In Auschwitz, there is such a man. An officer, high up in the SS."

"That's impossible," Miklos whispered.

"It is true, let me assure you. Please, don't abuse your intelligence or mine by thinking that such things cannot happen. They do, even in these insane times. This man is paid and paid well. Why does he accept? I don't know. Greed, guilt? It could be for any one of a thousand reasons. He came to us through the Slovaks, through Pauer and Weissmandel's network. Suffice it that he is there. He has done us good service before and is absolutely reliable. It was through this man that the maps were obtained. He arranged it all, and, as you saw, very quickly, too. So now do you believe me? Good. He will serve us again, as we may need him. He works as much for his own benefit as for ours. If it becomes necessary, he may be able to help you too. But only in an extreme situation."

"This man—how will I know him?"

"You won't. It would be foolish for his name to be known unless it is absolutely necessary. And if that happens, he will find you. He's been advised."

"A paid agent."

"If you like."

"I don't. Not at all. If this man knows who we are, if he has any idea . . ."

"He's trustworthy, Doctor. He's too well paid not to be."

"Paid by you?"

"With good Swiss francs, deposited to his name in a good Swiss bank. Along with a few hundred other good, numbered accounts that belong to other good, cooperative Nazi officers. He is also paid, by the way, by the Czechs and, I believe, by the Russians. You see, he too has hedged his bets."

"How much does he know?"

"Only that you may come and that we, all of us, wish you to succeed in your mission. He believes—and I doubt that anyone will disabuse him—that the 'all of us' even includes the gentlemen in Berlin and General Thomas's VW *Gruppe* in particular."

"Do you expect him to involve himself directly?"

Bor shook his head. "Not unless it is absolutely necessary. But he will be watching. At all times." Bor smiled his confessor's smile. "Good, now you know. Will you reconsider? This is good Polish vishniac. Paprocki found a case of it only last week, hidden away in the subcellar."

The German courier was one of the men who had been with Schragg in the forest above Rheinfall. He was a stocky, whey-faced man without a trace of humor, and with more than a little of the butcher's apprentice about him. A little after six, just as the clerks were preparing to close up for the day, he appeared at Grunewald's office with his message. The Paradeplatz was crowded with people going home. On the walls of the news kiosk at the corner of Banhofstrasse and the Nuenhof it was possible to see the huge black headlines that had been pasted up. SOVIETS TAKE MINSK. ALLIED TROOPS ON THE OUTSKIRTS OF CAEN.

No longer, Grunewald thought, was there any question of the final outcome. What really mattered now was what would happen afterward. That was the sole legitimate concern.

Grunewald dismissed the courier and phoned at once to the Baur-au-Lac, asking Stropp to meet him in the garden.

When he arrived, the doors of the hotel's main salon were open to let in the cool evening air. A little orchestra was playing Chevalier's latest, "La Symphonie des semelles en bois."

Stropp was sitting in a wicker chair, studying the headlines. They were the same as had been pasted up on the side of the kiosk. The British were descending on Caen in strength. Over a million men were ashore in Normandy. Zakharov's Belorussian front had swept General Busch's Army Group Center from Minsk and was debouching into Lithuania.

An attendant brought over another chair, and Grunewald sat down without a word and handed Stropp the tissue slip in its small blue envelope.

Stropp read quickly. He seemed oddly relieved. A great responsibility had devolved on him. It was all his and he was entirely on his own. There was no possibility whatever of going back now.

All of the arrangements had been made and confirmed. Director Schmitz regretted that his friends still entertained doubts concerning the venture, but he would do his best to satisfy everyone. Certainly he recognized the imperatives of prudence. A party would be received at the Monowitz installation. Up to three persons could be accommodated without difficulty. A stay of a week had been arranged. Any longer would be incautious. Dr. Krauch joined Director Schmitz in hoping that this would prove adequate for the examination. All necessary technical assistance would, of course, be provided. The safety of the experts was guaranteed. Security arrangements had been made through the highest authorities. Dr. Krauch hoped that upon the party's return arrangements could be concluded rapidly to everyone's "mutual advantage."

"Grunewald, what do you think, *really*?"

"It would not be proper for me to express an opinion. After all, I represent both sides joined together to constitute a third, distinct entity. An entity which well may have interests quite different from those of either of your people alone or I.G."

"Bullshit," said Stropp firmly. "I asked you, what do you really think?" Stropp took another sip of his whiskey. His tone had turned suddenly nasty. "Answer me, damn it. My neck is on the line, isn't it? I have a right to your opinion."

Grunewald looked him up and down. Stropp did not seem well. He appeared flushed. There was a little line of perspiration along his hairline. His eyes were dull, occluded.

More than that, Stropp now appeared to Grunewald in an entirely different light. Grunewald knew he would never again be able to see him as he had before.

Grunewald finally shook his head.

"You are doing all that anyone could do under the circumstances. Is that what you wish me to say?"

"Is that what you think?"

"I do."

"And will it be enough?"

"That, my dear Stropp, is another question entirely. And one, thank God, which I don't have to answer."

One lawyer's office was pretty much like the next, no matter what city they were in. To Baranyi's eye, Grunewald's chambers seemed no different from those he had seen in Budapest or Warsaw or, in films, in London or America. Perhaps a little neater. There was no doubt that the Swiss were generally neater. The files were nicely arranged, the papers neatly stacked, the lawbooks regularly dusted. Otherwise there was a sameness about the place that Baranyi found oddly comforting. He was considerably more at ease than he had expected to be.

Across the conference table from him sat a distinctly ill-at-ease Henry Stropp. Next to him was Eisner, doing his best not to seem nervous. Grunewald presided from the head of the table, speaking lazily in his gruff *Schweizerdeutsch* as though he were addressing a class of students. He hadn't so much as blinked when he had introduced Baranyi as an associate and an expert in Swiss patent law.

"Of course there can be no question of my traveling with you, you understand, Herr Stropp. I could not possibly leave Zurich for any length of time. On the other hand, our German client insists that some member of my firm be with the party. As a 'neutral,' you see, to protect *everyone's* interests. The interests of Chemihold, that is, which is all of your interests and at the same time not the interest of any one of you. As for myself, I certainly agree. Herr Baranyi is a Hungarian national, speaks excellent German, and is as good an attorney as I am or ever will be."

At first Stropp had protested. There was no need. It would be dangerous. It was too late in the proceedings to involve strangers. Eisner was perfectly capable of handling things alone.

To each of these objections Grunewald had a ready answer. There was indeed a need, and to establish it beyond any possibility of argument, he pushed forward a note on I.G. letterhead stating the case and signed by Carl Krauch. A perfect forgery. Stropp looked at it for only a second, no more. He did not wish to embarrass himself by laboring over the German. The letterhead and the familiar signature would have to suffice. As for the danger, what possible danger could there be to a Zurich lawyer who held both Swiss and Hungarian passports? Herr Baranyi would be treated as a guest, an ally. Nor was it a question of bringing in a third person at a late stage of the proceedings. As his associate, Baranyi had been privy to everything that had been done respecting the Criterion —I.G. Chemihold *Gemeinschaft*. Since the Rotterdam conference. Moreover, it had been through his diligent work that Landau had first been located. In the service of his clients, he had developed certain connections with various refugee organizations and a number of Jewish groups with offices in Zurich and Berne, and it was these very connections that had proven to be invaluable in "l'affaire Landau."

Finally, there was no question of Eisner being offended. He had, of course, known Herr Baranyi for over two years and had already expressed himself as being most willing to have the Hungarian accompany them.

As Grunewald talked on and on, Baranyi could not help stealing a glance at the photo of himself, on suitably aged paper, that had been provided by Bor's staff and now hung with the portraits of Grunewald's other associates on the conference-room wall.

From the photo, Baranyi's gaze returned to Stropp. He found that he could not take his eyes off the man.

How could such people as Stropp exist? How could they live with themselves? Stropp was not only now an accomplice in the murder of anonymous millions but he had taken a direct part in the murder of Zoltan Peshko. In all likelihood it was Stropp himself who had ordered the killing.

Or at least so Eisner had said.

He would pay for it all. In due course. When the time was right.

And he would begin paying very soon. Very soon now, Stropp would be in the Zurich Staatshospital, probably in intensive care and, if he were conscious at all, in fear for his immortal soul.

"I don't mind telling you," Stropp was saying, "I don't like this at all. Not one little bit. If Trilling had even the slightest idea that we—"

"But of course he doesn't, does he? And he won't unless you tell him. All he will know is that Henry Stropp was sent to do a job and did it very well. We shall all benefit from that, Herr Stropp." Grunewald sat back and gestured with his cigarette. "Do you realize how amusing that is, Herr Stropp? *You* are concerned that your superiors would disapprove of what you are about to do, and yet at the same time you recognize that they will be most pleased if you succeed. I don't envy you the ambiguity of your position, Herr Stropp. Not at all."

"There's nothing ambiguous about it, Max. As you say, I'm right in the middle and I know it perfectly well. And you, Eisner, if you think this is amusing, you'd better think again."

"Believe me, sir," said Eisner quietly. "I don't think any of this is in the least amusing."

"See that you don't," Stropp shot back. He coughed, already wheezing from Grunewald's cigarette smoke. "Can't you put that thing out?"

"A nervous habit."

"We're all nervous," said Baranyi. "This is not going to be pleasant for anyone."

"I want you to understand one thing, Mr. Baranyi. You keep in the background, do you follow me? You will do nothing unless you're *asked* to do something."

"I understand my own responsibilities, sir. I will know how and when to discharge them."

"See that you do," said Stropp. Then, as though pushing the unpleasantness he himself had generated aside like a completed item on the agenda, he turned to a review of the arrangments.

Grunewald produced his notes. The party would be taken by car to the border. It would be met there by an escort from I.G. in much the same way as had been done at the first meeting. From there they would proceed to the I.G. center at Freiburg and from there

by air to Vienna. The last leg of the trip would be accomplished by
regular passenger train. Air travel that close to the bombing corridors used by the Allies for their strikes at the oil installations along
the eastern reaches of the Danube would be entirely too dangerous,
no matter how carefully planned.

"And you think that they're going to let the three of them in
there to look around, just like that?" said Stropp, the old annoy-
ance returning.

"Yes, *just* like that," said Grunewald. "They don't really have
any choice, do they? You gave them none at all. And quite rightly,
too."

"Damn the whole business," said Stropp.

Grunewald ignored the outburst and went on. Everything had
been arranged. He himself had talked with Dr. Stellner at the
Oswiecim installation. Special quarters had been prepared. The
technical staff was awaiting its guests.

"And . . . oh yes, there is the matter of Herr Eisner's passport.
Just in case. Will a Swiss passport do?"

"I thought you didn't get involved with such things, Max?"

"Ordinarily I don't. But this is an extraordinary situation, isn't
it? After all, I don't want to lose Chemihold as a client."

For the first time, Stropp smiled. This, he understood.

It was an unpleasant smile, for all its blandness. Baranyi thought
that he would greatly enjoy what he would shortly have to do.

Grunewald took a bottle of cognac from a sideboard and pro-
posed a toast to the successful conclusion of the matter.

Baranyi watched carefully as Stropp drank. Sullenly and slowly.

Five ccs in all. It was the third dose in thirty-six hours. Another
five and the cumulative dosage would reach the critical level. Kagan would see to that the next morning.

An odd look passed over Stropp's face. Miklos tensed.

Had he detected the faint, bitter taste? No. It was impossible.
The cognac's own flavor was far too strong.

Grimly, Stropp reached for the bottle and poured himself
another glass, oblivious to the fact that everyone else was drinking
whiskey.

Dose number four.

Stropp hadn't noticed a thing.

DOCUMENT

From I.G. Farben, Work Report/Construction Totals, January 1944.

Buildings Completed: *Bunawerke*
916—Aldol factory
917—Aldol distillation
942—Contact factory
921—Butol distillation
850—Montan plant switchboard
856—Glycol building
854—Oxide factory
922—Butadiene factory

Oswiecim, Poland

The road ran straight as a die through the flat Silesian marshes. It followed the double railroad tracks which led through the vast complex of camps and factories, back past what had been the town of Oswiecim itself, and across the river to the wood-cloistered camp called Birkenau. The watchtowers and the hooked fence posts to which the electrified wire was attached extended as far as the eye could see. Here and there a tall tree, bulbous with unnaturally heavy foliage at the top, naked, bare, and blasted below, projected even above the watchtowers. The railroad tracks ran straight. The grass was pale, almost white. Ashes were strewn everywhere.

At night, with the floodlights on and the glow from within the low buildings of the Birkenau complex igniting the horizon, the entire scene became, to Schragg's eye, Boschian, otherworldly, and—in a way—almost beautiful. During the day it had none of this quality. During the day he could see the endless gray lines of workers moving at a jog trot, carrying heavy bags of cement, railroad ties, steel beams. The voices of the guards could be heard with their perpetual *"links, recht, links, recht."* The lines moved out before dawn and never stopped moving all day. They crawled across the desolate landscape like an endless infestation of slugs.

Schragg lowered the venetian blinds on the side window of the Daimler. There was no need to see it. It was disagreeable and it had nothing to do with him. It was simply the way things were. The *Baujuden* were there to be used up, and they *were* used up. He had thought about it all a great deal. He had no particular dislike of Jews, as long as they stayed away from him. The racial theories of Streicher were to Helmut Schragg no more than the ravings of a pitiful lunatic. No scientist could possibly credit them for a second. On the other hand, no man with any pretense to sanity could openly question them either. If the government had chosen to make them official policy, whether for political reasons or because they really believed them, then they had to be treated as a fact of life, like the incomprehensible anticartel legislation of the Americans or the findings of the geo-economic team that had decided on the Auschwitz site for I.G.'s Buna plant in the first place. The concentration-camp system existed; it would not vanish simply because Dr. Ing. Helmut Schragg disapproved and thought it an inefficient source of labor. Inefficient it was, but it was also cheap. And endless.

Surely the advantages were clear enough. What businessman could possibly think otherwise?

But it galled him to have had to deal with the likes of Felix Landau. Arrogant, demanding, unable to accept his position. Now there, he thought, was a Jew he could really detest.

He had also found the American, Stropp, disagreeable. But for an entirely different reason. Perhaps because he was too much like Schragg himself.

Well, Krauch and the others would have to make it up to him; it had been no easy thing, suddenly having to go out there by himself and see everything through. They would have to appreciate just what an effort it cost him and understand the risks to which he had exposed himself.

The car moved quickly past the double fences of wire that marked the perimeter of Camps VII and VI, and turned finally through a high iron gate and into the plant complex itself.

Construction work was in evidence everywhere. Would they never finish? Perhaps it might pay in the long run to feed the workers more. But why? There was an endless supply of them. The cost/production ratio had been carefully worked out. At only four Reichsmarks a day for each skilled worker and three a day for the unskilled, how much money could possibly be lost, no matter how low the level of production? True, the plant might never be finished. In fact, it would probably be far safer to let things go on as they had, slowly and inefficiently. Then no one could raise any questions about why no Buna was actually being produced.

The tall stacks of the butadiene storage tanks rose up on all sides like a convocation of giant chimneys. Huge potbellied polymerization kettles in all stages of completion crowded the spaces between the stacks. Pipes and conduits ran everywhere, connecting everything to everything else. Above it all towered the stripping columns that one day would belch steam and pump an endless flow of synthetic rubber into the rows of tanks that now seemed like so many silent, giant mushrooms.

Dust hung in the air. The Daimler was sealed. Schragg could not hear the shouts of the guards as they drove the construction workers back and forth between the towering silolike structures. He did not hear the clank of the steel columns, the groan of the cement mixers that ran from dawn to dusk. He heard no voices, no human sounds at all. He could hear only the calm hum of the car's motor as it turned down the packed gravel path that ran between two large office structures and stopped before a third building in front of which a small garden was being tended by a dozen or more *"Stücke"* in the remains of their ragged gray prisoners' garb.

Feeling the Daimler finally come to a halt, Schragg raised the venetian blinds on the side window and began, without thinking of the driver's sense of duty, to open the door himself. Before he had got it halfway open, admitting a pale rectangle of late afternoon Silesian sunlight, he stopped short.

In front of the main entrance to the sprawling two-story I.G. office building stood a staff car bearing the hood standard of an SS Standartenführer. Schragg knew the car. It belonged to Werner Neimann, chief security officer and liaison between the main Auschwitz *Lager* and the I.G. installation at Monowitz. It was through

Neimann that all labor consignments were arranged, through Neimann that all payments to the SS were arranged for labor supplied,
and from his office, more frequently than not, that complaints were
made—by the SS of all people—concerning I.G.'s mistreatment
of its labor consignments. Neimann had been pressing for months
to have control of the Monowitz *Lager* taken away from I.G. and
the whole installation placed under SS control. Berlin had refused
to even consider such a change, and a quiet war had been going
on ever since between Himmler's office and the Reich Ministry for
Armaments.

To make matters worse, Neimann was also in charge of external
security for the Monowitz camp.

No matter which way one looked at it, the Standartenführer's
car in front of the main office was not a good sign. Neimann was
one of the few people at the Auschwitz installation before whom
Schragg felt inferior. Though the tall SS man was not an aristocrat
by birth, he carried himself with a dignity and cold precision a
Prussian baron might well envy.

Gathering himself together and prepared for the worst, Schragg
got out and went quickly into the building.

The prisoners tending the garden on either side of the path
doffed their caps, thankful of even a few seconds' respite from
their labors. As Schragg passed, the Kapo mouthed the obligatory
greeting.

In the front corridor, hung with photographs and long graphs of
production and construction, bar graphs, "fever charts," multi-
colored diagrams, production schedules, and labor-consignment
tables, Schragg encountered not a single office worker. The door to
Deputy Production Chief Grossbart's office was open. Grossbart
was not at his desk. As always, the room was neat to the point of
absurdity; it was difficult to tell whether Grossbart had been in it
at all. Only a slide rule and a tin coffee cup testified to his recent
presence.

The corridor echoed ominously to Schragg's footfalls. Outside
the building the air had been heavy with the many and varied
sounds of construction—whistles, the dull clanking of beams being
unloaded, the huff of engines and the grinding of giant mixers
sloshing concrete down endless chutes, the mingled shouts of

guards, the Kapos, the hiss of steam rushing in and out of the stripping columns. Inside there was nothing but a deep, hermetic silence. Even the rap of his footfalls seemed to be absorbed by it.

Schragg's skin crawled. Where the devil was Stellner, where was Olmutz, the chief of Personnel Central? Had the entire engineering staff gone on holiday? There was no sign of Popitz or Raczewaca, or Thiessen or any of them. The doors to the drafting room stood open, the tables untenanted, heaped with half-finished designs like furniture in a house shrouded for the summer.

A wide iron staircase ran from the rear of the corridor up to the second floor, where Schragg had his office. As he approached the foot of the stairs he heard the sound of steps directly above.

In a second, the familiar stocky figure of Dr. Golo Stellner, assistant chief engineer and deputy production chief, came into view, feet first. The expression on Stellner's normally amiable face was by no means familiar. He was clearly upset. His eyes blinked rapidly behind his thick glasses, a sign of agitation.

"You're back, Schragg? Did you just arrive?"

"Just," said Schragg, suddenly acutely conscious of the briefcase that hung from his left wrist by a chain. "What's going on here, can you tell me please?"

"You don't know?"

"Stellner!" Schragg shot back; he was and had always been Stellner's superior and did not care to be put off.

"You'd better come with me," Stellner said, turning to go back upstairs. Schragg noticed that Stellner hesitated for a second, as though to make sure there was no one in the stairwell above him.

Neimann? Was he looking for Werner Neimann?

Stellner took Schragg by the arm and propelled him up the stairs. It was an unusual experience for Schragg; he did not like being handled, but he permitted Stellner the liberty in deference to his highly excited state.

"You really *don't* know, do you? You haven't heard?"

"Are you going to tell me what this is all about or not? My dear Stellner, I am not used to—"

"None of us are," snapped Stellner. There was an urgency in his voice that was most compelling. "Nothing like this has ever happened before."

"What *are* you talking about? Really, I must insist—"

Stellner shut the door. When he was sure that they were alone, he turned and with a chalk-white face confronted his superior.

"An attempt has been made to assassinate the Führer. For the moment, very few people know what has happened . . ."

The announcement, simple, terse, hit Schragg like a blow. He felt for an instant as he remembered feeling the last time he had tried to bathe in the frigid waters off Danzig. Simply unable to breathe.

"An attempt?" he managed to ask. "Tried? Then it wasn't successful?"

"He lives. Apparently he has only minor injuries."

Schragg's mind raced ahead. "And Krauch? Ter Meer? Speer? Were they injured too? Killed?"

"No, no. It was not at Obersalzburg that it happened. That meeting ended two days ago. The bomb went off at Wolfschanze."

Schragg sank into a chair, the briefcase yanking hard at his wrist. He glanced down. Stellner followed the direction of his gaze.

"The papers? Oh my God. You have the papers there?"

"What of it?" Schragg, for the moment, was dull, did not follow.

"Unlock that thing at once. We must put the papers away. Or destroy them."

"What are you talking about? What have these papers got to do . . ." He stopped in mid-sentence. It became suddenly, chillingly obvious just how the agreements with an American oil company might be viewed in the aftermath of an attempt on Hitler's life.

He fumbled for the key, got the chain and lock off his arm, and extracted a thin sheaf of papers.

"These are the copies only. The signed originals are in the hands of the Swiss lawyer who represents Chemihold."

"Give them to me. I'll get Noske up here. He can lock them away in the vault. They won't be found there, not among the mass of papers that's already down there. It would take an army of clerks—"

"It would be better to burn them."

"Not without a directive from Krauch. That would be unthinkable." Stellner's eyes narrowed; his face took on an expression of genuine indignation. "Really, Schragg . . ."

"Damn them. I suppose they're still in Berlin?"

"Berlin is no resort these days."

"Neither is this place, or hadn't you noticed?"

"And it's going to get worse."

"Neimann? Oh, God. I forgot about Neimann. He's skulking about the building, is he? That was his car in front, wasn't it?"

Stellner shook his head with something like relief. "Neimann is in Vienna for the moment, on leave. Even he cannot stand this place for more than a few months at a time."

"The car then? Who . . . ?"

"A captain named Lutze and two lieutenants. They are in the dining room with the rest of the staff, explaining to them what has happened. For the moment, there's nothing to worry about. Providing, of course, that you get rid of those papers."

"Of course. At once. What else can you tell me?"

"There was to have been an uprising, it seems. Hundreds have been implicated, perhaps thousands. The Führer has given orders to have everyone who was even in the most remote way connected with the attempt brought . . . to justice immediately. The SS have been hopping about like monkeys all day."

"Even here, in *this* place, they look for conspirators?"

"And," said Stellner dryly, "of course they would find none at all, would they?"

Stellner reached for the phone and called for Noske, the chief of the records department. He held a hand over the mouthpiece while a clerk went to get his superior. "Of course, after he brings the key we will put the papers away ourselves. Noske knows nothing about any of this."

Schragg nodded. His head was spinning. Ten minutes before, he had been tranquil, almost oblivious, pleased with himself and looking forward to a pleasant supper, a hot bath, a cognac, and some Haydn on the phonograph.

Now this.

Noske came to the phone. Stellner issued a few curt orders. Schragg detested people like Noske, clerks, pencil-pushers, accountants. Who understood nothing, cared to understand less.

Stellner slammed the phone down. Just then the sound of boots slamming against the metal floor of the corridor outside was heard.

"SS?"

"Our Werkschutzen don't wear boots, or have you forgotten?"

"Listen, Stellner. I am *not* a part of this establishment of yours. I work out of Berlin. Let me assure you, it is no pleasure for me to be here. I try to forget it all as rapidly as I can and to ignore as much of it as I can while I'm here. Sometimes I don't even remember your face."

"Thank you, my dear Schragg. That's very good," said Stellner dryly.

The heavy footsteps passed. Schragg sank back, relieved. He had half expected to see Neimann's figure loom up like the *Fliegende Hollander*'s ship in the doorway, a tall pyramid of greatcoat topped by a small, almost delicate face nearly invisible under the visor of his cap. Neimann was the sort of person who always seemed accompanied by sinister orchestral music whenever he appeared. Usually in E minor.

"Can we go to Waldeck's office? Are the construction charts up to date? I want to see just how much trouble we're going to be in with this . . . thing."

"What are you talking about?" It was Stellner's turn to be concerned.

"The Buna works aren't finished, that's what I mean."

"Of course not."

"How much more work is still to be done?"

"It depends entirely on how productive the *Baujuden* are. And that we can control easily enough. At a cost, of course—more food."

"If Neimann's people are going to be prowling about looking for plots, we'd better not give them anything to be suspicious about. We'll have to work things out, step up construction just a little, then ease it off. To make things look right."

"My dear Schragg, with over two and a half years of building, building, and more building, with billions of Reichsmarks spent, hundreds of thousands of laborers used up, everything done in the most monstrously inefficient manner—for no reason, other than the very fact of that inefficiency—you really think anyone will question us *now?*"

Schragg seemed not to have heard. "If there was a bomb, as you say, and that man was not killed, as you say, and he has given the orders that you say he has given, a single fart in the wrong key will be enough to land you in Flossenberg or in *this* place, on the other side of the wire. Do I make myself clear?"

Stellner considered for a long time without replying. He got up behind his desk, looked once again at the sheaf of copies Schragg had brought back from Waldshut and then at the map on the wall which showed in vivid red lines the advancing Russian front from the east and the Anglo-American beachhead that had now been firmly established in Normandy. He looked out the window and over the vast industrial installation of Monowitz, the forest of stacks and tanks, the pipes, the wires, the lines of gray figures toiling like ants all over the unfinished plant. The sun was sinking, dreary and stained, behind a mask of smoky clouds. Dust rose everywhere. Already the watchtower lights had been turned on. The scene was about to leave the earth and take its place on the moon.

"You make yourself absolutely clear," said Stellner dully. "My apologies, Dr. Schragg. You sometimes see things more clearly and more quickly than I do. Now . . ." He paused, licking his lips. "Shall we find Noske and the vault key and . . . get rid of these things?"

DOCUMENT

John Pehle, head of the WRB, recalling his thoughts at the time he made his first recommendations to the War Department that the killing installations at Auschwitz/Birkenau be bombed, and referring specifically to the Vrba–Wetzler report.

In a way, these [reports] were the first real verifications we'd had about what was going on in those camps. My letter to McCloy was an act of desperation. I guess we felt that if we wiped out the crematoria, it would take a while to rebuild them—at a time when the Germans weren't in a position to devote great amounts of men and materiel to that.

Washington, D.C.

"My hands are tied," said Pehle's assistant. His eyes clouded over with frustration and his earnest young face was fleetingly ugly with anger. "You don't know how many times I've been up there. John's gone to see the President himself three times already. So has DuBois. We've sent I don't know how many reports."

The bearded visitor listened quietly and with a stoical expression. He touched the fringes of his beard and absently twined a long strand around his finger.

They were an odd pair, there in the offices of the War Refugee Board, the young Yale graduate, pale, blond, crew-cut, and Methodist, and the rabbi from Slonim, Poland, now representing the Orthodox Rescue Committee in New York.

The rabbi smiled patiently, as was his custom.

"We do not ask the impossible, my young friend. For now, at least. We understand that in order for the bombing to take place there are serious problems that must be solved. But can aerial pictures be taken? It is very important to us, and not so much, I think, to ask where there is so much at stake."

"Why pictures? How will that help? We already have your diagrams. We *know* . . ."

"Ah, we know, yes we know. But there are some things we do not know. Some things we *must* know." He paused, then in a tone of the utmost earnestness said, "Tell me, can you do this for us?"

"It may be possible."

"One plane, on two occasions, say a week apart, that is all we ask."

The young man's face grew flushed. He seemed far more upset than the calm European who sat opposite him.

"I think so. Yes, I promise you, we'll do it. I'll see to it that it's done even if I have to camp out in General Spaatz's office myself until he agrees."

"Good. We will let you know when."

"The time matters?"

"Very much."

"Approximately when will it be? How much time do I have to arrange things?"

The rabbi was silent for a moment; then he said, "We must have the first series of photos within the week, the second set, of the same locations, ten days later."

"It's short notice."

"In ten days, over one hundred thousand will be dead. They gas us at the rate of ten thousand a day when the equipment is working well."

The young man looked away.

"All right, we'll do it somehow. We'll get the plane ready. With the best equipment we can obtain. The best photos."

"We will show you the areas we want photographed. Here." He pushed a marked copy of the Vrba diagram across the desk. It bore a large red circle in the center.

The young man looked puzzled. He touched the circled area.

"This isn't where the gas chambers are. And the crematoria are over here. Why do you want this part of the camp?"

"There is a reason, my young friend. It is just as well that the reason remain with us alone for the time being. If all goes well, you will know soon enough."

"I trust you," the young man said.

"And I trust God. That puts us both in good company."

Zurich

Stropp had been sitting alone at the bar at the Baur-au-Lac for over an hour, trying to decide whether he should contact Trilling. He didn't like the idea of Grunewald's not going, and he liked the idea of Grunewald's sending his associate even less. He had the distinct feeling, in fact, that everything was slipping out of his grasp.

There was no question of using the phone. The transatlantic lines were crowded with priority traffic and it would take days to get through, even from Zurich. Nor did he care to discuss what he had to discuss in the clear. He could, of course, go to the consulate and insist that Lorimer's next courier take a message across in the diplomatic pouch. But that would take too much time. A response would be days in coming.

A cable was impractical, even more dangerous than a phone call.

He ordered his third whiskey and soda. He knew that he'd had enough. The whiskey was already making him faintly ill. He hated drinking his whiskey warm, English style, but the Baur-au-Lac, for some unfathomable reason, had no ice. He laughed bitterly. Imagine, a Swiss hotel that didn't have ice? He covered his growing queasiness by making jokes with the bartender, a large, powerful man with the ruined face of an ex-boxer and flaming red hair.

The bartender managed a tentative smile and shook his head. He was sorry. He understood little English. Only enough to take drink orders. Not enough to converse.

How much English did you have to have to pour soda into a whiskey? Not much. Stropp grew sullen, agitated. He kept thinking about Trilling and what Trilling would say if he knew what was going on. Stropp knew the answer to that one perfectly well. "Just *do* it and get it over with. But don't tell me the details."

What choice did he really have? If he didn't take the risks there would be no deal. To proceed blindly, given the questions Landau had raised, would be to risk everything. They could come out with nothing more than they'd gotten at Rotterdam. His own future was on the line. If he failed, there would be no stock, no position on the board of directors of Hydro-Arc. Nothing. It would all be lost. But if he managed it, particularly if he did so by assuming the responsibility and taking the kind of risk he was now taking, he'd be a hero and the rewards would be even greater than Trilling had promised. He'd see to that.

It all went against Stropp's grain nevertheless. He was a lawyer, a very conservative person by nature, and not accustomed to taking chances. Certainly not accustomed to relying on others.

Now the success or failure of the entire operation would depend almost entirely on Eisner, a Hungarian he did not know at all, and a weaselly little German Jew.

He didn't like it at all.

As he sipped his whiskey and soda, he noticed that he was beginning to sweat. He felt a little dizzy, too. Had the room gotten suddenly warmer? It certainly felt as though it had. He shook his head violently, as though to dispel a ringing in his ears.

"Mein Herr?" It was the bartender, looking at him with a mixture of concern and disdain. "There is a problem?"

"No problem. I'm not drunk, if that's what you mean?"

"I did not suggest . . ." began the bartender.

Stropp reached out to steady himself against the edge of the bar. What the hell was happening to him?

All of a sudden the dizziness got much worse. He put the whiskey glass down hard. The glass shattered and the whiskey splashed over the edge of the bar and onto his trousers. His hand was cut and bleeding.

Other people, sitting farther along the bar, turned to stare.

"I'm all right," Stropp said weakly, trying to get off the bar stool. The dizziness became nausea. It hit him in successive waves, turning his stomach upside down.

He fell sideways off the bar stool and crashed into the man sitting next to him, then to the floor.

There was a triphammer inside his head going full tilt. His chest suddenly felt full of lead weights.

People were coming toward him from all over the room. The red-haired bartender had come around through the swinging doors and was calling loudly for a doctor. Someone came running from across the room, shouting.

Stropp looked up. The bartender had turned yellow. So had everyone else in the room. His pulse had gone crazy, rushing, then vanishing entirely, then rushing again.

The last thing Henry Stropp remembered was the man who had come running across the room kneeling over him and saying that someone should phone quickly please for an ambulance, this man had had a heart attack.

Then he lost consciousness.

"He did *what?*" Miklos screamed, taking Liebermann so high on the shoulders that he had him almost by the throat. "You couldn't have said what I think you did—"

"There was no choice," Liebermann protested, trying to free himself. His hands snapped up to Baranyi's wrists but he could not move them. For a moment, he was genuinely frightened. The Hungarian seemed to have lost control of himself completely. "Did you ever try to talk Itzhak out of anything? *Anything* at all?"

"You could have stopped him."

Baranyi's hands dropped away as though the muscles had been severed. It was true; he could not shake another, different truth out of Avner Liebermann. His head hung down, ashamed.

"I'm sorry, Avner."

"It's all right, it's all right. Someone should have told you before."

"I was just with him yesterday. How is it possible?"

"Right after they took Stropp to the hospital. It would be safer if he wasn't around for a while, he said, and if he had to stay out of sight, why not do something useful at the same time?"

"God, that's just like him, isn't it. How did he go?"

"The usual way. Through the Ticino, the way the two of you came out the last time. Once across the Drva, he'll have no trouble. The route up through Pecs is still open."

"But why, why—when I was about to leave, when everything—"

"He said that it wasn't enough. Both Bor and Sternbuch agreed with him," Liebermann said wearily, as though explaining something for the twentieth time to a recalcitrant schoolboy.

"Then why couldn't Bor have taken care of it? Or Pauer? Why send Kagan?"

"No one *sent* Kagan, as you put it. The idea was his. He *wanted* to go. I think that he could not sit here while you went into that caldron without doing something to help."

"He knew why he couldn't go with us. There was no point. He would have been too conspicuous. Stropp would never have agreed . . ."

"He knew," Liebermann said. "That's why he didn't argue with you. And that's exactly why he did what he did."

"Why not send one of Pauer's people?"

"Listen, Miklos. Itzhak is strong, he's clever. He'll pull it off. You talk as though he's dead already."

"Already?" repeated Baranyi dully. "Yes, *already*. What does he know of Budapest? He's a *Galizianer,* for God's sake."

"He knows as much as you, almost. How many times has he been there with you? What better teacher could he have had?"

Baranyi sat down on the edge of the cot, his head in his hands. It would have been better, altogether, had no one told him. He was to leave the next morning. He had composed himself, accepted his fate, was ready to meet it. He had no illusions. He was tranquil, at peace with himself.

Now this.

Liebermann's voice was calm, in a way reassuring.

"He will succeed, and he will come out alive," he said. "Even without you. Pauer's people could not do it because of the matter of timing—it would take too long to get one of Weissmandel's agents into Budapest. The borders are closed now, closely watched. Tiso's police are everywhere. Besides, neither Pauer's men nor the rabbi's people have the contacts in Budapest that you have."

Baranyi looked up, his chest tightening. Contacts? What need did Kagan have of contacts? To take the translation of the Vrba-Wetzler report in to Budapest, to see that it was duplicated, distributed to government and intellectual figures in the Hungarian capital—this took no "contacts." What was Liebermann talking about?

"*Avner* . . ." Baranyi said the name like an accusation.

"You may as well know now, Miklos," Liebermann said. "It's not only the report, though that's important enough."

"What else?" Baranyi could hardly breathe. Something else, and "contacts" . . . Liebermann's face, now deathly gray. Afraid.

"It was Bor's idea, actually. They spoke of it a few days ago."

"Without me?"

"Without you. Kagan said you had enough on your mind already."

"What, damn you? Are you going to tell me? What is it?"

Liebermann looked down, avoiding Baranyi's wild stare.

"It was decided that your mission needed support. If the Farben people are to believe you, even with everything you're bringing to them, the information had to come from another source as well."

"I swear, if you don't tell me straight out, Avner, I'm going to kill you here and now."

"It would be the most merciful thing you could do, Miklos. I'm very tired and I wouldn't mind. Particularly at the hand of a friend. There are worse ways. But it isn't necessary. I'll tell you. Here—it's simply this. At the right moment, after you've been given time to get in and do what you've planned to do, the German authorities in Budapest will receive certain information—that we've gotten hold of the railroad schedules and the routes. No names will be given, but copies of the documents we received from the Wehrmacht agents will be supplied. It will be absolutely convincing. They'll understand exactly how it happened even if they won't know who did it. It will be clear, of course, that it's no fabrication. You can be sure that the information will get to Poland at once, through the camp administration security office. And I.G. will have its confirmation."

"You're going to compromise the army people?"

"No, only the information they gave us, which no one can change anyhow."

"And how is Itzhak going to plant the information? Who is his contact?" Baranyi's eyes closed; he knew exactly what Liebermann was going to say. After all, he'd introduced Kagan to the man himself.

"Tibor Szekely. Who else?"

Who else indeed. And Kagan would walk right into a lion's den for far less important reasons than he had now.

Tibor Szekely. Third in command, Budapest sector, Hungarian political police. A man of extravagant intelligence, urbane, of consummate ability, the proper sympathies and cautions. And completely untrustworthy. An opportunist of the worst sort.

"It will be to Szekely's own best interest not to betray us," Liebermann said dismally.

"For the moment," replied Baranyi. "I suppose so. Let's hope the moment lasts."

He had said that he would be there by eleven, but it was almost a quarter to twelve and he still had not arrived. By the time she heard the sound of footsteps in the hallway outside her door, she had smoked eight cigarettes, filled her two little rooms with a dense, acrid pall of smoke, and cursed the Hungarian out roundly in three languages. She had bathed, scented herself with the last of the D'Orsay cologne that Bor had given her, combed out her hair, and straightened up her bedroom. All for him. And now he was more than a half-hour late and she stank of cigarette smoke and anxiety.

She pushed open the door to the dark hallway by the landing, not caring that she was in her slip and robe and that it might not be him after all.

"So, you took your time, didn't you? I shouldn't let you in," she said, whipping the cigarette from her mouth in frustration. "Damn you anyhow, brother-in-law."

Miklos sighed. A small man, he looked even smaller because of the large and obviously heavy cardboard box he was carrying under one arm and the huge bouquet of flowers he had under the other.

"You are a sight, aren't you," she said, letting him in.

He put the box down on the table.

"I hope you've got a phonograph," he said.

"Why?"

"In that box, mademoiselle, is every Hanka Ordonowna record in Zurich. I don't even dare tell you what I paid your friend Andrej for the last two or three he had. A czar's treasure."

She began to laugh, the hard-edged, slightly hysterical laugh that he knew he would never understand.

"And flowers too? . . . Thank you, Miklos. My God, you make me feel like a schoolgirl again. A difficult thing to do, believe me." She smiled and pushed her loose blond hair back from her forehead. Her eyes were all vulnerability. Her mouth relaxed.

"Come, sit. Tell me, what shall we do first? A brandy? Or shall we make love?"

Miklos shook his head and reached out for her hand. "What a one you are, Julie Malowska. Never before . . ."

"And never again . . . Come, let's go inside. You've wasted almost an hour already."

She took his hand and led him into the little bedroom, pleased at the surprise in his eyes when he saw how she had straightened everything up, how neat it all was. He knew that she had done it for him, for his visit.

The robe and the slip fell to her feet and she stood naked before him, with only her silk stockings still on, rolled to the knee. "Well? What are you waiting for?" She reached out to him, then drew back. "No, how could I be so thoughtless?"

She ran from the room and in a moment he heard the music, very low.

"Don't worry," she said, coming back into the room with an armful of the flowers he had brought. "The machine is one of those American marvels. It keeps playing the record over and over again automatically. I hope you like the song."

"Insane," he whispered, and took her.

Her lovemaking was amazing, frantic and violent. The first time, there had been an element of desperation in it, as though the act was done more out of hate than out of love or even pleasure. Now it was entirely different, a forceful, willful plunging that brought them both to the verge of hysteria time and time again before they finally spent themselves.

Even with Teresa it had not been like this.

He lay back, smoking, thinking guiltily of Teresa and their hesitant, always decorous coupling. There was such a contrast, and it was in fact a contrast of contrasts. Teresa had been strong, a strapping, thick-thighed woman, the complete opposite of her thin, nervous sister. All that the two women shared was the bleached straw color of their hair and their pale, gray eyes, the gift of the father, Adam.

He felt satisfied as never before, and guilty because of it.

She leaned over, the tips of her small breasts grazing his chest, the sheet down to her hips and a glistening of sweat on her belly.

His. She poured two tumblers of brandy and handed one to him, lit a cigarette, and pressed herself against his side.

"Why, Miklos?" she said softly. "Why do you have to . . . ?"

"Have to what?"

"Go there. To that place. Stay here, with me. The war could be over for you, couldn't it? Think how much you've done already. Stay, Miklos, stay."

"Impossible," he said, though it seemed to him that perhaps it was not quite as impossible as all that. It was all she needed, to hear that one word only. She went on.

"Why do you have to *go* there? Why can't you just leak the information back to them somehow? Wouldn't it accomplish the same thing to do that?"

He shook his head and touched her mouth with the tips of his fingers, then let his hand stray down across her breasts.

"In order to keep the agreement from being signed we had to do as Landau had suggested, let him tell Stropp that there was something wrong with the mechanism. He had to insist on going in to see it himself, to buy time. If he'd done anything else, they would have asked him to explain what it was that he thought was wrong and they would have known right away that he was lying and that it was a hoax. There isn't anything wrong, Julie. He says the mechanism is a marvel, as far as he can tell."

"So let *him* go if he must. Why do you have to go with him?"

"Eisner must go, as a representative of the company, because they don't trust Landau . . ."

"Yes?" She sighed deeply, and it was difficult to tell whether she was really listening; it was plain that no matter what he said, she would not change her mind, and, equally, that nothing she said could change his. They were simply going through the motions.

"And you, of course, don't trust Eisner."

"Exactly," he said. "Besides, the whole thing has been very carefully orchestrated. Someone must be there to make contact with Conrad's man inside the camp, and it would be unthinkable to let either Landau or Eisner know who it is. The man must be advised of what's going on so that the signal can be passed that will bring the planes in to photograph the removal of the equipment. No one else can do it. So, you see . . ."

"I see a suicidal man, doing his very best to kill himself."

"What is bravery but a suicidal urge gone wrong, eh? Who knows, these days, Julie?"

She reached down over his belly, surprisingly gentle, caressing him.

"So, so, so . . . try to forget these things for a time, yes, Miklos?"

"You make me forget, Julie. You make me forget many, many things," he said, thinking that perhaps she had in her strange way also made him forget some things that should not be forgotten.

But he did not care. An unfamiliar lethargy overtook him, not only a lethargy of the body—though he found himself quickly awakening again under her insistent fingers—but of his soul, his spirit. For the first time in years it struck him that there might be a reason to do something other than repeatedly try to throw his life away to save others.

. . . that there might, somehow, be a life for him too.

He closed his eyes. It was really too late, and that was the sad part of it all. Much too late to be thinking of such things.

In the morning, the plane would be waiting for them, somewhere north of Rheinfall, in the dark woods. A lumbering, three-engine, corrugated monster with a pig's snout.

It was much too late.

III

July 20, 1944
Germany, then Vienna, Ostmark

A dun-colored Junkers trimotor carrying private I.G. registration markings took them on at an abandoned Luftwaffe airstrip north of Freiburg. A perimeter guard of four armored cars and two dozen infantrymen with automatic weapons had been provided by the division of I.G. known as the Vermittlungstelle Wehrmacht. It was the function of VW, as it was commonly called, to coordinate affairs between the Gesellschaft and the army.

According to the usual protocols, no questions had been asked and the assistance requested had been given at once. The airstrip had been completely sealed off. The two roads leading in and out had both been blockaded by trucks, which formed a barricade through which the I.G. Mercedes that had picked up the party at the border passed with only the most perfunctory showing of papers. A heavy tank would have been needed by anyone trying to get by without papers.

Landau could not contain his curiosity; his head swiveled in every direction, his gaze lingering particularly long on the military equipment. He appraised it all with the practiced eye of a true technician. A faint smile lingered at the corners of his mouth, and when the Junkers at last lifted from the pockmarked runway, he leaned back, adjusted the seat straps, and emitted a long sigh of what was unmistakably satisfaction.

Baranyi, for his part, was too exhausted to react. He felt drained and therefore twice as wary as he might otherwise have been. Accustomed as he was to theatrics, to disguises, he found it difficult to get used to his latest ruse, being disguised as himself, the only lie about him being his purpose. His Swiss passport was legitimate, his papers were in perfect order.

Only Eisner gave evidence of discomfort. The pilot now and then looked back, grinned a wicked *Schadenfreude* grin, and chalked off Eisner's obvious anxiety to airsickness. It was, of course, a good deal more than that.

Samuel Morse Eisner was the only member of the party with forged papers.

In less than two hours, the trimotor lumbered down through a lowering sky and rolled to a stop before the administration building at Aspern airport outside Vienna. A gray civilian car moved out at once, beetlelike, and sped across the tarmac, still wet from an earlier rain. From the Weinerwald came the soft, musty smell of turned earth and budding trees; from the city itself a vague yet sharp acrid odor, a memory of explosives. In the distance, against the darker eastern sky, a few fires could be seen flickering against the low bellies of the clouds while long trails of smoke, like marking flares, rose up to flag the still smoldering evidence of the last English bombing raid.

A small, worried-looking man with the nondescript face of a bank clerk got out of the car, his oversized raincoat billowing in the stiff breeze. His shoes were soaked through and black with water.

"Herr Eisner? Herr Landau?" the man asked in a sharp but hesitant voice. He glanced at a sheaf of papers, then looked up again. "Herr . . . Bar-an-yee? I am Reinecke."

Landau spoke to him rapidly, with an air of authority.

"The arrangements," replied Reinecke, "have all been made. Herr Heidebroek will meet us at the station. He will accompany you on the trip." He turned. "You will come with me, this way, please. In the car, yes? You have luggage? Only the satchels? Good. There will be no room for luggage in any event. Now, quickly, please."

Eisner, his face white as wax, got into the car first. The man in the oversized raincoat was to be the driver. Landau sat in front with him.

Baranyi held up a hand in warning. Silence. Eisner pressed back against the seat and pulled his collar up.

Miklos looked around. He saw nothing unusual. The airport was jammed with military transport. Big six-engine Messerschmitts and fat, twin-boomed Gotha cargo planes lined the runways. In the distance he could see a file of big Junkers like the one they'd just been on, but with red crosses painted on their wings. Ambulances and hospital trucks by the dozen were weaving back and forth across the runways. The sky above was dismal and threatening rain. There were no aircraft coming in, only a few of the spidery Storches almost hovering overhead, nearly weightless against the gray sky.

The trip into the city was fast and silent. There was little traffic on the road, only the hospital trucks again and a few motorcycles and *Kübelwagens*. As they took the Nordbahnbrücke over the Danube into the Briggittenau district, Baranyi became aware of a sudden increase in military traffic. Dusty staff cars and open-back trucks loaded with steel-helmeted soldiers, all fully armed, rushed past with increasing frequency. All in silence. But many, many of them.

Miklos could see that the back of the driver's neck had begun to sweat. The collar was already sodden.

But there were no sirens, no planes overhead. No explanation for the sudden activity.

The little gray car swung down the wide street that ran past the north railway station, passed through the Prater–Stern intersection, and shot over the Danube canal at the Franzens bridge.

The streets again became almost empty. Though it was only late afternoon, there were few people about. A fine rain had begun to fall and the Volkswagen's windshield wipers were not functioning well. Now and then the driver had to stop and wipe the condensation from inside the windows with a handkerchief so they could see out. Every time the car stopped, Eisner swore softly under his breath and turned a shade paler. Landau, observing this, smiled vengefully. Of all of them, Landau should have been the most nervous, but, on the contrary, he seemed to be in complete control. He had even begun chatting with the driver, Reinecke, trying to find out just who the man was, whether he intended making the trip with them, whether he had a position with the engineering department or was strictly an administrative adjunct. Reinecke shook his head, excused himself, and concentrated on his driving.

They pulled up a little way past the station, opposite the side entrance of the War Museum on Arsenalstrasse.

"Now, you will follow me, please. I have your tickets and documents. Everything has been arranged, of course. However, you will try not to attract attention of any kind. It would be better if you kept still and let me do whatever talking may be required. For the moment, until we board the train, we are on our own entirely."

The west side of the station was lined with army trucks. Military police in gray uniforms and Orpo wearing the traditional high-crowned Viennese double-billed hats were everywhere. Long lines of soldiers had formed by the entrances to the building, whether coming in or going out was hard to say. Here and there were portable cookstoves on the back of trucks, their fires lit, smoke curling up from the corrugated chimneys. The air stank of grease and coal. From the yard beyond, steam rose and the sound of whistles and grinding steel wheels could be heard continuously. Somewhere, someone was playing an accordion and a young voice rose over the babel in a strong, steady melody.

The station itself was full of German and Romanian troops with their high-crowned, squashy field caps. Blanket rolls and knapsacks were stacked like cordwood between the waiting-room benches.

"Wait here," Reinecke said, pausing some distance from the gates that let onto the train platforms. The gates were shut and at each one a guard of helmeted Feldpolizei stood, carrying machine pistols. "This is not right. There is something unusual going on," Reinecke said, his eyes darting from side to side. The papers had disappeared into the capacious pockets of his raincoat. His sweating had gotten worse.

Landau said, in German, "It's nothing. Only the war," and laughed.

"Oh, it's something all right," said Reinecke. "Herr Heidebroek was to have met us right here. Your escort for Poland. But where is he, I ask you? Nowhere. Why is he not here?"

Just then there was a blast of whistles at the opposite end of the crowded station. Another group of armed field police pushed their way through. Officers, some in black SS uniform, others in *feldgrau,* spilled out of every door. The soldiers, waiting in sullen lines for their trains, stepped aside, grimaced, and went back to their brooding. The boy with the high tenor who had been singing "Lili Marlene" went right on singing.

"Ah, there," the driver said, seeing a stocky man in a leather coat and wide-brimmed fedora pushing through a group of Romanian officers. As he came up to them, a wicker hamper on one arm, there was a renewed slamming of bootsoles against the stone.

More armed Feldpolizei crashed into the station from the north entrance.

"Heidebroek, what the devil is going on here? This place is a madhouse," demanded Reinecke.

Heidebroek's face was white. "You don't know? No one's told you?"

"They landed only a half-hour ago. I've been at Aspern since early morning, sitting in the car. What's happened?"

"You'd better get these people out of sight for the moment. I can guarantee nothing, do you understand? Nothing," said Heidebroek.

"But *what,* for God's sake?" Reinecke was shaking, his head craning to and fro on his long sweaty neck.

Baranyi, from his years of experience, knew that the best thing to do was remain absolutely silent and listen. He'd seen enough to know that.

Heidebroek took a deep breath.

"There has been an attempt on the Führer's life. We have just had the news here. A bomb, I think. They say that there was a conspiracy. The head of the SD and the SS here have already been arrested. They've hauled off dozens, maybe hundreds. Who knows who'll be pulled in next. They themselves don't know who they're looking for." He paused. "The mad dogs are loose again."

"Perfect," said Landau, and then he laughed. "Why, it's absolutely perfect timing."

Reinecke stared at him, aghast.

Heidebroek took no notice. "Over fifty have been shot already, out by the Prater. It's a charnel house," he said with outrage.

Baranyi dug his fingers hard into Eisner's arm. "You don't make a sound, do you understand? Not a sound."

A squad of Feldpolizei came at a jog trot in their direction, attracted by the presence of a group of civilians among the troops of soldiers. Not far off an officer was being dragged by the arms across the floor by two SS men, head down, his toes leaving long black tracks of polish and leather on the concrete.

Landau's expression was utterly incomprehensible, a mixture of fear and malicious amusement. "Well, gentlemen, what do you propose we do now?"

The Feldpolizei were almost on top of them. A small man wearing glasses and a major's collar tabs pointed at them and began shouting.

"What are you people doing here? What? *What?* This is a restricted area. Your documents. At once!"

Two of the Feldpolizei clattered to a halt and held their weapons at the ready: machine pistols that could cut a man in half at that range.

"I assure you, everything is in perfect order, Major," said Heidebroek in a stiff voice.

"Nothing is in order today, as you can clearly see. Now, let us look at your documents. At once!"

A half dozen rifle bolts clicked behind him. Across the station another man had just been pulled out of line. He was screaming and pleading, but the words could not be made out.

Heidebroek seemed unable to extricate the sheaf of papers from his inside pocket.

The major was out of patience. His hand fell to his holster, his fingers spreading over the butt of his Walther.

"You are deaf apparently, yes? I said *at once.*"

"Really, Major, that won't be necessary," came a voice.

The major's head jerked around. He found himself looking up into the pale gray eyes of a tall man in the black uniform of the Totenkopf SS, the four bars and double oak leaves of an Oberführer on his collar.

"Herr Brigadier?" exclaimed the startled officer. He had been arresting SS all morning as well as regular army officers, but had yet to encounter anyone of such high rank. For a moment he was at a complete loss.

"I'm sure there must be some mistake. I know these gentlemen, Major. Herr Heidebroek is a representative accredited to General Thomas's office. Surely you have no business with General Thomas, Major? And so you could not possibly have business with the chief liaison officer between OKH and I.G. Auschwitz, now could you, Major?" The SS man turned to Heidebroek. "You should have let someone know you were coming through, Heidebroek. Lucky that I ran into you, isn't it?"

"I had no idea that you were here, Herr Oberführer," Heidebroek stammered.

"Of course you didn't, Heidebroek. Nor did I have any idea that you were here. That's where the luck comes in. I don't go back until tomorrow. I was here simply to check on the trains. My leave's at an end, but rank guarantees nothing these days. Poor working officers like myself have to look out for ourselves."

The major stood there speechless, his neck flaming above his stiff collar. His men were staring at him, obviously enjoying his discomfort.

"If you'll excuse me, Herr Oberführer, I am simply doing my duty. Which, of course, has nothing to do with General Thomas, as you suggest. But nevertheless, these men . . . for all I know . . ."

"You misunderstand, Major. It's what *I* know that is of importance here. And *I* know who these men are. Now, if you will stand aside, please?"

"We have strict orders," the major sputtered, growing even angrier as the SS officer turned and began to talk to Heidebroek as though no one else were in the vicinity.

"Herr Oberführer—"

"I am trying to be patient, Major. Please don't make me lose my patience." The SS officer took a leather document folder from his coat and held it out, though it was obvious from the brevity of the gesture that it was intended for form only. "Werner Neimann, Oberführer, as you see, Totenkopf SS. These gentlemen are all going to Poland. To Auschwitz. Would *you* care to join us, Major? No? I thought not. Poland is not a particularly pleasant place these days, and Auschwitz even less so. It's much more comfortable here in Vienna, arresting people, isn't it? Now, if you don't mind, you will tell your men to get away from the gate and let us pass. Before I insist on knowing *your* name. And let me assure you, once I take the trouble to learn your name, I won't be likely to forget it. Do you understand me, Major?"

"Orders," exhaled the major. "The attempt on our Führer's life . . ." He seemed close to apoplexy.

Oberführer Neimann shrugged, turned on his heel, and, with a gesture meant to draw the entire party into his wake, walked straight toward the line of Feldpolizei who were blocking the gate.

Under the steel arches that curved over the tracks and platforms, the trains rumbled and belched steam. A whistle blew, mournful but insistent. In spite of the chaos and the shouting, some of the

Romanians began to sing in rough chorus, oblivious to what was going on.

"This way, gentlemen. Allow me to escort you to the train," said Neimann. "It will be safer that way, I assure you."

"Perhaps it would be better to—" began Reinecke.

"To stay and argue with that scum? Hardly. Now get along before the train leaves without you. You have what? Ten minutes? No more. And by the way, Heidebroek, do give my regards to Dr. Schragg, and don't forget to mention to him that I've pulled his chestnuts out of the fire once again. Or so it seems."

The Feldpolizei stepped aside slowly. The major stood where he was, his hands at his sides, his fingers opening and closing spasmodically. Inches from the butt of his pistol.

"*Bon voyage,* gentlemen," Oberführer Neimann said cheerfully. "Tell Dr. Schragg to get out a bottle of his best claret. I'll be along to collect on my debts in a day or so."

The gate clanged shut again. Landau turned to stare at Reinecke and Heidebroek. They were both white and sweating.

Landau burst out laughing.

The moment the four men boarded the train, a young captain of transport appeared, carrying a portfolio of documents for the multiple crossings. Heidebroek in turn handed him a folder of papers with instructions that under no circumstances was the group to be disturbed. They were traveling under high-level authority. The orders bore the signature of General Thomas himself and were on the letterhead of the Military Economics Staff, Kurfürstenstrasse 63/69.

The captain took the papers, nodded perfunctorily, and vanished.

The moment they were alone, Heidebroek slumped back against the compartment seat and feverishly undid his collar.

"You have no idea," he said, "how close to disaster we have already come."

"Surely we had no reason to be concerned. Our papers were in order, weren't they?" said Landau.

"Our papers could have been our death warrant too. They may still be, for all I know. Who is to tell what names have been placed on the lists for arrest? Who knows who the Führer believes was implicated in the plot? Let us suppose, for instance, that General Thomas is suspect. His attitude is well known. It is *possible* . . ."

"Jesus," said Eisner. "Do you mean . . . ?"

"Exactly," replied Heidebroek. "Anyone who is even suspected will be arrested and most likely shot. It will make no difference whatever whether they are actually guilty or not."

"Under the circumstances," said Landau, "let us all pray that those who are guilty are quickly apprehended and brought to justice." Once again, there was a faint ironic smile on his face.

"So that the rest of us may be left alone? Yes, of course." Heidebroek looked suddenly around the compartment as though it had just occurred to him that there could very well be a microphone hidden somewhere. "And so that the Führer may be fully avenged and those responsible for this *outrage* punished as they deserve."

As the train rumbled over the Donau canal and cut across the southern end of the Prater, Heidebroek began to relax. He unfastened the catches of the hamper he had been carrying.

"You'll join me, gentlemen? A drink to the health of our leader and his narrow escape." He produced a bottle of brandy and four small glasses.

Eisner had not said a word all this time.

Landau took the brandy as it was offered.

"To the Führer," said Heidebroek.

"Of course . . . to the Führer," said Felix Landau.

The train raced on across Czechoslovakia, trailing darker and darker smoke as it passed through Ostrava and up into the foothills of the Tatra mountains. Steel-helmeted soldiers passed in shadow play behind the green curtains of the compartment. The baggage rack swayed. Once or twice the transport-command captain reappeared, each time bearing a solicitous gift. Something to make the trip a bit more comfortable. A bit of Westphalian ham, some precious cigarettes. He smiled ingratiatingly and did his best. He seemed, in an odd way, to be trying desperately to be friendly.

Eisner, over whom much of the conversation passed because of what he insisted was his limited German, sat by the window, his face pressed up against the sooty pane, looking out. Landau and Heidebroek soon were deep in animated conversation, having found a common ground in a love of Bruckner and a mutual dislike of Magda Behrens.

The landscape changed constantly, grew somber, twisted by repeated bombing raids. Fires lit distant, indeterminable horizons. Arcs of searchlights laced the deepening night with a cat's cradle of silver, catching and illuminating a soundless pattern of flak bursts over some unseen city to the northwest. Eisner shuddered and drank. An entire bottle of Riesling from the hamper.

As he reached for the second bottle, Baranyi intervened.

"Enough," he snapped.

"What else is there to do?"

"Let him be," said Heidebroek affably. "Surely there can be no harm in a little wine. He'll sleep better for it."

Miklos shrugged and handed Eisner the bottle, but gave him a warning glare that did not go unappreciated.

Eisner drank quietly and sullenly. Landau yawned and disengaged himself from the conversation. All at once, Miklos could see, tension had overwhelmed him. In a moment he would be asleep.

The landscape darkened. In the far distance, pulses of light could be seen now and then. Either artillery or bombing strikes. Occasionally a deep booming could be heard even over the steady ratcheting of the train wheels.

At last Miklos and the I.G. man were the only ones awake. Heidebroek reached over and retrieved the half-empty bottle of Riesling from the sleeping Eisner, corked it, and thrust it back into the hamper.

"So . . . you and I, we are the night owls, eh?" Heidebroek said. He stretched out, extending his legs. "Those with clear consciences sleep like children while we . . ."

"With guilty consciences?"

"Who knows? We are all guilty of something, aren't we? In the end there is not one of us who doesn't betray something or someone during his life. A cause, a man, more likely a woman. My God, what I wouldn't give for the opportunity to betray a woman just now."

Baranyi smiled appreciatively. He had yet to sort out all the betrayals of which he had or might have been guilty. They made a long, long list.

"You know," Heidebroek went on, "if Neimann hadn't happened along, that *Arscheloch* back there probably would have had the lot of us in a ditch in the Prater by now. They've been executing people all day long."

Baranyi nodded but said nothing. There ensued a long, painful silence. It seemed to Miklos that Heidebroek expected him to say something, was waiting for something in particular.

Finally Miklos said, "I don't think they would have, really. We are neutrals, after all. We have legitimate business with your people."

"Legitimate business at Oswiecim?"

"That surprises you?"

"Nothing surprises me anymore, Herr Baranyi. When I was a small child, yes, then things constantly surprised me. But not anymore. I have even lost the power to surprise myself."

July 23, 1944
Zurich

The two men walked slowly through the botanical gardens like old friends out for an afternoon's pleasure stroll, the one tall and courtly, gray-haired and elegant, with a slight forward stoop to his walk, the other short, stocky, and swarthy, who moved with anything but grace and whose gestures and voice seemed more appropriate to the machine room than to the genteel pathways of the park.

Bor clasped his hands behind his back and shook his head.

"If you really want my opinion, Pauer, you worry too much."

"It's our business to worry, isn't it? We must always think the worst and work for what we hope will be the best."

Bor smiled graciously and paused to inhale the fragrance of a newly blooming bank of flowers.

Pauer frowned. "What else is there to think now but the worst? At least from your point of view, I would imagine."

"And not yours?"

Pauer was silent. "Mine too, of course. What happens to Poland will determine what happens to my country. I have no doubts about that. The only difference will be one of time."

"And so?"

"And so, I think you must be very wary, Colonel. The Russians have encircled the Third Panzer at Vitebsk. Rokossovsky is even now less than two hundred fifty kilometers from Warsaw. With Petrov and Konev to his south, there is nothing whatever to stop the Soviets from overrunning the entire country."

"Do you consider that worse than allowing the Germans to remain?"

"It may be no better. They will push you and your kind out just as ruthlessly as the Nazis did. They will put their own people in control and wipe you out. Their so-called Lublin Committee of National Liberation will be the government in Poland before the year is out, mark my word. And you, my friend, will be dangling from a gallows."

"You do see the worst in everything, Pauer, don't you?"

"I see what's before my nose, that's all."

"Do you really think for a moment that the Americans and the English will stand by and let such a thing happen?"

"They may have no choice. Or it may simply be that their real interests lie elsewhere. After all, the English went to war because of Poland. Perhaps they've all had enough of war on your behalf."

Bor gave him a dark look but held his peace. What the Czech said was true enough. On all counts.

"We know," Pauer went on, "that some sort of arrangement was made at Teheran. Perhaps you already know more about it than I do. I won't ask you if you do. But what we both *do* know is that a great deal of Polish territory was promised to the Russians. It only stands to reason that they will wish to protect their gains by establishing a friendly government in Warsaw when the war is over. Where will you be then, you and Mikolajczk and his friends?"

Bor stopped. The color had drained bit by bit from his face, until now it was as pale as his hair. He bit his lip. His blue eyes, icy as always, turned full on Pauer with an almost disdainful glare.

"And what, exactly, are you proposing?"

"I'm proposing nothing. I'm merely suggesting that you be on your guard. People like you are a menace to them."

"Them?"

"Come now—the Russians, of course. You'll be ground up like corn between two stones."

Bor smiled indulgently. "You think so?"

Pauer was not to be put off. "Consider what happened at Katyn. Do you think that *that* augurs Soviet benevolence as far as you and your friends are concerned?"

"German propaganda. The Nazis must have done it. If it happened at all."

"God knows, they're certainly capable of it. But no, it was the Soviets, there's no doubt about it. Fifteen thousand of your best officers shot in the back of the neck and dumped in a pit. The same thing will happen to you."

"In Switzerland?"

"There are Soviet agents all over Zurich. You know that as well as I do. All I'm suggesting, Bor, is that you be careful, that's all. And that you and your woman get away from the consulate at the first sign of trouble. Before it's too late."

"Allow me some skepticism, Pauer. And allow me to ask why all of this should make any difference to you."

"If I said it was because I like you, Bor, or the Malowska woman, you wouldn't believe me. It's not a part of our business to form attachments. So I won't abuse your intelligence. Let's just say that it's a form of self-protection. I have no doubt that if Warsaw falls, Prague won't be far behind. I'd simply like to do my bit to keep that from happening."

"I'd rather you'd said it was because you liked me," Bor replied, smiling again that same gentle, irritatingly condescending smile. "In any event, I thank you for your concern. Believe me, Pauer, I shall know how to take care of myself when and if the time comes."

"As you wish," said Pauer, picking up the pace. He'd had enough of flowers and ferns. And enough of Bor, too. If the man wouldn't take what he had to say seriously, then the devil with him. And the woman too.

The worst of it, Pauer thought after he had shaken hands with Bor and gone his own way toward the gate that opened into the Talstrasse, was that he did like Bor and that really *was* the reason.

He liked Bor a great deal, and the pale, brooding Malowska woman even more.

Budapest

For Itzhak Kagan, Budapest would forever be a strange and unsettling city, unlike any place he had ever been before or was likely
ever to be in what remained of his life. There was, he thought, an
air of barely suppressed madness about Budapest that suffused
everything; it shone from the eyes of the city's citizens, flowed
uncontrollably through its music, its architecture, its politics. Bar-
baric, wild, totally unpredictable. It often seemed to him as though
the entire city existed by deliberate design on the bordeline of
insanity. It had none of the stabilizing dullness of the poverty-
stricken Galician countryside where he had been born, its primitive,
dependable brutality. Nor could he detect any common thread
running through the souls of its inhabitants, neither Slavic fatalism
nor Teutonic sense of order. Quite the reverse. Everything about
the place was flamboyant, exaggeratedly colorful, chaotic, from its
jaw-cracking language to the absurd chicken plumes in the caps of
the gendarmes.

Baranyi, of course, had understood such things instinctively. He,
Itzhak Kagan, son of Galician hill farmers, former foundry worker
in Varna, former truck driver in Berlin, would have to be very,
very careful. He understood nothing, and knew it.

Kagan walked slowly along the narrow streets near the Danube
embankment, his leather cap pulled down almost to his eyebrows,
but careful not to appear furtive. A man his size could hardly be
inconspicuous no matter what he did, so it was best not to try.

The wind was sharp and refreshing against his face. It would
keep him alert. There was a strange, unsettling hint of flowers in
the air. One did not think easily of flowers at such a time.

He kept his hands away from his jacket breast pocket; it wasn't
a good idea to be constantly checking one's papers. It attracted
attention.

A thick bank of *feldgrau* rain clouds hung low over the Svabhegy,
obscuring the upper stories of the Majestic Hotel. In front of the
hotel, a circle of pale sunlight fell, glinting from the hoods of the
Mercedes staff cars of the SS drawn up in an arc around the
entrance.

Elsewhere, the city was brushed alternately by washes of weak sun and isolated freshets of summer rain that whisked indiscriminately through the streets, dousing the queues of people waiting before the pastry shops and cinemas. The shop windows were emptier than they had been on Kagan's last trip to Budapest, the little yellow German police cars more in evidence. Only the shops which sold wine and brandy seemed well supplied. Trolleys, crowded far beyond their capacity, spit sparks from their overhead wires and groaned laboriously along the tracks.

From many an open window came the sound of German rather than Hungarian music—the radio and phonograph records—the childish soprano of Marika Rökk, the saccharine tenor of Willi Forst. German officers strolling in the streets below smiled in cautious recognition, hearing familiar voices. On the Field of Blood, the city's military parade ground, the band of the Sixth Silesian Jagercorps essayed the Rackozy March with only indifferent results before a thin crowd of onlookers pausing on their way back from a soccer game.

The city continued to bleed smoke into the gray summer sky, still-visible evidence of the Allied air raids that had dumped hundreds of tons of bombs on Budapest during the past two weeks. On the seven bridges across the Danube, bicycles, Honved trucks, and German military traffic moved with haste, the drivers' eyes ever cocked skyward, watching for yet more planes.

Men in Wehrmacht gray and SS black were everywhere, suspicious, prying. The Arrow Cross police, in particular, noticed everything. Kagan had no need to worry. His papers were in perfect order. Swiss passport, introductory letters from Himmelwasser & Sohne, Basel, baptismal certificate, letters of credit, letters from the director of the Swiss bank in which the Vaadah's numbered accounts were kept. All of it. He had nothing to fear.

For a time, Kagan had considered simply walking into the police office in the Margitkerut prison and asking to see Szekely. Sometimes the most direct approach was the best. But he knew where Szekely could be found after dark, and the idea of a few hours' rest was appealing too. He was tired. The trip had been longer than he had anticipated, though no more difficult. A few hours' rest would do him good, clear his mind, make him better able to deal with the police general.

He had considered making a clean contact, before getting in touch with any of the Vaadah agents. It would have been better that way. Any possibility of compromise could have been avoided. But time was short, and if he could combine two moves in one, then so much the better. The translation of the Vrba–Wetzler report, bound in oilskin, had been safely hidden under a landing on Margaret Island and could be retrieved easily enough when the time came. In the meantime, while he was clearing his mind and getting a few hours' rest, he could make the initial moves.

A quick phone call to one of the protected houses had been enough to set things in motion. The meeting would take place in the most obvious and visible way possible and because of that would not be seen. The right man was available. It was almost time.

Kagan paused in front of the Oriental mushroom cupola of the Vama bathhouse. He smiled grimly. The place was safe. For him and for his contact, a Sabbatarian Christian who had repeatedly helped the Vaadah Jews as service to his own religious precepts. The bathhouse posed no problem for Kagan either. The *mohl* in his father's village had died four days before Itzhak Kagan had been born and had not been replaced for months. Herschel Kagan had been a freethinker and a socialist and had had little use for Jewish ritual to begin with. What he did, he did for his wife's benefit, and there was little enough of that. By the time a new *mohl* had made his way up the goat tracks to Kagan's village, it was too late. Kagan's father would have no part of him. As a result, Itzhak Kagan had never been circumcised. A useful omission, considering the times. And one which guaranteed at least a measure of safety in the Turkish baths of Budapest.

The Vama was one of the larger, better bathhouses. In former times only the rich had gone there. War, however, even in an authoritarian, quasi-fascist country, had tended to democratize the goings-on there. It was crowded with all sorts of visitors, civilian and military, but it still remained an almost entirely Hungarian preserve. The Germans almost never went there. He got on line before the ticket window and waited.

"Hogy ez?" he asked. How much?

The attendant frowned and pointed brusquely to a placard. Three hundred pengos admission. He would have to be more careful about such little things. He should have noticed. A lapse like that could mark him fatally.

He disposed of his clothes in an alcove and made his way to the octagonal pool. A pleasantly mild steam rose from the surface of the water, obscuring everything. Naked men of all shapes and sizes, pale and ghostly, moved through the steam, giving the place a strange otherwordly appearance.

Lowering himself into the water, he looked around carefully. There was no sign of Etvos yet. He closed his eyes briefly, luxuriating in the muscle-easing warmth. He could stay there for hours without moving; paradise. He could not remember such a pleasant sensation, ever.

The gentle splashing of water, then pleasured little cries of men ducking their heads, drawing deep, satisfied breaths of contentment, all contributed to his sense of relaxation. He moved his feet, his arms.

Through the steam, which rose like a gauzy curtain before his eyes, he could see only vague pink blurs. Old men, a few young, but not many. Then there was a voice close by.

"Old friend, how are things in Varna?"

Etvos. Matyas Etvos.

He turned. A head, dripping, the hair plastered down over a high forehead, flat features that made the man appear at that moment more of a sea lion than a human. A hesitant, cryptic smile.

It was a good place to talk. The tiles blurred sound, the constant plashing of the water covered it.

"A surprise. But a pleasure," said Kagan.

"As always."

They turned, both of them, toward the tiled edge of the pool, lowering their heads. It would be impossible to hear them two feet away. Kagan poured water over his head as he spoke.

"Can it be arranged?"

"Difficult tonight. The Nyilas are out in force."

"Nevertheless," said Kagan, "if it is possible . . ."

"Yes."

"Where then?"

"Next door to the Little Majestic. On Fö Street," Etvos said, "to the right, as you face it."

Kagan looked at him sternly. Astonishing. The place Etvos had just named was right next door to the headquarters of the Hungarian Gestapo. The jail cells below the Little Majestic were well known.

Etvos smiled.

"Where better, old friend? Can you think of a better place?"

Kagan smiled too. Of course. Etvos was right. The Vaadah was right.

"Third floor," said Matyas Etvos just before he ducked back under the water. "Walk right in. The family will be expecting you. Anytime. The pot is always on the stove."

Then he was gone.

Kagan closed his eyes. After all, hadn't they established a field hospital right in the basement of the Arrow Cross building where Jewish doctors tended their own and, now and then, even Nyilas who had wandered in by mistake, not knowing where they were?

He shook his head. The Hungarians were a strange people. Budapest was a crazy city. Insane. All of them. Everything.

Insanity. But in such times, what else could be expected?

So the third floor of the house on Fö Street it would be. But first he would make his contact with Tibor Szekely, major general of police.

They had things to discuss that the Vaadah had no reason to know about.

DOCUMENT

From the testimony of a witness, I.G. Farbenindustrie trial transcript, pp. 576 et seq.

This food was absolutely insufficient for our existence in view of the work which was demanded of us at the I.G. Buna plant. Many prisoners died as the result of undernourishment and insufficient clothes.

The weight of some of my fellow prisoners at the I.G. Farben plant at Auschwitz dropped to 35–44 kilograms. The average weight was 55 kilograms.

Duerrfeld, the manager of the I.G. Farben plant at Auschwitz, was definitely informed about the bad food conditions. He tasted the soup on one occasion in the spring of 1943 in my presence. He praised the soup and I asked him whether he was serious about it and he said, Well, it can be improved.

The I.G. Buna camp listed 30,000 deaths during the 3 years of its existence while it had at the most 10,000 inmates. I obtained the information from prisoners who were employed in the orderly room at Monowitz and who had to be correctly informed about these things as, for instance, Stefan Hyman.

The heaviest work which I had to accomplish in the Buna plant was to carry cement bags weighing 100 lbs. at double time. This work, which was enforced by Kapos, was carried out on the initiative of the foremen and was a general custom. I myself was supposed to carry two cement bags simultaneously at double time.

If a prisoner collapsed at work, he was kicked and beaten in order to determine if he was still alive. If he was dead, the body-carriers would either come right away or he would be carried back to the camp at night on the shoulders of his comrades.

A large percentage of the deaths was also caused by accidents, insufficient protective clothing, and insufficient safety measures provided by the I.G. Farben plant at Auschwitz.

Oswiecim

The main rail line from Vienna to Cracow ran directly through the Auschwitz camp complex. Two times a day, sometimes three, depending on the frequency and accuracy of Allied bombing raids, the train would slow slightly as it passed the old Auschwitz station, then accelerate again and flee toward Cracow. From the windows of their compartments, travelers could see little or nothing unusual. Those to whom the name Oswiecim meant anything at all knew it as the former site of a tobacco factory, and the long, low buildings they glimpsed in passing were consistent with that remembered intelligence. Others, older passengers whose memories went back to the days of Franz Josef's Galician divisions, recalled that there had been military barracks at Oswiecim. Again, they found nothing in what they saw to distress them. The gray, shedlike buildings, some wood, some a solid purposeful stone, were reasonable enough when considered as barracks.

The station itself, past which most but not all of the Cracow-bound trains rumbled without stopping, was in no way remarkable, a typical provincial construction on which no particular care had been lavished, but solid and reassuring enough in its utilitarian shabbiness.

There were a few odd things about the place, though. Often there were extraordinarily long lines of freight cars to be seen on a siding facing away toward the birch wood about two miles off on the far side of the station. Whatever was in the cars—military or industrial equipment for the Krupp, Siemens, and the I.G. works whose towers and stacks could be just barely glimpsed above the roofs of the barracks and factory buildings—could not be seen because the unloading doors always faced the other way and the yard area was screened by the bodies of the freight cars themselves. Only their frequency in such a place was unusual; it was simply too much business for an abandoned tobacco factory. But then, only a constant traveler on the route would have noticed that, and there were few enough of those.

There was an odd smell, too. Most passengers who noticed anything at all—and it was hard to notice anything because the Vienna–Cracow express itself had become extremely malodorous due to a long-time lack of sufficient disinfectants and sprays—simply assumed that it was Silesia itself that stank. The area, after all, was marshy, ridden with peat bogs and fetid swamps. The ground was everywhere pooled with little lakes of stagnant water, and braky, unhealthy-looking grasses grew like stubble all over the flat fields. Three sluggish rivers wound through the nearby countryside, and those knowledgeable in geo-economy knew that there were substantial coal mines nearby. Such places always smelled, and if the particular combination of odors was a bit unusual, few gave it more than a moment's thought as the train whisked them toward the more hospitable regions to the north.

There was, too—by way of explanation—plentiful evidence of industrial development in the immediate area of the Auschwitz station. There was the Krupp installation, belching fire and noise, the Siemens plant, and farther on a vast enclosure, full of odd metal kettles, out of which jutted huge towers and a thicket of pipes; the place seemed to be perpetually under construction. Hordes of workers could be glimpsed distantly and imprecisely, toiling away, erecting yet more towers and kettles, trestles, bridges, sheds, and rail sidings. Here and there, at odd locations which seemed to have little to do with these industrial constructions, tall brick chimneys jutting above the barracks buildings and out of the birch wood in the distance gave off a constant scrawl of sooty black smoke.

It was from there, oddly enough, that the odor seemed to emanate.

It was not an attractive place, and travelers—if they noticed anything at all—were glad to be gone as rapidly as possible.

A half-hour north of Ostrava, the train came to a sudden rattling halt in the middle of a flat field of hard, red soil, surrounded closely on either side by low scraggly forest, the last greenery of the Tatras.

Baranyi sat bolt upright and stared out the compartment window. Why had they stopped? Here? There was nothing here, no reason whatever to stop. Out of the corner of his eye he saw

Landau pull the coat down from his face and struggle upright, bleary-eyed and, at last, visibly fearful.

Landau leaned over, pressed his face to the grimy pane.

"Can you see? What is it?"

Eisner, who had been awake for some time, shuddered.

Two trucks and a *Kübelwagen* had drawn up alongside the track embankment. A dozen or more men in blue uniforms the like of which Baranyi had never seen before were already clambering on board.

Heidebroek grinned in relief.

"*Werkschutzen,*" he exclaimed. "Company police. *Our* police. Nothing to fear, gentlemen." He began fussing with his necktie as though in anticipation of an official visit, preening, making himself presentable.

Landau said, "I don't like such surprises."

"Better such surprise than many others I could think of," said Heidebroek.

There was a rapping on the compartment door. It was the young transport-command captain.

"Gentlemen? How sorry I am to disturb you. It is I, Hauptmann Keisl, and I have someone with me who wishes to see you."

Before he could say anything more, a stocky, middle-aged man in a gray suit and a squashy fedora, both much too heavy for the sultry, almost malarial July of the Polish plain, pushed his way into the compartment.

"*Gott Gruss,*" he exclaimed. "Good morning, Otto. Good morning, gentlemen."

"What a relief to see you, Gunther," Heidebroek sighed. "You have no idea what troubles we have had."

Dr. Ing. Gunther Grossbart smiled disingenuously and introduced himself. The transport captain took his leave and slid the compartment door shut. The Werkschutz detachment on board, the train got underway again.

Grossbart settled himself next to Landau, opposite Otto Heidebroek.

"Considering the problems we have all been having since the unfortunate attempt on the Führer's life, we thought that some elementary precautions were in order. The Wehrmacht and the SS have been vying with each other to see how many people they can arrest these last two days. It's a wonder there's anyone left to fight the war."

"We had problems of our own in Vienna," said Heidebroek. "Of exactly that sort."

Grossbart's face darkened. Baranyi watched carefully for any sign . . . of what?

He wasn't really sure.

"But you managed to avoid any difficulties?"

"Only by chance. The Hangman was there, can you imagine? It was he who rescued us."

"Neimann?"

"Himself. He just happened along. And it was thanks to him and him alone that we are here. What a joke. Neimann, of all people." Heidebroek mopped his forehead; the handkerchief came away gray with perspiration. "We were almost arrested, simply for being civilians. As it turned out, we *were* almost the only ones in the entire place not in uniform."

Grossbart shook his head and sighed. "But you *are* here and all is well. The storm will pass in a few days, I imagine. But for the meantime, we will take our own precautions. This is not Vienna and we, here, have a little more control over things. So . . ." He reached into his pocket and took out what looked like a shipping manifest. "Felix Landau, Swiss citizen." He paused and looked hard at Landau but said nothing more. "Herr Eisner? Also Swiss citizen. Baranyi? Hungarian, and a Swiss passport in the bargain. How unusual. Everything would seem to be in order. I'm sure that there will be no further problems. You *do* all speak German, of course?"

"Not very well," said Eisner.

"French or Italian then?" replied Grossbart. "Obviously one of those."

"Poor French."

"Better that here than poor German. Speak French then, if you must speak at all," Grossbart said. "It would be advisable, I think. When we reach the station, you will be entirely in my hands. You will please not speak to anyone else but me until you are in the automobiles which will be waiting for us. This situation would be sensitive enough under ordinary circumstances but ever since the incident at Wolfschanze, things have been even more . . . unpredictable. I'm sure you understand. Here, have some breakfast, gentlemen."

The briefcase, it appeared, contained a thermos of hot, bitter coffee heavily laced with chicory, a half dozen hard rolls, and some excellent kielbasa.

There were three of them waiting on the platform with the sour Silesian wind rattling the long skirts of their leather coats. Schragg had contrived to look like a Bavarian gentleman ready for a boar hunt in a soft green hat with a small bristle-feather in the brim, sturdy, mud-clotted boots on his feet, and a pair of obviously unnecessary leather gloves dangling from his waist. He was, as he had invariably been in Switzerland, too warmly dressed. Heidebroek pointed out the man on the right as Stellner, shorter, stouter, but no less formidable.

It was clear from the way Stellner was staring at Landau that he recognized him. Miklos wondered if Schragg had been so foolish as not to warn him of what to expect.

Just then the third man stepped out of the platform shadows to a spot where he could be clearly seen. Baranyi blinked. Heidebroek went pale and choked. Grossbart simply looked puzzled.

It was Oberführer Neimann, resplendent in a fresh black uniform and polished boots.

"How did that bastard get here ahead of us?" Heidebroek whispered. "We left him in Vienna."

Neimann, too far away to have actually heard Heidebroek's remark, appeared nevertheless to have understood and smiled meanly. He knew that he was not a popular man among the I.G. staffers.

"You are surprised, Herr Heidebroek? Recall, our good German aircraft do make somewhat better time than the Polish rolling stock you've been riding on. I decided not to come back by train after all. That scene at the station was distasteful, to say the least, and I had no desire to repeat it. Your own people at VW were good enough to put a plane at my disposal. For which I am quite grateful, believe me."

"We're delighted to see you, Oberführer," Heidbroek managed. "We are all in your debt."

"I trust you had a pleasant journey, despite the unfortunate beginning?"

Grossbart chuckled. "At least a good breakfast."

"Certainly that," put in Landau elegantly. "For which we thank the firm most deeply. It cannot be easy to come by such excellent sausage in a place like this."

"Oh," said Schragg, his voice taking on a cutting edge every bit as sharp as the summer wind, "you'd be surprised. We have every amenity here. Perhaps you'll have the opportunity to sample more of them. Who knows?"

Landau returned the veiled threat with a smile and a brisk nod.

"We should get about our business then?" he asked. "The train was, of course, exactly on time."

"The trains here," put in Neimann, "are almost always on time."

"I'm sure," said Baranyi.

"There were no incidents along the way?" Stellner inquired.

Neimann did not allow Landau to answer. "There was no activity along the rail lines yesterday. There has been none since last Sunday, to be precise. The closest incident was a raid on Breslau which must have provided our travelers with a good fireworks display but no anxiety, I'm sure."

Baranyi followed the trio across the platform, struggling against a growing feeling of hopelessness. He knew that on the other side of the station, hidden from his view by the long line of boxcars that stood not half a mile distant, horrible acts were being committed. The only visible evidence of what was happening was a faint low cloud of dust that rose from the yards, a cloudy yellow distinct against the marsh mists, and the distant sharp yapping of dogs which could be heard above the whistling wind only because of the high pitch.

Schragg strode on ahead, leaving Landau to walk in the SS man's company. They reached the end of the platform and were about to enter the two waiting field cars that were to convey them to the I.G. complex when Stellner, perhaps more perceptive than the others, inclined his head toward Baranyi and asked if something was bothering him.

"Fatigue, Herr Stellner. It concerns me that I am very tired. I know that my mind should be keen if I am to be of any assistance to Herr Landau in this enterprise. Also, I am uncomfortable because we know that we impose on you by being here at all. Unfortunately, it *is* necessary."

"Of course. A matter of survival, yes?"

"Of survival, certainly," agreed Baranyi as the driver indicated that he and Eisner should enter the second and rearmost of the two automobiles. It occurred to him that what this meant was that they would be immediately separated from Landau, who was to ride with Neimann. It would be impossible to prevent it, but he did not like the idea at all. On the other hand, Landau could probably handle himself alone better with Neimann than, say, with Schragg, who had just gotten into the front of Baranyi's auto and settled in next to the driver. He took off his hat, mopped his forehead, and began to whistle an air from *Der Freischütz*. A trifle too insistently, Miklos thought. It was almost as though he . . . knew.

As the car eased out onto a hard-packed dirt road skirting the siding, Schragg hooked an arm over the back of the seat and addressed Baranyi.

"We have arranged everything for you gentlemen. You may begin your examination as soon as you are rested. A cold shower will be provided if you wish it. You may take lunch with you or return and eat with us in our private dining room if you prefer. We would be pleased to entertain you."

Baranyi nodded. It was impossible to tell anything from the tone of Schragg's voice, he didn't know the man well enough, but there was an edge to it that worried him.

Baranyi looked past Schragg, at the head car, the rear now hidden in a low, moving cloud of dust. He could barely see the SS man. Landau was hunched down low in the back, next to Stellner. Schragg caught the direction of his gaze at once.

His face displayed instant irritation.

"That man . . . we have to have *him* along . . ."

For a second, Baranyi wasn't sure to whom Schragg was referring.

Schragg waved a hand in frustration. "It is wiser in the end, I think, to make him a part of this. Especially as he has already joined us, though without invitation. The Wolfschanze episode makes everything rather sensitive. I'm sure you can understand . . ."

Baranyi understood why perfectly and said so.

"He will be at dinner with us tomorrow night. I trust I can rely on you, Herr Baranyi, for the utmost discretion, yes? I look to you, as a gentleman, as an ally of ours . . . of sorts . . . to keep that other person, that . . . *disgrace* . . . in the other car . . . from creating any unpleasantness. In short, keep him silent. It is bad enough that he must be here at all."

Baranyi smiled. It was astonishing but should not have been beyond prediction. Schragg had transferred to him, as a Hungarian, the responsibility for Landau's behavior. He, Baranyi, was now to be Schragg's confidant. He felt like laughing.

"I will tell you outright, Herr Baranyi, if I had my way we would deal with that pig's fart in an entirely different manner. And he would certainly not be dining with us or sleeping in a clean bed tonight."

"I understand completely. But the times, unfortunately, are such that we all have to make . . . unpleasant compromises now and then. To ensure the ultimate good."

"Nicely put. I hope you are as adept at other things as you are at fending off my intemperate remarks."

"I'm sure everything will be in order," Miklos said, tightening his grip on his briefcase; it was as though he could actually feel the tiny rolls of microfilm that had been inserted in the tubular handle. It was the first time since leaving Zurich that he had even thought of the films.

How strange . . .

"I will look to you, Herr Baranyi," Schragg said. He turned and contented himself with staring straight down the road in front of them and moving his shoulders to relieve the cramp that hanging over the seat for so long had caused him.

The road passed alongside a vast complex of low buildings bordered by twin rows of barbed-wire fences which were punctuated every fifteen or twenty meters by tall, skeletal guard towers.

"As it is," Schragg said by way of afterthought, his voice low and barely audible, "we must keep that pig away from anyone who might recognize him. There are a number of his former colleagues at the installation, and since Wolfschanze, we cannot be too careful."

Baranyi stared out the window. All that was visible now were shifting gray shapes, almost obscured by a dense ground haze that steamed up from the marshes. The outlines of the low barracks stretched away as far as he could see, almost lost in the mists. The towers alone could be clearly made out, their dark silhouettes defined against the gray morning sky. Over the smooth purr of the Mercedes's engine he could hear distant, unidentifiable noises. Railroad cars groaning in an unseen yard. Couplings smashing together. More dogs barking. Now and then the hoot of a siren. But no voices, no trace of human activity. He knew from Vrba's sketches that he should at least be able to make out the smokestacks of the Krupp works, those of the Siemens factory, and perhaps the general outlines of the I.G. installation pushing up high above the barracks. But in the close mists, he could make out almost nothing.

For one terrible moment he had the feeling that they were driving off the edge of the world and into a great abyss.

"Shortly," said Schragg in a bored, almost inaudible drawl, "you may shower if you wish . . ."

Shower.

Vrba had written: "When everybody is inside, the doors to the shower room are closed . . . after which SS men with gas masks climb on the roof, open the traps, and shake down a preparation in powder form out of tin cans. . . ."

". . . shower if you wish. It is now"—Schragg held up his hand, displaying an elegant gold-cased Patek-Philippe—"exactly eleven thirty. We have arranged for you and . . . Landau . . . to begin your inspection at two. Perhaps by evening you will have seen enough so that"—and here he paused meaningfully and turned once more, his face flushed with anxiety—"so that we can all rest comfortably, yes?"

Zurich

She had gone shopping and bought herself a new dress, a plain inexpensive cotton print, nothing remarkable, only thirty-five francs, but it was the first time since coming to Zurich that she had done such a thing. By herself.

The morning was warm, the breeze from the lake gentle and

scented with mountain wildflowers. The shop windows glistened in
the pure morning sunlight. Posters advertising a plague of Viennese
operetta films and sentimental Gigli movies were everywhere. People whistled waltzes and hummed maudlin Italian tunes. Over the
constant buzz of traffic she could hear a distant clatter of cowbells
and the hooting of the ferry just then nearing the Alpenquai.

She was aware that her mood was suspect. There could have
been a number of reasons for it, all equally arguable; she did not
want to know whether it was because she had finally made her
peace with Miklos, or because he had gone and probably never
would return, thus relieving her of an almost impossible problem.
Or because the weather had finally turned really warm and lulling.

Or because she had simply grown terminally exhausted with
hating.

She walked slowly along the Bahnhofstrasse, smiling at passers-
by, breathing in the fresh morning air. It was wonderful to feel at
peace. Even if the sensation did not last.

She pressed the parcel under her arm. It was, in a way, a symbol
of her deliverance. What a shame that Miklos would not see it.

She tried to remember what it had been like but could not, and
for the first time in years could not summon up an accurate remem-
brance of her sister's face either.

All of that was gone, irretrievably. Unwanted now.

Unneeded.

She had no idea what to do with herself. She would, of course,
go back to her room and try on the dress, perhaps even spend some
time looking at herself in the mirror. She might even go to a store
that sold phonograph records and buy some of the new popular
songs, the kind Conrad Bor detested, and sit for a half-hour or so
with the window open, listening to them as she had done when she
had been a girl in Warsaw.

She rounded the corner and headed without really thinking
about it in the direction of the Frankengasse. With Baranyi gone,
there hardly seemed any point in her going there. If another load
of children was to arrive, Liebermann would get in touch with her
soon enough. In the meantime, she was free. No one needed her
and no one demanded anything of her.

As she came opposite the Municipal Building, a car eased to the
curb alongside her and followed, slowly, a little way behind. At

first she did not notice. Then out of the corner of her eye she saw the dull green, then recognized the car as the old Packard that belonged to the Polish legation.

The Packard pulled in a little way ahead of her and stopped. The door opened.

More annoyed at having her peace of mind disturbed than anything else, Julie Malowska went over to the car and peered inside. She neither expected to find Bor nor found him. It was Semkowski, one of Bor's underlings.

"The colonel wishes to see you," he said flatly, expecting her to get into the car at once.

"I'll come over after lunch."

"I don't think you understand, Pani. He wants to see you *now*."

There was an edge to Semkowski's voice that eliminated the need for further discussion. Julie got into the car.

It was hot. The windows were rolled up. Semkowski was sweating and looked uncomfortable. She refused to look at him. He was a decent enough person and was quiet and did not complain about the things he was asked to do. Perhaps it was this perpetually accepting manner that made Julie Malowska dislike him. She had never accepted anything in her life without a fight.

It was not far to the legation building. Semkowski was wise enough not to attempt conversation. Julie stared past him, intent on the driver's head. She could not see his face and did not care who he was. It simply gave her someplace else to look.

"Where is he?" she said as they came up to the front of the building. "With the consul?"

Semkowski shook his head.

"He's in his own office, Pani. Please, go up at once."

Much to her surprise, Semkowski got out behind her and followed her into the building and up the stairs.

She turned on him at the landing.

"Are you afraid I'll run away? This is amazing."

"Please, Pani. Don't make things difficult."

"*What* things?"

She was cut off by the peremptory sound of Bor's voice from within the office.

"Come in, Julie. At once."

She went in. Semkowski followed and shut the door behind them, leaning against it and looking acutely uncomfortable.

"So," said Bor, looking up from his papers. *"So . . ."*

"I don't like being ordered about in this fashion," she said.

"I regret the necessity, but as I have been trying to reach you for almost twelve hours, I thought it might be the simplest thing to send Semkowski to find you."

"Since when do we talk of 'necessity,' Conrad?"

"Since Tuesday night," he said.

"Oh?"

"Tuesday night," Bor repeated dully. "Really, Julie, I thought I could count on you to be more sensible."

"What *are* you talking about? And whatever it is, do you really think that it's appropriate to have *him* here?"

"Under the circumstances, yes."

"I don't understand you at all."

"Of course you do," Bor said. The tone was very unusual for him. Weary and hollow. His normally sardonic manner had deserted him entirely. He seemed genuinely injured.

She glanced at Semkowski. He looked away.

Then she knew.

"Tuesday night, Julie. I asked you about Tuesday."

"You know already, so why ask?"

"I want to hear it from you."

"Apparently you've already heard it from poor Semkowski here. You were having me watched, Conrad? Spied on? I never would have believed you'd do such a thing."

"After the episode in the alley—the man *you* killed, Julie—I thought it prudent. I was trying to . . . protect you."

She laughed, stridently and angrily.

"You do have a nerve, Conrad, don't you?"

"I'm too much older than you to be offended by the mere fact that you choose to sleep with someone younger."

"Thank you very much, Conrad."

"But," he went on, "when your choice of a partner is a direct insult to me—"

"Get *him* out of here and we'll talk about it," she said.

"He is here to corroborate—"

"There's no need for that. If it's any of your business who I sleep with, and I suppose you feel that it is, I have no secrets. So please ask him to leave, or I will." Without waiting for an answer, she turned on the embarrassed Semkowski. "Jan, do you mind? Please go. *Now*. I'm sorry if this offends you."

Semkowski went out, breathing a sigh of relief. The door slammed shut.

"Look at that," she said. "He didn't even wait for *you* to give him his orders. Well, neither did I. Very sorry, Conrad."

Then she noticed that there were two suitcases standing by the window—the suitcases she had dragged with her from Warsaw. She had left them, a long time ago, at Bor's apartment.

"All your things," he said, noticing the direction of her glance.

"Very thoughtful of you."

"More thoughtful than you were, Julie," he said.

"Why, Conrad? Why?" she demanded, feeling very foolish standing there with the parcel containing her new dress still under her arm. "Jealousy? You never cared before what I did, or what I'd done. You knew it all."

"I'm too much older than you to be jealous. I've said that already."

"What then?"

"Taste, Julie. An absolute lack of taste."

She stared at him, still not understanding.

He went on, his eyes closed, a pained expression creasing his elegantly planed face.

"A Jew," he said. "Or have you forgotten? Helping them, working with them, particularly as we have a common cause at the moment, that is understandable. But to sleep with the man?" He shook his head. "What was it, an act of revenge, or did you really want to do it? No, don't even try to explain. I'm sure you don't know yourself."

She took a deep breath. It was complete now and she felt suddenly and tremendously relieved.

Bor was no different from all the others. Only more polished. More urbane. Cleverer.

What a fool she had been all along to think him any different.

But then, had she really? She had gone to him at first because there had been no one else. He had known her father, however slightly. He was in a position of power. It had been the natural thing to do. It had been very good for her. Then.

It no longer was.

"Take your suitcases, Julie," Bor said. "If you need anything from me, if you are in difficulties of any kind, you must call. I won't turn you away. But the other . . . thing . . . is finished."

"It was finished a long time ago. Probably before it started."

He nodded. "Possibly. But we shall never know, shall we?"

She went over to the window, picked up her suitcases, and went out.

On the landing Semkowski offered to help her with the luggage. She accepted. It was difficult to manage both the suitcases and the package containing the dress.

She didn't want the dress to become creased.

Bor sat for a long time behind his desk, his eyes closed, rubbing his forehead with his fingers, breathing deeply.

It had been very difficult to do. He hated lying and he hated hurting her as he knew he had. He did not want her, ever, to be disappointed in him. But it had been the only way. And it had to be done.

He had no wish to involve her in what was to happen next.

Inevitably.

For that, he had to be alone and under no obligation to anyone.

It would be better for her. That was the only saving grace. It would definitely be better for her.

Budapest

The brothel which police Major General Tibor Szekely regularly frequented was located in the old section at the foot of Castle Hill in the Taban, a district of ancient houses, inns, and innumerable staircases ascending the steep slope of the hill itself. The house was neither distinctive from the outside nor marked in any way; it might easily have been mistaken for a small hotel closed for renovations.

Only the faint sound of music—a phonograph record, deeply scratched—gave evidence of life behind its shuttered windows.

Kagan had changed his clothes. The house was by no means reserved for the rich, but there was no point in calling attention to oneself by looking like a drayman either. In his breast pocket was a fat wallet, full of bank notes obtained by calling on the Zurich bank representative at his home and taking a quick walk through Telecki Square to intercept a courier.

He entered the little court, went under a stone archway, and rang the doorbell. After a moment, a man in a neat gray suit, clearly of French cut, opened the door, looked him up and down, and hesitated. Kagan knew the ritual. He pressed a hundred-pengo note into the man's hand. Not a word was said. The door swung wider and he went in.

A short corridor opened onto a large room. One side was occupied by a piano, the opposite by a sort of bar. Settees and chairs were disposed all over the room in no particular order. A dozen young women in various stages of undress lounged about, all of them good-looking at least, some truly beautiful. The men were the usual mixture: Hungarian civilians, a few Romanians, a few officers of the Honved. In one respect, it was the same as the bathhouse. It was not a place where Germans were welcome, and they obviously stayed away. By mutual consent.

The music was clearer now. An old song. "One Hundred Red Roses." Imre Nagy's throaty voice. The air was heavy with cigarette smoke, dark and fragrant. Miriams. From the number of wine and brandy bottles in evidence, it would have been hard to tell that there was a war on. It was already well past curfew, but no one seemed to notice. If it mattered at all, it mattered only to the civilians.

A woman came over to ask if Kagan wanted anything to drink. He gave her a thousand-pengo note and asked for a bottle of Debröi Harslevelü. The woman raised her eyebrows, smiled, and disappeared into the next room.

Kagan looked around. The proprietress was nowhere in sight; he wondered if it would be the same woman who had been in charge when he had first come to the place with Baranyi the year before. A few of the girls gave him approving glances; he was by far the biggest man in the salon. He smiled back but did not motion any of them over. When the wine was brought, he sat back and drank quietly, looking things over. The music ground on, the record impossibly scratchy. The women were an odd mixture, some obviously Hungarian, some just as clearly Slavic. One of the Honved officers was drunk and trying to play a Chopin prelude on the piano. The woman he was with kept pulling at him, and after a while he went with her up the stairs at the rear of the room. Someone put the needle back at the beginning of the record again. "One Hundred Red Roses."

For the fifth time. That makes five hundred roses at least, Kagan thought. It was difficult, in such a place, to remember why he had come. Difficult, but not impossible.

After a while, the proprietress made her appearance, a pretty woman with dyed blond hair, the only blond in the room. She was well over forty, and tending to fat. She wore her rings and bracelets with flair and her make-up without caution.

"You're the only one alone," she said. "Don't you see anyone you like?"

"Magda," Kagan said quietly.

The madam's eyebrows went up.

"Which Magda? We have three."

"The one with red hair," he said. Magda with the red hair was the general's whore. She was available to no one else. Everyone in the house knew that.

The madam shook her head, squinting at Kagan, trying to remember if she'd ever seen him before.

"Red-haired Magda," he said. "No one else."

"It's impossible. Drink your wine and leave, if that's what you want."

"I can't. It's past curfew. Why, I'd need an escort to get by the patrols. Say, a police officer. A general." He smiled. "What d'you say? Tell him it's Varna."

Somewhere in the back of the woman's mind, something stirred. She remembered. Her face turned several shades whiter under the make-up.

"All right. But you'll have to wait. He's busy at the moment."

"I assumed he would be. Why should this night be different from any other?"

"That's an odd way of putting it, wouldn't you say?"

"Perhaps," he agreed, getting up to follow her, taking his bottle of Harslevelü with him.

The proprietress led him to the third floor of the house, down a short corridor, and into a small room containing only a bed, a table with a washbowl on it, and a chair.

"He may be a while. Don't you want some company while you wait?"

"This will be company enough for me," he replied, patting the wine bottle. The woman shrugged and went out, closing the door firmly behind her. The lock, however, did not click.

Kagan got up at once and went to the door, listening for the sound of the woman's footsteps receding down the hall. Then there was quiet. He heard nothing but labored breathing in the next room, on the other side of the wall, then the sound of a woman counterfeiting pleasure. The sounds were harsh, unpleasant. They continued for some time. Szekely was known as the "black bull of Budapest" by both his admirers and his detractors. It was said that he was at the brothel punctually every night at eight, except on evenings when he was detained by affairs of state or police matters, and never left before midnight. If he ate out or went to the theater, it was always after his trip to the Taban.

Kagan had no weapon but his documents, spoke only limited Hungarian, and had no idea whether the woman had really understood what he had said. It was a chance, of course, but it was still the best way to make contact. Obviously the proprietress was accustomed to meetings of this kind, otherwise why would she have shown Kagan to an empty room, on the third floor . . .

The third floor.

He tried to remember what the building had looked like from the outside, but it had been dark when he'd approached it and he had had no clear view of the upper stories or the adjoining structures.

He went to the window, and looked out. Normally, in the Taban, the buildings were crowded close, one on top of the other, the roofs almost adjoining. It would be easy to slip out of a window, climb down, make one's way across the rooftops in the dark.

He looked out, then smiled.

The room to which he'd been shown overlooked a courtyard. It

was a straight three-story drop down to the cobblestones, with no
rooftop within reach. A man could leave the room only the way he
had come in. There was not even a drainpipe to hang on to on the
exterior of the building wall under the window, nor a single ledge.

Fine. She was taking no chances with him. That meant only one
of two things. Either he was being set up—and there was no earthly
reason why she should have done that—or he was going to receive
the general shortly.

He glanced at his watch, a small, steel-jacketed Swiss. It was
after ten. Even a man of Major General Szekely's reportedly pro-
digious energies should have spent himself by now.

A door slammed close by. Next door, in fact. Footsteps in the
hall, heavy, unconcerned. Not furtive at all. The doorknob turned.
Kagan found himself looking into the swarthy, mustachioed face of
Tibor Szekely, major general of police, who was just then tucking
in his shirt and adjusting his suspenders. He wore an expression of
satisfaction on his face, a deep flush, and little else.

He squinted, as the proprietress had done, the same questioning
narrowing of the eyes, then grinned.

"You take quite a chance, coming here," he said, in German.

"I take a chance being anywhere in your city," said Kagan.

"Why? I assume your papers are in order."

"Oh yes," said Kagan. "I wouldn't want to embarrass you by
being arrested."

The general laughed appreciatively, finished tucking in his shirt,
and sat himself on the edge of the bed.

"We have business, then?"

"We do."

"Let me warn you, now that we have a city full of German tourists, there's very little I can do for you."

"I don't want anything from you. I want to make you a present."

"Oh?"

The two men sat there, eyeing each other for a long time, without saying anything. Both were massive, Kagan slightly larger; both
were powerful, had hands that could bend iron. Szekely had been a
field commander under Horthy when the regent had seized power.
He'd killed men with his bare hands. Many. Kagan understood
such people; he preferred them by a considerable margin to the
ones who killed by orders, telegrams, phone calls, and memoranda.

Finally, the policeman said, "Well then, what kind of gift do you bring me from wherever it is you come from?"

"Would you like to set the 'tourists' fighting among themselves?"

"It would be amusing, certainly," Szekely said.

"It could be done. If you like, I can give you a gift that will have the SS and the army at each other's throats. But you must promise me one thing in return."

"And that is?"

"That you'll really use it for that purpose. That you'll pass it on and not use it to blackmail someone. That's my condition."

Szekely was becoming interested. He leaned forward, his black eyes dancing with anticipation. As unreliable as he was generally, there were two things Kagan knew he could count on—a keen sense of self-preservation and an intense dislike of the Germans.

"You're aware of the transports, of course," Kagan said. "The trains taking the Jews east . . ."

"There is nothing we can do about it. You must understand. Between the Arrow Cross and the Germans, our hands—"

"I didn't ask you to do anything about it. We know you can't. We do not expect miracles. We try to make them ourselves."

"Has what you're going to tell me something to do with a self-made miracle?"

"Perhaps, but that needn't concern you."

"What *should* concern me, then?"

"Only this—that the Wehrmacht wishes to put an end to the commandeering of rolling stock by the SS. That the Wehrmacht considers the supplying of its eastern front with men and ammunition more important than the slaughtering of women and children by the carload—"

"For the moment," interrupted Szekely.

"Always the realist," said Kagan. "All right. For the moment. I grant you that. But it may be the last moment. They'd like to keep the Russians back as long as possible. A sentiment I'm sure you share—am I correct?"

Szekely nodded. His face had taken on a distinctly more sober expression in the last sixty seconds.

"To achieve this end," Kagan went on placidly, "certain elements in the Wehrmacht—and let me tell you straight off, I don't know who . . . we had nothing to do with the contacts—these certain elements have provided us with detailed plans, maps, schedules, all of the information necessary for the Americans and the English to bomb the rail lines leading into the camps in southwestern Poland. The ones to which the Jews from here are being sent."

"The proof?"

"You're interested?"

"Of course. It would be a real pleasure to see the swine fighting among themselves. Over railroad cars. Ha! It would give me one of the few enjoyable moments I've had this year, believe me. What's your condition?"

"You've just complied with it, I think. I'll give you the proof and you pass it on to the SS. To that bastard up in the Majestic if you like. He'll thank you for it. Maybe you can get something useful for yourself in return. *But pass it on.* We want them to know what we've got and where we got it from."

"Why?" Szekely said very softly.

"It's one thing to have secured the information." He chose his words very carefully now, testing, watching the police general's expression. "It's one thing to know that the lines will be bombed. But there are still carloads leaving every day. It may be weeks before the air strikes can be mounted. The Germans can't do anything about them, they haven't the strength to stop them anymore. But in the meantime, who knows how many more trainloads will go through? If we can stir them up, set them at each other's throats, who knows what may come of it? We've nothing to lose, and if we stop or delay even one train, one transport, it will be worth it."

Szekely nodded gravely. It made enough sense for him to accept it. And where there were holes in the logic—and he sensed that if he gave it some thought, he would find many holes—the anticipation of benefit to be gained was enough to plug the gaps.

He was ready to believe. It suited him to believe. Kagan saw it and knew that he'd said enough.

"When can you deliver?"

"I'll see that the documents are in your hands by morning. Never mind how. You'll have them."

"Have I ever asked you people in the past?"

"No. And you've at least been honest with us. That's why we come to you."

"If one cannot have honor in these times, at least one can try to remain honest."

"The honest thief is worth far more than the devious saint."

"Where did you hear that one, my friend?"

"I just made it up," Kagan said.

Szekely laughed. "Very good, really excellent. I'll remember it, I promise you."

"Remember better what you promised *me*. You'll have the proof in a few hours."

"It will be a pleasure to use it, never fear."

"Jo ejszakat . . ."

"Good night," answered the policeman. "And by the way, your accent isn't bad at all. Come back after the war and we'll make a Hungarian out of you, I promise . . ."

Oswiecim

Two technicians in white laboratory coats accompanied them across the courtyard that fronted the administration complex. From there they proceeded down a narrow pathway of hard-packed cinders flanked on both sides by high walls of corrugated metal. The sounds of activity were everywhere. Steam hissed, motors rumbled, concrete mixers groaned, beams clattered against beams. The plant area, still in the process of construction, stretched ahead of them for what seemed like three or four kilometers. A forest of gray fuel tanks, silvery silolike structures the height of a three-story building, rose among the iron kettles, the striped towers, and the steel piping. Every so often a concrete blockhouse appeared; into these buildings a clustered run of pipes would disappear, emerging from the other side, separating and branching off in a dozen different directions, to be joined at varying distances by yet other pipes issuing from yet other blockhouses. In the middle of this metal jungle, larger structures rose at irregular intervals, two- and three-story wooden buildings with wide glass observatory windows and curious clusters of machines on their roofs, like giant water tanks.

The technicians walked briskly ahead, leaving Baranyi and Landau to follow. There was no need for Eisner to accompany them, even in aid of the charade. He had been represented as what, after a fashion, he actually was, an agent of Swiss Chemihold. Landau and Baranyi had been identified to Oberführer Neimann as technicians from a Swiss petrochemical firm which was interested in the postwar licensing of the Buna process from I.G. There could be no harm in such a visit. The approval of the Reichsminister for Armaments had been obtained through VW. The SS security office at Auschwitz proper had been handed an order signed by SS Major General Wolff of Himmler's personal staff authorizing the visit. Dr. Krauch had been nothing if not thorough.

And so Herr Eisner, very tired after his long journey, sat alone in his room on the second floor of the administration building living quarters while the technical experts made their inspection.

Everything was quite in order.

At the end of the path was an iron gate and a movable barrier striped red and white like those used at railroad crossings. Beyond this point, surrounded by high fences of double-strung electrified wire, spread the industrial facilities themselves. Over two square miles of buildings, works in progress, towers, smokestacks, and sheds. Nearest, and occupying approximately half of the total area, were the Buna works, still very much under construction. Much farther out, to the north, were the stacks of the synthetic fuel plant, thick against the murky sky, like a forest of telephone poles. Once, on a hunting trip in the foothills below Mount Kekes, Miklos had come upon just such a place, a few square miles of forest which had been ignited, perhaps by a lightning bolt, and had burned to a skeletal, blighted ruin of tall, black trunks half hidden by a pall of smoke that refused to dissipate.

It seemed that a similar malevolent act of nature must have been responsible for this terrible place.

Wherever he looked, Miklos saw crowds of bent men in striped prison pajamas and shapeless "blackberry" caps, laboring over piles of beams, hammering, hauling, mixing, raising. Concrete, steel, vast scaffoldings of wood rising latticelike against the sky, gridding off the turmoil of buildings and installations beyond. Here and there a group of these men, clay-faced and skeletal, would go trotting by, sometimes carrying awesome loads but always at double-time. There seemed no intermediate stage—either the actual work at a slow, exhausted pace or frenetic, desperate rushing to get from one area to another. I.G. foremen in civilian clothing stalked through this forest of uncompleted construction, stomping through the muddy ground, gesturing, shouting instructions. The special plant police, the Werkschutzen, were everywhere, giving orders, blowing whistles. The Kapos drove their squads with cudgel blows and vicious slashes of their dog whips, even interrupting work that seemed to Miklos to be proceeding as fast as humanly possible in order to make examples.

The entire site, as far as he could see, resembled a vast hive. Dust rose, voices were raised in constant and unrelenting anger. The clanking of heavy building materials and the grinding of machines raised a din so constant that it was almost impossible to hear.

Landau's head swiveled back and forth. He peered from side to side. Every time a group of I.G. workers appeared, he squinted quickly at them, turned his head and looked away. A bit too guiltily, Baranyi thought. Stellner, who had joined them at the path's end, just before they entered the main section of the complex, where the polymerization kettles stood like giant milk bottles, noticed Landau's odd behavior. He plucked Landau by the sleeve and spoke hurriedly to him.

"Listen, you don't really think we'd be so foolish as that, do you? Everything's been arranged. No one you see will know you. We have a whole new generation of technicians here. New men, Felix." He gave these last three words a hard emphasis. Yet he had called him Felix and not Herr Landau in that derisive way of Schragg's.

Baranyi noticed that, and it worried him.

They entered one of the larger buildings, a metal shed perhaps half a city block long, equally as wide, and two stories or more high.

"Here," said Stellner, "here is where the aqueous-phase emulsion is prepared. What do you wish to examine? There must be something in particular that troubles you, yes? I assure you, we have the process completely under control. As you will see." He called after the elder of the two technicians who had gone ahead into the building. "Dieter, show our visitors the catalyst injection equipment."

The building was filled with pipes, drums, and yet more of the oddly shaped kettles. Baranyi tried his best to counterfeit a knowing expression and followed as fast as he could behind Landau. He had no little difficulty keeping up with the man, so rapidly did he dart about. Didn't Landau remember where he was and why they had come? A look of near transfiguration had spread over Landau's face the moment he had entered the building. He was close to tears.

Of joy.

But why not? From everything Baranyi and Peshko had been able to learn, from all the entries in Bor's dossier and the Swiss police records, Felix Landau had indeed been one of the leading chemical engineers in his field, second only to such bona-fide geniuses as Ambros and Ter Meer. Take such a man away from his life's work by force, pen him up as a common pharmacist's assistant for four years, then suddenly drop him into a place where he can see his theories realized, and why shouldn't he weep for joy?

Even under such circumstances as these.

It was a reaction he should have anticipated, and the fact that he hadn't sent a violent chill through Miklos's body.

He stood back, growing more and more apprehensive, as Landau fired question after question at the two technicians. He fingered valves, pushed at coils and fittings, checked switches. He asked for calculations, whipped out a pencil and covered sheets of paper with figures of his own.

Stellner watched all of this with a nervous smile.

Now and then Baranyi would take Landau aside and whisper to him, to make it appear as though he too were asking questions. He took down scraps of what the technicians were telling Landau. Stellner seemed satisfied. It didn't really matter.

By evening Schragg, and Stellner, too, would know what they had really come for.

A network of iron stairways and catwalks surrounded the polymerization kettles. Liquids bubbled through conduits the diameter of sewer pipe. Needles flickered back and forth across the faces of endless dials and gauges. Open transparent tubes like level gauges on water tanks or furnaces registered the passage of various chemicals as they were pumped into the mixing tanks.

The interior of the room was very cold. Baranyi found that his hands were growing numb, and thrust his fingers deep into the pockets of his coat. The surface of the kettles showed a tracery of ice crystals. This was because the polymerization process was carried on at temperatures as low as five degrees below zero centigrade.

Landau did not seem to notice the cold. He ran from one piece of equipment to another, asking his questions, probing, boring in. The technicians became flustered, could not answer rapidly enough, grew confused. Landau was too much for them.

And he was obviously overdoing it. That was bad, very bad.

Stellner, watching this performance, became visibly alarmed, as did Baranyi, watching Stellner.

Landau turned and came over.

"Would it be possible to see Dr. Krauch? There is an aspect of the temperature-depression apparatus that—"

Stellner was shocked. "Krauch? Impossible. Impossible. Dr. Krauch is not here. He does not *come* here."

"And Otto?"

"Ambros? No, no, out of the question also."

"He doesn't come here either?"

"Not frequently. It is not necessary. Felix, please, consider—do you really need—"

Landau cut him off, a look of almost childlike disappointment on his face. "No, I suppose not. I can manage quite well without them. Still, it would have been nice . . ." His voice trailed off.

Baranyi watched with growing concern; to Landau it was obviously no longer a deception, a time-marking operation. He was taking the game seriously, reveling in the authority that his knowledge and pretended position gave him, in being back among the machines and the men with whom he had spent most of his adult life.

It was, Baranyi thought, a most dangerous development. He would have to take Landau aside very soon and caution him.

About what?

Just at that moment, Miklos looked up and saw a man standing high above them on an iron catwalk running between two ice-covered towers that reached almost to the ceiling of the shed. At first he could make out no more than a vague outline, a dark shape in a greatcoat. Then the light coming through the upper windows shifted, grew momentarily more intense as clouds gave way to the east and permitted a brief lightening of the sky.

It was Neimann, his arms folded over the railing, his cap pushed back on his bullet head, rubbing his hands together and watching them. Silently.

For how long?

Baranyi touched Stellner on the arm, lightly, so as not to make him start. Stellner turned, and Baranyi, with his eyes only, indicated the catwalk.

Stellner turned his face upward and saw what Baranyi had seen. The color drained from his face, but he said nothing.

He took Landau by the arm.

"Felix, are you finished here? We must move on. You will want to see the reaction arrester, yes?"

"But the temperature controls—we haven't seen them yet."

"We will see the reaction arrester now. *Now,* Felix. It is most important that we do so."

Baranyi signaled that Landau should do as he'd been told. As they hurriedly left the huge shed, Stellner was heard to mutter under his breath.

Baranyi caught only one word, or thought he did.

". . . *Henker* . . ." The Hangman.

Budapest

In the cellar of the house next to the Gestapo building on Fö Street a small printing press ground on remorselessly, turning out one leaflet after another. Kagan watched the young Vaadah in the bunker with undiminished amazement. It was like watching the backstage of a theater during the performance of a historical pageant. But the time of the pageant was now and the purpose far from entertainment. No two people in the cellar were dressed alike. A few wore the paramilitary dress of the Hungarian youth corps, the Levante, with their forage caps and red-white-and-green metal badges. A gendarme with plumed hat still in place bent over the press, now and then inking the plates. In a corner, a young man in the familiar uniform of a Nyilas captain stuffed leaflets into envelopes. Two nurses from the Bethelen Street hospital—by their arm patches—affixed stamps. Honved officers, policemen, even German army uniforms. Everything but Jews.

Runners came and went, carrying a few of the slender envelopes at a time. Only a few. Otherwise they might attract attention. It was tedious and time-consuming, but the leaflets were going out. By regular post, which still functioned despite the increasingly severe air bombardment.

A leaflet was going to every man or woman in Budapest who could be considered even remotely sympathetic. Comprehensive lists had been drawn up. Copies had been taken the day before to the papal nuncio's office.

So far, no one had been caught, though over three thousand of the leaflets had been mailed.

A young man in Levante uniform came over to Kagan. His face was hard, set in a counterfeit of arrogance that had by now become second nature, a regular part of his appearance. No names. Not a single person in the Fö Street house had a name as far as Kagan was concerned.

It was better that way. Just in case.

The young man in Levante uniform lit a cigarette, then handed the pack to Kagan. The printing press ground on, issuing a soft clacking noise.

"It can't be heard over there?" Kagan asked, indicating the walls on the other side of which lay the Gestapo cellar.

"Can *you* hear it? Just barely, from over here. The wall on our side is three feet thick, of stone. On their side there are steel plates and more stone. They were afraid someone might try to tunnel into the torture chambers so they took precautions. There isn't a better-insulated cellar in all of Budapest than this one."

Kagan smiled grimly, took a drag of the young man's cigarette. He would be leaving as soon as it got dark. By truck to Szigetvar, then by foot over the border and back to Zurich. It was a route he knew well. Though he hated to leave, it was time. This day or the next. How he would have liked to have remained; these young men and women were different even from those he had left in the city two months before. There were no illusions anymore. Weapons were being accumulated in secret storehouses. Let the others, the older ones, try to escape. Let them continue to believe in their ideals and bargains, to believe that they could buy their way out, that in the end logic would prevail. These young men and women knew better. They were ready to deal with Eichmann on his own terms when the time came.

It had been a long time since Kagan had killed a German. He envied the Vaadah here their opportunities.

For a moment, briefly only, he thought, Why not? Why shouldn't he stay? He had obligations to no one but himself anymore.

But that wasn't true.

How many times had Miklos Baranyi saved his life? He owed that man a thousand times over. And he would have to live to be able to repay the debt.

An older man in the uniform of a Wehrmacht major touched him on the shoulder.

"It's getting dark," he said.

"The truck?"

The ersatz major nodded. "Across the river, by the brickyards." He had been a butcher before the Germans had shut down all the kosher butchers in Budapest. Now he used his knife for different purposes.

"Here," said Kagan, handing the man his baptismal certificate, Christian birth certificate, and residence card. "I won't need these."

"Keep them. Who knows what will happen, eh? We'll do all right here with one baptismal certificate less, believe me, but who knows how *you'll* do? Besides, we make them just as well."

"This one is real. From the Turkish nuncio."

The Wehrmacht major laughed. "So are ours. You see? There's no difference at all."

Oswiecim

The pilot sucked on his oxygen mask, squinted once at his instruments, and pulled the Liberator up to twenty thousand feet. Thin fingers of cloud lay like smudgy tracks all over the Silesian plains below. The co-pilot checked his hydraulic-system gauges and relaxed. It was going to be very easy, very routine, very uneventful.

To the north, a low pall of smoke hung close on the horizon, marking the still burning Breslau area, the target of a massive strike only a few days before.

Not a single German fighter was in the air.

There was no flak, either.

The pilot turned slightly and spoke into his chin mike.

"Getting ready, Charley?"

"Another minute. How's it look up there?"

"Clear, clear, clear. Not even sparrows."

"Too high for sparrows. They get beak bleeds," said the aerial photography specialist back in what would normally have been the bomb bay but was now crowded with high-resolution camera equipment.

"You want to take her down for me a little?"

"Anyone tell you what the flak over Breslau looked like?"

"This isn't Breslau," said the photographer. "Looks like there isn't much of anything down there, in fact."

"You'll see it soon enough."

The pilot nosed the big bomber back down a little. He could afford to give the cameraman a little tighter range. The German flak, if there was any, couldn't touch them where he was, and there had been hardly a sign of the Luftwaffe since they'd left base. Only once, near Breslau, a Focke-Wulf had flirted with them for a while and then decided to stay clear.

"It's a picnic, Charley."

He heard a whistle on the intercom and knew that the Auschwitz installations and the factories must have come into view. From where he sat, he could see only his instrument panels and a lot of sky. But he'd seen the camp and the factories before in pictures, spreading like a city over the marshy plain between the two rivers. Why they were going back for yet more pictures he couldn't figure out, but he'd long since given up worrying about such things. He just did as he was told and didn't argue. The order, they said, had come direct from Washington, and you simply didn't argue with such things. Besides, they'd have to go back in a week or so and do it again. He didn't understand the reason for that either.

There was plenty of sun, big yellow patches of it, all over the long rows of barracks and the sheds and the industrial areas. Particularly the big factory area right on the rail line, on the east side of the camp complex.

He checked his course with the navigator and called back to the photographer to get ready.

"Way ahead of you," came the reply. "We're rolling already."

In the bomb bay, the cameras were clicking away, on automatic, every second or so. Like a clock ticking. Through the viewfinder, the photographer could see the industrial areas that lay to the east, the railroad tracks and the barracks clustered around them. The tracks ran straight alongside the area they were photographing; the siding was a little farther toward the river. A hundred or more boxcars waited there.

It was odd, but even from that altitude he could see what looked like long lines of people outside a complex of buildings on the other side of the river, near a heavily wooded area. Some kind of factory, he thought. Big smokestacks jutting up out of concrete buildings. He shrugged and checked the cameras. The weather was perfect. The flight was level and the air smooth. The pictures would be just perfect.

The pilot held his course, true and level, like the professional he was.

"How's business, Charley?"

"Run's finished. All out of film."

The pilot pulled the nose of the B-24 up again, seeking more altitude. The sky remained clear, empty and beautiful.

It was like taking a walk in the country on a sunny summer day.

Zurich

A pale, uncertain morning light filtered in through the window of room 4D at the Zurich Staatshospital. Henry Stropp turned uneasily on the bed, reaching for the water glass with its odd cover and bent glass straw. Through the spaces between the venetian-blind slats he could see a gray church spire rising into a grayer sky.

For a moment he was unsure where he was. Then it all came flooding back to him. The bar at the Baur-au-Lac, his collapse, the doctors hovering over him.

How long had he been in the hospital? Six days, eight, perhaps ten? He had difficulty remembering. For a long while he had been kept in a special section of the hospital with a round-the-clock nurse, surrounded by all sorts of machines the purpose of which he did not understand but which he knew had to do with the possibility that his heart might stop at any minute.

Heavily sedated at first, he had drifted in and out of consciousness on successive waves of nausea. Gradually the nausea had subsided. Doctors had come and gone, a whole army of them, it seemed.

He dimly recalled being shown a cable from New York which had read, simply, "No expense too great. Get the best. Marcus."

They had told him that he had had a serious heart attack. They had hooked him up to machines with little needles and long rolls of paper tape like stock-ticker machines.

The possibility that he might die had, for the first time in his life, become a present reality. He had become like a child, submissive, doing exactly what he was told to do. Constantly fearful.

The door to his room opened. A nurse came in, a colorless, briskly efficient woman who inspired confidence but generated no warmth. And warmth was what Henry Stropp felt he needed just then. Something to push away the loneliness and the fear.

The nurse was carrying a folded newspaper.

"Dr. Vincenzi says you may have this today, Herr Stropp. He trusts you not to excite yourself, yes? The news, at any rate, is very good. From your point of view, I would think."

He took the paper gladly. It was the first contact he had had with the outside world since they had brought him here.

"Will I have visitors now, nurse?"

"Not as yet," she replied. "You will have to make do with Dr. Vincenzi and myself."

Stropp elbowed himself upright. The nurse adjusted his pillows. She had a pungent medicinal odor about her.

"Has anyone asked to see me?"

She shook her head.

"Are you sure?"

"I can check at the desk if you like, but I am sure. No one has called."

Stropp was confused for a moment. Where was Eisner?

In Poland.

He hadn't come back yet. Of course not.

And Ellsworth? Where the devil was Ellsworth? And Grunewald?

There was no one else in Zurich who even knew he was in the
city. Trilling had cabled. But no one had come over to see him.
He knew that he should not have expected anyone, but it hurt him
nevertheless. Even Bard at the embassy in Berne had stayed away.
Probably he didn't even know there was anything wrong. Who was
there to tell him?

The nurse went out.

Stropp unfolded the paper. All at once he felt a hundred anxi-
eties pressing in on him. His pulse began to race, then slowed. He
pushed the paper away angrily. Then, very slowly, retrieved it and
started to read.

Do not get excited. Under no circumstances allow yourself to
become excited.

The headlines were terse and violent. There had been an uprising in Warsaw. The Soviets were camped on the opposite side of
the Bug, waiting for the Poles and the Germans to destroy each
other. The Americans were in Florence. The British had landed on
the Riviera.

The *Riveria?*

What were they doing on the Riviera? *They were supposed to
land at the head of the Adriatic, near Monfalcone.* They were on
the wrong side of the Alps now. The drive north would take them
into France, to link up with the invasion force that had landed in
Normandy, not up into Austria, across Czechoslovakia, and into
Poland.

Frantically he pushed the buzzer button for the nurse. He had
to place a phone call. It was imperative that he speak to Trilling.
In the clear if he had to. Dimly, he realized that it was almost too
late to matter now.

Even as the nurse popped her head in through the door he knew
what the answer would be.

"Of course you cannot make such a call, Herr Stropp. Dr. Vincenzi—"

". . . has left strict orders."

"Precisely."

"Damn Dr. Vincenzi! I must make the call, don't you understand?"

"You must rest, Herr Stropp, that is what I understand. Here, your arm please. This will help you relax."

Before he could stop her she had jammed a needle into his arm. He closed his eyes and inhaled the sharp alcohol smell, felt the cool touch of the swab on his skin.

He barely noticed it when the nurse scooped up the newspaper and, shaking her head disapprovingly, carried it out with her.

DOCUMENT

From Weekly Report No 82/83, I.G. Farbenindustrie/Ausch-witz.

General Direktor Falkenhahn, Pless
Bergwerkassessor Duellberg, Feurstengrube
Director Heine, HGW, Brzeszoze
Dr. Riedenklau, with three companions from the estate of Saybusch
Estate owners Fryda and Tschenin as neighbors of the estate
Bezirkslandwirt (district agriculturist) Hoffmann
SS Lt. Colonel Hoess with 3 chiefs of the concentration camp and gentlemen of I.G. Auschwitz

The following were shot: 203 rabbits, 1 fox, and 1 wildcat.

Herr Duerrfeld was proclaimed champion hunter, with a total of 1 fox and 10 rabbits. The hunt supper (*Schuessel-treiben*) took place in the recreation center "Zum geschlif-fenen Pokal" (The Crystal Goblet). A good time was had by all. The result was the best in the district so far this year and will most probably only be surpassed by the hunt the concen-tration camp is holding in the near future."

[*I.G. Farbenindustrie trial transcript, p. 492; exhibit.*]

Oswiecim

It was not until almost nine in the evening that they arrived at Helmut Schragg's country-estate house on the far bank of the Przemse River. It was here rather than in one of the *Gesellschaft* dining rooms that the dinner of which Schragg had earlier spoken had been arranged.

The house had belonged to a director of one of the Polish concerns which had earlier worked the coal fields to the north. The house was typical of the area, a mismatch of the worst elements of Teutonic and Polish architecture. The interior was rustic, with the ceilings braced by heavy beams. A multitude of animal heads hung from the walls. The huge stone fireplace was flanked by tongs that would not have been out of place in a foundry. Antique hunting rifles hung on racks near the casement windows, whose panes were so heavily leaded that they appeared barred.

The mists had finally cleared. Just before sundown the clouds had drifted away toward Wola and the sky had turned a pale steely blue tinged with ocher. This, in turn, had dwindled to a dull gray and been gradually replaced by a night made soft by moonlight and a plenitude of stars.

The four of them, Baranyi, Landau, Eisner, and Stellner, had driven up from the Buna works along the south road that skirted the main Auschwitz installation. The night had become so clear that it was possible to see for miles across the flat Silesian plain. Far to the south, illuminated not only by the pale moonlight but by a haze of reflected searchlights, a vast wood of silvery birch could be seen. A double line of railroad tracks issuing from the I.G. installation pointed like a finger at the heart of the forest.

It was from there that the stench arose. And the smoke.

Baranyi could not bear to look at the birch wood. In the moonlight and at that distance there was an obscene beauty about the place. He found himself suspended in a strange, hallucinatory state: none of what was happening was actually real. He understood violence, he understood death. With a man like Kagan by his side nothing was impossible, nothing foreign to his nature or understanding. Herding truckloads of people out of Budapest, bringing refugees across heavily guarded borders, climbing mountains, guiding the desperate through forests as interminable as the war itself—all of this he understood. What he did not understand and never would was this—riding in an open car toward a country house perched romantically on the banks of a river with an unpronounceable name, sitting down to dinner and calmly discussing business transactions with men like Schragg.

"We do not concern ourselves with what goes on in that place. It is not our business," Stellner had said firmly, following Baranyi's gaze to the birch wood. "Our business is to manufacture synthetic rubber. Anything that does not involve that business is not . . . our concern."

They arrived at the country estate shortly before ten. The house was set by itself at the edge of a wood overlooking the river. There were no guards, no barbed wire, no electric fences. The whole scene reminded Miklos of a country hunting lodge in the Carpathians.

They were met at the door by a servant in a crisp white jacket and formal black tie who ushered them at once into the main salon. A small fire crackled in the hearth, just strong enough to take the damp edge off the evening air.

Schragg, attired in a gray business suit that would not have been out of place in his Unter den Linden office, rose and came warily to meet them.

No one else was there, though Schragg had said that the SS officer, Neimann, had been invited.

"A profitable afternoon, I trust?" Schragg inquired, not looking directly at Landau as he asked the question. "Have you seen enough to convince you that you were mistaken, that the process *will* work?

"I'm by no means finished, Dr. Schragg. I've been shown a great deal, true, but not everything I need to see. Not yet."

Schragg frowned at the aggressiveness in Landau's tone.

"And you, Herr Baranyi? You also have reservations?"

"I must leave such decisions to Herr Landau."

"Dr. Schragg, you have shown us the body but not the heart," Landau said.

"Yes?" Schragg's face clouded over. Stellner gave him a look that counseled caution and diplomacy. He knew exactly what Landau was talking about but was not quite sure that Schragg did.

"Whiskey, gentlemen? What is your preference?"

Without waiting for an answer, Schragg went over to an elaborately furnished bar and gestured to the servant. "Karl will prepare anything you wish. We have here what is probably the best-stocked bar in Silesia. The Adlon could do no better."

After a time the guests were ushered into a small dining room off the main hall. It was obvious that the pictures had been changed, for the pale outlines of the earlier decorations could be plainly seen on the walls. Now, in place of whatever had pleased the Pole who had earlier owned the house, the walls sported a series of forest landscapes and hunting scenes. All very much in keeping.

From somewhere came the sound of music, a phonograph record: a Mozart string quartet. Tall crystal goblets stood on the table. The setting was rich, elegant, the silver highly polished, the napery crisp and white.

"Gentlemen?" said Schragg, taking his place at the head of the table. "Yes, you too, my dear Landau. Why should we continue this childishness? You are here. Perhaps it is all as it should be."

Landau nodded. A faint smile informed his lips. He seemed suddenly humble, grateful.

Schragg's manner grew expansive. As the guests sat in silence, he began to apologize to Landau. Miklos was amazed. Obviously, Stellner, who had been the only one of the I.G. staff to accompany them during the afternoon, had sensed what was under Landau's aggressive questioning, his eagerness, his attention to detail, and had convinced Schragg to behave accordingly.

The man simply wanted to be accepted. Welcomed back.

And Schragg, it appeared, was more than willing to accommodate him. For the moment at least.

Landau sipped his wine, guardedly pleased and growing flushed.

"You understand," Schragg said, "that Ambros still maintains a correspondence with Professor Willstaetter, that we have arrangements with the Weinbergs as well. Unfortunately, Arthur has died. We did our best. Even I.G. Farben cannot be held responsible for the state of a man's gall bladder. But Carl is in Italy. Just where, it would not be prudent to say. But he receives over eighty thousand Reichsmarks a year from us. There are others, too. We are not entirely insensitive." He raised his glass. "Why, after all, should you not be treated the same way?"

Landau beamed. Baranyi looked away. Schragg was coming perilously close to taking things out of his hands.

"The way you behaved at Waldshut," Landau began, "I would not have thought—"

Schragg cut him off with a broad, conciliatory gesture.

"It would be foolish for me to tell you that I am moved by a sudden feeling of friendship. Or regret. Or any such thing. I have discussed these things with Krauch and Ambros many times. And with others. We do not always see eye to eye. As for myself, I have no feelings whatever toward you Jews, one way or the other. It is immaterial to me what a man is. It is also immaterial, I must admit, what is done to that man if it does not involve my work. In your case it would seem obvious that I allowed myself to become too angry too quickly. I admit that my views are based strictly on self-interest. But what better basis for an understanding can there possibly be?"

"Self-interest changes," Baranyi observed quietly. "With the times, yes?"

"Of course, that's true. But the times do not change now as rapidly as they did in past years. Things are settling down, you might say. If we both understand what is meant by 'the times' and I think we all do."

"The Russians are *where,* precisely, at the moment?" Baranyi asked.

Schragg laughed throatily. "You are very perceptive, Herr Baranyi. Perhaps you know even better than I do where the Soviets are at the moment. Could that be? They tell me the line is just west of Lublin at the moment. I do not normally bother myself with military matters, but, of course, the present situation is unquestionably of concern to us here. I would not deny that."

"Indeed," said Baranyi and took a sip of his wine. A very small, cautious sip. He watched Schragg carefully for any sign that his remark had been taken for more than an idle response. There was a furtive movement of his pale blue eyes, a faint tremor along the cheeks. Surely Schragg was well aware of what would happen if the Russians reached Oswiecim first.

Miklos remained silent. It was enough for the moment that the seed had been planted. By Schragg himself, ironically. Let nature take its course.

Unless, of course, Landau's bizarre conduct forced his hand.

An excellent dinner was served, a fine cutlet in Madeira sauce, peas, and boiled potatoes in cream. Two or three excellent wines followed. The I.G. staff obviously did not want for anything. No doubt others of the hierarchy enjoyed similar privileges: the com-

fortable dining rooms at the administration complex showed clearly
that the lower echelons were also well cared for.

Once or twice during the meal, Landau veered back toward the
topic with which he had begun the evening's conversation. He had
been shown a great deal, he said, but not what he had come to see.
The Buna works themselves spread over the better portion of a
square kilometer, but what he was interested in, what I.G.'s friends
were interested in, would be found in one or two small buildings
at most. The highly sophisticated antioxidant feed equipment. All
the rest was as it had been five years before.

Schragg would nod, agree that this was in fact a matter to be
considered, and then change the subject. Landau, each time, drew
back, cautious, afraid to offend. He grew loquacious with drink,
obviously unused to alcohol in such quantity.

Stellner remained quiet, ate little, and tried to avoid being
drawn into the conversation. After a dessert of fresh fruit and
pitch-black, bitter coffee, the party retired to sit by the fire.

"Let me come to the point at once, my dear Landau," said
Schragg, balancing a balloon glass of cognac on his stomach. "I do
think that we understand each other now well enough for me to be
absolutely frank with you, yes?"

Landau nodded meekly, pleased by the air of confidence.

"So," said Schragg, "we all understand what the outcome of this
unfortunate situation must be. The war, I mean. It is not necessary
to dwell on *that* aspect of things. It is enough that we all perceive
it clearly. We will survive it, of course, for various reasons and in
various ways. Things will eventually be much as they were before.
In making the demands upon us that you did, you showed as keen
a realization of that fact as any of the *Vorstand* have ever shown.
I admit, I grew too angry that first time. I was rebuked by Krauch
when I told him of what happened, and I deserved that rebuke. It
was galling for me to admit that you, whom we had been forced
to eject, and who—I admit—we had convinced ourselves *deserved*
to be ejected, should have shown such an understanding of things."

"By which you mean exactly what?"

"By which, my dear Landau, I mean that tomorrow I will show
you the antioxidant feeder installations. You are quite right, of
course. The equipment is located in two small blockhouses. It is
the heart of the system. All the rest is expendable. And the equip-

ment I shall show you, as you will immediately recognize, owes much to the designs that you initiated before you . . . left us. Herr Landau, we were candid with your people before. We *did* give them everything. Apparently you have certain reservations. So be it. A scientist should never take anything on faith. We all understand that. Look. Satisfy yourself. Ask whatever you wish. We will answer. But one thing I insist on, for our mutual good—that the report you send back to your people be accurate. That you tell them that everything is as it was represented to them, that we have not tried to cheat them, and that we *will* keep our part of the bargain. It is absolutely essential that you do this. As I have said, it will be to our mutual advantage. Do you understand that, Felix?"

Landau flushed. Just then the servant in the white jacket came back into the living room. He did not appear pleased.

"Karl?"

"Herr Dr. Schragg, there is an officer . . . he wishes to see you."

"Tell him to wait in the study, Karl. I'll be with him in a few moments."

"No need," came a voice from the doorway. Oberführer Neimann ambled into the room, his greatcoat slung over his arm, his uniform neatly pressed, his shirt fresh. He carried with him a faint odor of cologne.

"Gentlemen? I'm so sorry to be late. The Wolfschanze business, you understand. There have been so many inquiries to attend to. I'm afraid there have been a few arrests even here. Don't look alarmed. No one you know was involved. Only some of my own staff." He put his coat down. "I've missed dinner, it seems. What a pity. But you've saved me some of that excellent claret of yours, haven't you, Helmut? I assume that Heidebroek conveyed my message?"

Schragg's face was a study in restraint.

"Karl, will you see to the claret at once?"

Neimann laughed. "Delightful. A man who honors his obligations. How rare in today's world. I'm always pleased to be in the company of such a man, even if it does mean a long ride in this foul country air. I can't say that the air here is too good for the health, is it? It gets more and more like Essen every day. Which can't be helped, I suppose."

"The invitation was . . . delayed, then?" Schragg drawled. "Your subordinates are getting very inefficient, Werner."

"Oh no, your invitation was put on my desk early this afternoon. I simply wasn't there to receive it. We do have things to do now and then. We don't just sit about looking at charts and adding up columns of figures. No insult intended, of course. You people do work hard. But it's the kind of work a plain soldier like me doesn't understand too well."

"A plain soldier indeed," said Stellner quietly.

"Yes, Dr. Stellner? You said something?"

"That you were not a 'plain soldier.' That's what I said."

"Not a soldier or not plain? Well, it doesn't matter. What about the claret, Helmut?"

"Karl, could you find something to eat as well? I'm sure there is plenty left in the kitchen."

"In these times," said Neimann, "one should not waste food, should one? I'm sure that you observe all the necessary precautions against waste. Why should there be anything left over?"

"You *were* expected, you know," Schragg said.

"Ah yes, well . . . in that case . . ."

"I'm sure that there is at least the claret."

Neimann sat down opposite the fire and, as if in imitation of Schragg's earlier posture, extended his even longer legs. "What a pleasant convivial evening this is. I imagine that your guests have been complimenting you on the technological marvels of your installation. I understand none of it. Perhaps someday, when all of this is settled, I shall have the opportunity to learn. Tell me, me, Herr Baranyi, what did *you* see? You can explain it to me, perhaps?"

Miklos hesitated, stared for a moment into the pale, cloudy eyes of the SS man. The face, oddly enough, struck him as not at all evil, and this made him all the more wary. He knew such faces, and it was a terrible danger to take them as they appeared.

Then an odd thing happened: before he could speak, Neimann smiled, tossed his small, close-cropped head back, and chuckled.

"Ah, no, what would I understand? And why should you be imposed on to such an extent, Herr Baranyi? You have had a long trip. You have gone directly to work, you are finally at a pleasant dinner, and I come in here and ask you to go back to work again.

At such an hour. No, no, that isn't right. Besides, I wouldn't understand a word you said. I too am tired. Even if I weren't, I still wouldn't understand. Idle curiosity. For a moment I thought that you might care to instruct me. These gentlemen always intimidate me. They assume that I won't understand, which is correct, and they make no bones about telling me so. Why explain such things to an idiot, eh? Well, I do understand claret. Helmut, you said there was claret to be had, didn't you?"

The servant, Karl, had meanwhile come up with the bottle and a glass on a tray. Neimann had not noticed. Then, finally, he did, and poured the wine for himself, a tall glass, full almost to the rim.

The fire sputtered. Stellner rose to poke at it with the long iron tongs. They had the look of industrial implements, heavy and formidable.

Landau looked away, confused.

The conversation slowly warmed. Schragg began to grow expansive again. More wine was offered. The officer accepted, grew visibly bleary. The situation at the front was not all that it could be. The Russians were proving unexpectedly stubborn.

"A retrograde advance. Most unfortunate," Neimann opined. "Our good General Model's troops are advancing backwards so fast that it is difficult for him to keep up with them. Soon they will have advanced all the way back to Berlin."

Schragg did not find that amusing. Neither, on reflection, did Neimann. "A very poor jest," he agreed. "One which we may all regret sooner or later."

Brandy was brought. Stellner grew morose and returned to the fireside. Landau and Schragg, finally accustomed to Neimann's presence, began a complex discussion about emulsifying agents and temperature controls.

Baranyi found himself standing under a huge bison head with Neimann. His eyes moved casually over the uniform. He had worn just such a uniform once. It had been at great risk; his appearance was not that of the usual wearer of such uniforms. But then neither was Colonel Eichmann's. Nevertheless, he had gotten away with the ruse. Two hundred Jews had been peeled right off the end of a column of Ruthenians already on the road, already half dead.

Neimann seemed determined to be amiable. A common ground was shortly found: hunting. Neimann was fascinated by Baranyi's descriptions of boar hunts in the Carpathians. A faraway look clouded his eyes. He grew rhapsodic over forest, wildlife, and the mountains.

Finally he said, "Ah, all this talk, it makes me hungry. To think of the fresh air, the forests. This damned war, it keeps us from doing all the things we really wish to do. I should have accepted our good doctor's offer of leftovers. My own fault, for being late. Well, what can one do? This, at least . . ."

He dug into the pocket of his breeches and came up with a small paper bag.

He smiled, self-deprecatingly.

"I developed a taste for these some while ago. In Slovakia. Oh yes, I was there for quite some time. We were invited by Tiso's minister of police to assist in setting up . . . certain departments."

He poured the contents of the little bag onto his palm and held it out to Baranyi.

"Have a few. They're really excellent," he said. "I understand that you too have a great fondness for them."

What an odd thing to say, Miklos thought. Then he looked down into the German's hand.

Neimann held a little mound of blanched almonds.

In Slovakia? *Blanched almonds?*

Miklos was painfully aware that the SS man was staring straight at him. The hand did not waver.

Neimann said, "One develops an insatiable craving, an almost . . . religious fanaticism . . . over such things."

White almonds. *Weisse Mandeln.* Weissmandel. Rabbi Michael Dov Weissmandel. Slovakia.

Neimann's hand did not budge. Miklos took a few of the almonds.

"It is almost uncanny that you should just happen to have some of these in your pocket. I have always been very fond of them. As you say. Almost an . . . obsession."

Neimann nodded.

"Now, is it not good that we understand each other, Herr Baranyi? That we have so many tastes in common is a good omen, yes? It brings one back to the old days when Hungarians and Austrians were all part of one great empire. It will be so again, mark my word, someday in the future."

There was no doubt whatever in Miklos's mind. It was all he could do to keep himself from an outburst of relieved laughter. How absurd it was, but how perfectly reasonable.

Oberführer Werner Neimann, SS, Security Division, Oswiecim, Poland, was Colonel Bor's man.

It was well after midnight when Neimann drove away. Landau dozed near the fireplace. Stellner and Eisner had occupied themselves with a stamp collection that had belonged to the house's former owner.

Baranyi took Schragg aside.

"I find it a little stuffy here. Perhaps some night air?"

He had made up his mind. Landau's behavior was creating too many risks.

"As you wish," said Schragg.

They passed through a set of glass doors and into the garden. Here the persistent burning smells of the camp and the plants were gone. There was only the deep, timeless odor of woods and river.

"You wanted to speak to me, alone?" Schragg said when they were outside. "That means we understood each other this morning? I had hoped so."

Baranyi held back for a moment, still not entirely certain of his timing. Yet why should he wait? Neimann had extended his protection. Schragg himself had supplied the last necessary link in reply to Landau's question earlier in the evening: the critical pieces of equipment were indeed movable. A few dozen railroad cars and it all could be on its way out of Poland in a few days.

Leaving the men in Wilmington with no reason to protect the camp. Particularly at the risk of being charged with treason.

Baranyi began.

"You must promise me that you will hear me out before you say anything. I must have your word on this."

"Go ahead."

"You must remember also that what I will tell you must make no difference in the way you act toward us. It *cannot*."

"What, exactly, are you talking about, Herr Baranyi?"

"I mean to say that you must keep in mind the precariousness of your own position before reacting to what I tell you. I am sure, in any event, that you will be grateful."

"Please say what you mean, *at once,* Herr Baranyi."

"What I have to say is, to put the conclusion first, Dr. Schragg, simply this: the Americans have betrayed you."

Schragg inhaled sharply. Then, for a second, he did not breathe at all.

"Go on," he said. "Tell me."

"I not only can tell you, I can *show* you. I have the proof. Here." He thrust a hand into his pocket and took out a small metal cylinder the size of a pencil. "They are going to bomb this place after all, Dr. Schragg. Their promises to you are about as good as the promises you made to them five years ago."

"Impossible. What could they conceivably gain by betraying us?"

"You yourself explained it, Doctor. The Russians are the answer, of course. They are already at the gates of Przemsyl. Do you think your General Model can hold them? If you do, you're the only person in Germany besides Adolf Hitler who does. How long will it take them to get here? Obviously they will come in this direction. They want both Prague and Budapest. They will be all over you here in Silesia within three months, perhaps even sooner."

"Many things can happen in three months."

"One thing that will not happen is a drive up from the Adriatic by the Americans. Your army intelligence knows that. You have your own intelligence, too. Surely they have told you the same thing. The Americans and the British cannot possibly get here before the Russians do. No, Dr. Schragg, they are going to bomb you out of existence, your American friends. Not because they have had a change of heart—oh no, they'd still prefer to honor their deal with you, I'm sure. But the fortunes of war make it . . . impractical . . . for them to do so. If they cannot have the Buna equipment and the new process, they certainly don't want the Russians to have it."

"The proof?"

"Here, as I say. On microfilm. I assume that you have a lens in the house? If not a microfilm reader, then a magnifying glass and a strong light?"

"Let us go inside. At once, if you please."

With Stellner looking over his shoulder and Landau and Eisner pressed against the wall by the fireplace, Schragg examined the documents one by one, reading and rereading them with the aid of a large ground-glass screen, of the kind normally used for viewing slides, and an ornate gold-rimmed magnifying glass.

The bombing schedules.

The three maps with all of the industrial installations in the Auschwitz complex targeted.

The letters from Stropp to Criterion's Wilmington office advising them to lift their interdiction of the bombing.

The memorandum from Trilling to OPD.

The Pehle letter to McCloy of the War Department and the newspaper article that had accompanied it.

Schragg sighed and shook his head. His face seemed to have collapsed. Stellner's eyes blinked constantly behind his glasses.

Schragg turned to Landau, who had all this time maintained a wary silence. Baranyi stared hard at him, waiting.

"Yes," Landau said finally. "It was for *this* reason that we came. There was no other way to tell you."

"All that talk about the low-temperature controls—all of that meant nothing?"

"Nothing at all."

"But why? Why should *you,* of all people, do this for us?"

Landau understood at once what he had to say. But he did not understand why Baranyi had moved so rapidly and without any warning.

"I believed it wise," Landau said, "for me to honor my bargain with you, just as—I am sure—you will honor yours with me. As you said, things will be different soon. When the time comes, when the war is over, we will both know what to do."

"Landau, damn it, say what you mean," Schragg spat.

"I *am* saying what I mean. I'm sure that you will know what must be done. The Buna process will be important to you afterwards. If it is important to you, it will be important to me, too. You *will* honor your bargain with me. Perhaps even you will better it."

"And you, Herr Eisner, what do you expect to gain?"

"Nothing."

"Nothing?"

"I had no choice," Eisner said slowly. "They threatened to inform on me if I didn't cooperate. He said they'd turn me over to the Poles or the British, and if they didn't murder me, they'd go to my own people. I don't think the Gestapo would care to know what you're up to, do you? It wouldn't be very good for your image as fine upstanding servants of the Reich. Well, we have people who would feel the same way about me. Look, I'm only a lawyer. I got sucked into this business against my will, and I don't want a bullet in my head or to spend the rest of my life rotting in prison somewhere for dealing with the enemy."

Bravo, thought Miklos. Just the way it had been rehearsed. And he sounded so convincing, too. Why not? Every word was true.

Landau nodded. "Herr Eisner was good enough to provide us with the memoranda and the letter of Trilling, the chairman of the board, that you see here."

"And how did you find out about all of this? These maps, these schedules, they are not the sort of thing that would normally come into the hands of people like you."

Landau shook his head. "The maps came later. Herr Baranyi was able to obtain those for us. He has certain contacts. As for finding out, it was discovered in the simplest way imaginable. They simply refused to pay me. Your American friends who are so generous with their promises are less than generous with their money. I got half my fee before and was to get the other half afterwards. When Stropp refused to honor his bargain and threw me out, it was not hard to discover why. From our young lawyer friend over there."

Eisner looked away. He hardly needed to pretend.

"And so," said Stellner, "it is all as simple as that?"

"It's just that simple."

Schragg lifted the roll of microfilm and lit it with the end of his cigarette. He held it up as the celluloid was consumed.

"Well, gentlemen," he said, "I suggest we all give some serious thought as to what we should do next, yes?"

"You have very little time. A few weeks at most," said Baranyi.

Schragg looked despairing. There was no question in Miklos's mind that he believed them.

"But one thing bothers me," Schragg said. "Why do you trust *us?* Why do you trust me not to turn you over to Neimann or the others? Or to deal with you myself?"

"That too is very simple," said Baranyi. "If you do not behave properly toward us, a copy of the agreement that you and Stellner and Krauch and the others signed will be on the desk of a Gestapo section head within twenty-four hours. But more important, and apart entirely from that, you are men of intelligence."

"Which means?"

"Which means that you know, as I do, where your best interests lie."

As he spoke he noticed that there seemed to be something wrong with Stellner. His head was cocked back at an odd angle; his eyes appeared to be focused on the ceiling, searching for something.

Then they heard it.

A distant rumble, a rattling sound, like pebbles being tossed inside an oil drum. It seemed to be coming from somewhere outside, to the north.

Schragg jumped up and ran through the double doors into the garden. The rumbling was louder there.

"No, you can't see . . . it's in the front. Beyond the river."

They followed Schragg around the corner of the house to the front, where there was a clear view over the low forest toward the north.

By then a dull, hollow booming was coming from somewhere just beyond the horizon, from the same place the rattling had come from before. The air itself seemed to move, and on a dark line, dimly visible across the flat plain above the river, wide, hazy bursts of light rose like phosphorescent mushrooms. At first there were only a few of them, then more and more until they joined together into a web that extended almost the entire width of the horizon. Above them a faint tracery of lights formed a delicate arabesque across the sky. The drumming sound, at first composed of distinct pounding noises which bore no relation to the appearance in the sky of the yellow-white mushrooms, settled into one long continuous roar which grew in intensity until it hurt the ears, even at that distance.

Spears of brighter orange and red light, high geysers of flame, shot up through the aurora borealis of the bomb blasts.

Schragg turned with a look of horror on his face.

Baranyi's heart beat wildly. He knew from the sour smell that he was drenched with sweat.

It could not have come at a more perfect time. It was the earnest of the information he had just given Schragg. The first massive raid.

Schragg's jaw hung slack. It was a full moment before he found his voice.

"Blechhammer," he said. "They're bombing the refineries at Blechhammer."

"How far away?" Baranyi asked in a whisper.

"Thirty kilometers, no more."

Baranyi nodded but said nothing.

He didn't have to.

Budapest

The truck carrying Itzhak Kagan out of Budapest sped across the suspension bridge, crossed Clark Adam Square, and plunged into the dark tunnel that pierced Castle Hill. At the other end of the tunnel lay the truck route south to Dombovar and then to Pecs. They could not have picked a better time to start out: no sooner had the truck pulled away from the yard behind the old Pest brick works than the air-raid sirens had begun to squall. In a matter of minutes the city was once again in chaos. It was the third time since Kagan had been there that the British bombers had come over: twice during broad daylight, and now a third time at night. The burning oil refineries at Pestsentlörinc threw a ghostly flickering glow on the underbellies of the clouds, lighting up a whole arc of sky, across which the long black fleets of bombers seemed to pass endlessly.

Kagan munched on a pastry he had bought only hours before in a little shop off the Clark Adam Ter. Why not? A little luxury. Feast in time of plague. But, too, it had been his final act of defiance. He had been wearing an Arrow Cross uniform when he'd purchased it and had enjoyed the look of dismay in the shopkeeper's eyes when he'd walked in. He would have liked to have strangled them all, every one of them. Three thousand leaflets had gone out so far, and not one life had been saved. The good citizens of Budapest, unable any longer to hide their heads in the sand, had looked the horror square in the face, shrugged, and done nothing.

It was up to Baranyi and his people now. If the rail lines could be smashed, if the gas chambers could be destroyed, then at least a few lives might still be saved.

The truck sped out of the end of the tunnel and onto the main road south. A factory was burning nearby, the flames violent and swirling, large chunks of wreckage being thrown into the air, dropping, then rising again on successive waves of intense heat. He could hear the clamor of fire trucks over the steady drumming of the bombs and the pulse of the flak guns.

The driver, whose face he had not seen clearly, hunched over the wheel, squinting into the dark. The conditions were ideal. Even if they should pass a new German checkpoint it was unlikely that it would be manned while the raid was going on.

They passed a huge gas tank that stood like a giant drum in the dark, miraculously untouched.

"That will make one devil of a bang if it goes up," Kagan said, nudging the driver. "Let's move out of the way."

"You don't have to tell me," muttered the driver as he floored the accelerator.

Scraps of black shadow ran across the roadway in front of them, lifting like windblown paper. Chickens, loose from someone's yard. Kagan laughed. It was little things like that that kept one sane. Chickens, in the middle of an air raid.

He had gotten rid of the Nyilas uniform before leaving. It would do more good in Budapest than out. A fair exchange, he thought: the ersatz Wehrmacht major had traded him a Tommy gun for it, a Soviet Pepesha. How many more months would it be before there were a few hundred thousand Pepeshas in Budapest? Not long, he thought. Poor Szekely. He wasn't much looking forward to the Soviets. But he'd always been an adaptable sort; he'd manage well enough. Better than the Jews, at any rate. At least he'd be alive.

He could see the profiles of the bombers against the illuminated sky, very low now, coming in in droves through nets of searchlight beams.

Suddenly a beam of light speared across the roadway in front of them, much lower. It wasn't an antiaircraft searchlight but the headlights of a car.

The driver cursed and slammed on the brake, wrenching hard on the wheel. The shoulder of the road was too high at that point to

mount, and the car whose light had struck them was halfway
across the road, blocking the way. It hadn't been there a moment
before, or at least it hadn't turned its lights on.

Waiting for them . . .

Kagan's fingers tightened on the stock of the Pepesha.

"Stop," he whispered. "I'll manage whoever it is if you can't."
The driver pulled the truck up so close to the car that the mud-
guard was almost touching its fender. As he came to a full stop,
Kagan reached over and flicked on the running lights so that they
shot, full force, over the car, blinding its occupants. At the same
time he raised the muzzle of the Pepesha.

It was no accident. Whoever it was had *known.* They'd been
waiting. There was no other explanation for a lone car there on
the highway in the middle of a raid.

Kagan peered through the windshield and drew a sharp breath.
His hand shot out and he pulled the driver's arm back; the man had
been reaching for a shotgun he kept under the dashboard.

The car was an open-back touring car, military model, from the
old Manfred Weiss works. Honved or police, it was impossible to
tell in the dark.

Standing in the back in full uniform was Major General Szekely.
He was waving.

"Mother of God," said the driver.

"He'd be amused to hear himself called that," Kagan said. "Just
wait. Be ready to hit the accelerator and plow him under if it's
necessary. I'm getting out."

"What?" the driver breathed, incredulous. "He's *police* . . ."

Kagan nodded and clambered down, the Pepesha in his arms.

"Greetings," Szekely called. "I've been waiting for you for quite
a while. It was getting cold."

"What are you doing here? This is insane."

"No more so than anything else that's happening," the police
general said, getting down from the back of the car. He was alone;
he hadn't even taken a driver with him.

"So?" said Kagan, still wary, expecting at any moment to be
caught in a cross fire and staying very close to the general as a
precaution. "Explain, why . . . ?"

"I thought that you shouldn't leave without seeing these," Szekely said, smiling wickedly. He handed Kagan a sheaf of message tissues. In the light of the truck lamps, Kagan could read them easily.

"It's an excellent start," said the police general. "Quite amusing, too. I understand that Eichmann was livid with rage. They say he's quite a sight when he's angry."

The Wehrmacht, it seemed, had won the first round. The trains had been rerequisitioned, two hundred cars. Orders for the detention of a number of Eichmann's staff had been issued. So had orders for the immediate arrest of half a dozen senior army group officers by the SD. The pot was already at full boil.

"It's nice to see the mad dogs biting each other for a change, isn't it?"

"This is why you came all the way out here?"

"And to remind you who your friends are," Szekely said, suddenly very serious. "As you see, I knew exactly where you were going, exactly when, and exactly how to find you. We have most of your routes under observation the same way. Just remember, later, that we did nothing, that we *let you go*. If you're stopped, it will be by the Germans, not us."

"I understand," Kagan said.

"When it comes time later, if your friends get here before the Soviets, please do me the kindness of reminding the right people about it, will you?"

Kagan raised two fingers in salute. He found it exceedingly difficult to dislike the man, opportunist though he was. He began to climb back into the cab. Szekely stopped him.

"There's this, too." A package wrapped in a towel flew through the air. "Careful," Szekely called. "Don't drop it."

Kagan caught it. He could tell by the shape that it was a bottle.

"Thanks," he called, slamming the cab door. "We'll remember. Everything. I promise you."

"It's an excellent vintage," Szekely called as he backed the staff car out of the road. "Harslevelü, 1939. You hardly touched yours at Irma's the other night. I finished it. This is to replace it. Good luck."

The truck lurched forward onto the clear road. In a second it had been devoured by the darkness.

Zurich

Stropp walked slowly and uncertainly into the bar of the Baur-au-Lac. The evening was warm. The windows were all open to admit the freshening breeze from the lake. The babble of voices in a dozen or more languages was reassuring. The lounge pianist was playing "That Old Black Magic." That, too, was reassuring.

And Stropp was very much in need of reassurance. He had been released from the hospital only that afternoon. With a stern warning from Dr. Vincenzi and instructions that on no account should he go back to work for at least a month.

He had no intention of doing any such thing, but he had nodded obediently, signed the necessary release forms, and allowed himself to be escorted out of the hospital in a wheelchair to a waiting taxi.

At the hotel, the head porter had handed him the few letters and cables that had accumulated in his absence. One letter was from his firm, advising him of a decision in an important case he had entirely forgotten about. There was a bank draft. A cable from Trilling, dated two days before, advised that he would be arriving in Zurich on Saturday evening by plane from Lisbon. One phone message from Grunewald. Nothing else.

So Trilling was coming to Zurich. It was only natural; actually, it was surprising that he hadn't come over sooner, or at least sent someone in his place. Probably he hadn't any real idea of how serious Stropp's seizure had been. Probably he'd thought it would only be a matter of days. He hadn't been ready for the two weeks it had taken and he was getting nervous.

Considering what was at stake, he had every right to be.

Stropp crossed the foyer and sat down in a *Telefon* cubicle to call Max Grunewald. At home.

A servant answered. After a moment, Grunewald himself came to the phone. As always, he was annoyed at being disturbed after office hours.

"Damn it, you could have come to the hospital," Stropp said.

"You were not allowed visitors, you know that."

"You could have come," Stropp insisted.

"I phoned. They told me most emphatically that if I came I

would not be allowed to see you. What would have been the point? I know Dr. Vincenzi. He is a very able physician."

"All right. But yesterday or the day before, they said I could have visitors."

"Listen, my friend, you are behaving like a child. Who do you think has been taking care of all your arrangements? Who do you think advised your New York office of your problem? Who do you think made sure there were adequate funds to cover your expenses? Emil Vincenzi is one of the most highly regarded specialists in the canton."

"I'm sorry, Max," Stropp said. The Swiss was right, of course. He was being unreasonable.

"If it was important to you that someone come to hold your hand, I'm sorry."

"I apologize, Max. I said that already."

"You're well now?"

"Yes, of course. They let me out this afternoon. But I've got to talk to you. I've been a prisoner in that place for almost two weeks."

Grunewald anticipated the question. "Nothing's happened that you haven't already read about in the newspaper. Assuming, that is, that they've let you see the newspaper."

"There's been no word from Landau?"

"You wouldn't have expected that, would you?"

"In two weeks?"

"Things may be a little more complicated than we expected, my dear friend. Since the attempt on Hitler's life . . ."

He'd read about that. But the full meaning of it hadn't really penetrated until just that second.

"Over two thousand have already been arrested, so we understand. No branch of the government has been spared, including the Economic and War Materials Ministry."

"General Thomas? Any of the *Vorstand*?"

"There's no way of knowing yet. But to answer you as best I can, yes, probably yes. All of them. Either arrested already or they will be shortly."

"Christ," Stropp said. He took the receiver away from his ear for a moment. His forehead was bathed in sweat and he felt as though he was going to have another attack.

"Henry? Are you there, Henry?"

"Thanks, Max. I'm glad you're concerned."

"Listen, there's nothing else I can tell you," came Grunewald's voice. "Tomorrow perhaps."

Stropp agreed to meet him for lunch and hung up.

He sat for a moment, staring at the wall and the potted plants. The thought of having to confront Trilling and answer for all that had happened and was still happening, even now, made his blood run cold.

And there was one other thing that had been bothering him even more. A question that he hadn't been able to ask Grunewald.

Where the hell was Ellsworth?

With Eisner gone, who was there to ask? The concierge at Ellsworth's pension had no idea where he was. She said she hadn't seen him for almost three weeks.

Even thinking about the possibilities brought on a wave of nausea and cold sweats. But he'd read nothing in the papers that even hinted at a murder. Normally the Swiss made a terrible commotion about such things. Either Ellsworth had done his work very carefully or he hadn't done it at all.

He got up and went into the bar. Dr. Vincenzi had said that alcohol in moderation would be good for him. So much the better. He needed a stiff one.

He sat at the bar. At least he'd have a chance to thank the man who'd helped him the day he'd been stricken.

The big redhead.

The man behind the bar came over to take his order. He was small and dark and wore glasses.

Stropp ordered a whiskey.

"Where's the other fellow?" he asked.

"Bitte?" replied the bartender.

"The other bartender."

"Excuse me, sir. There is not another bartender."

"The red-haired fellow, the big red-haired fellow."

"There is no red-haired 'fellow,' sir," the bartender said. "I am the only bartender. This is my job for the last five years."

Stropp stared at the man for a moment. The bartender shrugged and turned away.

Stropp downed his whiskey and went out hurriedly.

* * *

Maximilian Grunewald finished his dinner, told his manservant to go out to a *Kino* for the evening, and then called the Vaadah office on Frankengasse.

Liebermann answered. In a moment, Kagan was on the phone.

"I've just heard from Stropp, Herr Kagan. He's out."

"I know—this afternoon. We have someone at the hospital."

"There's something you should know . . ."

"I probably do already. What is it?"

"He's had a cable from Herr Trilling in New York."

". . . who is arriving tomorrow evening from Lisbon."

Grunewald snorted. "You know it all, you Jews."

"Thanks to our Polish friends. You forget, the Poles have people at the hotel." He was about to say "at the front desk as well as in the kitchen," but thought better of it.

"What will you do?"

"It will all be taken care of, don't worry."

Grunewald wasn't going to worry. There was a hard edge to Kagan's voice that told Grunewald that he didn't want to know, either.

"Is there word from your friends?"

"Nothing," said Kagan. "But we have the first set of photos already."

"Amazing."

"Excellent shots. The Americans are very good at that sort of thing. Their cameras are even better than those of the Germans."

After a pause, Grunewald said, "When Herr Trilling arrives, I may have difficulty . . ."

"With Stropp? There will be no difficulty," Kagan said. "None at all, I promise you."

Grunewald was silent for a moment; then he said, "Good luck, Herr Kagan."

"Thank you, friend. Lose no sleep over the prospects ahead. Everything will go well."

"God willing," said Grunewald.

"Hopefully we will not need God's help in this," Kagan said.

Then he hung up.

DOCUMENT

From: Office of the Asst. Secretary of War, John J. McCloy
[*August 14, 1944*]

To: A. Leon Kubowitzki, World Jewish Congress [*who had written to the War Department, passing on a request from the Czech government-in-exile for the bombing of the gas chambers and crematoria at Auschwitz*]

Dear Mr. Kubowitzki

I refer to your letter of August 9 in which you request consideration of a proposal made by Mr. Ernest Frischer that certain installations and railroad centers be bombed.

The War Department has been approached by the War Refugee Board which raised the question of the practicability of this suggestion. After a study it became apparent that such an operation could be executed only by the diversion of considerable air support essential to the success of our forces now engaged in decisive operations elsewhere and would in any case be of such doubtful efficacy that it would not warrant the use of our resources. There has been considerable opinion to the effect that such an effort, even if practicable, might provoke even more vindictive action by the Germans.

The War Department fully appreciates the humanitarian motives which prompted the suggested operation, but for the reasons stated above, it has not been felt that it can or should be undertaken, at least at this time.

Sincerely,
John J. McCloy
Assistant Secretary of War

Oswiecim

A pall of smoke fully twenty kilometers in breadth had hung over the northern horizon for over twelve hours. The bombers had come and gone in vast waves that had lasted from midnight until almost dawn, and the flak had turned from brief yellow-white bursts to dirty, infrequent smudges on a gray dawn sky. For a long while after the bombers had gone the sky above Blechhammer trembled with rising waves of heat so that it appeared as though the horizon itself had risen up and there were now mountains where before there had been nothing but the flat Silesian plain.

By the time they had returned from Schragg's house in the gray foulness of morning, the bombing had ended. But somehow the echoes seemed still to reverberate. Miklos sat in the back of the open touring car, his hands damp and a chill seeping through his bones. He saw the smoke to the north and saw, also, thin columns of a darker smoke rising from the birch wood. Nothing there had stopped. Everything was as it had been before.

Landau watched the smoke. He knew what it meant, what it was. The play of emotions on his face was so complex that after a time Baranyi could no longer bear to watch him. There was no telling any longer what was going on in the man's mind.

They had not slept for over two days. The time on the train had been a period of fitful, unsatisfying dozing only. When they had left the house, after the klaxons from the camp had stopped whooping and the searchlights over the nearby Krupp works had surrendered to the dawn, Schragg had gone to the closed-line phone and called first Berlin and then the Buna works. After that they had been led out and put in the car.

The rooms reserved for them on the third floor of the administration building were clean and orderly. They could hear the determined tramping of boot soles on the corrugated metal decking of the building as the technicians and workers came and went, those who had worked all night returning, those who were just starting going out. They passed many whose eyes were ringed from watching all night as the bombers had passed time and again over the synthetic fuel works at Blechhammer. There was a hollowness in their gaze that had not been there before.

Landau had fallen into a deep, exhausted sleep. Baranyi, tired as he was, could not rest. He stood at the window overlooking the administration compound and the towering mass of stacks and kettles beyond. From one corner of the room, just beyond the cot where Eisner lay, twisting and turning in an agitated doze, he could see at an angle that permitted a glimpse of the track line running back to the main station. In the far distance, perhaps five kilometers back, he could make out the low huddled outlines of the siding and the station. A long row of boxcars stood there, their blank backs turned toward him. Others moved by slowly on a spur line. Dust trembled above the tracks. There was motion beneath the dust. Many, many people. The dust did not rise because of the movement of the trains; it was not related to it. It rose because of what was going on on the other side of the station. The side he could not see.

There was a whistling in the corridor: someone going by, pleased to resume his work. Whistling a popular tune.

And the dust cloud continued to rise, then—slowly—to settle again.

Schragg had believed them. It was, in a way, probably all true. It was unlikely that the Trillings and the Stropps could hold out forever. Sooner or later there would be bombers over the gas chambers. The ovens would be smashed, the crematoria blown sky high. Copies of the Vrba–Wetzler report had gone out to the neutral embassies, to the Red Cross, to the Vatican, the newspapers, to the broadcasting stations. Surely *someone,* sooner or later . . .

In the meantime, another trainload would arrive. And another. And another. From Budapest, from the towns and the villages of Carpatho-Ruthenia.

But Schragg had believed them. He had gone to the phone and he was doing exactly what they had hoped he would do. The men of I.G. were frightened now, not of losing something they needed at the moment but of losing something far more important, something that was precious for their future. The war had nothing to do with it. The war was lost. They all knew it. It was only a question of time. Afterward, things would have to be done. New alliances would be required, new arrangements made under new conditions.

The Buna process was important. It would be a counter, perhaps even a ransom.

He could not contain himself: the tears moved down his cheeks. His hands shook. He stood in the clean neat room with its hospital bed and looked out over the factories and the towers and saw the gangs of men in their prison uniforms struggling with impossible weights and the Kapos everywhere, shouting and beating them. And the barking of the dogs, and over it all the endless pall of smoke.

Now, if it was going to be, if they were going to move the heart of the Buna equipment, if then the bombing would be possible because there would no longer be any reason *not* to bomb, then please, God, let them do it before another trainload arrived.

He wondered if Landau understood it all yet, whether he really *felt* it. By now, he, Miklos Baranyi, once-upon-a-time doctor of medicine and God only knew what since then, should have grown so used to suffering that he could no longer feel it himself. They had always said it would be like that. Kagan had said it the first few times they had gone back into Hungary. For every ten you bring out there are a thousand who will remain and die. You can not think about the thousand, only about the ten who can be saved. Or the one. If you think about the others you will go mad. Or else simply cease to feel anything at all.

Which would be the worst thing that could happen.

So it was better to think only of the ten. Or the one.

He lay back, his head in his hands. And, oddly, he thought then not of the trains or the birch wood, but of a woman.

He could not tell exactly who she was. She might have been Teresa, his wife, or Julie Malowska, the sister. He was not certain. The features were unclear. Only the impression of womanness was clear. If he ever got back to Zurich, he would have to try to sort it all out.

As it was, he was ashamed that he should have even thought of such a thing at such a time. It was wrong. Unless it was his exhaustion speaking to him.

He fell, finally, into a deep sleep. Relieved, anxious to escape the guilt that the brief vision had caused him.

Zurich

The desk porter at the Baur-au-Lac called for a Winterhalder taxi, and within a half-hour Henry Stropp was on his way to the airport to meet Trilling's plane. Not one of the Swissair commercial flights than ran regularly between Lisbon and Zurich with their bright red aircraft and big white "HB" letters painted on the side, but a company plane with Portuguese registration. Private and discreet.

Stropp sat in the back of the taxi, crossing and uncrossing his legs. He could not get comfortable. His body still felt strange all over. Perhaps it was all in his mind, but there seemed to be a heightened sensitivity, an awareness of the inner workings of his body that hadn't been there before. He heard and felt things, noticed sounds, pulses, all sorts of small matters that didn't seem to him to have returned quite to normal.

The bars and cafés on the Bürkliplatz were full and the lights burned brightly. The news of the last few days, the breakthroughs both in Normandy and on the Russian front, had stirred the city's refugee colony to a near frenzy of expectation.

It was hard not to be caught up in the excitement, and Stropp had constantly to remind himself not only of the priorities of his client's interests but of the damage excitement could cause to his health.

The taxi made good time. There was little traffic, and within ten minutes they had cleared central Zurich and were on their way out to the airport.

Shortly, the lights of the main terminal buildings came into view, and the red and yellow landing lights, running like cat's eyes off into the darkness. A commercial transport, a big four-motor Swissair Wibault still in service on the Rome–Zurich–Vienna run, was just coming in, its motors thrumming over the wireless antennae above the control tower building. A number of big transports and liners stood by on the edge of the field, some being refueled, others dark and waiting.

Stropp told the taxi driver to take him past the main passenger terminal to the row of private hangars at the north end of the airport. The runway lights there were less bright and there were far fewer people about. Most of the big hangars were dark. A few trucks were parked out on the tarmac to service incoming craft. A half dozen light planes of mixed nationalities, old British Tiger Moths, French Dewoitines, and Swiss-made Fokkers, stood parked in neat rows.

The airport proper seemed very distant, a splotch of light barely visible much farther down the line of runways, like a ship floating on a dark sea.

"Ah," said the driver. "Here? *Mein Herr,* this is where you wish to get out?"

Stropp barely heard the man. He was trying to remain calm, and finding it very difficult. What in God's name was he going to say to Trilling? He had absolutely no information. He'd had no word from Eisner and the others. Grunewald had been singularly uncommunicative. Ellsworth had vanished from the face of the earth, and there had not been a word about the Jew, Peshko, in any of the Zurich papers all the time he'd been in the hospital. He'd gone to the library and checked the back issues.

All he had to show for his labors was a receipt that Grunewald had given him for a bank vault that couldn't be opened until after the war. That and a few draft agreements and patent assignments that didn't even have signatures on them.

The cab driver's voice cut through his thoughts.

"You have transportation back from here, *mein Herr*? There is no way to get a taxi from this place."

"Thank you for your concern," Stropp said, paying the man and getting out. "You needn't worry."

"Would you like me to wait?"

"Please go."

"As you wish."

The cab moved off, leaving Stropp standing before the empty hangar. The door was open. A light burned dismally at the far end of the hangar, illuminating a worktable, a pile of piping, an engine on a rack. A converted EKW biplane, rigged for courier service, sat in the shadows, its engine partly disassembled.

The company rented space here. The hangar was large enough to service the two-motor Electra that Criterion used for the Lisbon–Zurich run. But there was no one about. The place was empty.

Stropp had expected that there would be someone there, at least a dispatcher or a few mechanics. But apart from the light, there was no sign whatever of activity.

Yet the hangar door was open.

He called into the long, empty building. His voice echoed, as though from a mountainside. Oddly metallic.

The phosphorescent dial of his watch showed 10:30 P.M. The Lisbon plane was due at any minute. Then where was the ground crew? He knew from many years' experience that the Electra required fueling, service, a crew of a dozen or more to handle it properly. It wasn't like the little Moths, which could be tended by their pilots.

Puzzled, he walked back and forth outside the hangar. The runway lights were on. Someone had seen to that at least.

Perhaps there was a telephone in the hangar. He could call, find out what was going on, why there wasn't anyone there.

He found it, on the wall by the workbench next to the engine rack. He jiggled the dial. There was no tone. The line was dead. As he put the receiver down hard, he thought he heard a sound. Turning suddenly, he saw only the long, empty expanse of the hangar, full of shadows. Nothing moved.

What a damned fool he'd been to let the taxi go. What harm would there have been in having the man wait for him? Criterion was picking up the bill.

He went outside again. Far down the field, the administration building, the control tower, and the main terminal were all aglow. Perhaps he should walk over and see what he could find out. Surely the main dispatcher would be able to tell him something.

It was a long way, though. And dangerous. It would be foolish to try it.

Just then he heard the sound of motors and looked up. In the dull glow that rose like a fog from the runways of the airport he could see the familiar silhouette of the heavy-bodied Electra coming in high and to the right.

With an enormous sense of relief, he moved a little farther out onto the runway, as though to position himself the better to meet it when it taxied up after landing.

The wing lights of the Electra flashed and the plane dropped lower, making its approach. The roar of its twin Pratt and Whitneys grew louder, blotting out everything else. The plane banked and began to settle toward the runway, almost drifting down through the calm summer sky.

Stropp did not turn his head, not even slightly, when another, much nearer engine turned over somewhere to his left and behind him, along the row of parked planes. He continued to stand where he was, watching the Electra coming in and wondering what he was going to tell Trilling when he stepped off the plane, all grim and anxious.

How was he going to hold the man to his promise of a place on the Hydro-Arc board, how hold him to his promise of a majority stock position? Things were almost as bad as when the Rotterdam deal had fallen through.

Suddenly a flicker of movement caught his attention. A long finger of shadow seemed to rush out of the hangar. Someone had moved into the entrance, between the light over the workbench and the door.

Stropp turned. His heart began to race.

A man in flight mechanic's overalls was standing there. A sense of relief swept over Stropp. A mechanic. He belonged there. Everything was all right after all. He was getting too damned nervous. Ever since the heart attack . . .

The man raised one hand. He was holding something.

A gun.

Stropp instinctively backed away. The roar of engines settled over him like a heavy blanket. He could not take his eyes off the man in the overalls.

The man had red hair. Just like the bartender in the Baur-au-Lac.

Stropp thrust out his hands, palms up, as though to ward him off. The mechanic walked slowly out of the hangar toward him.

"No—no!" Stropp cried.

Suddenly a cloud of dust swept around him. His jacket billowed out, his glasses flew from his face. He half turned, and only then saw the light plane that had been taxiing toward him from the line of parked aircraft. At that moment, it was less than ten meters away.

He didn't even have time to scream before the propeller blade took off the entire upper part of his body.

The pilot switched off the motor and clambered down.

"Don't look," said Kagan, unzipping his overalls.

"I have no intention of looking," replied Semkowski. "Besides, there is nothing left to look *at,* is there?"

The two of them walked off together to the waiting car and were gone before the Electra touched down.

Oswiecim

Schragg was flaming mad. He'd been trying to raise Colonel Seidl of Transport for over half an hour and wasn't about to take no for an answer. Unlike Heinrich Beutefisch and most of the others on the *Aufsichtsrat,* he held no SS rank. At a time like this being strictly a civilian was an absolute liability. Even the sergeants talked back to him.

At the end of his tether, he uttered a string of obscenities that made even the surly noncom on the other end of the phone line gasp.

"Moment, bitte . . ."

Schragg continued swearing. How the devil was he supposed to arrange for the boxcars needed to move the antioxidant equipment if he couldn't even get through to Seidl? He glanced out the window of his office and grimaced. The chimneys in the birch wood were sending up long black columns of smoke again and the air was heavy with the stench. He could smell it even in his office with the windows closed.

"Who is this?" demanded a harsh voice at the other end. "Who wants to speak to Colonel Seidl?"

"Helmut Schragg, I.G., here. Who's this?"

"Major Fritzsche. Who did you say you are?"

"Schragg, Willi. Where's Seidl?"

"What the devil do you want Seidl for?"

"What does anyone ever want him for? I need rolling stock."

"Listen, you'd better come over here right now. I'll explain it all to you in person."

"Explain what?"

"Seidl's not here and he's not going to be here."

Schragg hesitated. He knew Willi Fritzsche well enough to understand what that tone of voice meant.

"Will you wait for me?"

"At the junction office."

Schragg slammed down the phone and clattered down the iron stairs outside his office. Passing the construction control rooms, he shouted for Waldeck, who, as usual, was not there.

In fifteen minutes he pulled the little *Kübelwagen* up next to the corrugated metal shed that served as field office for transport headquarters at the railroad junction just above the Auschwitz station proper. He could hear the barking of dogs not far off. The unloading area was hidden from view by a line of empty boxcars and a high-roofed shed that was over fifty meters long. A cloud of yellow dust rose from the siding. Whistles blew.

He flung open the door of the main office and stamped in. He was in no mood to be put off and was only vaguely aware that he was behaving in a manner almost calculated to focus attention on himself.

Major Fritzsche jumped up at once. He was a lean, bookish-looking man with a receding chin and a small, uneven mustache. He had been a marine engineer before the war.

"Willi . . . ?"

Fritzsche met him halfway across the room.

"We'd better go outside," he said in a subdued voice.

"Really, I must speak to Seidl."

Fritzsche's face went white. "For God's sake," he hissed.

Schragg allowed himself to be pushed back outside but would go no farther than the steps. The sun beat down hard through the dust clouds. He could hear people shouting and dogs barking again. He tried not to listen. He hated dogs. The shepherds that the guards used made his skin crawl. He'd been bitten by a shepherd when he was a boy and had never forgotten the experience.

"You're crazy," said Fritzsche, "bursting in there like that. Worse yet, to do that on the telephone . . . my God . . ."

"Do what?"

"Rothke told me you were on the line for over a half-hour, insisting on talking to Seidl."

"Well, what's wrong with that, apart from the fact that I still haven't been able to speak to him?"

"You really don't know?"

"Willi, please, enough of this."

"Seidl's been arrested."

Schragg stopped dead in his tracks. His hands fell to his sides. Of course. He should have thought of that himself. Why not? Hadn't Stellner said that the number of those arrested was up over two thousand now? Why not Seidl? Why not anyone? Did they really think they were immune just because they were in Poland?

"Who else?" Schragg asked. "There were rumors . . ."

"Whatever you heard, it's probably true. If there was enough for there to be a rumor, there was enough for an arrest. They took Schacht yesterday. Can you imagine? Hjalmar Schacht."

"If Schacht, what about General Thomas?"

"Half of the War Economy and Armaments section of OKW has been taken. About Thomas I don't know yet. There's no telling where it will stop. The Gestapo and the SD have gone absolutely crazy."

Schragg took a deep breath. What the devil was he going to do now? If Thomas was arrested, they would most assuredly go through his papers. That meant that all of the I.G. personnel who had been involved with the Vermittlungstelle Wehrmacht would come under suspicion. By association. Which had always been more than enough for the Gestapo.

And that meant Grossbart, Stellner, Krauch, Ter Meer.

And Helmut Schragg.

Who was still without the needed transport.

He put an arm around Fritzsche's shoulders. The major looked uncomfortably in the direction of the unloading area, as though there was something going on there that required his immediate attention. Schragg withdrew his arm.

"You've got to help me, Willi."

"Whatever I can do, I'll do. But be careful what you ask."

"I won't compromise you, don't worry. Just tell me, what are the chances of getting hold of, say, thirty or forty boxcars strong enough to take heavy industrial equipment? And some cranes for loading?"

"Impossible," said the major, shaking his head.

"Those cars there . . .?" Schragg pointed to the long lines on the siding, sitting silent in the middle of the yellow dust clouds.

"They're from Budapest. We have strict orders from Colonel Eichmann."

"If he had his way he'd have every railroad car in the Reich running between here and Budapest." Schragg paused to consider. There was no point in even thinking about Thomas or VW. And it would take days to get hold of Ter Meer or Krauch in Berlin.

Or Speer. If they hadn't been arrested. "How soon before they have to go back?" he asked.

Fritzsche looked puzzled.

"D'you know, we haven't gotten any dispatch on that yet. It's odd. The first time. Not a word so far."

Schragg nodded; he knew why. The deal for the trucks that Eichmann was trying to make with the Jew, Joel Brand, that was the reason. He was in deadly earnest about the trucks, and as long as there was a possibility that it might go through he was going to have to show the Jews he was reliable. It was even possible that he'd ordered the deportations slowed down or stopped altogether for the moment.

"It would only take two days," Schragg said.

Fritzsche grew wary. "How much?"

"Whatever you wish. Name your own price. I'm sure you won't be unreasonable. Our people will be most grateful, you can rest assured."

"When could you have them back?"

"Three or four days at the outside."

"It could be done. They need repairs, of course. They have to be cleaned out and patched up. Why, it's not uncommon these days for trains to be shunted off onto some spur line and get lost for days. We had a thirty-car train arrive last week that'd been sitting on a siding for four days. No one even knew it was there. Except for the *Stücke* in the cars, of course. They were dead, most of them, by the time they got here."

Schragg looked away. What bothered him was not that Fritzsche could report such things without any apparent discomfort but that he chose to mention them at all. Schragg did not care to know where his workers came from or what happened to them after they could no longer work. That, as he viewed it, was not his affair.

"We should be most grateful," Schragg said again.

"Understood," said the major, turning back to the shed. "Send some of your technicians over in a few hours. I'll see what I can do for you. Do you have your own engine?"

"Yes," Schragg said. They had more than enough engines. A dozen, perhaps fifteen, that hauled the flatcars loaded with cement and steel beams to the unloading sites, where the prisoners could pick them up and move them to the construction sites. At least four of the engines then in service could be used for the haul.

"Say, two hours?"

"Done. I'll send ten of my best people. They'll take complete charge. You won't have to be involved. And I'll send a work gang along too."

"Guards also, please. I haven't any to spare here."

"Don't worry. And thanks, Willi. Thanks very much. You won't regret it."

"I don't expect to," said the major. "And, Helmut, for your own good, don't go around asking for Seidl anymore. I can keep Sergeant Rothke quiet, and the others you spoke to, but don't do it again. You can never tell who's listening or where it will all end."

As he drove away, Schragg thought that there was only one other thing that had to be tended to now: where was the equipment going to be sent? Even that didn't really matter. As long as it was sent well away from Oswiecim before the American and British bombers came over and did to the installations there what they'd done to Blechhammer.

He didn't even give Horst Seidl a second thought.

DOCUMENT

Operations Division, War Department (U.S.), June 1944 [*In response to a proposal to bomb railheads near Auschwitz.*]

The War Department is of the opinion that the suggested air operation is impracticable for the reason that it could be executed only by diversion of considerable air support essential to the success of our forces now engaged in decisive operations.

The War Department fully appreciates the humanitarian importance of the suggested operation. However, after due consideration of the problem, it is considered that the most effective relief to victims of enemy persecution is the early defeat of the Axis, an undertaking to which we must devote every resource at our disposal.

Oswiecim

By afternoon of the next day, strings of empty boxcars had begun to move unobtrusively onto the spur lines leading into the Buna works. The cars were empty except for oddly shaped metal cradles and empty packing boxes stuffed with excelsior. A dozen large cranes had been shifted from the construction areas to the central complex where the antioxidant-apparatus blockhouses were located. Gangs of prisoners in ragged gray pajamas and blackberry caps made their way out of the Farben complex in a steady stream, back into the sewer of Monowitz. No sooner had the gates closed behind them than troops of I.G. technicians and mechanics converged on the blockhouses, brandishing wrenches and blueprints.

All along the rail lines leading into the camp, trains were being uncoupled. Motorcycles carrying couriers in sidecars moved like beetles through the marshy fields, carrying messages which were not to go out over the phone lines. A shroud of secrecy descended over the administration building.

Schragg, in sole command of the installation during the continued absence of Ambros and Krauch, sat alone in his office, frantically issuing orders over the closed lines leading to the *Gesellschaft*'s outposts up and down the rail lines. Oberführer Neimann's mocking warning burned in his ears. It was all true. He could no longer even raise General Thomas's Kurfürstenstrasse office on the VW lines. Fear bred a desperate energy. Less than forty-eight hours, he knew, stood between success and a typhoon of SS wrath. And who in Berlin—if such persons existed anymore —could possibly protect them there in the swamps of Poland?

They had to move rapidly; there was no other way. Storage facilities had been arranged in a warren of bunkers far to the west, near Görlitz. The bunkers had been built to store rockets, but the rockets had not been built and it did not seem likely that they ever would be. The bunkers, thus, were of no strategic importance. Their location was a secret, and there was no reason whatever to expect that they might be bombed. Even if they were, no possible harm could come to anything stored in them.

The boxcars moved. Behind them came the small engines with their hoists and winches. Canvas screens went up around the blockhouses. Portable generators fed batteries of searchlights that had been hastily set up inside the barrier for night work.

There were no gangs from the camp. All of the workers were either I.G. personnel or foreign draft-workers, mostly French and Czech. The workmen ate quickly, drank their coffee, and got on with the job. Men in gray business suits carrying sheaves of blueprints moved in and out of the blockhouses at regular intervals. The air trembled with muted hammering and the sound of electric saws.

It was still light out. Night would not fall for some time yet. The light was intense, clear, the shadows precise and deep blue.

Baranyi, Landau, and the American stood on a little hummock near the spur line loading platform, watching the activity as they had for most of the afternoon. Cranes swung large crates of machinery overhead. The engines labored. Baranyi regarded it all with a feeling of amazement and a growing sense of calm.

The boxcars were filled with machinery, moved out, were replaced by other cars. Empty. Soon filled.

The day had been unexpectedly hot, far more typical for this time of year than the past few days had been, and it had caught everyone by surprise. Landau looked haggard and worn. The American was almost at the point of collapse. His expression had grown more and more agitated every hour.

Landau, despite his exhaustion, seemed satisfied.

"It will take two days, perhaps three," he said. "If they work quickly. And these people *always* work quickly when they're protecting themselves, oh, let me tell you, they do."

Baranyi barely heard him. Nearby he could see Stellner directing a loading gang in the performance of some particularly delicate operation. Huge pieces of machinery whose purpose was completely unknown to Baranyi kept emerging from the block houses; he had not been aware that there was so much machinery within. Perhaps some of it had been underground.

An engine, spewing steam, hooted and moved toward them on the loading track. Just then there was another, more distant hooting. A klaxon, somewhere to the south in the direction of the main camp.

Stellner stopped what he was doing and looked up.

It was the second time since they had arrived at Oswiecim that the klaxon had sounded. Baranyi smiled fleetingly. It was almost impossible to believe, but everything was working, everything was proceeding right on schedule.

High above, almost invisible against the long streaks of cloud that had begun to spread from the northern horizon, a tiny dot moved. The machinery halted, the engines were switched off.

It became very still. The workers put down their loads and turned off their machines, stood waiting, expectantly staring into the sky.

At the single dot.

At the airplane high above them.

The sound of the motors could now be heard, very distant but quite clear. Baranyi knew the characteristic whine of the Jumos and the Daimler-Benz engines that powered the big Heinkels. Neither gave off the sound he was hearing.

The plane was definitely American or British.

He turned to Landau.

"Now they know," he said. "In a day, they will *all* know."

Landau nodded. Baranyi was hard put to divine his expression.

But now it made no difference. Landau had done as he had promised. In a way, he had more than redeemed himself. The plane had gone over the second time. The pictures had been taken. The words would be simple and direct: *the equipment is gone.* Here is the proof, in black-and-white. There is no reason to be an accomplice to mass murder any longer. *We* have acted as your conscience. Now you can do the right thing without fear of personal loss.

We have solved your moral dilemma for you.

The phone rang in Helmut Schragg's office on the third floor of the administration building overlooking the *Bunawerke.* It was Oberführer Neimann. He sounded mildly amused.

"I thought you should know, Helmut," he drawled with exaggerated pleasantness, "the pot seems to be boiling over."

"Speak like a human being, if you please. Not a peasant."

"Really," said Neimann. "I'm calling to do you a favor. Don't abuse me."

"It wasn't my intention to abuse you."

"That's good, Helmut. That's very good."

"What did you want to tell me?"

"Just this. I hear from Berlin that your Wehrmacht friends are in a little trouble."

"What are you talking about?"

"Something that affects you rather directly, I think."

"Yes? What is it?"

"It may be simply more paranoia brought on by the unfortunate episode at Wolfschanze, but then, on the other hand . . ."

"Are you going to tell me or not?" Schragg was almost shouting now, something that he instantly regretted; he could almost hear the *Schadenfreude* dripping from Neimann's voice. He'd have to be more careful in the future.

"Someone—probaby a good deal more than just one—has been passing railroad dispositions to the enemy. Schedules of the crossings, routes, switching yards, what's to be expected where and when. That sort of thing. The information went through Switzerland, apparently with a courier from Army Group N, the Ukraine."

"My God, for what possible purpose?"

"To make it impossible to continue the transports from Budapest to Auschwitz, it would seem. They—whoever 'they' are—gave the Americans everything they need to put all the rail lines in and out of this place right out of business in a day. Coordinates, schedules, timetables, bridges, everything."

"But *why*, why would they do such a thing?" Schragg cried in genuine indignation, even though the answer was perfectly clear.

"To free up the trains for other purposes, of course. Such as carrying troops and ammunition to fight the Soviets."

"Whom do they suspect?"

"Everyone, of course," replied Neimann pleasantly.

"It's treason," Schragg breathed. "There is no other word for it."

"I'd think so, wouldn't you? The Reichsführer SS is screaming mad about it, of course, and Eichmann's people in Budapest are literally foaming at the mouth." Neimann paused for a long moment. Schragg could feel the sweat starting to trickle down from his hairline across his broad, sloped forehead. His hands had suddenly grown cold.

"The trains," Neimann went on, in a very casual tone.

"Trains?"

"The ones you're using over in the Buna S plant. The ones you talked our dear friend Willi Fritzsche into lending you . . ."

"Yes? Yes?" Schragg groaned.

"I hope for your sake they weren't part of Eichmann's lot. It wouldn't look very good, your taking them, I mean. Not with all that's happened, Helmut. It wouldn't look good at all."

Schragg took a deep breath. He had to ask.

"Has General Thomas been arrested? Do you know for certain?"

"If he hasn't been already, he certainly will be after this mess gets sorted out. There's only one place our army friends could have gotten the information. It had to be Supply and Armaments, wouldn't you think?"

Schragg could hardly breathe. For ten years the carefully nurtured Vermittlungstelle Wehrmacht connection had been I.G.'s armor against the lunatics of the SS. Now, suddenly, the armor had turned to a millstone.

"The trains," Neimann said softly. "Really, Helmut you must do something about the trains."

Then he hung up.

Zurich

She had not been able to sleep. When the phone rang at two thirty in the morning, she was sitting by the window, her knees drawn up to her chest, a cigarette slowly turning to ash in her fingers, unsmoked. She had not expected to feel the loneliness so acutely. The presence of another human being was essential. Better Bor than no one at all, and the prospect of there being no one at all for a long, long time to come terrified her.

For a moment she did not realize that the jangling sound was the phone in her room. The sound of the Swiss phones was not like that of the phones in Warsaw, and she had never quite gotten used to it. Her head was full of vague, muddled thoughts, and what clarity of understanding she had earlier achieved had been dulled again by fatigue. She had sat there for hours, too emotionally drained to move. Too leaden to even get a coat or a robe. Her teeth were chattering slightly, and the flesh on her bare arms had turned blue from the night chill. Even in July, the nights in Zurich could be cold.

Like Warsaw. Like Plotzk.

Finally the insistent phone claimed her attention. She gazed at it blearily, an antique black contrivance sitting on the floor amid a welter of newspapers and discarded underclothing. Had it been ringing a long time? Possibly it was Conrad. He had changed his mind, that was it. He had forgiven her. He hadn't really been wrong, and he'd had every right to despise her. She couldn't even give an explanation of her conduct that satisfied herself. How could she have expected him to understand?

It occurred to her that it was the first time in a long while that she understood what it was like to want forgiveness from another human being.

She picked up the phone.

The voice on the other end was not Bor's. It was Pauer from the Czech legation.

". . . you must go over there. The phones have been ringing
. . . no one picks up."

"What's that? Say again, please?"

"Listen to me, Pani Malowska, please listen. What is the matter
with you?"

"Nothing, nothing. I'm all right. Just repeat, please."

The receiver was cold against her ear. Things were starting to
clear. Her heart raced.

". . . for at least an hour I have tried . . . we have news . . .
they must be made aware, at once . . . but there is no answer."

"News of what?"

"We had it from our underground radio only a little while ago.
He cannot possibly know yet. The Russians have recognized the
Polish liberation committee in Lublin as the sole authority in the
country. Do you understand what that means?"

"What do you want me to do?" She was suddenly alert, her body
tense as a bowstring. "*Me,* of all people . . ."

Pauer did not understand, of course. He had no way of knowing
what had occurred between Julie Malowska and Conrad Bor. His
tone expressed both confusion and desperation.

"You must get over there and tell him. There are men here,
downstairs, outside the building. Russians, I'm sure. Watching us.
It is quite impossible for me to go myself. But you, you can go. If
anything is wrong, don't go inside, call the Swiss police at once.
You can do that, can't you?"

She put down the phone and without even thinking pulled her
coat from a hook on the door, flung it over her nightgown, and
went down into the street.

Her room was not far from the Polish legation building. She had
chosen it precisely so as to be near Bor's office, available to him
whenever he wanted her. Whenever she wanted him.

She found herself running through the street. It was warmer
than she had thought; her room had been cold, the stone retaining
the chill of the earlier, rain-swept daylight hours. There was a stiff
breeze up from the lake, carrying with it the scent of mountain
flowers. Almost chokingly sweet.

As usual at that hour, the streets were nearly deserted. A child
cried somewhere. A dog barked in response. Somewhere, a tower
clock chimed the half-hour.

She ran, barefoot, past an old man who was rummaging in a trash barrel at the mouth of an alley.

The Polish legation building was its usual nighttime dark, the only lights a dull amber glow in the entryway and a single light in Paprocki's upstairs office. There were no cars in the street, no sign of anyone at all, much less Russians. Besides, what could the Russians do there in the middle of Zurich? If what Pauer had said was true, if the prediction in his voice became fact, Bor would simply become an exile again, this time a double exile. Alone in Zurich, he would need her even more.

She pushed open the front door. Unlocked. That was odd. She stopped for a moment in the front hall, thrust her hand instinctively into the pocket of her coat, looking for the gun. Why should she need a gun, of all things? Pauer was a foolish man, paranoid. Well, didn't he have the right? Didn't they all?

But the *Russians*?

She went upstairs to the second floor. The night clerk was nowhere to be seen.

The door to Paprocki's office was a little ajar. Without knocking, without thinking, she pushed it open and went in.

There was one light burning, on a side table. The light she had seen from the street below.

"Jerzy?"

Paprocki was sitting behind the desk, his head back against the chair. He seemed to be caught in an attitude of thought, his hand to his mouth. She took a step forward.

Then she saw the blood, all over the back of the chair.

The gun was still in his mouth. The back of his head was a ruin, spread all over the upholstery, against which the force of the shot had thrust him.

On the desk lay a message tissue. She didn't have to read it to know what it said; it must have contained the same news that Pauer had phoned to tell her.

Paprocki's eyes were wide open as if in surprise at what he had done. She wondered for an instant what her father, who had known Paprocki when he was administrator at the Bank Pantswa, would have said.

She waited for some reaction beynd curiosity and a faint feeling of disapproval.

There was nothing.

She closed her coat, suddenly aware of her near nakedness and bare feet. Then she went downstairs, slowly, so as not to make any noise. Now she was almost afraid to call out.

She had not noticed, but there was also a light showing under the door to Bor's office. Of course. She could not have seen it from the street. The window faced the rear court.

That door, too, was ajar. This time she hesitated. If Bor had done the same as Paprocki . . . No, it was impossible. Not Conrad Bor.

She pushed the door open.

Bor was kneeling before a filing cabinet whose drawers had all been pulled out. There was an open satchel by his side and another bag, stuffed full of papers, by his foot. He was emptying the remains of the file drawers into the satchel.

At first he did not hear her, or notice the door opening. Then she coughed, and he looked up.

For a moment neither of them said anything.

Then Bor said, "You saw him? Upstairs?"

"You can read my face like a map, can't you, you bastard."

"You were always rather poor at hiding your emotions, Julie."

"You *know* and you can talk that way to me? So calmly?"

Bor shrugged and stood up, slender, graceful, almost courtly. His silvery hair was brushed well back from his forehead. The only disorder about him was his expression, halfway between amusement and contempt.

"I am neither so foolish nor so pessimistic as poor Paprocki."

"The Russians . . ."

"We shall survive the Russians as we have for the last hundred years or so. Surviving the Russians should be a fine art with us by now, don't you think? Besides, we've had lots worse in the last few years, haven't we, Julie?"

"Conrad . . . he blew his head off and you . . ."

"So he did," Bor said quietly. He seemed to be waiting for something but was not sure himself just what.

"I want to go with you," she said finally.

He shook his head.

"There's only room for one of us in this particular cart, I'm afraid." For a second he seemed genuinely moved, even regretful. All the bitterness vanished. His tone was soft, almost gentle, as one would use in speaking to a child who had misbehaved badly and whom one would not now see for a long time.

"Where are you going, Conrad?" She knew the answer before she had finished asking the question.

Bor nodded toward the satchel stuffed with files and smiled. "To our new masters, of course. I'm sure they'll find some use for me. And for the information I bring them. I am truly sorry, Julie."

"You swine," she whispered.

"Call me whatever you like." He closed the last file drawer and picked up the satchel and the bag. "If I were you, I'd put something on, really. You can catch a bad cold like that, even in July."

"I came to *warn* you . . ."

"But, as you see, I needed no warning. I already knew."

"Pauer said . . ."

"Pauer has his own problems. They are not necessarily mine. Now, if you please, step aside. You can call the police if you like, about poor Paprocki, but please wait for a while, until I'm gone. I don't think I need the added inconvenience of the Swiss police just at the moment." Then he added, "You needn't be concerned. It's clearly suicide. They won't bother you at all."

"Conrad, please . . ." She was close to tears.

He walked up to her and stood patiently, waiting for her to step aside as he'd asked. Finally she did so, very hesitantly, her eyes narrowed, her lips compressed and trembling.

"Go to the Jew," Bor said as he walked down the hallway. "If he survives. You'll make a good pair, the two of you."

With that, he saluted, in the old Polish manner, with three fingers—one for the Father, one for the Son, and one for the Holy Ghost.

Oswiecim

Oberführer Werner Neimann sat back in his desk chair and stared for a moment at the little spool of wire on the table in front of him. He turned it, letting it catch the light of his desk lamp and send little jagged reflections bouncing off the walls of his room.

He took a sip of brandy, then opened his desk drawer and turned on the recording machine. The little cat's-eye glowed green, ready to wink at him as the volume waxed and waned.

He put the spool on the spindle, turned on the motor, and closed his eyes. It was the third time he had listened to the wire.

The voices were indistinct, muted, without clearly identifying timbre. They could have been anyone.

But they were not. Neimann nodded in quiet recognition. He knew them both.

The two men were speaking without haste and without passion, like merchants bargaining with each other over a hundredweight of grain or a thousand kilos of pig iron.

"The machinery must *not* be moved. *You must stop the trains.*"

"Why should we stop? How else will we save the equipment? The Americans will bomb it. You've seen the maps, the schedules, the letters."

"They will not bomb the Buna works. The oil installations, yes. But not the Buna works. It's all a lie, a clever forgery. No bombs will fall."

"How do you know this?"

"Believe me, I know it. I know it as surely as I know who I am and who you are."

"But why? Why should they do this?"

"They have fooled both you and the oil company. They have tricked you, or so they think. If you move the equipment, your partner can be told, can be *shown,* that there is no reason *not* to bomb. Because the Jews and the Poles wish to stop the killing and this seems to them the only way. They must make your friends withdraw their protection. Only then can they stop you." There was a long, significant pause. "The plane that went over this afternoon took photos, as did the plane that went over four days ago. They will show your partner the photos and they will convince them that you have betrayed them once again. Then, in a short while, the bombs *will* fall. It is their only chance."

"But why should you tell me this?"

"The Russians will come. They will take the machinery."

"Only if we leave it here. I don't understand you."

"It is accepted that the equipment must be left here and that the Russians will take it. It doesn't matter. It can be rebuilt, later."

"Only at great cost."

"The cost can be met."

"By whom?"

"Does that really matter? It can and will be met."

"No, it doesn't matter. If the payment is made, it doesn't matter who pays. The important thing is what happens in the end."

"The equipment may even be destroyed, though the Russians wish to have it. If that should happen, what is needed in order to rebuild it, to make the Buna S flow?"

"Knowledge. Nothing but knowledge. The same knowledge that is needed whether the equipment is destroyed or not. It cannot properly be operated by men without that knowledge."

"Which you have."

"Yes."

"And what do you think will happen to you when the war is over? You and your colleagues here? Do you think you will be allowed to go about your business as though none of this has happened?"

"Why not? We are businessmen. We have done nothing but carry on our affairs."

"Really? What about Monowitz? The camps? These are not 'nothing.' No, no, you will be tried. Depending on who catches you, you will either be hanged or put in prison for a long, long time. Certainly you understand that, don't you?"

There ensued a long silence.

Then: "Yes, I understand that."

"Suppose I could assure you that this will not happen? That I can see to it that you will be safe, all of you. In return for the appropriate action on your part, after the war. To make the Buna S flow. And other things too, perhaps."

"Why should we do this? Why should I trust you?"

"Because you have no other real choice. And because it makes good business sense, which may be just as good a reason."

"How can you assure this . . . if we agree? How can we be sure it will work?"

"You will have to trust me. It is very much in our own best interest to make it work. Beside, you cannot really move the equipment. You can try, but if there is one false move, one mistake, you will all end up on an SS gallows. As you yourself said, the situation has become very sensitive since Wolfschanze. Are you willing to take the chance? My odds are much better."

"The offer is attractive, I will admit that."

"I would say so."

"And, also as you say, it makes good business sense. Very good business sense."

"What about the agreement that Schmitz and Krauch signed? There was a specific threat that if anything happened, copies of those papers would be turned over to the Gestapo. We can hardly afford that."

"The Hungarian is not in control. You have my word, there will be no problem with respect to the agreement. It can be handled very simply."

"By *you?*"

"By me. Believe me, there's nothing to worry about."

"I will have to believe you about a good many things, it seems."

"It's up to you. I assure you, I can manage it. I have the necessary . . . connections."

"It's absolute madness. But in these times, who knows? To be mad may be the only way to stay sane."

"You can give the trains you are using to move the equipment back to the SS. Eichmann will thank you for that."

"Yes, yes, you think of everything, don't you?"

"I do the best I can."

A laugh, harsh, edged with sarcasm.

"A little gratitude from the SS might not be amiss. There are rumors that General Thomas has been arrested. Being in bed with the Wehrmacht is no longer quite as comfortable as it once was."

"You'll have to have us all arrested, of course. Can you manage the necessary theatrics?"

A laugh, the second time, mirthful now, a little more relaxed.

"You will not be compromised."

"Good. One never knows . . . later . . . what may happen."

"Everything we do now is for later, isn't it?"

"A sound business proposition, wouldn't you say? Everyone profits, according to his needs."

The wire spool came to an end. There had been more, but it was not important. Badinage. Grotesque attempts to be witty.

Neimann turned off the machine and sat back again, smiling. The light from his desk lamp spread comfortably over his bare desk. He retrieved the little spool and put it away in a steel container.

Everything would be just as it should be. A dozen different men, a half dozen different organizations, all working at cross-purposes, were all pushing events inexorably in one single direction.

It would all come out well.

The equipment would not, after all, be moved.

Stellner came clattering down the catwalk at the rear of the low-temperature blockhouse, streaming sweat and puffing like an engine. Close behind, a roll of blueprints under his arm, came Waldeck, the construction manager, and three of his staff. The buildings were already half gutted; the concrete mounting pads lay bare, anchor bolts jutting up like spikes. Racks on which rows of motors and compressors had been hung were stripped and empty. Coils of wire, freshly spooled, lay in stacks, all tagged and ready to be loaded and shipped. Crews were disconnecting runs of pipe.

At the end of the blockhouse, the overhead door had been raised. A rectangle of smoky light from the floods on the roofs of the adjacent buildings crawled across the loading bay. The night air was warm, humid, and swarming with midges. Above the complex, a sky heavy with dust and smoke hid an anemic moon and a scattering of stars. A dull glow on the horizon toward the west illuminated the birch wood.

Landau was squatting next to the main compressor regulator, examining the couplings, when Waldeck and his crew came over.

"This will have to be removed now. You are finished, Herr Landau? I hope so. We must get to work here."

"As finished as I need to be," said Landau pleasantly.

"Efficiency. A good thing," replied Waldeck. "Good that you are efficient, Herr Landau."

He gestured and a work gang dogtrotted over, all husky Silesian Germans and Slovaks who looked as though they'd all been truck drivers or longshoremen before the war. Tools clattered, wrenches emerged from toolboxes. Another gang went to work disconnecting electrical lines and tagging the live cables so that the men who came after them to remove the remaining equipment wouldn't electrocute themselves.

Stellner looked wary but pleased. The work was going well.

Outside, Thiessen from the engineering department was directing the actual loading. A big boxcar had been backed up to the bay on a single-spur track. Cranes swung the crated equipment into place.

Landau had watched the start of this particular phase of the loading from the beginning. When the boxcar had come up and the doors had been opened, a strange smell had issued from the interior. A mixture of human feces and disinfectant, possibly carbolic acid. When the workers had pulled the sliding doors open a tiny object that had been caught in the door track, tumbled out.

A child's doll.

Landau remembered, then, what the cars had been used for. He remembered a great deal at that moment. It had all been very difficult for him; his mood had seesawed with dizzying speed—elation, a weird sense of comradeship with these men in their laboratory jackets and gray suits, then a violent hatred not only for them but for himself as well.

It took all the self-control he could muster to continue doing what he had to do.

Baranyi and Eisner appeared at the end of the track, together with Dr. Grossbart of the production division and another man from Thiessen's staff. They had just come out of a field office hastily erected at the end of the loading area.

Stellner called out to him, and Baranyi came over.

"Amazing," he said. "When you decide to do something, you let nothing stand in your way, do you?"

"We like to think of that as a distinctly German trait. Perhaps it is just a trait of the successful businessman, regardless of his nationality. Who knows?"

"You have a sense of proportion, Dr. Stellner. One does not always find a sense of proportion in men of position these days."

Stellner smiled guardedly.

"And such men, Herr Baranyi, do not maintain their positions long, do they?"

"It is important for a man to know just what can be accomplished and what cannot. He must know his limitations, yes?"

"And also the limitations imposed on him by others."

"To be sure, Herr Doctor."

"We deal with limitations imposed by others all the time. Often we deal with them by ourselves. Sometimes we have help. Sometimes even luck plays a part. Today we have luck, Herr Baranyi. Did you know? Freight cars. These freight cars are our luck. We have all we need, and just at the right time."

"How is that?"

"How indeed when freight cars are more precious than gold, eh? You may well ask, and the answer, again, is luck. Politics, if you will. Cars are available, right here. Instead of being sent back, they have been given to us, on our requisition. Forty cars from Budapest. No longer needed there. Your city, is it not?"

"I was born there, yes."

"You would find it a different place now, Herr Baranyi," said Stellner. "The population has shrunk substantially. The Jews, of course. But the shrinkage has now stopped for a time. Your government is upset and so there is a respite, and in that respite, look, there are the cars. They do not need to be sent back for another shipment because, for the moment, there is no other shipment. And for the moment, the cars are ours. Excellent luck, wouldn't you say?"

"I would say so."

Stellner smiled again, and Baranyi realized that the reason the smile had seemed so odd before was that Stellner did it so rarely.

Eisner looked on warily. Since their arrival, his face had grown noticeably older, harder around the edges. It was clear to Miklos that the experience had not left him unmoved. He was, Baranyi thought, perhaps beginning to learn some things. Even about his own conscience.

As he had been instructed, Eisner remained silent in public, simply looking on. No one noticed him. He had, after all, the kind of coloring, the flat Aryan rear cranium, the bearing that made him totally inconspicuous in such company. Probably some German ancestors, Baranyi had decided. Or Scandinavian. Possibly both. He wondered what the man might have been able to accomplish if he had been stronger and had not been thrown into the company of wolves at such an early age.

But wasn't that the problem that afflicted half of mankind? How to avoid picking up the habits of wolves when you lived among them?

Baranyi watched the loading operation. Landau came over with his rolls of plans and his notebooks. He was making a good show of it, wandering from area to area, taking notes, examining things. If anyone had looked at his notes they would have found nothing either unusual or offensive, nothing suspect. Only brief, nontechnical descriptions, notations that he had examined everything and found it eminently satisfactory. Brilliant engineering, etc., etc. Not even the Gestapo could have found fault. There were no secrets. Only praise.

In twenty-four hours they would be on their way out of Poland. And not a minute too soon. Baranyi could almost see the tension rising in Felix Landau's eyes, like the water in the level gauge of a boiler. Who could tell just how much longer the man would be able to control himself?

Or how much longer the I.G. men would continue to believe?

The logic and directness of Baranyi's story had stunned Schragg and the others. Yet, overwhelming as the proof appeared to be, he could see that it was still hard for the Germans to believe that Landau could have taken so great a personal risk simply for the sake of an uncertain future gratitude. To be sure, he had his "insurance policy"—the signed agreement—but still, the audacity of it all was almost too great for the cautious, phlegmatic chemists to comprehend. He could see them still struggling with disbelief. Sane men simply did not take such risks.

Baranyi sighed and looked around him.

They *did* believe. The equipment *was* moving. The reconnaissance planes *had* come and gone. The pictures *had* been taken.

Perhaps something had been accomplished, against all odds.

The engineer, Waldeck, was gesturing. Baranyi raised his hand to acknowledge the signal, then realized that the gesture had not been meant for him at all. Waldeck was waving at something which he, from his slightly elevated position above the loading dock, could see and the others could not.

Then, over the grumble and rattle of the freight cars and the creak of the crane's chain-link sling, Baranyi heard the high-pitched whine of car motors, a squealing of brakes, then a din of voices coming closer by the second.

He turned sharply. Something was happening; something was wrong.

Above the din of machinery and the new clamor of cars, banging doors, and booted feet in the gravel, one voice rose distinct and sharp, shouting orders as yet not quite comprehensible—Helmut Schragg's voice.

Around the end of the freight car into which, just then, a massive crate containing one of the huge bottle-shaped polymerization re-actors was being carefully lowered, trotted a dozen men in the blue uniform of I.G.'s Werkschutz. Behind them, coming in fast and fanning across the spur-line tracks, ran a squad of steel-helmeted Totenkopf guards from the main camp. They carried Schmeissers and automatic rifles.

There was a sudden, characteristic rushing sound. The searing beam of a portable flaklight snapped across the yard, then another and another, both intersecting the first at the dock where Baranyi, Eisner, and Landau stood with Stellner. The chemist shielded his eyes and shouted in protest. The workmen dropped their wrenches where they were, blinking at the rapidly moving shadows just be-yond the blaze of blinding light. Unable to understand what was going on.

Schragg stepped forward, a half dozen armed Werkschutzen be-hind him.

"Step aside, Golo," he snapped. The nasty tone was back in his voice. The eyes were very narrow. He waved at Waldeck. "Stop everything. *At once!*"

Waldeck's voice came back over the groan of the crane engine. "What's that, Dr. Schragg?"

"Unload. At once. *Everything!*" Schragg shouted. He turned on Stellner with a vengeful vehemence. "We all make mistakes, Golo. Fortunately, some of them can be rectified. Sometimes even the worst of them . . ."

Baranyi pressed back against the wall of the blockhouse.. "Oh my God," said Eisner quietly. Landau blanched. Baranyi blinked into the searchlight glare. A dozen trucks and *Kübelwagens* were drawn up alongside the compound fence.

"These men are frauds, Golo," Schragg cried. "It is a lie. Every word they've told us is a lie."

"Please, please, I don't understand." Stellner backed away, flustered and angry; after all, he had just been talking to them, all three of them. Why did Schragg have to come up at just that moment and make his announcement in public? As though he, Golo Stellner, were somehow an accomplice.

He could feel the eyes of the SS men on him. Even the Werkschutzen were looking at him oddly.

"Obersturmbahnführer Lautmann? Do what is necessary."

"I demand an explanation of this outrage," Baranyi exclaimed in his most authoritative voice. He stepped forward. "As a Swiss citizen, as a Hungarian as well, *as an ally,* I demand—"

Schragg struck him backhanded across the mouth. The blood spurted.

"What you'll get is an explanation all right. In Monowitz, that's where. In the *Straflager.* You'll get a fine explanation there, that I promise you. We'll see to it. And if there's anything left after Lautmann gets finished with you, why then, I'll be happy to give you a personal explanation too." He waved angrily. "Now do as you're told."

Landau's voice rose, high-pitched with indignation. "But Herr Dr. Schragg, surely you see that this is wrong. You *must* see—"

"I see it all too clearly now. As you will also very shortly, you pig-shit Jew bastard. It's all finished, don't you understand? Finished. *Done with.*"

He turned on his long, spindly legs. "Lautmann?"

"Zum Befehl, Herr Direktor . . ."

The SS officer gestured sharply, and three guards launched themselves at Baranyi and the others.

Miklos sprang back, not considering for a second the impossibility of his position, the absolute futility of any attempt to escape. Beyond the blaze of blinding searchlights there was a darkness pocked only by the dull red warning lights on the tops of the butadiene storage tanks and the skeletal superstructures of the buildings still under construction. That was all he could see. A tangle of dark tracks, cars, huge industrial buildings, fences, beyond them the flat gray marshlands, sweltering and fly-ridden in the Polish summer night. A few misty searchlight beams probed the darkness in the direction of the main camp. The birch wood glowed, as always, phosphorescent in the night.

It was *not* impossible.

Not to *try* was impossible.

He saw Eisner go down, driven to the ground by a rifle butt, blood jetting from his forehead. Landau vanished under a pile of blue-uniformed Werkschutzen. Baranyi's hands shot out, fingers fastening hard around Stellner's neck. He yanked, twisted the shouting German between himself and the oncoming guards.

The searchlights, he realized instantly, had been a mistake. A grand stroke of theater, but a mistake. Their brilliance obscured everything beyond the periphery of their blaze. Center stage was lit brightly, the wings were in deep darkness.

Gravel flew up. He felt the railroad ties under his feet, stumbled, caught himself, and ran past the corner of the boxcar. A crate swung perilously overhead. A rifle bullet sang past him, pinging hard against the iron latch bar of the car door. It ricocheted off into the darkness. A stutter of automatic weapons fire followed. The gravel around him leaped away in all directions.

"You idiots, hold your fire! There are chemicals—don't shoot!" Schragg's voice, suddenly stark with terror.

He had a chance then. The chemicals—they could not fire . . .

If he could reach the edge of the light and be swallowed up . . . only a few meters away now.

Schragg's voice came again, distorted by outrage.

"*Insane!* You are insane!"

It was true. He was insane. Where could he go? How could he hope to escape?

Vrba had escaped. Wetzler had escaped. Others had gotten away, even from the main camp, which was much more heavily guarded. Here there were only a few fences. No machine-gun towers, no electrified wire . . .

He thrust past the edge of the light, his breath a hard, immovable mass in his throat. His heart slammed against his rib cage.

More shots, automatic weapons again. Schragg shouted in protest. Something slammed against the cab of the crane. The operator shrieked in pain and pitched forward against the control panel. With a violent metal roar, the cable drum let go and the huge crate spun down like an anchor, crashing into the SS and the Werk-schutzen who had just cleared the spur-line tracks. Men screamed in sudden, surprised agony.

Baranyi went down almost on all fours. Ahead of him, the out-lines barely discernible in the darkness, were the reactor tank pads and a jungle of steel pipes thrusting up from the buried main lines, creating an almost impenetrable tangle of metal.

His head whipped around. There was only one way to go—straight ahead. Beyond the tank field, the shadowy outlines of the butadiene storage tanks suddenly loomed up. No one would dare fire there.

Safety? Even for a moment . . .

Boots slammed the gravel close behind him, fracturing the darkness. Schragg's voice came again, one long, unending shout.

"*Insane* . . ."

Then he saw it, only seconds before he would have collided with it had he not looked up at just that instant—a small automobile parked across his path, blocking his way to the tangle of pipes. A staff car of some kind. It had been sitting there all the while. Whoever was inside had been watching.

He spun to the left. A sharp, jarring pain erupted across the side of his head and his left shoulder. He had caromed into a wall of pipes, unseen in the darkness. For a second, he could see nothing but bright purple flashes. His arm felt as though he had broken it.

Gasping, he fell back.

The car door opened. Though he could not make out the face of the car's occupant, he could see that the man was holding a pistol. Pointed directly at him.

But there was no report, no need for the man to fire. The ten seconds Baranyi had lost when he had hit the pipes had been enough.

His arms were wrenched violently behind him and he felt a length of wire twisted hard around his wrists. His hands, all at once, were sticky and hot with blood.

"It is unavoidable," said Neimann softly, stepping away from the car door. Baranyi was dragged backward by the hair. His head yanked back, he saw—upside down—the blaze of light again, very close. He had managed to get less than twenty meters from the loading dock.

Twenty meters.

He heard Eisner making weird noises deep in his throat and Landau still pleading, shouting incoherently at Schragg, at Stellner, at anyone within earshot.

"Bring them back," Schragg called. "If there's anything left of them. Liars, cheaters, swine . . . By all means, bring back what's left."

Baranyi closed his eyes. The pain in his head was overwhelming; it felt as though his scalp were being peeled from his head. It had all happened too fast for him to understand either what had happened or why.

He wondered at that moment whether he ever would.

Epilogue

November 10, 1976
New York City

The lights in the police interrogation room had been turned down a long while before, when the first of the three containers of coffee from the all-night deli on Lexington Avenue had been brought in. Senator Trilling had drunk his ninth cup by the time Baranyi had finished his story. His craggy face, very much the image of his father's but tending now to fat, had gone wax white. A blue vein pulsed irregularly along his right temple. The look of loathing he had first bestowed on Baranyi had given way to an expression of inner-directed horror. He was seeing with a sickening clarity his own private visions of disaster. Not historical, not past, but immediate and future.

Eisner hadn't touched his coffee at all. He hadn't moved, either, not once during the whole time.

Now, finally, Eisner's head turned slightly as he took his eyes off Baranyi's strangely placid face and sought cautiously for some evidence of understanding in the senator's eyes. It was there all right, clear and unmistakable.

Baranyi sat back in his straight metal chair, his hands knotted together and hanging down between his legs. He did not look up. A thin spiderweb of blood had begun to ooze down again from his lacerated scalp, but he did not make a move to wipe it away.

"They took us to the main camp," he went on in a distant, detached tone, "where the SS had all their special facilities. The Punishment Bunkers, they called them. I saw the others only twice after that, and then only from a distance. They tortured me, naturally. I don't even remember the things they did to me, and there would be no need for you to hear them even if I did. They were very inventive. It was interesting at the time to try to guess what they would do next. There was no point to it all, of course, because I told them all that I knew right away. There was no reason not to. But they went on, and on, and on . . . perhaps because they didn't believe me, perhaps for other reasons.

"I never saw Schragg or Stellner again, or Neimann either. Landau, I believe, was not badly treated. They were practical men. If you were valuable to them, they managed to restrain themselves.

And Landau was certainly valuable to them. If there had been enough time, I'm certain he would have done as he had promised Stropp and made it work for them. But, of course, there was not time. You, Samuel, I know what they did to you. I could hear it through the walls, all day and all night. But at least you survived. You could have been shot as a spy, I suppose—not that they required any legalistic justification for killing you, though I imagine that because you were an American it would have made them more comfortable to have an excuse—but then there was the matter of the agreement with the signatures of Krauch and Schmitz on it. They could not afford to risk that, yes? Wherever it was, whoever had it, it was a danger to them, a terrible danger.

"Finally, when they'd finished with me, they sent me back to Monowitz. But by then they had many other things with which to occupy their minds. The Soviets were already in Sandomierz. There had been no American advance up from the Adriatic, no third front. No push north through Vienna. There never was to have been. The Soviets had seen to that. So, in September, after I had been at Monowitz a month or two already—it's hard now to tell how long it had been, really—the Americans did finally start to bomb some of the plants. First the synthetic oil works, then the Krupp plant, the Siemens works. The Farben installations were the very last to be hit, and then only very reluctantly—only after it was perfectly clear that the Soviets would take the whole of southern Poland. By that time it was too late. The Russians captured the Buna works almost intact.

"So you see how futile the whole thing was. It was all for nothing. Between that July and the next winter, another quarter million died in that terrible place. In the gas chambers that could have been destroyed in half an hour and probably never would have been rebuilt. *A quarter of a million people, and two million before them.* That, sir, is quite a record. It is a very heavy load of guilt for any man to live with, wouldn't you say? But—surprising, isn't it— so many *were* able to live with it. They managed quite easily, your father and Herr Stellner.

"I, however, found it more difficult. There were a number of things that I needed to understand. First, how was it that we had not been able to save at least that last quarter of a million? Was it Landau who had betrayed us? I was not sure. There were many possibilities. It could have been Landau with his insurance policy safe in a Swiss vault. Or Bor? There was that possibility too. I found after the war that the good Colonel Bor had gone to work for the new Polish government, the one that the Lublin committee and the Soviets had put in power. It was in the Soviets' interest to keep the Buna works intact, of course, just as it had been in your interest to do so as long as you thought that your own troops would get there first. There was, therefore, that possibility too— the Bor possibility—and it was a very strong one, so it seemed at the time.

"Finally I realized that it really didn't matter. I could not afford to pick the wrong man, so I had to have them both. And if there were other possibilities—and of course there were—I had to have them, too. They were all involved in one way or another. You've seen the clippings I collected. My 'dossiers.' Just like Wiesenthal. In my own small way. But privately, of course. I could not afford to become involved with governments, tribunals, statutes of limitation.

"Bor was quite difficult, Landau far less so. By the time I was released, the war had ended. Kagan was gone. He had vanished during the last days of fighting in Budapest. I was told afterwards that he had been betrayed by the very man who had earlier helped us so often—the police general, Szekely. When the Russians took Budapest, they had little interest in the Jews either, and little love for anyone who had helped them, particularly if American money had been involved. The Polish woman was gone, utterly vanished. Peshko was dead. Liebermann said that I was mad and threatened to denounce me to the authorities. The times were too precarious, there was too much at stake, he said. If I had proof, he said, I should go and see Wiesenthal or the occupation authorities, or the Mossad. I tried to make him understand that the authorities were the last people to whom we could look for justice, that this was a very personal matter, something only I could attend to. He never did understand that. Liebermann died of a heart attack in '49. By then I had settled accounts with Landau. Bor followed two months later. It was ironic. The man who helped me the most to finish Conrad Bor was Szekely himself—his opportunism again. The intricacies of the political system to which he had now sold himself were such that with Bor gone he would have a significant advantage. I never asked what or how. It was enough to accept his aid. Perhaps it was also an act of penance for him. Who knows? Bor, the landlocked Pole, died in a fishing accident off the coast of Riga. There were no questions asked. Szekely saw to that. Grunewald, to my regret, died in his bed before I was able to get to him.

"You remember, of course, what happened at Nuremberg. The second series of trials, after the world had grown bored? They *all got off,* every one of them, every one of the defendants from I.G. Farben. Oh, there were a few light sentences. Ambros received eight years. So did the petroleum expert, Beutefisch. Krauch got six years. Ter Meer seven. *Seven years in a comfortable prison in exchange for two million lives.* If one is useful, if one is a scientist, then it is all right. Everything is permitted. That, gentlemen, is the lesson of the second Nuremberg trials. The sentences, such as they were, were all commuted shortly thereafter. By 1951, every one of the I.G. men was out of prison. Krauch became an 'export consultant' for the Bonn government. So did Dr. Ambros, who was put in charge of the new I.G.'s southern plants. Schragg became chairman of the Federal Association of West German Industry. Stellner, as you saw, remained as chief chemist and became a member of a half dozen boards of directors of the 'new' Farben combine. The rest of them . . . here is a full list, in my file . . . they were all dealt with. One at a time. Over the years. *I* dealt with them, gentlemen, with much efficiency, much skill. Perhaps they would have been pleased to know just *how* efficiently, *how* skillfully. They were all men who appreciated efficiency above all else.

"Even those who died of apparently natural causes were mine, Senator. Recall . . . I was once a very skilled physician. Your Herr Hayklut, for instance, with his terrible cancer. There are many ways of inducing cancer, Senator. I thought it was a particularly fitting end.

"I suppose that in your eyes I too am a murderer. I choose not to look at it in quite that way. The people I helped to die had all committed suicide a long time ago. It was only a matter of time before that decision took effect fully. It was, in each case, quite inevitable. Your father and Stellner, they were the last ones. For a long time it was impossible to get near them. As it seemed to me that I had little time left myself, I could not afford to let any opportunity pass by, even though it meant coming out into the open.

After all, it would hardly matter after that. There are no more. They have all paid what they owe, all those who were directly implicated. Murder is a crime restricted to the killing of a human being, is it not, Samuel? By definition. That was *their* view too, if you remember. Jews were considered subhuman, vermin, scum. Consider—what makes an animal a human? A moral sense, a soul, the ability to determine destinies, to make moral choices. Consider whether any of these people had any right to think of themselves as human beings by such criteria. If not, then, as they themselves argued at the time, to destroy them was nothing more than to exterminate a lower form of life. Not murder, certainly."

Senator Trilling's face was deeply flushed. He had entered the room, five hours before, no longer young—he was well over forty. Now he appeared distinctly aged. His eyes darted in Eisner's direction. He pulled anxiously at his tie. Sweat slid down his neck and stained his collar a blotchy gray.

"Sam, do you realize what this can *do?*" His voice was barely audible.

"I realize," replied Eisner levelly. "Of course I do."

"It's finished now," said Miklos Baranyi. "They were the last, Stellner and your father. Your father was in a way the worst of them all, Stellner perhaps the least evil. It was ironic that they should have gone together."

A silence settled over the room. Trilling's face was black with signs of an impending explosion. He fought it back. Eisner wondered what exactly he was going to do.

Finally the senator spoke again, his voice throttled, on the edge of panic.

"I simply don't believe it," he said. "I don't believe one word of your God-damned lies."

"There is proof," Baranyi said, a thin smile on his lips.

"Oh hell, sure there's proof. We all know about that kind of 'proof.' It's the same proof you people have been talking about for the last thirty years. But its all ancient history now."

"I do not mean *that* proof. I mean *direct* proof of the part your father played in all of it. Proof of the guilt of the oil company. A million lives, Senator. And treason in the bargain."

"You haven't got any such thing," said the senator, his eyes narrowed. "You lousy Jew bastard."

"Ah, it comes out at last."

The senator rose suddenly. His arm swung back as though he were about to strike the old man. Eisner's hand shot out, the fingers driving hard into the senator's wrist. Trilling swore. For a moment he stood stock-still, breathing very hard, his mouth going purple around the corners. Then he went to the door and began to pound.

Baranyi looked up at Eisner.

"This is a man who wishes to run for President of your country?"

"Maybe," said Eisner. "And maybe not . . . anymore."

"I see," said Baranyi. His shoulders relaxed and he looked at peace with himself. Resigned, Eisner would have called it if anyone had asked him.

A policeman pulled open the door and asked if Eisner and the senator were ready to come out. They'd been in there for five hours, did they realize that?

The senator realized it. He wanted to leave. At once. If there were still any reporters outside would it be possible to go out through the back? He didn't want to talk to any reporters. Not under any circumstances.

Basharian was waiting for them in the corridor.

"Are the reporters still there?" Eisner asked quickly.

"More than there were when you went in, I'm afraid. The street's full of them."

"Does anyone know he's here?" Eisner pointed to Trilling.

"You'll have to ask them." The detective shrugged.

"Damn," Trilling said. "I should have known better." His face was dark, the panic beginning to show clearly.

"Is there a back way out of here that we can use?"

"No back way," said the detective. "But I can get you out through the basement. You'll come up in an alley next to the church. There's a red door that's always open. You know what I mean. It's a service of theirs. Go in, go through the church and then out next to the sporting goods shop."

"We won't be seen?"

"Not a chance," said Basharian. "What about him?" He hooked a thumb back at the room where Baranyi sat. "Are you going to represent him, Counselor?"

Eisner nodded, without even looking to Trilling for confirmation.

"Good luck, Counselor," said Basharian, grinning. "Me and ten million other people were eyewitnesses. As many as with Ruby, I guess."

Eisner shrugged. Basharian had no idea of how it was going to be. Eisner knew. He didn't like it but he knew, and he knew that it couldn't be any other way.

The detective led them down the hall to a small door crossed by a panic bar. Trilling looked terrible—almost as bad, Eisner thought, as his father. Odd, Trilling hadn't even asked to see his father's body. No, it wasn't odd. That was the way it had always been with them. Even in death, the son disliked the father. It was just as well. Eisner hated morgues and bodies. He refused to look, ever. He'd seen enough of corpses in his time. He could still see the stacks, like cordwood, in his dreams.

By the crematoria.

They came out in the narrow alley next to a church, just as Basharian had said. The police officer who had accompanied them through the basement asked if they needed anything.

The senator shook his head. Eisner said that the senator's car was parked nearby and the only thing they'd need, maybe, was to have a ticket fixed if they'd gotten one. The officer laughed and said they didn't give out tickets after six, so there wasn't anything to worry about.

The side door of the church was open, just as the detective had said it would be. They went in and walked quickly down the aisle between the pews. A shabby old woman was kneeling at the rear, next to a bank of candles. She looked up and stared at them as they went by, then lowered her head and resumed her solitary prayers.

The night air hit them in the face, snapping Eisner wide awake. He could see down the street. There was still a crowd in front of the precinct house. Lots of cars. Lights and TV cameras.

They went quickly around the corner.

The car was there, right where Trilling had left it—one of Moedler's fleet. It belonged to Criterion, just as the Lear jet that had brought Trilling up from Washington belonged to Criterion.

Just as Eisner, in his own way, belonged to Criterion.

But who did the company really belong to now that the old man was dead? Eisner wondered. Would the Eastern–Sunrise merger go through in the morning as planned? He supposed it would. That was the way people like the Trillings operated. Those who would succeed Trilling would be no different.

It was 5:29 A.M. The closing had been set for 10:00. There wouldn't even be time to retype the papers for someone else's signature.

They walked to the car and got in without a word. When Trilling had pulled himself behind the wheel and turned on the motor, Eisner said quietly, "There *is* proof, Wayne. You must know that."

The senator was sunk in his own private despair and seemed almost not to have heard. He was silent for a long time while his foot worked up and down on the accelerator. Finally, he said, "You know what this can do to me?"

"I know, Wayne. I'd have to be an idiot not to know."

"I have to make some calls. And damned fast. Can I come up to your place?"

"You can come up to my place, but not to make calls. You want to make phone calls, you use a phone booth."

"What?"

Eisner took out a handful of change and handed it to the senator. "For those kind of calls, you use a booth, Wayne. Not my apartment."

Trilling seemed at a loss. He stared at the handful of coins.

"You haven't got dimes."

"Jesus," said Eisner. "Use the quarters then."

He drove along Madison Avenue until they were in the low Eighties.

"There's a booth on the next corner," Eisner said.

They pulled up. Trilling got out. The street was deserted. A doorman dozed, huddled in his thick green-and-gold coat, in a lobby across the street. The booth was at the corner, shielded from the light. Anyone making a call would be in darkness.

"I'll drive around and come back for you in ten minutes."

"It won't take that long," Trilling said.

"Ten minutes, Wayne," Eisner said.

"You know it's *necessary,* Sam. You can see that, can't you? It's going to be damned hard to manage, but it has to be done."

"I can see it," said Eisner, "but I don't want to know anything

about it. Look, Wayne, let's not talk about it, all right? You make
your calls. Then I'll pick you up and we'll go back to my place. If
I can manage to wake Ilse up, she'll make you some coffee. If not,
I'll make it for you myself."

"Listen, why shouldn't I talk to you about it? What the hell is an
attorney for? What about the attorney–client privilege? What about
that?"

"Let's not stretch it, Wayne . . . please. If you stretch it, you'll
have to get someone else, not me."

Trilling got out and went into the booth. Eisner sighed and
slipped behind the wheel. He was dead tired, but somehow he felt
exhilarated, almost to the point of trembling.

The sky was getting lighter but the day would not be bright. A
low-pressure zone had settled on the city and there would be rain
for at least two days.

Three days had passed. It was shortly after 8 A.M. when Samuel
Morse Eisner pushed open the double glass doors of Hayklut,
Bard, Winston & Stropp and walked as briskly as he could across
the thick brown carpet of the reception room. He had not slept at
all well that night. As he often did, he had stayed overnight at the
Manhattan Athletic Club, brooding alone in the steam room until
the bleary-eyed attendant closed the place for the night, then taking
an icy plunge in the deserted pool and a stiff nightcap in the
deserted lounge. He had sunk into a troubled sleep in one of the
bedrooms on the eighth floor reserved by his firm for their private
and exclusive use.

Now, the receptionist looked up quickly from her desk, an expression of urgency on her normally bland, institutional face.

"Oh, Mr. Eisner, where *have* you been? They've been trying to
reach you all night." She was pointing a sheaf of yellow telephone
message slips at him like a bill of attainder.

He recalled, with a sinking, icy feeling, that he had told his wife
only that he would not be home, not where he was going. She had
undoubtedly assumed that he was headed to one of the "places"—
as she put it—that he often frequented, and of course she would
have been too ashamed to have told anyone that he was gone for
the night. God only knew what lies she had told. Of course, no one

would have had any idea how to locate him. Even in case of an emergency.

The receptionist thrust the phone message slips into his hand as he went quickly into the corridor that led to his office.

"They've called six times since we opened, sir. They're very anxious to speak to you—something's happened, I think . . ."

As he entered his office and switched on the light, he riffled the message slips.

Three from the Manhattan district attorney's office.

Two from the *New York Times*.

One from the office of the chief medical examiner.

He felt as though his blood pressure had dropped to 30 over 90. Ice water filled his legs. He held his hands together to keep them from shaking.

"Jesus," he breathed. It had happened. Already. He had known that it would happen. It had been expected. Inevitable.

But so soon?

Of course. Before Baranyi could be indicted. Before anyone could be summoned to testify. Before Trilling himself could be questioned about what Baranyi had said in the interrogation room. No privilege attached to *that*.

Eisner glanced down.

Efficiency. It was there on his desk. The city edition of the *New York Times*. On top of the usual morning pile of advance sheets and correspondence. One of the associates had thoughtfully circled the news item with a yellow marker.

He poured himself a long drink of whiskey from the silver-banded bottle on his desk and read the piece slowly and carefully.

The only real surprise, he concluded, was that it had taken three days to happen.

During that time he had visited Miklos Baranyi only twice, each time taking with him two associates from the firm's criminal division, conducting only the most cursory of interviews. Baranyi seemed to understand. A look of undisguised amusement had lit the Hungarian's eyes each time Eisner came into his cell. A look of disdain. Cold, cynical, and knowing.

But he had behaved soberly, answered the questions put to him, never once inquiring how Eisner planned to manage the defense of a man whom half the nation's prime-time audience had seen shoot two other men in cold blood.

Insanity?

Hardly. No one who heard Miklos Baranyi's story could possibly consider him insane. Quite the contrary.

Eisner had an uneasy feeling as he talked to the man that he was being tested, that Baranyi was almost challenging him to find a way to defend him without telling his story in open court. Withdrawal as attorney was impossible now. Too many questions would be asked. Reporters would press. His too-ready agreement to serve as counsel that first night had been picked up instantly by the papers. What had seemed to him the most discreet thing he could do subsequently seemed to be leading him into a trap from which he could see no way out.

But now none of it made any difference at all.

Eisner poured a second whiskey, told his receptionist to hold all calls until further notice, and read the front-page piece again.

> Despite precautions as great as any since the arrest of Sirhan Sirhan for the slaying of Robert Kennedy, the accused killer of Criterion Oil Company's retiring Chairman of the Board, Marcus Trilling, and award-winning chemist Dr. Golo Stellner was found dead in his cell at the 51st Street station house early this morning. The Chief Medical Examiner, Dr. Morris Drescher, was called to the scene from his bed at two in the morning and immediately confirmed the apparent cause of death, though just how the potassium cyanide capsule with which accused killer Miklos Baranyi committed suicide had escaped detection continues to baffle police. Officials have privately admitted that Baranyi was not searched in a way that would have revealed a hidden poison capsule, particularly if it had been concealed in a tooth or a body cavity. The possibility had not even been considered, admitted Chief of Detectives Sidney Goldhaber. The method of death recalls the suicides of Nazi war leaders before and after the Nuremberg trials. The motive for the shootings remains obscure, though the

accused is now known to have been a Hungarian national who was active in Switzerland during the war. Attempts to obtain comment from the office of Baranyi's counsel, Hayklut, Bard, Winston & Stropp, have thus far been unsuccessful. The Mayor's office, in conjunction with the office of Manhattan District Attorney Santucci, has announced that a full inquiry will be made.

There was a second, smaller piece directly below.

A private service for Marcus Trilling was held yesterday at the Church of the Heavenly Rest on upper Fifth Avenue. The service was attended by a small group of political and industrial notables, including the late oil man's son, Senator Wayne W. Trilling. The body of West German scientist Dr. Golo Stellner was returned yesterday by plane to Wiesbaden for interment in the Stellner family vault. The West German Government and the entire West German scientific community have expressed their regrets.

Having Trilling make his phone calls from a booth was one of the better ideas he had had in a long time, Eisner concluded, putting down the paper with a still-palsied hand. There would be no inquiry, of course. Where men like the senator were involved, there never was. It wasn't and couldn't be the way it had been with Nixon. They'd gone all out after *him* because he was a usurper. But wealth protected wealth. No one had ever even pointed a finger at Roosevelt for any of the things *he'd* done. Or at Kennedy or even Johnson. And the Trillings had done more than all three of them put together.

He would have to go down to the district attorney's office, of course. He'd probably end up having an uncomfortable lunch with Benjamin Santucci and one of his eager assistants. The DA would understand, and they would exchange meaningless aphorisms over the zabaglione at Forlini's. Hopefully, the assistant would be too impressed with having been invited along to ask any embarrassing questions. Even if he did, a disappointed look from Santucci would quiet things instantly. And the assistant would quickly realize he'd been asked along as a matter of form, not for any real assistance.

Eisner made his calls. No comment for the *Times*. The reporter would understand. Of course he could say nothing. Of course he was deeply shocked. Of course his firm would remain involved. A sense of duty. A strange case. Perhaps there never would be any answers. Only more questions.

He told his secretary to make the necessary reservation at Forlini's for the next day. Lunch with the district attorney would be on the account of Hayklut, Bard, Winston & Stropp this time.

It was six hours later that the call came, within minutes of his having told his secretary to release the hold on incoming phone calls.

"Well, Miss Bergen, who is it?"

"He won't say, sir."

"Give the call to Mr. Stern then."

"He says it's important, sir. He has an accent, sir," the secretary said hesitantly, as though unsure whether that particular piece of information was really relevant.

He took the call.

The voice on the other end did indeed have an accent, a sort of vague, general-purpose European accent that reminded him, suddenly and uncomfortably, of Max Grunewald. It wasn't Max, he knew that. Max had been dead over a decade. But it was the same sort of accent. Possibly German, possibly not.

The voice sounded old, very tentative.

"I am speaking to Mr. Eisner? Advocate Eisner?"

"You know who you're speaking to, don't you?" Eisner replied coldly.

"I beg your pardon? Excuse me . . . this *is* Herr Eisner, yes?"

"Who is this, please. Who *are* you?"

"It is not important, my name."

"Nevertheless . . ."

"It is Palfy, if you must know it, if it is important to you."

"I don't know you, do I?"

"I have something left to you by a friend, sir."

"A friend?"

There was a hesitation. "You *are* Samuel Morse Eisner, yes?"

"Yes," he said dully. It sounded to him as though he was pleading guilty, not merely admitting to his name.

"Then it is for you, unquestionably, sir."

They met on the Eighty-first Street esplanade, overlooking the East River. It was night, though not as dark there as it was elsewhere in the city. The neon sign on the hamper factory across the river sent a wavering red glow over everything. To the north one could see the outlines of the Bronx-Whitestone Bridge festooned with tiny silver bulbs, and the Triborough, cutting across in front of it, an unilluminated shadow of girders and cables marked only by the shifting headlights of the traffic it bore.

The man had been waiting for him. He was as he had sounded, small, elderly, and tentative. And unidentifiably Middle European. He wore thick lenses, a pointed, goatish beard and mustache, and a shabby overcoat much too large for him. He looked like an elderly professor of music. During the war the West Side had been full of men who looked like that, but there weren't too many of them around now. It would take another war in Europe before they would come again.

"I am Palfy," the man said, coming right up to Eisner as he turned onto the esplanade. Eisner experienced a momentary twinge. He was sure that he had never met the man before, yet this Palfy, whoever he was, knew *him* by sight. "You are Eisner, yes?"

Eisner nodded. The man nodded back, his yellowish little beard catching the red neon light from across the river.

"This was left to me in trust," the old man said, handing Eisner a little package wrapped in brown paper and fastened with cellophane tape. "Mr. Baranyi said, 'Istvan, if anything happens to me, this must be delivered to *one* man. You must put it in his hands and the hands of no one else.' And that man, sir, is you."

"You've done very well," Eisner ventured, considering carefully what was to come next. Then he asked. "You were a friend of Mr. Baranyi's?"

"Oh no, sir. What a fine man—I only wish it could have been that I was the friend of such a man. But it was not. I was a neighbor

only. We took walks sometimes, to feed the pigeons beneath the
Verdi."

"I beg your pardon?"

"The Verdi, sir. The statue at Broadway and Seventh-third
Street. Also, we played chess now and then. That is how I know
Mr. Baranyi."

"He was an acquaintance then?"

"Such a word could be used. No more."

"And yet you do this for him?"

"Who would not? It was terrible, what happened to him. Who
can believe the things the papers have been writing? They cannot
be true."

"They're true," said Eisner softly. "They're very true." His hand
trembled when he took the package. "You don't know what's in
here, do you?"

"Would Istvan Palfy violate a trust in such a way? Never. It is
for you, the package, and now you have it. Good night, sir."

"Can I do anything for you? I owe you for the service . . ."

"Nothing at all," the man said, and he hurried off.

Eisner stood by the railing, watching him go. When the old man
had descended the stairs and vanished into the shadows of the
apartment buildings along East End Avenue, Eisner undid the
little package.

Inside was a folded letter and another, smaller envelope.

He read the letter first.

Samuel,

If this is delivered to you, you will know what has happened to me and why. You, of all people, will understand
exactly. Risks were accepted and taken. I have no regrets. It is all for the best. In the package is the key to
the vault in Zurich. I got it from Grunewald when I came
back from Auschwitz. He did not tell your people where
the papers really were, only that he had not kept them
and that he thought that Landau had taken them with
him to Poland. This was not true, as you know, but the
matter was dropped there. After the war, the Buna process was worth nothing, as you also know. The Oswiecim

plant and its equipment was in the hands of the Russians and the need of your country for the rubber was no longer great. You had all the natural rubber you needed back again from the Japanese, and your own synthetics as well. Consider how many lives could have been saved if Mr. Trilling's chemists had been a little smarter a little earlier. Or had Mr. Trilling been a little less greedy and a little more enterprising himself.

In the vault are all the papers and the agreements which Dr. Schragg gave to Stropp in Waldshut as well as the signed letters of instruction from Delaware. It is enough to prove it all. The involvement, the incredible greed, the indelible stain. If you are reading this letter, then you will know that the son is as bad as the father. Perhaps worse. You will know what to do with the documents. I am sure.

Eisner didn't have to open the small envelope now.
He put it in his pocket and walked away.

The stones of the cemetery rose on every side, a vast necropolis that went on seemingly forever, spilling endlessly over the mounds and slag heaps of Long Island City. The soil was gray under a low, swirling gray sky, and runneled by rain. It had been drizzling on and off for three days. The billboards that hemmed in the Express-way along the west flank of the vast cemetery were hung with tatters of mist, the warehouses and factory buildings decapitated by surging low clouds as filthy-looking as the ash-strewn roads all around. A neon sign announcing the presence of a bread factory winked balefully on and off in the gray weather. The incongruous, friendly odor of baking bread seeped through the rain-soaked atmosphere.

Eisner had left his wife sitting in his Lincoln at the gate to the cemetery. Poor Ilse, she had no idea what was going on, or who the man being buried was. There had been no reason to tell her, to explain anything and bring back long-repressed memories that would be imprecise at best, and ultimately very painful. There was no reason to resurrect the child Ilse Landau. She had learned to play the piano well since those days, but that was the only part of her time in Zurich that she still carried with her, nothing else.

A shapeless old woman wrapped in a slicker tended a small flower stand at the gates, selling wreaths, bouquets, and potted plants that could be quickly shoved into the soft soil of graves to assuage the guilt caused in too-infrequent visitors.

Eisner bought a few flowers, gave the woman a five-dollar bill, and walked quickly down the asphalt path that wound aimlessly through the vast ocean of headstones. A ground mist rose in some places, obscuring the graves. In other places the outlines of the stones were clear and precise, the stones themselves washed clean and touched with an occasional beam of light, pale and watery as the sky.

At the crest of a small hill a good quarter mile into the cemetery, he found a solitary gravedigger just finishing his work. A big man in a yellow raincoat and boots, shoveling away at the syrupy ground, straining against the mud and swearing under his breath. The digging machine stood idle nearby, a backhoe with an incongruously cheerful yellow body and steel bucket. The grave had to be finished by hand; there was no other way in such weather.

The coffin had already been loaded onto the lifting rig on the other end of the backhoe, a forklift like those used on the docks. There was one other man there, an official from the Department of Health. He stood, miserable and dripping. The backhoe afforded him some small shelter from a wind that continued to send clouds of stinging rain slanting across the field.

There was no priest, no rabbi, no relatives. Only the gravedigger and the man from the health department.

Eisner introduced himself and stood back from the grave's edge.

"Well, I suppose there's no one else coming, is there?" said the man from the health department, consulting his watch. "May as well get on with it."

Eisner nodded. The health department man signaled to the gravedigger, who stuck his shovel in the mud, rubbed the dripping water from his nose, and mounted the machine.

The forklift grumbled and turned heavily through the wet soil until it came alongside the grave. Slowly, it lowered the coffin. The sides of the grave began to slide in, not even waiting until the plain pine box had touched bottom.

A momentary vision of the service at the Church of the Heavenly Rest flashed through Eisner's mind. He hadn't been there. And he was glad that he'd been too tied up to go. The senator hadn't given a damn.

The digger climbed down from the forklift and moved away to the crest of a nearby rise, standing there in his rolled-top galoshes, trying without success to light a cigarette, waiting until the visitors had gone so that he could return and fill in the grave.

The health department man glanced up miserably. Rain ran down his glasses. He looked as though he needed a set of miniature windshield-wipers.

"Are you a relative, sir?"

"No, just his attorney."

"What a terrible business," the man said. "He never did explain why he did it, did he? Well, even if he had, *you* couldn't say, could you? I have a nephew at Fordham Law. He says that the attorney-client privilege doesn't go on after death . . . well . . . These old people, you know, it happens so often. They go crazy, they imagine all sorts of things. We see cases like this all the time. Usually they hang themselves or take sleeping pills."

"I'm sure," said Eisner, pulling the collar of his raincoat up around his ears. He wasn't young enough to stand in the rain like this anymore. It was cold, and he began to shiver.

The gravedigger came down from his hill and got into the cab of the backhoe again, ready to begin filling in the grave. He didn't want to stand in the rain either. Eisner couldn't blame him. Some more dirt slid into the hole, washed down by the increasingly strong rain. It made a sucking noise as it hit the coffin.

The health department man shrugged and walked off.

Eisner waited until the health department man had gone down the path a ways, though there was no reason, really, for him to wait. He took out the little packet that Miklos Baranyi had sent him and undid the paper.

The key smelled of oil; Miklos must have put it away very carefully, sealed up somewhere all this time. He held the key up to the light and looked at it.

The tiny engraved letters said, "Crédit Suisse, Zurich," followed by a number.

With his other hand, he reached again into his pocket. For a moment he fumbled, looking for something. Then he found it, among the change, the wadded tissues, and the crumpled cigarette packages.

The other key.

The one Grunewald had given him when he'd gone back to Zurich after the Soviets had liberated Auschwitz. Max had died a rich man because of that key. Because he'd given it to Eisner, who had known what to do with it.

Poor Miklos. He'd never gotten it quite right. He hadn't understood anything at all. Not in all this time. Miklos probably didn't even know about Ilse. He certainly hadn't mentioned it. Well, Eisner had looked after Ilse Landau until she was old enough to marry, and then he'd married her. And a week later he'd gotten the agreement that Felix Landau had made the I.G. people sign. He'd put that away for safekeeping in the vault with all the other papers. It hadn't been too hard to make good on the promises he'd made Schragg and the others. The arrangements were a little complicated, a little cautious, but then, they had to be. In the end, it had all worked out as he had assured them it would. The I.G. men who'd developed the Buna process had gone to work for Criterion's subsidiaries and affiliates all over Europe, scattered so that there was no hint of a concerted plan. But their work had all been concentrated. And they'd gotten away from the Soviets; that was the most important thing.

Just as he'd promised.

Miklos had gotten it all wrong. Poor Miklos.

Eisner lifted the two keys so that they were both pressed together, ridge to ridge. They were identical. The indentations matched perfectly. It was a wonder Miklos had never figured it out. How did he think a man like Samuel Morse Eisner—a man who had come close to being disbarred, a secret drinker with no great legal talent—how did he think such a person had gotten to be a senior partner in a firm like Hayklut, Bard, Winston & Stropp? In a way, it was sad to think that Miklos had died not even knowing that the process Criterion had come up with after the war— "on their own"—the process that Miklos had thought would have saved so many lives if it had only been developed earlier—*was the I.G. process.* If they couldn't have the know-how and the equipment, then at least they could have the men and the brains.

Eisner had seen to that.

Oh yes, they had owed him for what he'd done for them in Poland. And they feared him, too, for what he could still do to them all with that key.

It was a perfect combination. Gratitude and fear.

It had been that simple, but Miklos had never understood it. He'd never guessed that it hadn't been Bor at all, or Neimann, or Landau, or anyone else either.

It had been him, Samuel Morse Eisner. All the time. Not very smart, not a very good lawyer. But, as Helmut Schragg had said such a long time ago, a man with "good business sense."

He tossed the two keys into the open grave and watched them sink into the saturated soil.

The backhoe moved over to the graveside and began pushing in the dirt just as the rain finally ceased.

Eisner turned and walked slowly along the path toward the cemetery gate where the car and his wife, née Ilse Landau, once of Zurich, Switzerland, and before that Berlin, Germany, were waiting for him.

He could see her sitting there in the front seat of the blue Lincoln. She had a bouquet of asters in her hand. She must have bought them from the old woman by the gate. He could see the wet footprints leading up to the car from the little stand and the old woman back huddled behind her barricade of potted plants, shivering in the cold wind.

Eisner shook the water from his coat and slid into the front seat next to his wife.

"How much did you spend for those?" he asked, looking at the asters.

"They're so pretty, Samuel . . ."

"How much?" he insisted, out of sorts.

"Why, nothing. The old lady gave them to me. Wasn't that nice?"

He reached down to turn the key in the ignition, thinking, "Nice? Yes, that's very . . ."

As he turned the key, he saw in the rear-view mirror that the old woman had stood up behind the heaps of flowers and plants. He saw her face clearly, as though for the first time. He hadn't really noticed before, but there was no question in his mind about it now. It was the same old woman who had been in the church the night he and Trilling had come out of the police station through the basement. It was a face, moreover, that he seemed to know— had *known*—years before. Just as he had known the face of the old man, Palfy. . . . When both faces had been much different, much younger . . . .

He froze, a current of horror running through his body like an electric shock. He pulled his hand violently away from the ignition key.

But it was too late.

Smoke and flame rose a full twenty feet into the air, carrying the car roof and the instantly incinerated bodies of its occupants with it in a billowing geyser of wreckage. In two seconds, there was nothing left but a mass of twisted metal engulfed by snapping, gasoline-fed flames. Embers and blazing bits of wreckage were scattered for fifty yards in all directions.

The health department man, who had been almost to the south gate, stood transfixed and then began to shout in terror.

On the rise by the newly dug grave, the burly gravedigger in his yellow mackintosh leaned on his spade with one arm and with the other pushed back his cap a bit so that a few locks of hair, now shot through heavily with gray, but still discernibly red, fell over his streaming forehead. He did not smile, but as he rubbed the little duplicate key that was the only thing he had in his trouser pocket, there was a look of satisfaction on his face.

Below, by the gate, the old woman had no such inhibitions. She had already thrust the few bits of leftover wire and blasting caps into the soil of one of her potted plants. Now she threw back the rain hood that had covered her pale, gray-blond hair. Julie Malowska's mouth opened in a wide, angry smile, and she waved at the gravedigger with the once-red hair. He smiled back. Liebermann-Palfy would be so pleased. They'd gotten them all now, every one of them. There was no possibility that the guilty one had escaped. They'd all been guilty, one way or the other.

It was just as Miklos had said. Cemeteries were a place for judgment.